PRAISE FOR *BABY JAILS*

"A powerful work that uses a rich combination of litigation documents, personal interviews, noncitizens' stories, and case law to trace the development of child and family detention in the United States."—Pooja R. Dadhania, Assistant Professor, California Western School of Law

"A novel and thorough historical account of an issue of enormous importance." —Geoffrey Heeren, Associate Professor and Director, Immigration Clinic, Valparaiso University School of Law

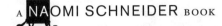

A NAOMI SCHNEIDER BOOK

Highlighting the lives and experiences of marginalized
communities, the select titles of this imprint draw
from sociology, anthropology, law, and history, as well
as from the traditions of journalism and advocacy, to reassess mainstream
history and promote unconventional thinking about contemporary
social and political issues. Their authors share the passion, commitment,
and creativity of Executive Editor Naomi Schneider.

The publisher and the University of California Press Foundation gratefully acknowledge the generous support of the Anne G. Lipow Endowment Fund in Social Justice and Human Rights.

The publisher and the University of California Press Foundation gratefully acknowledge the generous support of the Lawrence Grauman, Jr. Fund.

Baby Jails

Baby Jails

THE FIGHT TO END THE INCARCERATION
OF REFUGEE CHILDREN IN AMERICA

Philip G. Schrag

UNIVERSITY OF CALIFORNIA PRESS

University of California Press
Oakland, California

© 2020 by Philip G. Schrag

Cataloging-in-Publication Data is on file at the Library of Congress.

ISBN 978-0-520-29930-6 (cloth : alk. paper)
ISBN 978-0-520-29931-3 (pbk. : alk. paper)
ISBN 978-0-520-97109-7 (ebook)

Manufactured in the United States of America

28 27 26 25 24 23 22 21 20
10 9 8 7 6 5 4 3 2 1

To the courageous children and families
who flee persecution and torture in their homelands
to seek safety in the United States of America

Contents

Figures

Acknowledgments

As the many endnotes to this book reveal, a great deal has been written about the long effort to end the detention of migrant children, though this is the first book-length treatment of the subject. It explores the issues by combining journalistic accounts with research done by nonprofit organizations, close analysis of court records, and interviews with key participants. I am grateful to all of the lawyers, journalists, and other authors who have documented the many dozens of moving pieces and thereby made it possible to reconstruct the history of the struggle. Constructing the backbone of the book depended, however, on my interviews with many of the nonprofit and former government lawyers who played important roles in the conflict. They each volunteered hours of their time to explain the sequence of events and the work they did. In many cases, they also shared documents that are quoted or cited in this work. The individuals whose cooperation was essential to this narrative included Cheasty Anderson, Michelle Brané, Bridget Cambria, Robert Doggett, Carol Anne Donohoe, Leon Fresco, Lee Gelernt, Denise Gilman, Manoj Govindaiah, Laura Guerra-Cardus, Lindsay Harris, Barbara Hines, Robert Libal, Cristina Parker, and Peter Schey. Carlos Holguín and Jennifer Lee also contributed valuable background information.

I am grateful for additional help from Pooja Dadhania, Mary Ann DeRosa, Geoffrey Heeren, Lisa Lerman, Michael Meltsner, Karen Musalo, Mabel Shaw, and Anna Selden. I appreciate the constant support of my Georgetown colleagues Andrew Schoenholtz and David Koplow. This book was inspired in part by the excellent case study of the legal battle against compulsory sterilization, *In Reckless Hands*, by my colleague Victoria Nourse. A special shoutout goes to Naomi Schneider, my wonderful editor at the University of California Press, who held my hand at every stage of this process and gracefully allowed me to expand the projected length of the book and to accelerate its production when, during the writing of this manuscript, President Trump suddenly turned the "Flores Settlement" from a term known only to immigration specialists into a household phrase.

.   .   .   .   .

I am pleased to acknowledge these individuals and institutions for granting permission to use their copyrighted images. Those images may not be reproduced further without permission from the copyright holders.

The INS detention center at the Mardi Gras Motel, 1985: Lisa Hartouni.

Judge Robert J. Kelleher: Gary Miyatake/Toyo Photography.

Carlos Holguín: Peter Schey.

The seizure of Elián González: AP Photo/Alan Diaz, copyright Associated Press.

Dianne Feinstein: courtesy of the office of Senator Dianne Feinstein.

Prof. Barbara Hines: courtesy of Barbara Hines.

A family cell in the L. Don Hutto Family Residential Center: AP Photo/ L.M. Otero, copyright Associated Press.

Judge Sam Sparks: *The Federal Lawyer*. The photograph first appeared in a profile of Judge Sparks in the May 2010 issue of *The Federal Lawyer*.

Vanita Gupta: Courtesy of The Leadership Conference on Civil and Human Rights.

Michelle Brané: courtesy of Women's Refugee Commission.

Children in CBP custody in 2014: AP Photo/Ross D. Franklin, copyright Associated Press.

Judge Dolly Gee: Gary Miyatake/Toyo Photography.

Leon Fresco: courtesy of the law firm of Holland & Knight.

Family separation editorial cartoon: used with the permission of Jeff Danziger, the *Washington Post* Writers Group, and the Cartoonist Group. All rights reserved.

Cover photo, migrant child: AP Photo/Gregory Bull, copyright Associated Press.

Introduction

In January 2019, many federal agencies were shuttered for weeks, federal services were curtailed, and 800,000 federal workers were furloughed because President Donald J. Trump refused to approve a budget plan unless it included funding for a wall between the United States and Mexico. In the midst of the turmoil caused by the closure of vital federal agencies, Trump sent a letter to Congress outlining the two "most pressing legal changes" that he wanted legislators to enact in order to deter people, including asylum-seekers, from trying to come to the United States.[1] These were, first, to "terminate the Flores Settlement Agreement," and, second, to "amend the Trafficking Victims Protection Reauthorization Act (TVPRA)" that Congress had unanimously passed, and that President George W. Bush had signed, in 2008. The Flores agreement is a 1997 legal settlement under which the United States had agreed not to jail migrant children for more than a few days. The TVPRA reinforced the Flores agreement by preventing the Border Patrol from holding unaccompanied children in its custody for more than seventy-two hours and by providing procedural protections for those who applied for asylum.

The Flores agreement and the TVPRA had limited, but not entirely ended, the incarceration of migrant children. The TVPRA required that the government transfer *unaccompanied* children promptly to the custody of the Department of Health and Human Services, which then reunited them with parents or other family members in the United States or, failing that, housed them in shelters where they were usually well cared for. But the TVPRA did not apply to *accompanied* children, those who arrived in the United States with a parent or other adult.

The Obama administration hired private prison companies to build two large jails in Texas for the mothers and children in these families. A court interpreted the Flores settlement agreement to mean that the children could not be incarcerated in those jails for more than twenty days. But the Trump administration wants to be able to jail these asylum-seeking families for years,[2] until the backlogged immigration courts can hear their claims. It has sought, successively, to persuade Congress to terminate the Flores agreement, to get a court to reinterpret it, to repeal it by regulation, and to circumvent it by making Central American families wait for their hearings in Mexico rather than allowing them to enter the United States.

This book arose out of my brief volunteer experience in one of the family jails. In the fall of 2015, I left the comfort zone of my Georgetown University office for a few days to provide legal services to mothers and children confined in the immigration detention center in Dilley, Texas. The place I visited was no ordinary jail. The women and children had not been charged with crimes. Each of the mothers with whom I talked had fled dreadful violence in Central America. They had come north, making an arduous trip through Mexico, to seek the safety afforded by the United States and its asylum law. After crossing the Rio Grande, they were quickly apprehended by the Border Patrol. Initially, they were confined in the Border Patrol's holding facilities in what they described as miserable conditions. Then they were put into the custody of Immigration and Customs Enforcement (ICE), which transported them to what was euphemistically called the "South Texas Family Residential Center," a name suggesting some kind of resort. It was in fact a corporation's private jail, operated under a contract with ICE.

Along with several other lawyers, I worked in a trailer set aside for conversations between the women and attorneys. While we talked, their children, most of whom seemed to be between three and eight years old, played with a few toys on the floor. It was hard for me to get my head around the idea of a jail full of toddlers, but there they were. The children also looked longingly at the vending machine that was stocked with candy for the legal representatives, but they were not allowed to have any. In fact, the lawyers had asked for the vending machine to be removed, but ICE had refused. The mothers reported that many of their children were ill. Conjunctivitis seemed rampant among the confined youngsters. The mothers also said that children who developed fevers or diarrhea had to wait for a long time to see a nurse or doctor, and then were most often told that the children should drink water. Many of the children seemed terrified of being in jail after their harrowing trips through Mexico, often at least partly on foot.

The role of the lawyers was to prepare the mothers for screening interviews conducted by asylum officers of the Department of Homeland Security (DHS). These interviews were called "credible fear" interviews, because to avoid deportation, the mother would have to show that she had a "credible fear" of persecution. "Credible fear" was a term of art, signifying the asylum officer's determination of whether the mother had no case at all or whether she could seek asylum in immigration court. An asylum officer could find that a mother had "credible fear" if the officer thought that, in a court hearing months or years later, an immigration judge might well conclude that she was telling the truth about her experiences in her home country, and that she reasonably feared being persecuted, if deported, on account of one of the grounds identified as acceptable in U.S. law.

For example, a mother who persuaded an asylum officer that she did have credible fear of being persecuted because of her political opinions might be released from the jail, along with her children, so that the family could live with a friend or relative until an immigration court hearing took place. But if she could not persuade the officer that she had credible fear, her family would remain in jail until deportation, which could take place within days. In that case, there was one last chance. The day after the asylum officer interview, she could make a teleconference appeal to an immigration judge, who could either affirm or reverse the asylum officer's finding that she lacked credible fear. Immigration law permitted a lawyer to prepare her for the asylum officer's interview and the appeal, and to sit with her in front of the camera and the video screen, but it barred the lawyer from "representing" her.

Most of the mothers were very anxious about these legal proceedings, in which they had to relate—and relive—horrible experiences, including knifings and rapes. Their small children were equally unnerved by the process. One video hearing that I attended with a six-year-old child's mother had to be postponed because the boy would not leave her side even for the mother's half-hour court appearance. After the child screamed for forty-five minutes, a guard tore the child, still screaming, from his mother's arms. The distraught mother had to go directly from that scene to the courtroom, where she would testify to a camera. There her fate was decided, on the spot, by a judge in Miami, Florida, more than a thousand miles away.

The mothers related experiences in El Salvador, Honduras, and Guatemala that are almost unimaginable in the extremity of the violence visited upon them. One of the women I advised, whom I will call Maria, had been eleven years old when her father, who was employed but very poor, refused to give a portion of what little money he had to the local gang. One night, Maria was sitting in their small house holding her two-year-old sister on her lap. There was a knock on the door. Her father called out to find out who it was. A male voice said that the group had come for its money. Maria's mother rushed from the living room into the bedroom to collect the family's meager savings. Her father tried to stop her, refusing on principle to pay extortion money. He wanted to bar the front door with furniture. Her mother insisted on paying, to avoid danger to the family. Her parents scuffled in the living room. Maria's mother broke free and was carrying the money to the door when the gang members became impatient and fired several shots through it. She was killed instantly. A bullet hit Maria's baby sister, but the wound was superficial, perhaps caused by a ricochet. Maria herself suffered a graze on her arm. Her father was also hit. He did not die right away, but he later perished from the wound because he could not afford medical care. Her aunt heard the shots and called the police. When the shooters heard the siren, they fled. Maria took care of her father until he died and then moved in with her grandmother. Years later, when she was an adult, a gang extorted money from her. She was raped and threatened with death. At that point, she fled to the United States with her youngest child, leaving three other children behind with her grandmother because she didn't have enough money for them to make the trip.

Hundreds of volunteer lawyers were taking turns providing legal advice to the mothers in this facility. Along with its sister jail in Karnes City, Texas, and a very small facility in Berks County, Pennsylvania, Dilley was then one of the three facilities in the United States known to immigration lawyers as "baby jails."[3] Most of the lawyers who volunteered at Dilley traveled to Texas for a week at a time to counsel the detainees, prepare them for the screening interviews, and help them with their last-chance videoconference appeals.

Dilley started housing mothers and children only in 2014, but mothers and children fleeing for their lives to the United States have been detained for decades. Lawyers had been trying to prevent the incarceration of migrant children ever since 1985, when Peter Schey, a California lawyer, was asked to help Jenny Lisette Flores, a Salvadoran teenager. Jenny was languishing in a Los Angeles motel that the Immigration and Naturalization Service (INS) had converted to a jail by surrounding the building with barbed wire.

When Schey agreed to represent Flores, he could have had no inkling that her case would go to the United States Supreme Court or that it would still be going on thirty-five years after it began. Nor could he have predicted that the settlement he would eventually negotiate on behalf of migrant children would become a significant target for an American president intent on making it much more difficult for Salvadorans and other victims of violence abroad to obtain asylum in the United States.

This book is a history of the Flores case, its aftermath (including related legislation and litigation) and, more generally, of the efforts by lawyers, legislators, and others to end the detention of migrant children and to alleviate the conditions of their detention. These efforts often have been successful, at least for periods of time. Though the long-term trend of political and legal developments has favored the interests of the children, there were also many setbacks for the children, their parents, and their advocates. The federal government's decades-long effort to keep immigrant children in jail, among other harsh measures to deter them from seeking asylum, has become extreme under the Trump administration. It first attempted to separate families (keeping the mothers in jail while sending the children to shelters or foster care) and then, after an international outcry, it concluded that it would be better to keep entire families imprisoned for years. More than three decades after Jenny Flores became a plaintiff, the issue of what to do with migrant children, including those who have fled to the United States to escape persecution and violence, remained a controversial legal and political issue.

In 1980, Congress made asylum available to almost anyone in the United States or at its border who could prove that he or she had a well-founded fear of persecution on at least one of five specified grounds.[4] Hundreds of thousands of people subsequently sought and won protection. Under the law, even those who entered the United States without visas can seek asylum, though people apprehended for entering the United States surreptitiously, or who ask for asylum at a border crossing, can be detained—jailed—until their cases are heard. Many immigration advocates oppose the jailing of adults pending their asylum hearings because it is very difficult for those confined in ICE facilities to obtain legal representation or to collect evidence to corroborate their claims. It is also very costly to house and feed migrants in ICE's detention facilities. Special considerations apply to children, because the consensus among mental health professionals is that jailing children, even for relatively short periods of time, can cause permanent developmental and emotional damage. Children have fled to the United States from Central America at least since the early 1980s, sometimes by themselves and sometimes with an adult. Since 2005, and particularly since 2013, the numbers of such children have been substantial, presenting successive administrations with the problem of what to do with them until their claims could be adjudicated.

One way to avoid detaining children would be to station judges at the border to decide within days whether their claims for asylum were valid. But this would be unfair to the children and their relatives, because it is difficult to win an asylum case without a legal representative who can assemble corroborating evidence. It can take several months for an indigent migrant to find a lawyer who will provide free representation, after which the process of collecting evidence often takes many weeks. In the clinic that I co-direct at Georgetown Law, my students, working day and night on a single case, need about three months to obtain enough evidence to persuade an immigration judge of the validity of a client's claim. If either the government or the client appeals the judge's decision, the case can go on for as long as three years.[5]

A second possibility would be to release the children (and any accompanying relatives) to live in the community until their cases can be heard, perhaps monitoring them electronically or through periodic required visits to ICE officials to ensure that they will appear for their hearings. Monitored release is actually what the government does with many families, because it doesn't have enough space in its family jails to house all of them, even for the twenty days permitted by a court order in the Flores case. A third option is to incarcerate the children (together with an accompanying parent) until the hearing; a fourth is to jail the parents until then, but to release the children, thereby separating families. The government has used all of these approaches—humanitarian release, long-term detention, and family separation—from time to time. Indeed, as this book shows, these three "solutions" to the problem of what to do with children awaiting hearings on their asylum claims have been the subjects of advocacy by numerous administration officials, legislators, judges, and immigrants' advocates for more than three decades. The TVPRA requires that with rare exceptions, unaccompanied children should promptly be taken out of detention and placed in the "least restrictive setting possible." The treatment of children who arrive with family members, on the other hand, remains the subject of fierce political contestation.

Chapters 1, 2, and 3 of this book relate the early history of the Flores case, which is remarkable in two respects. First, although the case hasn't quite set the record for longevity, it is still alive after nearly thirty-five years. Second, after eight years of litigation, the case was decided by the United States Supreme Court. Usually, a case that goes to the Supreme Court ends shortly thereafter, because there can be no appeal from that court's decision. In its decision in *Flores,* the Supreme Court decided that children did not have a constitutional right to be placed with a responsible adult who was unrelated to them, but it left open one aspect of the case. It assumed that the government was honoring an agreement it had signed regarding the conditions of confinement for migrant children, an assumption that turned out to be incorrect. Ms. Flores's lawyers drove a truck through the small opening created by the government's failure to honor its initial agreement. They first obtained a second settlement of that aspect of the case, four years after the Court's decision. They then enforced the settlement through motions, beginning in 2015, that challenged the government's policy of long-term detention of families with children. Chapter 1 tells the story of Jenny Flores's incarceration, how the case began, and its initial, partial settlement in 1987. Chapter 2 explains the appellate history of the case, including the Supreme Court's decision. Chapter 3 reveals how, even after the Supreme Court ruled against Ms. Flores, the case resulted in the second settlement, against which President Trump would rail more than twenty years later.

Chapter 4 concerns the first intervention by Congress, largely at the initiative of Senator Dianne Feinstein. In its 2002 Homeland Security Act, Congress began to address the issue of confinement of unaccompanied migrant children. It divested the Immigration and Naturalization Service of responsibility for their custody and transferred that duty to the Office of Refugee Resettlement in the Department of Health and Human Services. This change led to a much more humane system for the care of these children until their cases could be decided.

In Chapter 5, the book briefly explores the law of asylum and explains the alterations that Congress made in 1996 in the process for adjudicating asylum claims for migrants who arrived without visas. The 1996 amendments to the immigration law created the expedited removal procedure. This process for summarily deporting some asylum seekers was never imposed on unaccompanied children, but it was an important change for mothers and fathers who arrived with one or more children, adding an additional obstacle to their obtaining asylum.

Chapter 6 discusses the establishment of the nation's first large family detention center during the administration of President George W. Bush, and of the lawsuit that sought to shut it down. The judge in that case declined to end family detention, but his orders did bring about substantial reforms in children's treatment.

In Chapter 7, I explore how Congress revisited and expanded the rights of unaccompanied migrant children who seek asylum or other relief from deportation,[6] extending them beyond the provisions of the 1997 Flores settlement. Through several provisions of the TVPRA, Congress limited the amount of time that those children could be kept in rough border facilities and provided that full hearings on their asylum claims should be conducted by DHS asylum officers, who receive specialized training in interviewing children, rather than by immigration judges.

During his first year in office, President Barack Obama closed the family detention center that the Bush administration had opened. Five years later, however, after the arrival of many more families and children seeking asylum because of gang violence and domestic violence in Guatemala, Honduras, and El Salvador, the Obama administration opened three new family detention centers, first in New Mexico and then, in 2014 and 2015, in Texas. Chapters 8, 9, and 10 reveal how the community of immigration advocates, assisted by an Internet that did not exist when the Flores case began, rallied to the defense of the incarcerated families, and how the settlement came back to life to prevent their long-term detention.

Chapter 11 concerns the small family detention center in Berks County, Pennsylvania. It had operated since 2001, but because of its size (only eighty-four beds) and the rapidity with which it released most of the children held there, it initially attracted little attention. That changed in 2015, when the government started sending families to Berks to avoid having to release them, pursuant to a court order in the Flores case, from imprisonment in Texas. At that point, litigation in Pennsylvania over state licensing of the Berks facility began to parallel ongoing litigation in Texas.

Chapter 12 surveys the policies of the Trump administration on detention of migrant children.[7] The administration has sought to reverse nearly all of the reforms of the previous thirty years. As part of a broad anti-immigrant effort, it tried to deter migrants, including children and families with children, from coming to the United States to seek asylum. It called for repeal of the protective provisions of the 2008 law that Congress passed to assure humanitarian conditions for unaccompanied children awaiting hearings. It unsuccessfully sought reversal of the 2015 court decision that held that the Flores settlement applied to accompanied and unaccompanied migrant children. When that failed, the government embarked on a politically and legally disastrous program of criminally prosecuting mothers who brought their children to the United States. This had the effect of separating children from their parents. In many instances, the government failed to keep records of where the children were sent. When a court ordered that the children be returned to their parents, this failure made the order difficult to implement.

Unable to persuade Congress either to amend the 2008 law or to over-turn the Flores settlement, the administration sought to overturn it unilat-erally by issuing an administrative regulation, an initiative guaranteed to lead to many more years of litigation. Attorney General Jeff Sessions also issued an edict purporting to bar most victims of domestic violence or gang violence from asylum, prompting a lawsuit that enjoined DHS from imple-menting his decision. President Trump followed with a regulation with-holding asylum from immigrants who cross the border without permis-sion, even as his administration prevented more than a limited number of people from seeking asylum at legal border crossings. The administration also adopted a plan to force Central American families to "remain in Mexico" for months or years while waiting for immigration court hearings. It also threatened to impose crippling tariffs on Mexican goods unless Mexico curbed the number of migrants transiting through that country or signed a "safe third country" agreement with the United States. Under U.S. law, the existence of such an agreement could deny asylum to any non-Mexican refugee who passed through Mexico. Central American as well as other refugees would instead have to seek asylum in Mexico, even though Mexico lacks the resources to process or protect very many refugees. Mexico resisted signing such a pact. But the Trump administration pres-sured the government of Guatemala to agree to accept the transfer of all non-Guatemalan adults whose asylum claims the Trump administration does not want to consider.

A conclusion assesses the impact of the Flores case and the state of play in the continuing struggle between the government and immigrants' advocates over the duration and conditions of confinement of children who seek safety in the United States. It includes my recommendations for reforming a system that over the years has caused anguish and trauma for parents and children alike in our nation's baby jails.

1 Jenny Flores

1985–1988

HAROLD EZELL'S JAILS FOR CHILDREN

In 1985, fifteen-year-old Jenny Lisette Flores traveled alone from war-torn El Salvador to the United States, hoping to be reunited with her mother, who was living in California. Like many children who had fled the civil war in her country, she had no visa. The Immigration and Naturalization Service (INS) apprehended her and took her into custody shortly after she crossed from Mexico into California, but she could not be deported until she appeared before an immigration judge to determine whether she had any basis for being allowed to remain in the United States. The judge might find, for example, that she had a claim to U.S. citizenship based on the citizenship of one of her parents, or that she was eligible for asylum. Or the judge might decide that she had no valid claim and should be sent back to El Salvador. But months might pass before such a hearing took place. For children seeking asylum, it could even be several years before their cases were finally concluded, because either the child or the government could appeal a decision that it didn't like.[1]

At the time, in most regions of the country, when the INS apprehended an unaccompanied child traveler who had never received permission to enter the United States, it would release the child to a parent or legal guardian in the United States until an immigration court could decide whether the child was eligible for asylum or other relief from deportation. If no parent was present in the country, it could release the child to an "other responsible party" who would promise to bring the child to court when required.[2] Such a "party" could be a relative or a child welfare agency. But things were different in the INS's Western Region, which included California.

The INS Regional Commissioner was Harold Ezell. He had been an executive for Wienerschnitzel International, a hot dog franchising company, before he joined the Reagan administration in the early 1980s.[3] He believed that "illegal immigration will destroy what we know as a free society in the next five to ten years"[4] and was "among the first to start the drumbeat against what he called an 'invasion' of illegal immigrants."[5] He reportedly stated in a 1985 newspaper interview that some undocumented immigrants should be "skinned and fried" and then deported.[6]

Notwithstanding the child detention policy in effect elsewhere, in 1984 Ezell had adopted a stricter policy for the release of children apprehended in his region. He decided that in California and the other Western states, which happened to be the location of most of the nation's unaccompanied child migrants, the INS would routinely release a child who was in deportation proceedings only to a "parent or lawful guardian." His office would release the child to a different responsible adult only in "unusual or extraordinary cases."[7] It didn't consider Jenny's case unusual or extraordinary. Therefore, Jenny could be detained for as long as it took for her to get a hearing before a judge.

Jenny's mother would have been happy to be reunited with her, but she was herself undocumented, so she was afraid to report to any INS office or facility, such as the one where Jenny was being held, fearing that both she and her daughter would then be deported to El Salvador, where a civil war was raging. Her fear was reasonable, because INS officials acknowledged that undocumented adults who showed up to claim their children were "subject to arrest and deportation."[8] In fact, undocumented mothers who went to INS jails to post bond[9] for their children were sometimes put into deportation proceedings along with their offspring.[10] Decades before the phrase made headlines, Jenny and others like her were subjected by immigration authorities to family separation.

The INS detention center at the Mardi Gras Motel, 1985.

But Jenny's mother had an alternative. Jenny's aunt and uncle lived in Los Angeles and were willing to look after Jenny.[11] The uncle was a U.S. citizen, and the aunt had a green card. Because Jenny had been captured in the Western Region, however, the INS would not release her to someone other than a parent.

Jenny was not in an ordinary jail. The INS had hired a private for-profit contractor, Behavioral Systems Southwest, to house detainees in Los Angeles.[12] That company had taken over the Mardi Gras Motel in Pasadena, "drained the swimming pool, covered the front of the property with chain-link fence, and strung up concertina wire."[13]

Male and female adults and children inhabited this makeshift jail. The children mixed freely with the adult detainees. Jenny shared sleeping quarters with seven other children and five adult women, none of whom were related to her. Like her fellow detainees, she was given no educational instruction or recreation and no reading materials except some English-language magazines that she could not understand.[14] Visitors were not allowed.

The children at several of the other INS jails in California and Texas fared even worse. They were strip-searched when they first arrived and when visited by anyone other than lawyers.[15] At one detention center in Texas, girls were vaginally and rectally searched as well.[16] At another large detention facility for immigrants in Southern California, the staff would "bring minors into the gym every morning, erect a screen between boys and girls, and search everyone . . . [though they] never found anything in body cavities."[17]

When the INS first took Jenny into custody near the border, on May 15, 1985, she had refused to sign any documents without the advice of a lawyer. The INS officials told her that "all Salvadorans were idiots and pubic hair." When she asked where she could remove the fingerprint ink from her hands, an official told her to wipe them on her face, and she complied; the official then laughed at her. Eventually she was transferred to the Mardi Gras Motel. A doctor who examined her after she had been there for two months concluded that the stress of her confinement had resulted in "intermittent preoccupation with death, anorexia and depression."[18]

Jenny was one of about five thousand children detained by the INS each year in the late 1980s, most of whom did not have lawyers.[19] Many of them were sixteen or seventeen years old, including teenaged boys who had fled from violence associated with military forces. One such youth was "Francisco" (not his real name). When he was eight years old, Sandanista soldiers in Nicaragua had killed Francisco's father, older brother, grandfather and uncle. His mother sent him to Honduras, where he lived on the streets before fleeing to the United States at the age of seventeen. Another boy saw his parents and three sisters shot in a village square; he had walked from El Salvador to Texas to escape the same fate.[20]

Some of the children in INS custody were much younger. In 1988, for example, the Border Patrol picked up three Honduran girls, ages seven, five, and four. The oldest one had "a tattered slip of paper in her pocket" with a Miami phone number that turned out to belong to the parents of the younger children.[21]

Jenny Flores was unusually lucky, however, because she was only three degrees of separation away from a lawyer who could make a difference. Imprisoned with her was Alma Cruz, the twelve-year-old daughter of Alma Aldana, a housekeeper for the actor Ed Asner, who had starred in *The Mary Tyler Moore Show*. Like Jenny, Alma Cruz was being held in the motel because Aldana, who was also undocumented, was afraid of claiming her.[22] Asner knew that he could help to solve the girls' problem by calling an attorney whom he knew well.

PETER SCHEY

A vocal critic of the Reagan administration, Asner had been active in promoting peace in Central America and had co-founded an organization known as Pax Americas to lobby for an end to the region's civil wars.[23] He also had been involved in protests against the administration's efforts to deport Central American refugees. In connection with one such protest, at which arrests were expected, Asner had consulted with Peter Schey, a lawyer who had founded the National Center for Immigrants' Rights, which later became the Center for Human Rights and Constitutional Law. To help his housekeeper and her daughter, Asner called Schey.[24]

Schey had dedicated his legal career to the defense of immigrants. His father, a Jewish opponent of the Nazis, had fled Europe in 1938, on one of the last planes from France to England. He had ended up in South Africa, where Peter was born in 1947. As a young teenager, Peter participated in protests against apartheid. In 1962, when opposition to apartheid had become too dangerous even for white activists, the family moved to San Francisco.[25]

Schey was arrested in a protest against the Vietnam War while he was an undergraduate at Berkeley. He went on to study at the California Western School of Law in San Diego, where he received his law degree in 1973. While in law school, Schey enrolled in a legal aid clinic. In his first case, he discovered that the San Diego County hospital was notifying the Border Patrol when an undocumented pregnant woman wanted to give birth there. The Border Patrol would then deport the woman to prevent her baby from becoming a U.S. citizen. Schey threatened to sue the hospital. As a result, the hospital stopped cooperating with the Border Patrol.[26]

After finishing law school, Schey began to represent immigrants, first in San Diego and then in Los Angeles. This work quickly became full-time. His first class action was a successful suit against the INS to force it

Peter Schey in 2017.

to provide everyone who was in deportation proceedings with a list of free local legal services.[27] Over the years, he initiated other important class actions on behalf of Central American immigrants and refugees. In the late 1970s he brought a case against the Houston Independent School District, the largest school district in Texas, challenging its denial of secondary education to undocumented children. He argued that refusing to educate these children was a denial of the equal protection guaranteed by the United States Constitution. While the suit was pending, Schey discovered that state officials were getting federal funding for migrant children that they had expelled from school.[28] The case was consolidated with a similar suit in another district, and it went all the way to the Supreme Court.[29] In 1981, he was one of two lawyers who argued for the children in the Supreme Court. By a 5–4 vote, the justices agreed that the Constitution required states to allow undocumented children to attend public schools.[30]

THE FLORES CASE BEGINS

After receiving Asner's call, Schey went to the converted motel in which the children were incarcerated. He was horrified by the prison-like conditions. He quickly contacted the next of kin of several of the children in the motel, including Jenny, and offered to try to help all of them, without charge.

Jenny Flores had been jailed for nearly a month at that point. The government had set bond for her at $2000. If she did not raise the funds or agree to return to El Salvador, the government would detain her indefinitely.[31] And officials had not told her about Ezell's policy, which would keep her in jail even if she did raise the funds. Schey's co-counsel, Carlos Holguín, the second-most experienced lawyer in Schey's office, asked for the bond amount to be reduced, and a judge reduced it to $1500. Only then did an official reveal that even if she paid it, she would not be released until a parent or legal guardian picked her up, a condition that she could not meet.[32]

On July 11, 1985, after taking statements from several of the children and their relatives, Holguín filed a federal lawsuit titled *Jenny Lisette Flores v. Edwin Meese III*, Meese being President Reagan's Attorney General, whose Department of Justice included the INS.[33] Over the next thirty-five years, however, many subsequent attorneys general would be named as substitute defendants in what would become an apparently never-ending case. Holguín named Ezell and the private prison companies in California and Texas as additional defendants.

JUDGE KELLEHER

The case was assigned to Judge Robert J. Kelleher. Although he had been appointed by a Republican president, Kelleher had become famous as a young lawyer for his own personal challenge to the status quo. An avid tennis player, he'd been a member of the U.S. Davis Cup teams in 1962 and 1963 and had then become president of the U.S. Lawn Tennis Association. At the time, amateur tennis players were not allowed to compete in major international tournaments such as the U.S. Open. With British counterparts, he had pressured the International Lawn Tennis Federation into changing that rule. The result was an immense boost in the incomes of

Judge Robert J. Kelleher.

American tennis players, and the emergence of tennis as a major spectator sport. Kelleher was later honored for his role in the matter by being inducted into the International Tennis Hall of Fame. In 1969, he returned to a law practice that he'd left for his Tennis Association work, but the next year he was appointed to the bench by President Richard M. Nixon.[34]

Holguín took the lead in making arguments to Judge Kelleher. No legal theory would have prevented the government from jailing child migrants, so he didn't ask the judge simply to order an end to all such detentions. Instead he wanted Kelleher to order three specific reforms. First, Holguín asked that his clients and other unaccompanied immigrant children be released, if they posted bond, to the custody of responsible adults other than their undocumented parents. Holguín argued that Ezell's policy hadn't been authorized by any regulation. It was just an arbitrary practice that had been adopted by the INS in California and some other Western states. Holguín suspected that in the region he directed, Commissioner Ezell was using the children as bait to arrest their undocumented parents.[35] Holguín also offered a more expansive argument for releasing his clients to relatives other than parents. At the time, immigration law distinguished between two categories of individuals (including children) who came to the United States without permission, such as that provided by a U.S. visa.[36] Those who were apprehended at the border and allowed into the country until their claims (such as asylum claims) could be adjudicated were said to be in "exclusion" proceedings. Those who were apprehended after crossing the border were put into "deportation" proceedings. The rules for releasing children differed for these two types of cases. A federal law specified that children in "exclusion" proceedings could be released to a sibling, aunt, or uncle willing to sponsor the child.[37] No such law mandated release to those relatives for those who, like Jenny Flores, were in "deportation" proceedings, leaving Ezell free to make his own rule for the Western Region. Holguín argued that the distinction between these two categories was arbitrary, and therefore an unconstitutional denial of the children's right to the "equal protection" of the laws.

Second, Holguín wanted to end the strip and body cavity searches. He argued that the searches were unnecessary and unreasonable and therefore a violation of the Fourth Amendment's ban on unreasonable searches and seizures. Finally, he asked for a third change in detention policy. To the extent that children remained in detention, he wanted the court to require the government to provide them with reading material, education, recreation, and visitation rights. He argued that keeping children locked up without the basic amenities afforded even to convicted criminals violated the guarantee of "due process of law," and on the much narrower (and more winnable) claim that the conditions of confinement administered by the private prisons violated the INS's own operations instructions and manuals.

Although Schey and Holguín had named only four children, including Jenny Flores, as individual plaintiffs, Holguín asked the judge to certify the case as a class action, so that if he won, the court would order the INS to make policy changes for all similarly situated children. Under federal procedural rules, this would require him to show that Jenny and the other children he represented suffered hardships similar to those held by the INS elsewhere, and that he and Schey could provide "adequate representation" even for children they had never met.[38] Holguín expected that the lawsuit could easily satisfy these requirements. By 1985, class actions to change government policy were a well-established tactic. *Brown v. Board of Education* was a class action, and in 1966, the federal procedural rules had been amended to make it easier for lawyers to use class actions to ask for changes in government policy. The class action was a good vehicle for this lawsuit because, unlike individual cases, class actions can't be made moot and dismissed simply by giving the particular plaintiff or plaintiffs what they are asking for. Even if the INS released Jenny, and even if she won asylum and eventually became a naturalized American citizen, the case would continue so long as the government was jailing other children under similar conditions and restrictions.

Lawsuits often involve a good deal of skirmishing through motions to the judge long before they go to trial. As a preliminary matter at the very outset of the case, Holguín asked Judge Kelleher to order the INS to release Jenny Flores on bond to her aunt, and to release her fellow plaintiff Dominga Hernandez on bond to an adult family friend.[39] Holguín knew that the case could drag on for a long time, and he wanted his clients to be free while the legal wheels turned. Even Ezell's restrictive policy allowed release to a "legal guardian" of a child. Family law is the province of state courts, and it wasn't clear that a *federal* judge, as opposed to a state judge or an INS administrative judge, could designate someone as a legal guardian. Nevertheless, Judge Kelleher designated the aunt and the family friend as "temporary legal guardians" of the children. He also stated that Ezell's bond release policy violated equal protection,[40] apparently because children in other parts of the country could be released to adults other than parents.

Kelleher was unwilling, so early in the case, to make a broad ruling affecting other detained children, so he stated that his order applied only to the two girls.[41] The INS released Jenny and one of Holguín's other clients immediately, just nine days after Holguín filed his complaint. Because of the judge's "temporary legal guardian" designation, Ezell's policy had not been modified. Ezell held a press conference to say that he was pleased with the judge's decision because adults would be legally responsible for the care of the two girls.[42] Other INS officials crowed that the judge's designation of adults as temporary guardians "vindicated" their policy of releasing children only to parents or legal guardians.[43]

The next step for Holguín was to persuade the court to certify the suit as a class action on behalf of all children incarcerated in the Western Region. As mentioned above, this would prevent the government from mooting the case by releasing all four children named in the original complaint (and any others added later). Also, it would ensure that discovery would extend to information about all of the INS's juvenile detention facilities in the region. Holguín would be able to obtain sworn testimony and documents about detention conditions and policies for all the immigration jails in the region. The judge did not immediately rule on the class action request, but he allowed discovery to begin.

Discovery began and continued through 1985 and 1986. Holguín enlisted law students to interview children who had been detained. For example, Pegine Grayson, then a student at the University of Southern California, interviewed fifteen children in INS detention at a border patrol station in Chula Vista, California. In a report filed in court, she stated that the facility was a "living hell" for minors who had nothing to do while in detention "except sit there and stare at the walls. All were despondent and depressed." She asserted that the facility failed to meet state and federal standards for the detention of children, which called for them to be separated from unrelated adults and provided with educational materials and recreation.[44] Paul DeMuro, a juvenile justice and child welfare expert who visited several of the facilities, testified at a deposition that "none had specially trained staff, adequate educational program, adequate recreational program (particularly for younger children), adequate medical services, privacy, appropriate menus, etc. The norm for each program was sterility, boredom, and confinement." At Chula Vista, he found, "boys were awakened in the middle of the night for roll call and threatened with seclusion in a cold room if they failed to cooperate," and "teenage girls on some shifts are stripped completely naked and visually inspected."[45]

Ian Fain, the assistant U.S. attorney handling the case for the INS, told the court that the claim that INS detention conditions were inadequate was meritless. He said that no educational materials or programs for the children in detention were warranted, because "the INS is not in the business of educating children," and because most of them were released after a short time. Besides, he said, while she was in detention, Jenny Flores "never asked for books nor did she complain about lack of schooling."[46] But after reading all the evidence about detention conditions, Judge Kelleher had become fully engaged in addressing them. He ruled that the case could proceed as a class action.[47]

A PARTIAL SETTLEMENT

Behind the scenes, the INS regarded the detention of unaccompanied children as "the biggest headache the service has"[48] and had been trying to divest itself of responsibility for caring for children its agents had arrested. For years, it had sought to arrange for the Community Relations Service of the Department of Justice to take on the task of finding appropriate placements for the children until their court hearings could be held. But early in 1987, these efforts failed. The Reagan administration was not willing to spend the money either to improve conditions in the detention facilities or to add funds to the Community Relations Service so that it could secure better placements. "Budget priorities scrapped the program," one of Ezell's assistants reported.[49]

By the end of May 1987, Holguín and Schey were ready to return to court. Judge Kelleher ruled that the INS should release children to certain relatives other than parents, but he postponed ruling on the other issues in the case. He ordered the government to allow relatives other than parents (or legal guardians) to post bond and take custody of detained children. Finding Ezell's restriction unreasonable, he ordered the INS to release the children not only to parents but also to siblings, aunts, uncles, or, if necessary, even to nonrelatives who had accompanied the children to the United States.[50] As to Schey's complaints about the conditions of confinement of the children while they awaited release, or of those who had nobody to post bond for them, Kelleher decided not to make a decision until a trial could be held, which could take a year or longer.

For Schey, the broadening of the categories of adults who could come for children represented a foot in the door but only a partial victory. For example, some detained children had relatives, such as grandparents, who were willing and able to take responsibility but remained ineligible to do so because they were not listed in the judge's order. One of the defendants gave Schey an opening to try to pry the jail door wider. Behavioral Systems Southwest filed a motion to dismiss the claims against the company. It made a "just following orders" defense, arguing that the company "followed whatever procedures or lack of procedures that the INS had for housing of juveniles."[51]

Two months after he had extended pick-up privileges to siblings, aunts, and uncles, Judge Kelleher held a pre-trial conference to discuss Behavioral Systems' motion. Holguín argued against it on behalf of the plaintiffs. He disputed Behavioral Systems' claim, noting, for example, that the INS did not have a rule barring visitation, but Behavioral Systems "had in fact taken it upon itself to have an absolute no visitation policy."[52] Judge Kelleher denied the company's motion.[53] The lawyers for all of the parties were in court with the judge, so Holguín took the opportunity to urge that the judge's previous order should be extended to "clearly responsible adults, such as grandmothers, priests, other persons whose reputation and responsibility is beyond question."[54]

The transcript of the hearing reveals the judge's reaction. "Hold on," he said. "Priests are not very well equipped in any respect to provide the kind of shelter, care, custody and control that ought to be required. Grandmothers may not, either, be respectively able to do that."

"We're not saying that the INS ought to release a minor to a grandmother who is completely unable to take care of the child," Holguín responded. "Simply that they not adopt the hard and fast rule saying that we will not release this child no matter how reputable the adult is and how much evidence you show that you are able to take care of this child."

Holguín's argument apparently caused the judge to recall that his prior order extended the categories of responsible adults beyond blood relatives to unrelated persons who had accompanied children to the United States. "There was an order of this court, was there not," he asked the INS's lawyer, "which required the release to a person unrelated in blood . . . who at least stated or represented to the court that he had the ability to take care of the child?"[55] Nevertheless, he declined to issue a further ruling on the issue that day.

Holguín's reference to priests had not been fanciful. Many of the children did not have any relative in the United States, so Ezell's restrictive conditions of release presented them with the prospect of lengthy or indefinite detention. But the Roman Catholic Archdiocese of Los Angeles was concerned about their plight. The church had declined an INS request to create its own detention facility for unaccompanied children, citing a "moral conflict" because it did not believe that they should be in INS custody at all.[56] A few months after the court hearing at which Holguín had raised the custody question, the INS agreed to release two dozen children to the church, which undertook to put them in foster homes. Aside from this special arrangement, the INS continued to be unwilling to make that option available to other "responsible adults."[57]

While trying to liberalize INS release policies for children, Schey and Holguín had been quietly negotiating with government lawyers to try to settle the issues regarding conditions of confinement.[58] Neither side wanted a trial of those issues. The INS at last persuaded funding officials in the Department of Justice to allow the Department's Community Relations Service to create an "Alien Minors Shelter Care Program" (AMSCP) under which it would contract with nonprofit or for-profit agencies with child care experience to operate detention facilities for children.

The policy anticipated that in most cases, the period of detention would be about thirty days, though long-term care might also be necessary. Agencies that won the contracts would have to meet detailed standards for care, including:

- Children detained by the INS would be transferred to facilities meeting the required standards within seventy-two hours of arrest except in extraordinary circumstances.
- The children could be accommodated in foster homes, group care programs, or residential facilities, but for residential facilities, the shelter care was to be provided "in accordance with applicable state child welfare statutes" and "in an open type of setting without a need for extraordinary security measures."
- All facilities had to meet "applicable state child welfare licensing requirements."

- Children would follow an "integrated and structured daily routine" with education, recreation, work or chores, a study period, counseling, group interaction, free time, and access to religious services.

- The contractor would have to provide "suitable living accommodations," food, appropriate clothing, and routine medical and dental care (including a complete medical examination within twenty-four hours of admission).

- Each child would have at least one individual counseling session per week conducted by trained social work staff, and a group counseling session at least twice a week.

- The children would have to have classroom education five days a week, led by a licensed teacher, focusing on science, social studies, math, reading, writing, and physical education.

- Each child was to have at least an hour a day of large muscle activity and an hour of structured leisure activity, not including time watching television. The facility should have equipment such as "a basketball, volleyball, softball, tetherball, punching bag and soccer ball."

- Visitation and contact with family members was to be encouraged.

- The agencies could not provide legal assistance to the children, but were required to restate to each child information that the INS would give them regarding their right to be represented by an attorney, their right to apply for asylum, and their right to a hearing before a judge.

- The agencies would have to try to identify family members for potential reunification. The standards stated, however, that if undocumented parents were identified, "the child would be released to the parent's custody after the parents were processed by the INS and subsequently assigned to a deportation docket."

- Children housed in an agency facility would remain in the legal custody of the INS.

- The agencies would have to maintain detailed records regarding each child and would have to report quarterly to the INS.[59]

As we shall see, although the government did not at first implement the standards, they were precursors for more detailed rules that eventually were put into place and lasted well into the twenty-first century.

Six months later, Schey agreed that the standards in the AMSCP were reasonable, and certainly a big improvement over the conditions in the

Mardi Gras Motel and other INS facilities. He had high hopes that the INS would hold contractors to them. He agreed to a settlement of the part of the case dealing with conditions of detention. The settlement provided that by June 1, 1988, "except in unusual and extraordinary circumstances" any child detained by the INS for more than seventy-two hours would be housed in a facility that met the standards in the AMSCP. The exception would apply only if the child's interests was served by being placed in some other facility or if the child could not be housed in a contract facility "because of unforeseen events."

For the first year, all exceptions would have to be reported to the court. The settlement also provided that in addition to the AMSCP standards, Spanish-speaking children would be given educational and reading materials in their own language. The INS would make "reasonable efforts" to provide such materials in other languages as needed.[60]

THE STRIP SEARCH ISSUE

Nothing in the settlement pertained to the first seventy-two hours of detention. In some of the INS facilities in the Western Region, children were strip-searched during that time. Because strip searches were so damaging to the children's psychological wellbeing, Schey and Holguín focused on them for the next skirmish in the case. Holguín asked Judge Kelleher to order an end to these searches. Holguín and the government's lawyers agreed that there was no factual dispute about whether the searches occurred and were authorized by law. The only issue was whether they were unconstitutional under the Fourth Amendment's prohibition of unreasonable searches. Therefore, it was appropriate for the judge to decide that legal issue without putting it to a jury, through a procedure known as summary judgment. In a summary judgment, where no facts in a case are in dispute and the only issue is a legal one, the judge decides all issues. Because Holguín was still pressing for a more liberal ruling on who could post bond for children and take them out of jail, he asked the court only for a partial summary judgment that would ban the strip searches.

The government justified the searches in two ways. First, it claimed a "need to maintain security in detention facilities by preventing aliens from bringing in weapons on contraband." Second, while Americans have a right not to be searched unreasonably when they have an expectation of privacy, people from Central American countries "may have little or no rights" and therefore "carry no actual or subjective expectation that they would not be subjected to unreasonable intrusions into their privacy" in the United States.

Judge Kelleher disposed of these arguments with ringing rhetoric. He deemed a strip search to be "perhaps the most severe intrusion on personal rights," one that another court had described as "demeaning, dehumanizing, undignified, humiliating, terrifying, unpleasant, embarrassing, repulsive, signifying degradation and submission." He noted that "children are especially susceptible to possible traumas from strip searches." He dismissed the security claims as factually unfounded, noting that the INS strip-searched about 7,300 children a year, but in 1987 had found only one instance of contraband as a result—a teenage girl with a piece of a broken mirror. In that instance there was no evidence that the girl had planned to use it as a weapon. As to the argument that Central American children had no expectation of privacy, he said that many of them came to the United States with "the expectation of liberty, opportunity, and a better life, the embodiment of which is in our Constitution." Therefore, unless the INS had a reasonable suspicion that a particular child was hiding contraband that could be found only by a strip search, the search would be unconstitutional.[61]

JUDGE KELLEHER DECIDES

Judge Kelleher still had to decide whether to expand further the categories of persons who could take custody of children released from INS detention. On May 17, 1988, perhaps anticipating that the judge would rule against it, the INS changed its policy, conforming it to the judge's ruling a year earlier. Regional commissioners could now release children to certain relatives other than parents. The INS issued a new regulation stating that they "shall" be released "in order of preference, to (i) a parent; (ii) legal guardian or (iii) adult relative (brother, sister, aunt, uncle, grandparent) who are not presently in INS detention" unless it determined that release would result in the child absconding rather than appearing in court. Judge Kelleher's ruling had covered the siblings, aunts, and uncles listed in the new policy; grandparents were an addition. If a relative who was not in detention couldn't be located, INS officials could consider, "on a case by case basis," releasing the detained relative as well as the child. If continued detention was necessary to prevent absconding, a "juvenile coordinator" would find a "suitable placement" in a "facility designated for the occupancy of juveniles," which could be a state juvenile detention center.[62] The new regulation applied this policy nationwide, in both deportation and exclusion cases. This mooted Schey and Holguín's argument that INS procedures were riddled with irrational distinctions. It left them only the argument that INS refusal to allow unrelated adults and nonprofit agencies to assume responsibility for the children violated the due process clause of the Constitution.

From Schey's perspective, this policy change was an improvement, but it did not go as far as he wanted. Many incarcerated children did not have any close relatives in the United States with whom they could stay. Also, the government's announcement of its new policy might cause Judge Kelleher to accept the half loaf that the government offered and therefore to deny his request that responsible nonrelatives be allowed to assume responsibility for detained children.

But Schey had persuaded the judge to go for the full loaf. Seven days later, nearly three years after the lawsuit had commenced, Judge Kelleher finally gave Schey and Holguín almost everything they had asked for. He ruled "on due process grounds" that in the absence of a reason to believe that the child would abscond, the INS had to release an eligible minor to his parents or guardian, or an "other responsible adult party." The person need not be a blood relative; even a responsible priest would do. In addition, the court ordered that every child taken into custody had to be given an administrative hearing to determine probable cause for his or her arrest and the need for any restrictions on release, even if the child did not affirmatively request such a hearing.[63] This was an important addition, because most children did not know that they could request a hearing at which an immigration judge might lower the amount of bond to secure their release. The government had argued that in the absence of a request, it had no duty to bring the child before a judge until the final hearing on deportation.

An elated Holguín told the press that "this ends the practice of . . . using the children as bait in order to capture their undocumented parents." The INS was not at all happy. William Odencrantz, the INS's top lawyer for the Western Region, signaled that the INS was unwilling to accept the ruling, particularly the indefinite boundaries of the phrase "responsible adult party." "What defines a 'responsible adult?'" he asked a United Press International reporter. "We will have to make those kinds of calls and judgments in releasing these kids. We're not a child welfare agency and we're not possessed of expertise in making those calls." He offered a hypothetical situation in which a border patrol officer might stop a motor home and arrest twenty-three undocumented children inside it. "Then someone comes in off the street and says, 'I want those children released to me.' How do we judge it?"[64]

The plaintiffs had won and the case seemed to be over. But from where Odencrantz sat, it was just beginning.

2 "Good Enough"

1988–1993

Peter Schey's victory in the first stage of the Flores case was far from complete. There were two problems. First, although the settlement agreement promised an improvement in the conditions under which children were detained, the government disagreed with Judge Robert Kelleher's decision that the Constitution required releasing detained children to the custody of responsible adults other than their parents or close relatives. It decided to appeal the judge's order to the U.S. Court of Appeals for the Ninth Circuit, which includes California. The second problem, which I will discuss in chapter 3, is that the government failed to live up to its promise to improve the conditions of detention.

A few days before Judge Kelleher rendered his decision, the government had issued its new regulation establishing the same standards for release for children in deportation cases and those in exclusion cases. The original issue in the case—whether the disparity in the standards for release was arbitrary—was rendered moot by these new regulations. Therefore the government's appeal of Judge Kelleher's decision focused on two other issues.

First, did federal law allow the Immigration and Naturalization Service (INS) to bar the release of children to responsible adults if there were no available close relatives? Second, if the restriction on who could take custody of children was valid, was the government constitutionally required at least to offer every detained child a hearing, whether or not the child requested one? If such a hearing was required, an immigration judge would have to decide whether there had been probable cause for taking the child into custody and determine any conditions for release, such as the amount of bond that would have to be posted.

The first issue broke into two parts. Did federal *statutes* require the INS to release children to any responsible adult? If they did not, was the government's restrictive release policy so unreasonable as to violate the Constitution?

CARLOS HOLGUÍN

Schey and his partner Carlos Holguín worked very closely on all aspects of the Flores case; they agreed that Holguín would take the lead in defending Judge Kelleher's decision on appeal.

Holguín had been a lawyer for five years when the Flores case began. His father was a Mexican-American public school teacher who had been involved in protests, sit-ins, and confrontations with administrators to protest substandard education of Mexican-Americans in Los Angeles. Rather than seeking admission to any of the nationally accredited law schools in California or elsewhere, Holguín had chosen, instead, to get his law degree from the People's College of Law, accredited only in California, which was founded for students who "demonstrate a commitment to progressive social change, have an awareness of working class issues and [are] willing to employ the skills gained at the school to further these progressive causes in their own way."[1] While there, he began working at what is now the National Immigration Law Center. By 1984, he was a full-time immigration lawyer at the National Center for Immigrants' Rights (later named the Center for Human Rights and Constitutional Law), which Schey had recently founded. Holguín and Schey had worked together earlier in a legal services office funded by the federal Legal Services Corporation. In 1980, Congress barred most of those offices from representing undocumented immigrants or initiating class actions.[2] Both

Carlos Holguín in 1987.

lawyers quit their legal services jobs to seek a way to work for immigrants' rights in a nonprofit institution unconstrained by politics.[3]

The Orantes-Hernandez Case

By the time he met Jenny Flores, Holguín already had handled a major class action suit. When Holguín was two years out of law school, he had learned from individual Salvadoran clients that while in detention, they had been pressured by INS agents to agree to return to El Salvador voluntarily. They had not been told of their rights to seek asylum under the federal Refugee Act of 1980 or to consult with a lawyer before agreeing to return. For some of them, the government's intimidation had begun at the moment of arrest.

The experience of Crosby Wilfredo Orantes-Hernandez was typical. While he was in El Salvador, government soldiers had come to his house and kicked the door down. They accosted his mother and asked where the men of the house were. When she refused to answer, they grabbed her by the hair and hurled her against a wall. She fell, and a soldier stepped on her neck and smashed her face with his rifle. Then they found Orantes-Hernandez and his uncles and brothers in a back room and beat all of them with rifles. They took the uncles away. Two days later, the uncles' bodies were found. Their eyes had been gouged out and their sex organs had been cut off. Orantes-Hernandez fled to the United States, where the INS captured him as he got off a bus in Culver City, California. An INS agent grabbed his arm and twisted it behind him and held him against an INS van while a second agent hit him twice with his revolver.[4]

The law gave Orantes-Hernandez and others like him the right to apply for asylum, enabling him to avoid deportation and start a new life in the United States. It provided for a grant of asylum if an applicant proved that he or she had a "well-founded fear" of being persecuted on account of race, religion, nationality, political opinion, or membership in a particular social group, such as a union.[5] Orantes-Hernandez had a good chance to win asylum, because by 1982, the U.S. government was well aware that the Salvadoran military was committing horrific human rights abuses, including torture. The State Department had reported to Congress that disappearances were common, that bodies with signs of torture had been discovered, and that members of the government's security forces may have committed the unsolved murders.[6] Amnesty International had similarly found that the security forces had been killing civilians who were innocent of any participation in guerrilla activities.[7]

During one of Holguín's visits to the detention center, Orantes-Hernandez and his fellow detainees told him that immediately after being detained, INS officials had presented them with statements to sign. The detainees did not know their rights or the significance of the documents, but the officials told them that if they did not sign, they would stay in jail for a long time and then be deported. At least one woman was told that she would be placed in a cell with men. None were told that they could talk to lawyers or seek asylum. The detainees were talked into signing "voluntary departure" agreements authorizing the INS to deport them immediately without a hearing or any other process. Most signed them, but a few who had some knowledge of asylum refused. Some Salvadorans managed to contact a lawyer after they had signed the agreements and before they were whisked away, but at least 75 percent of them just vanished from the detention facilities,[8] often "in a matter of hours," and ended up back in El Salvador.[9]

For those who refused to sign, jail conditions were awful. In some facilities the detainees were not allowed any reading or writing materials except the New Testament. Some had no access to telephones, even for attorney calls. Lawyers' paralegal assistants were barred from visiting. The detainees were sometimes put into solitary confinement for several days, without an opportunity to contest charges of misconduct, for minor infractions such as not standing in a long line at mealtime.

Holguín sued. The government did not seriously contest the facts. It relied on legal arguments. It claimed that the Salvadorans could not sue in federal court and could only raise their complaints in the asylum hearings that most of them had waived by signing the agreements. The government also argued that courts could not challenge INS's procedures because if Salvadorans knew about the right to seek asylum, more Salvadorans would apply, which could affect U.S. foreign policy. The government also told the court that it should not hold the INS responsible because "the agency is powerless to completely control its employees."[10]

The court rejected the government's arguments. It found that "INS agents routinely give incomplete, misleading and even false advice to Salvadorans regarding their legal rights," that they engage in "coercive tactics," that the agents had deprived the detainees of due process, that they had imposed unreasonable restrictions on their access to lawyers, and that placing them in solitary confinement without prior hearings was unlawful. The court issued a preliminary injunction which barred the use of coercive tactics to obtain voluntary departure agreements; required that detainees be read a specified statement of their rights; permitted lawyers to rescind any voluntary departure agreements that their clients had signed; permitted paralegal assistants to visit represented detainees; and barred use of solitary confinement for more than twenty-four hours without written charges and an opportunity for a hearing.[11] Six years later, after other lawyers had replaced Holguín as the representatives of the Salvadoran plaintiffs, the preliminary injunction was made permanent and somewhat expanded.[12] That decision was upheld on appeal.[13]

THE FLORES CASE GOES TO THE NINTH CIRCUIT:
ROUND ONE

With the Orantes-Hernandez victory behind him, Holguín became responsible for defending Judge Kelleher's decision in the Flores case. The government was represented in its appeal to the U.S. Court of Appeals for the Ninth Circuit by Ian Fain. Fain and Schey had worked together, years earlier, at the Legal Aid Society of San Diego. Schey regarded him as "a very sweet guy, well balanced."[14]

Fain's brief argued that the INS was well within its statutory authority, because an act of Congress gave the Attorney General the discretion to release an alien on a bond of at least $500. The law also authorized the Attorney General to make regulations necessary to enforce the immigration laws.[15] Holguín countered that the only legitimate purpose of a bond requirement was to ensure that the detained person appeared for a subsequent hearing. The amended regulation, which did not permit release except to close relatives, exceeded the authority that Congress had delegated as it was not tailored to achieve that narrow objective.

Judge Kelleher had based his ruling on the U.S. Constitution. Both sides agreed that the Constitution imposed some limits on the government's ability to incarcerate individuals. The Fifth Amendment barred denial of a person's liberty without due process of law; this applied to foreign nationals on American soil as well as to citizens. The issue to be litigated was what standard should be used to determine when governmental action exceeded permissible limits. If a migrant child had a "fundamental right" not to be jailed pending an immigration hearing, the government's rules on who could take custody of the children would be subject to "strict scrutiny" by the courts. If the right was not "fundamental," the INS regulation would be upheld if the government could show some "rational relationship" to a legitimate purpose. So how the right was described could determine the outcome of the case. Fain asserted that the child's right was best characterized as "the right to be released to an unrelated adult," while Holguín argued that the right was, more fundamentally, "the right to be free from physical restraint." The government claimed a legitimate purpose for its regulation, urging that it lacked the resources to do "home studies" to determine whether unrelated adults were sufficiently responsible to care for a released child, and that limiting release to close relatives would foster the safety of such children.

Finally, the government urged that no automatic hearing on conditions of release was constitutionally required. Judge Kelleher had not explicitly stated why he had thought that such a hearing was legally necessary. However, his ruling was consistent with the 1975 decision of the Supreme Court in *Gerstein v. Pugh*. In that case, a person had been arrested without a warrant and incarcerated under a Florida law which allowed jailing of accused persons for extended periods of time without probable cause review by a judge. The Court had held that "the Fourth Amendment requires a judicial determination of probable cause as a prerequisite to extended restraint of liberty following arrest."[16] Fain argued that this rule for criminal cases did not apply to deportation cases, which, although involving incarceration, were civil in nature. Holguín relied on the unqualified statement of the nation's highest court.

Most lawyers believe that the fate of appellate cases involving public policy issues often depends on which judges are assigned to decide it.[17] In the federal courts of appeal, three-judge panels are created through a random process, and cases are randomly assigned, after briefing and shortly before oral argument, to one of these panels.[18] But there is one exception to this randomness. The chief judge of the court may create a panel consisting of two judges of the court of appeals and one visiting district judge (though such a panel would not hear a case being appealed from a decision of that very district judge).[19] Allowing district judges to sit on appellate panels has two ostensible purposes: to reduce the workloads of the appellate judges, and to give the district judges insight into the thinking and operations of the courts above them. The chief judge has discretion to appoint a particular district judge to participate on a panel. The panel that would hear the appeal in *Flores v. Meese* included a district judge.

THE NINTH CIRCUIT PANEL

One of the judges was J. Clifford Wallace, known as a "law and order" judge.[20] Appointed by Richard Nixon, Wallace was "a noted conservative who has earned the enmity of liberals." One criminal defense lawyer complained, "You get the feeling, 'Why are you wasting the court's time?' by raising cases before him." Wallace described himself as one who "would not want to modify what I think is the law that governs me under the feeling that I want to show my compassion."[21] A devout Mormon, he "sought inspiration day by day from his Heavenly Father."[22]

A second member of the panel was Wallace's ideological opposite: Judge Betty Fletcher, a Jimmy Carter appointee who would be called "a liberal stalwart of [the court] for decades." A native of Tacoma, she had graduated from the University of Washington's law school and then experienced discrimination first hand. "The professor who was supposed to get interviews for graduating students never got one for me," she remembered, but she insisted on seeing the hiring partners of the firms that she wanted to work for, and was hired at one of them. She practiced law in Seattle and later became the first female president of the King County (Seattle) Bar Association.[23]

Given this ideological divide, the third member of the panel was likely to cast the deciding vote. That was District Judge Lloyd D. George, whom Chief Judge Alfred Goodwin had appointed to the panel. George was a Nevadan and, like Wallace, a Mormon. He had attended Brigham Young University, become president of its student body, and then served as a fighter pilot in the Air Force. After graduating from the law school at Berkeley, he practiced law before Ronald Reagan appointed him to the bench in 1984.[24]

Schey was "somewhat taken aback" when he learned which judges would be on the panel, because two of the three members were likely to be more deferential to the government than most members of the court.[25] "I think we realized that this could be a problem," he said, because "in general conservative Republican judges are going to tend to side with the Department of Justice more often than a liberal, non-religious judge may. But you just soldier on."[26]

THE NINTH CIRCUIT DECIDES

On June 20, 1990, more than a year after Holguín and his INS counterpart Fain argued the case, the court overturned Judge Kelleher's decision by a vote of two to one, with Judge Fletcher dissenting.

Judge Wallace, writing for the majority, began by broadly affirming the authority of the INS to issue regulations in general and, in particular, the regulation that barred releasing children except to close relatives. He noted the Attorney General's statutory authority to make regulations that "he deems necessary," and added that "Congress intended the Attorney General's power to detain and formulate bond conditions to be exceptionally broad." He also noted that nothing in the law limited the government's discretion regarding individuals to whom children could be released.[27]

Then he turned to the critical constitutional issue of whether the regulation infringed a "fundamental" right. He cited *Bowers v. Hardwick*,[28] in which the Supreme Court had recently held that Texas could criminally penalize homosexual sex despite the claim of a protected liberty interest. In the Bowers case, he wrote, the court had "advised against expanding the list of fundamental rights which have attenuated roots in the language of the Constitution." He agreed with the INS that "the right at stake is the right to be released to an unrelated adult," one that was not as fundamental as the right not to be incarcerated at all.[29] Since, narrowly framed, the children's rights were not fundamental, only "minimal scrutiny" of the regulation was appropriate. The restriction on who could take custody of detainee children was rationally related to the asserted purpose of protecting the incarcerated children from unrelated adults who, despite being found "responsible," might harm them. If Judge Kelleher's order stood, "there would be no way to ensure that the children would not be released to child abusers, sexual deviants, or adults that would subject the children to severe neglect."[30]

Finally, Judge Wallace rejected the argument that the Gerstein decision required giving every child a hearing. "*Gerstein* does not apply to deportation hearings," he wrote, because the Court hadn't said that it applied to civil cases. Moreover, deportation proceedings are "a unique kind of civil proceeding" with "fewer procedural due process protections than a criminal trial" and in which "the full panoply of due process right are not applicable." On this issue, however, the court left a door open, sending the case back to Judge Kelleher to weigh the interests of the children, the value to them of a hearing, and the burdens on the government if its regulation was modified.[31]

It is often possible to discern the contrasting perspectives of the majority and the dissent simply by reading how each opens its opinion. Judge

Wallace began the majority opinion by stressing the government's administrative burdens: "this case arises out of the INS's efforts to deal with the growing number of alien children entering the United States. . . ." Judge Fletcher's dissent framed the case very differently: "The facts of this case are among the most disturbing I have confronted in my many years on the court. Children are being held in detention by the INS for as long as two years in highly inappropriate conditions out of a professed concern for their welfare."[32] She disagreed with every aspect of the majority opinion. She noted that although deference to the Attorney General's authority to write regulations was appropriate for immigration decisions that might affect foreign affairs or national security, that did not apply to the cases at hand. The issue here, she said, was how the INS should treat people awaiting deportation decisions. Since foreign nationals, a group traditionally subject to discrimination, were being deprived of physical liberty, the regulations should be reviewed closely.

Judge Fletcher was appalled by the court's narrow definition of the right involved in the case which, she said, was "very simply, wrong." "Constitutional rights are not characterized at that level of specificity. To define the right as the majority does defines it out of existence."[33] She believed the regulation should be strictly scrutinized, but even under a relaxed standard of review, she would strike the rule down as irrational. "The INS's assertion that children's welfare is better served by remaining indefinitely in jail stretches credulity," she wrote. "Common sense as well as expert testimony tells us that keeping children in jail, even under 'ideal' jail conditions, is not a rational way for the government to fulfill its responsibilities as 'surrogate parent.'"

Judge Fletcher also disagreed with the majority about whether *Gerstein* required hearings for the children. She noted that in a subsequent case,[34] the Supreme Court had cited *Gerstein* several times while evaluating (and upholding) the adequacy of New York's civil juvenile detention procedures. In addition, even if the district court balanced the benefits of release to the children against the burdens on the government, it would have to decide in favor of the children.

She closed by noting that some of the incarcerated children would be deported, but some would be granted political asylum. "Even if we were so unfeeling[35] as to be unconcerned with the tragic effects on children who in the end will be returned to their home countries, at the least we ought to be alarmed at the effect on those who will remain."[36]

The usual recourse for a lawyer who thinks that a Court of Appeals got it wrong is to seek review in the Supreme Court. However, it is also permissible for the losing party to request the court to reconsider its decision and further to request that all of the active judges of the court, not just the panel that rendered the decision, participate in the reconsideration. In the case of the Ninth Circuit, the nation's largest, the court had so many members that reconsideration by all of the judges was impractical, so the court had devised a rule under which eleven of the active judges, rather than all of them, could consider such requests.[37] Requests for en banc reconsideration are common in the Ninth Circuit (about fifteen hundred a year) but are rarely granted (fifteen to twenty-five cases a year).[38]

Holguín decided to seek en banc reconsideration of the Ninth Circuit decision. He had unluckily drawn a three-judge panel that was more conservative than the court as a whole. Judge Fletcher had written a powerful dissent in his favor. And a random selection[39] of eleven Ninth Circuit judges was likely to be more favorable to his case than the Supreme Court of the early 1990s.

THE NINTH CIRCUIT: ROUND TWO

The court granted Holguín's motion for rehearing en banc. During 1991, a year in which the INS detained 7225 immigrant children,[40] the lawyers for each side rehashed their arguments. Holguín would need six votes to sustain Judge Kelleher. President Carter had appointed five members of the en banc court. Another member was Judge Wallace, who had been appointed by President Nixon. Four others were Reagan appointees. One, Pamela Rymer, had been appointed by George H. W. Bush. Holguín needed the support of the Democratic appointees and to persuade one other judge to win the case.

In fact, he got seven votes, or perhaps six and a half. One of the Reagan appointees sided with the five Carter appointees in overturning the panel decision; Judge Rymer agreed with the majority in part and dissented in part.

Judge Mary Schroeder wrote the majority opinion. In 1971 she had become the first female associate at a major law firm in Arizona. Shortly after she was made a partner, she wrote Arizona's law barring sex discrimination. She also lobbied for enactment of the federal Violence Against Women Act. Schroeder was appointed to the Arizona Court of Appeals; she was the first woman judge on that court. There, she caused a stir by bringing her infant daughter to court and nursing in her chambers.[41] Schroeder was appointed to the Ninth Circuit by President Carter in 1979.[42]

Judge Schroeder rejected the panel's narrow definition of the right asserted on behalf of the children. She relied on the Supreme Court's foundational case on the rights of children, known as In re: Gault, which held that children detained for delinquency had due process rights with respect to their detention.[43] The case held that children have fundamental liberty interests, just as adults do. Schroeder noted that the Supreme Court had said, in another context, that legislative abridgement of fundamental interests had to be achieved by the least drastic means to achieve a legitimate governmental end. The interest of the child was broadly in "freedom from unjustified governmental detention," not (as the panel decision had put it) in the narrower "right to be released to an unrelated adult." As a result, she reasoned, "governmental confinement of a child to an institution should be a last resort." In addition, deference to the judgment of the INS about what was necessary was uncalled for because "child welfare is not an area of INS expertise."

She acknowledged that the INS could not conduct "home studies" of the unrelated adults to whom children might be released, but she rejected the INS's claim that "since it is unable to do such an evaluation, the best interests of the child must lie in detention rather than in release." On the contrary, she said, the due process clause of the Constitution requires the opposite conclusion. The INS could make individualized determinations that particular adults were inappropriate hosts for detained children, but its "blanket policy" of refusing releases to all unrelated individuals had to fall. Judge Schroeder also opined that Judge Kelleher decided correctly that a hearing was required in every case, both because most children would not know to ask for one, and because a hearing was needed to determine whether giving custody to a nonrelative would present a danger to the child.[44]

Two of the judges who agreed with Judge Schroeder wrote concurring opinions expressing their views even more strongly. Judge Thomas Tang, the son of a Chinese immigrant,[45] wrote to emphasize that in the United States, the right to release, subject to narrow exceptions, was fundamental: "liberty is the norm: arrest, detention or restraint by the state is the exception." Judge Tang also pointed out what was at stake in the case. "Detention by the government stigmatizes children, regardless of the ultimate resolution. . . . [They] enjoy, at best, very limited educational and recreational opportunities. They are away from family and friends; every aspect of their daily life is regulated by strangers. They have very little privacy, may be shackled and handcuffed, and lead a very regimented life."[46]

Judge William Norris wrote the other concurring opinion. Norris was an active Democrat before being appointed to the bench by President Carter. He had been with Senator Robert Kennedy when the Senator was shot to death at the Ambassador Hotel in Los Angeles and he had taken the stage after the shooting to try to calm the alarmed crowd. In 1974, Norris ran for attorney general of California but lost. A few years before sitting on the Flores court, he issued an opinion holding that discrimination against gays in the military was barred by the U.S. Constitution. At the time, that opinion was highly controversial.[47] He excoriated the INS for its claim that its regulation was necessary because it could not perform home visits. "What the INS's justification for its policy boils down to is money," he wrote.

> It claims that it does not have the 'competence' or 'resources' to 'conduct meaningful screening' of [homes]. . . . Translated, this means that our government chooses to hold children in detention facilities, despite the INS's lack of competence to care for them, rather than pay for the services of qualified social workers to conduct home studies of the kind that county social service agencies perform routinely.

He noted that the INS hadn't made any effort to show that the cost of paying for such studies would be greater than the cost of keeping the children in detention.[48]

Judge Pamela Rymer, the Bush appointee, agreed that the INS's regulation did not meet the demands of the Constitution, but relied on narrower reasoning than the majority. She thought the discussion of the right to liberty was unnecessary because "the regulation itself creates a liberty interest in freedom from constraint," and the only issue that the court had to decide was whether a hearing was necessary to protect that interest. On that point, she concluded that the regulation was deficient because "there is no process there." A child with no close relative "is left in procedural limbo" and "there is no provision for reasoned consideration [of continued detention] by a neutral hearing officer."[49]

Writing for the four dissenting judges, Judge Wallace reiterated what he had written in his panel opinion. He also would have deferred to the INS's "estimation of the risks" to released children, arguing that "no one on this court can be sure there is no evil awaiting an unsuspecting alien minor in the custody of an unrelated adult."[50]

THE SUPREME COURT

Schey was pleased but hardly jubilant after the Ninth Circuit ruled in favor of the class. He knew that the government might ask the Supreme Court to overturn the ruling. Although the Supreme Court agrees to consider only about 1 percent of the appeals it receives, several factors suggested that the court would agree to review the Flores decision. The federal government was the party seeking review, the case involved a constitutional question, the case had been heard en banc with several judges dissenting strongly, and the case came from the Ninth Circuit, a court with which the Supreme Court very often disagreed.[51]

Schey realized that if the Supreme Court accepted the case, it was likely to be less accepting of his claims than the Ninth Circuit had been. He therefore tried to negotiate with the INS before the government decided whether it would ask the Court to take the case. Schey thought it was more likely that the political leadership of the INS, as opposed to its litigators, would agree to a favorable settlement. He therefore sought and obtained a meeting with the head of the agency, Commissioner Eugene McNary.[52] In 1989, President George H. W. Bush had appointed McNary, a Republican politician who had lost elections for governor and senator in Missouri, as the INS commissioner. Lawyers who represented immigrants thought that McNary was more accepting of immigrants' rights than his predecessor. McNary appointed another moderate, Grover Joseph Rees, as his general counsel. Schey, McNary, and Rees met in Washington in November 1991. But unbeknownst to Schey, Rees and his subordinates had already sent a memorandum to the Justice Department's chief appellate lawyer recommending that the Department ask the Supreme Court to review the case, because, among other reasons, thanks to the Ninth Circuit's decision, "the INS will be required to schedule and conduct hearings before immigration judges . . . to determine whether release of the juveniles is appropriate. This will require the expenditure of significant resources by INS."[53]

In his negotiations, Schey wanted the 1987 settlement, which technically covered only the INS's Western Region, extended nationally. Rees wanted Schey to consent to vacate the Ninth Circuit's decision, which held that at least some immigrants had a due process right to be free from detention.[54] McNary gave Schey some encouragement that things could be worked out. There never was a second meeting, however. Before it could take place, the Supreme Court agreed to hear the Flores case. The government was no longer interested in negotiating a settlement. After the court announced early in 1992 that it would take the case, Holguín prepared to argue it for a third time, more than seven years after the litigation had begun. It was to be his first Supreme Court argument.

In its brief to the Supreme Court, the government presented itself as a victim of circumstance. "The problem has been thrust upon INS by the combination of socioeconomic conditions in Central America beyond its control—which cause huge numbers of unaccompanied alien juveniles to flee their homelands. . . ." It reiterated that the INS "has neither the administrative resources nor the expertise to conduct the home visits necessary to make reliable guardianship determinations." But the government also made a new argument. A child who is not released immediately "does not remain in a correctional institution," it said. As a result of the government's 1987 agreement with Holguín, it noted, the INS now placed the child in a facility that meets or exceeds the standards in the Alien Minors Shelter Care Program (AMSCP) of the Justice Department's Community Relations Service (CRS).[55]

The government provided the Court with a copy of that agreement, which appeared to require humane conditions of detention.[56] AMSCP detention was a reasonable alternative to the custody of unrelated adults, it argued. INS's detention program, including placement in shelter care, therefore should pass constitutional muster. A hearing was not constitutionally required, either, because INS did provide hearings for children if they requested them. By not requesting a hearing, a child was waiving the right to one. Since the Court had held that a child "has the capacity to waive his Miranda rights in criminal proceedings, it also must be true that a juvenile can waive the much less significant right" to have a judge review his continued detention by the INS, a detention in connection with a "civil" rather than a criminal case. On top of that, the "fiscal and administrative burdens" of providing hearings to each child, even when not requested, "are substantial."

The government's invocation of the shelter care agreement threatened to convert a main focus of the case from a theoretical discussion of how to frame the liberty interest into a factual inquiry into whether AMSCP was at least as good as release to an unrelated adult. Holguín then had to decide how much of his argument to address to the legal question and how much to challenge the government's claim that the AMSCP agreement was a fair substitute for care in the home of a responsible adult.

In the district court, where the official factual record of the case had been made, Holguín had introduced plenty of evidence showing poor conditions of detention for children like Jenny Flores. All of that evidence, however, predated the creation of the AMSCP, which was established only as the district court phase of the lawsuit was ending in 1987. If the AMSCP in fact created suitable conditions of detention for all the children in INS custody, the pre-1987 evidence was likely irrelevant. But Holguín had little information about conditions of detention after the INS invited private companies to offer proposals for detention facilities in 1987. His brief addressed this issue only in one footnote, in which he tried to throw the burden of proof onto the government. He stated that "there is no evidence that [education, reading materials, commingling children and adults, recreation, and visitation] have actually improved," and he asserted that in the Ninth Circuit, several immigrant and refugee rights groups had "presented voluminous evidence . . . showing that conditions in INS camps remain deplorable. . . . [B]elated improvements the INS made in its detention camps under the compulsion of this lawsuit cannot save a policy that was punitive and harmful [to start with]."⁵⁷

Most of Holguín's brief was instead devoted to his argument that the INS detention policy violated the due process clause of the Constitution. He pointed out that nothing in the INS regulations limited the amount of time that a child could be confined or required INS to convince a judge that continued detention was in the child's best interest. He noted that before 1984, the INS had released minors to nonfamily adults and shelter programs without incident. He rhetorically asked: "if INS cannot manage to screen potential custodians [to avoid harm to the children], how can it possibly expect to care for the physical, emotional, spiritual and developmental needs of children during months of open-ended confinement?"⁵⁸

The party appealing a lower court's ruling—in this case the government— has the right to the last word. The government's reply brief reiterated that the 1987 settlement, which had been embodied in a consent decree from the court, had changed everything; the fact that it had agreed to the settlement should tip the scales of justice against release to an unrelated adult sponsor.

> If [Flores and her lawyers] wish to contend formally that INS has failed to comply with the consent decree, they should initiate proceedings in the [district] court that entered that decree. If the district court concludes that the INS has violated the decree, it is fully empowered to require INS to comply with it. . . . Notwithstanding [Holguín's] frequent reference to INS 'jails,' the facilities in this case resemble shelter-care facilities more than they do highly restrictive secure facilities.

And as for Holguín's claim that recently arrived children are ill-equipped to request hearings, "the juvenile will receive a hearing unless he either checks a box specifically indicating he does not want a hearing, or refuses to complete the relevant form."⁵⁹

At the oral argument, the justices seemed more interested in the impact of the AMSCP agreement than in the abstractions addressed by the Ninth Circuit. Maureen Mahoney, the Deputy Solicitor General, noted that just before Judge Kelleher ruled, the INS had established its shelter care standards. The AMSCP "had been adopted and [was] being implemented at the time that the district court found [the government's policies] to be unconstitutional." Therefore, all the evidence of dreadful detention conditions before 1987 were "simply irrelevant." Now, half the "care providers" were "group homes and foster homes established by the Catholic Church. . . . They don't have barbed wire. . . . They offer specialized programs to help the children . . . as well as educational efforts and medical treatment."[60] One of the justices then asked: "why wouldn't your opponents just throw in the towel and say, well, they're taking such wonderful care of the children that we have no reason to litigate?" By continuing with their case and defending the appeals, Mahoney responded, "maybe they were influenced by ancient history."[61]

Holguín had a different view of what was going on. "In California," he said, INS detainees are kept in a facility in El Centro . . . remote from anywhere, surrounded by desert. . . . When minors are released, they are free to go to church services, they're free to attend public schools, they're free to go to the park. None of these things occur from the middle of the California desert." But Holguín was trapped by the consent decree he had wrangled from the government, and as the oral argument progressed, Holguín came to understand that despite receiving some sympathetic questions from Justice John Paul Stevens, he would lose the case.[62] A justice asked: "there isn't any dispute that the order has been complied with?" Holguín conceded: "That's correct, your Honor, at this time."[63]

That was the concession the Supreme Court jumped on, overturning the Ninth Circuit decision by a vote of seven to two. Justice Antonin Scalia wrote the majority opinion. He quoted from the AMSCP standards at length, noting that the facilities had to be licensed by the state for the provision of shelter care, foster care, group care, and related services, in an "open setting," and that the provider of care had to provide many listed services. Holguín, he observed, had told the court that conditions were in fact severe, but "whatever those conditions might have been when this litigation began, "they are now . . . presumably in compliance with the extensive requirements" of the part of the case that had been settled by agreement. The government need not look after the "best interests of the child," which was a typical standard in state custody proceedings but not a constitutional requirement. In addition, the majority accepted the way the dissent in the Ninth Circuit had characterized the children's claims—not as a fundamental right to live in freedom until judged to be deportable, but only as the right to be released to an unrelated adult. "In short," Justice Scalia concluded, "There is no constitutional need for a hearing to determine whether private placement would be better, so long as institutional custody (as we readily find it to be, assuming compliance with the requirements of the consent decree) is good enough."[64]

Justices Stevens and Blackmun dissented, pointing out that the INS itself relied on the "best interests of the child" standard to justify its refusal to allow unrelated responsible adults to accept custody of children in detention. They noted that although the average time in detention might be, as the INS stated, thirty days, some children were kept for up to a year in institutions. They also took issue with the majority's description of the legal issue in the case: "the right at stake is not the right . . . to be released to one particular custodian rather than another, but the right not to be detained in the first place." And they mocked the majority's "good enough" standard: "as long as its cages are gilded, the INS need not expend its administrative resources on a program that would better serve its asserted interests and that would not need to employ cages at all."[65]

3 The Second Settlement

1993–1997

Was the settlement agreement actually "good enough," as the Supreme Court claimed? Except for his description of the desert facility, which the court ignored, Holguín hadn't been able to tell the Supreme Court much about what had happened since the agreement was signed. Under court rules, an appeal is limited to the facts established by the record in the original court—Judge Robert Kelleher's court—and only the legal issues are supposed to be argued at the appellate level. The settlement agreement had been signed in 1987, a year before Judge Kelleher's "unrelated adults" ruling that was being appealed, so there was no evidence in the record about the actual conditions of detention in 1992 when the Supreme Court case was argued.

The conditions under which children were being held were increasingly important because more unaccompanied children were arriving annually than when the lawsuit began. By 1989, INS was detaining about nine hundred children a month in California and another two hundred in Texas, up from thirty-two a month in Texas a year earlier.[1] Only about half had at least one relative in the United States; the others knew nobody and therefore could not be released even if bond could be posted.[2] Bond was sometimes set so high that it could not possibly be raised. For example, twelve-year-old MacDonald Caballero, a Nicaraguan orphan, had no relatives in the United States. Even if he could locate an adult relative, it was unlikely that anyone could afford the $25,000 bond set by immigration judge Rose Collantes Peters. The judge said that someone resourceful enough to ride a freight train from Central America to the United States might be a flight risk.[3]

Because the part of the Flores case dealing with conditions of confinement had been settled by agreement, the Supreme Court's ruling siding with the government with respect to which adults could care for a minor who was released did not affect how minors were treated while they were incarcerated. The agreement required the INS to follow rules for detention of children laid out in two government documents issued by the Community Relations Service (CRS) of the Department of Justice (DOJ). One was the "Alien Minors Shelter Care Program—Description and Requirements," dated April 28, 1987, and filed with the court as part of the 1987 settlement.[4] The other was the "Alien Minors Shelter Care Program—Guidelines and Requirements," which the CRS issued somewhat later, with more specific rules for institutions receiving federal funds to house detained migrant children.[5]

CONDITIONS IN THE DETENTION FACILITIES

In fact, the INS began to violate the settlement agreement and its own Shelter Care Guidelines almost as soon as the agreement was signed. For the most part,[6] the agency did honor the requirement that detention of children in a border patrol lockup not exceed seventy-two hours, but what happened after the first seventy-two hours became a matter of concern.

The agreement contemplated that the children would be housed in an "open type of setting" that met "state child welfare licensing requirements." The Guidelines described an "open type" as one "without security fences and security hardware or other major restraining construction typically associated with correctional facilities." The guidelines also directed that institutions should "discourage runaways and prevent the unauthorized absence" of the children. The INS had represented to the Supreme Court that detained children did not remain in institutional facilities but were in "community based shelter care programs" where "restrictions on their freedom are quite minimal."[7]

By November 1993, six months after the Supreme Court assumed that the settlement agreement was being honored by the government, Holguín had obtained many signed statements from children who had been held in INS detention while the settlement was supposedly in effect. These statements showed that with the exception of the Casa San Juan facility in San Diego housing fifteen boys,[8] none of the facilities in the Western Region met state licensing requirements for dependent children. The settings were not of an "open type." The government had contracted with Los Angeles County, for example, to put detained children in trailer modules within high-security lockups for youthful offenders. Fences with barbed wire surrounded the trailers.

When children arrived, all their possessions, including writing material, were taken away. Although the settlement required that children be given "appropriate clothing," they had to wear the uniforms that the prison used for offenders. There was little privacy; showers and toilets were communal with open doors.

The settlement mandated education and daily recreation for the children. In at least three of the lockups, children had no textbooks or other reading materials. At one facility in southern California, a child reported being allowed outside only three times in sixteen days. In another facility, the indoor "structured leisure activity not including time watching television" consisted largely of watching television. The guards woke many children at 3 A.M., handcuffed them, and took them to court for early morning hearings. The guards then handcuffed the children again to return them to their trailers.

In the facilities that the INS contracted with in Arizona, the children were not segregated into trailers but housed with the general juvenile offender population. In one facility, they had to spend most of every day sitting at a table, playing cards or reading the one available Spanish-language book. At one detention center, the children were strip-searched on arrival and after every court visit. They spent of most every day in a locked room with only a bed and a toilet.

Under the settlement, each child was supposed to receive an individual counseling session at least weekly and a group counseling session at least twice a week. Children reported, however, that counseling services were either non-existent or available only on request.

The settlement required INS contractors to restate to the children that they had a right to legal representation (though not at government expense) and that they could apply for asylum. A lawyer could have helped a child to apply for bond. The children reported only being given some papers in English that they could not understand. Many children had no idea of what was transpiring in their cases, much less how to defend themselves or to be released.[9]

Michael Olivas, a law professor at the University of Houston, wrote that in 1990–91, the INS held 2400 children in California alone, and that

> The facilities are ramshackle: one site in Texas has been sardonically dubbed 'El Corralon' (The Corral), while another is a former Department of Agriculture pesticide storage facility. These shacks, tents and makeshift housing are fenced in, and are not even as safe or as commodious as Manzanar [a major internment center for Japanese Americans] was in World War II. A 1991 study of the children in these facilities revealed that virtually all suffered from advanced and untreated cases of post-traumatic shock syndrome.[10]

When Olivas organized students and lawyers to try to provide at least some assistance to the children incarcerated at the former pesticide storage facility (with skulls and crossbones on the doors), "INS moved the children around to hide them from us, took public payphones out of operation, would not let us interview privately, refused us bathroom accommodations, and in general compromised our ability to serve clients."[11]

In the course of collecting declarations from children to use as proof that the government was violating the settlement, the lawyers visited some of the institutions in which children were confined. They also held periodic individual and conference calls with "most advocates in the United States" who were "involved with assisting apprehended [immigrant] minors."[12] These advocates' organizations helped to supply information about conditions in facilities that were far from Schey's Los Angeles headquarters. In November 1993, the lawyers filed a motion to enforce the settlement. They attached the evidence that they had collected.[13] The government's response was, in essence, that the plaintiffs' lawyers had cherry-picked their anecdotes; in other words, that the children's reports that tended to show violations of the agreement might not be true, and if they were true, were "aberrational."[14] Schey notified the government that he wanted to take depositions of INS officials to prove that his motion should be granted. He agreed to postpone the depositions, as well as a hearing on his motion, while the parties discussed a further settlement. Those discussions dragged out for four years and involved the exchange of at least fourteen settlement proposals.[15]

In 1996, Human Rights Watch independently investigated the conditions under which migrant children were being held.[16] The INS allowed the group's staff members to visit two detention facilities in or near Los Angeles, California, and one in Arizona. They spoke with some detained children, with staff at the facilities, and with INS officials.[17] Human Rights Watch had a hard time collecting information, though, because of "passive resistance" by INS officials in California and "deliberate falsehoods, along with a wide variety of blatantly obstructive behavior" by INS officials in Arizona.[18]

Human Rights Watch reported that the "most fundamental problem" with the Los Angeles facilities was "that they are prisons," in violation of the Flores agreement. They were all surrounded by barbed wire fences. Authorized visitors had to enter "through several guard stations and locked doors."

- At one location, the children had to wear white or orange uniforms with the words "Detention Bureau" stamped on the legs and sleeves despite a statement in the CRS "Guidelines and Requirements" that each child had the right to "wear his or her own clothes, when available."

- At that location, girls were housed along with adjudicated offenders in "barracks-like" rooms with forty beds. There were toilets without doors at the side of each room.

- At another facility, boys and girls were housed in two rooms off the same corridor. The lower halves of the windows of each room were painted black "so that only the sky could be seen." Each room had eight metal cots, each with a thin blanket, and a toilet without a door. The walls were blank cinderblock, as the children were prohibited from displaying personal possessions. All books were in English, and the television showed only English-language stations. Children who used bad language were sent to "the box" (solitary confinement). Spanish-speaking children could occasionally find Spanish-speaking staff, but some of the children spoke only Chinese and could find nobody who could talk with them. The children received no counseling and were seldom visited. One legal representative reported that "kids get brought in [to holding cells to wait for court hearings] at weird hours, like three in the morning. . . . So they miss breakfast because they are being transported, and they miss lunch because of the hearing."

The New York Post profiled Angel Avila, a fifteen-year-old boy who was detained in Los Angeles. He had been abandoned as a baby in Honduras and years later had trekked to the United States. He crossed the border without being apprehended and went to live with relatives in New York. He was arrested for shoplifting. Although the charge was dismissed, it brought him to the attention of the INS, which sent him to one of the juvenile jails in Los Angeles. His relatives could not afford to visit him there. In the jail, he fought with bullies and was often sent to solitary confinement as a result. In 1991, after three months in detention, he gave up, preferring deportation to Honduras rather than enduring more months of detention before he could see a judge.[19]

Excessive punishments of children in INS custody also became an issue. Children at one facility in California, run by a private company under an INS contract, were punished for talking while standing in line, for forgetting to wear a required hat, or for going to the bathroom without asking for permission. The punishments ranged from being allowed to drink only one glass of water with a meal to having to run a hundred times around the building in slippers. The facility also had a "punishment room." When six people protested that all of the detainees had to run fifty laps because some had forgotten their hats, they were consigned to this room for seven days, during which they could not have education, exercise, radio, television, or telephone calls.[20]

In 1996 (nine years after the settlement was signed, and three years after Holguín filed his motion in federal court to enforce it), the Department of Justice, which housed both the INS and the CRS, entered into an agreement with a Texas-based company, Southwest Key, which operated juvenile detention centers, to create a "shelter care" facility in Arizona that would meet the requirements of the settlement agreement.

DOJ officials allowed Human Rights Watch staff members to visit this facility and speak with fifteen children for ten minutes each, provided that they would not give the children legal information or reveal the location of the facility. It isn't clear why the government sought compliance in only one facility, but the cost of compliance or DOJ's limited staff for monitoring may have played a role.

Human Rights Watch reported that despite the CRS "Guidelines," the building was locked and surrounded by an eight-foot-high fence, with access controlled by a guard and monitored by surveillance cameras. The children were allowed outside for only an hour a day, except when they were punished by being required to work outside in the desert heat for hours. The guidelines stated that children could "talk privately on the phone, as permitted by the house rules and regulations," and the director of the facility assured Human Rights Watch that the children had unrestricted private access to phones to obtain legal representation and to contact family members. In fact, the children were permitted to use the telephone only once every other week. They were told that telephone use was a reward for good behavior, and that they could not receive calls from relatives abroad. Attorneys were barred from visiting the facility to inform the children of their rights, and any telephone calls with lawyers were monitored by the staff. INS officials told Human Rights Watch that all detained children had legal representatives, and named organizations that supposedly were representing certain children. Those organizations said, however, that they had no contact with the children or the facility.

The settlement provided that all children should have access to religious services, but the Arizona facility had only a "small and uninviting altar" in a corner of the lot outside the facility, offering no protection from the sun, and no visits by clergy.

In a follow-up report a year later, Human Rights Watch also reported on conditions at an INS juvenile detention center in Berks County, Pennsylvania, which had both shelter care facilities and a secure detention wing.[21] The shelter care facility, it reported, had "comfortable furniture . . . a wide range of activities, and a caring staff." But at any given time, a third of the children were kept in the secure wing, which was "surrounded by a fifteen-foot razor wire fence." Children arrived there "in handcuffs and leg irons and [were] strip searched" and forced to give up their own clothing. Then they were assigned to "cells with concrete walls, ceiling and floor, completely bare except for bedding and a Bible" and told nothing about legal services or hearings. The immigration judges wouldn't hear children's cases unless a lawyer or family member was present, and the children were unrepresented and far from family. As a result, they remained in detention for "months and months." In violation of the Flores settlement, children were transported to court along with adult inmates and sometimes were handcuffed for more than eight hours. Kids were sometimes punished for failure to follow staff instructions given in English, but many did not speak English. Physical exercise was used as punishment for disciplinary violations even when the child was ill. Children in the secure facility reported having few activities; they spent "hours each day in their bare rooms with no books."[22] An INS spokesman responded to these concerns by noting that "conditions at the facility have always been more than adequate" and that "if my kids had nowhere to go, I wouldn't be concerned about having them go there."[23]

In 1997, the Women's Commission for Refugee Women and Children did another study of detention conditions. It found that the INS was unprepared to house family units. If a parent and child were apprehended together, they were sent to separate detention centers, which caused "extreme distress" to both. It also found troubling conditions in several INS "children's shelters." The Flores settlement stated that children could be placed in secure detention only if they had been charged with crimes or had run away from shelter facilities. In the Liberty County Juvenile Correctional Center, an hour and a half from Houston, Texas, few of the eighty immigrant children had ever been charged as criminals or identified as runaways. The facility was surrounded by concertina wire. The children were housed with juvenile offenders. They were required to wear prison uniforms and were kept in cells for up to twenty-three hours a day. The facility provided three hours of classroom instruction on weekdays, but only in English.

The commission visited one eleven-year-old girl in another detention facility. She had been abused by her parents and then sold for child labor. An immigration judge had granted her asylum, but the INS had appealed. Because of this, she was kept in jail for fifteen months.[24]

THE NEW SETTLEMENT

From November 1993 until January 1997, Holguín negotiated with the Department of Justice to draft a new and more detailed settlement agreement. Both sides were willing to negotiate because (as reported in their settlement) they realized that a trial would be "complex, lengthy, and costly to all parties concerned, and the decision of the district court would be subject to appeal by the losing parties with the final outcome uncertain."[25] The government also may have been willing to negotiate because the Clinton administration would have been embarrassed by the publicity associated with a trial. Schey claimed that he would relish such an event, telling the government's lawyers that

> 'We're going to have a factual feast here, you know. And it's going to be on the front page of the newspaper every day. Every day we're going to subpoena twenty government witnesses [to] explain what the government interests are in treating children harshly, inhumanely. It's going to go on and on about the abuse. You guys are going to painted as child abusers.' That's what I think drove them to serious settlement [talks].[26]

For their part, Holguín and Schey were actually reluctant to try to press the court to decide their pending motion to enforce the 1987 agreement, or to hold a lengthy factual hearing, because Judge Kelleher, then over eighty years old and in semi-retired "senior" status, seemed to have little interest in moving the case along. They put more of their effort into negotiations for an improved federal commitment, and they let their pending motion "go by the wayside."[27]

The new settlement agreement, which they concluded in 1997, included a definition of a "minor." Under the agreement, a minor was "any person under the age of eighteen (18) years who is detained in the legal custody of the INS" except for any child who was incarcerated after being convicted as an adult for a criminal offense. As we shall see, that definition became extremely controversial two decades later, when the government claimed that the term did not encompass children who arrived in the United States together with an adult.

Even though the "class" that Judge Kelleher had approved a decade earlier included only children held in the Western Region of the INS, the

INS agreed that the new settlement would become "nationwide policy" and would replace all INS policies inconsistent with the agreement. The government also stipulated to extend the class of plaintiffs nationwide, which meant that every child in INS custody had a right to be protected by, and could ask a court to enforce, the agreement.

The new settlement stated that children could be held immediately after arrest for up to five days[28] in an unlicensed but safe and sanitary facility. Then they had to be placed in the "least restrictive setting appropriate to the minor's age and special needs." If that was an institutional setting, it had to be one licensed by "an appropriate state agency to provide residential, group, or foster care services for dependent children." The facility had to be "non-secure as required under state law" except that a child could be held in a secure facility in special circumstances, such as when the child had drug or mental health problems. The institutions that housed child detainees also had to satisfy other conditions specified in the settlement. These conditions included some requirements from the original agreement, such as academic classroom education five days a week, outdoor recreation for at least an hour per day, individual counseling once a week, group counseling twice a week, and information about the availability of free legal services. The new agreement also included certain additional requirements, some of which had been written into the government's 1987 guidelines. The children had the right to wear their own clothes, when available; to talk privately on the phone and visit privately with guests "as permitted by the house rules and regulations"; and to be offered a bond redetermination hearing before an immigration judge (unless the child refused such a hearing in writing). If the INS originally set bond at an amount that a child's family could not afford, the child could ask a judge to reduce the amount of bond to the minimum necessary to ensure that the child would appear for a hearing.[29]

If an "emergency or influx of minors into the United States" occurred, "the INS could take longer than five days to place the children with an adult relative or legal guardian, or with a state-licensed institutional facility." If the INS had more than 130 minors eligible for placement in a licensed program, that was deemed an "influx."[30] Even then, the agency was obliged to transfer the minor to such a person or facility "as expeditiously as possible." As we shall see in chapters 6 through 10, the lawyers who drafted this definition did not foresee that a much larger number of children might flee from increased violence in the Americas.

Because the INS had apparently violated the earlier agreement, Holguín insisted that the new settlement should provide for compliance monitoring. The INS was required to establish a "juvenile coordinator" in the Office of the Assistant Commission for Detention and Deportation who would ensure compliance with the agreement. That individual would maintain a record of minors who remained in custody for more than seventy-two hours and of the reasons for each child's detention. The coordinator would collect statistical information from INS district offices and border patrol stations weekly, and report to the court on INS compliance annually.

Two other provisions of the new agreement were noteworthy. The federal government had to pay the plaintiffs' lawyers $374,000 for its costs in enforcing the 1987 agreement by filing its 1993 motion. The agreement specified that it would terminate at "the earlier of five years after the date of final court approval of this Agreement or three years after the court determines that the INS is in substantial compliance," except that the INS had a permanent obligation to care for institutionalized children in its custody in "facilities that are state-licensed facilities for the care of dependent minors."[31]

Schey wasn't happy about agreeing that the settlement would end after five years, but, he reported, "the government pretty much always insists on a sunsetting clause in these settlements. . . . They didn't want to bind the next administration." The government's negotiators refused to settle without this clause, and Schey accepted it because "if at the end of five years, they went back to their old ways, we could just file a new suit."[32]

In fact, it turned out that the five-year sunset clause never went into effect. Four years after the Clinton administration reached the settlement, the Bush administration agreed to amend the sunset term to keep the deal in effect until forty-five days after the government issued final regulations to implement the agreement. Once again, the government agreed that the obligation to care for the children in state-licensed facilities would be permanent, even if final implementing regulations were issued and the rest of the agreement was terminated. For decades, the government never even tried to issue such regulations, so in 2018, the 1997 agreement remained in force. As we shall see, the Flores settlement became the subject of renewed litigation in both 2006 and 2015.[33] In 2018, the Trump adminis-tration began a process to try to nullify the agreement by issuing a regula-tion that would "implement" it.[34]

In April 1997 Schey, Holguín, and senior INS officials held a press con-ference to announce what seemed to be a landmark agreement. "We are committed to a humane and effective program to care for minors taken into INS custody without their parents or family members," INS Commissioner Doris Meissner said. Harvard's Professor Rosa Ehrenreich, who had written the Human Rights Watch report, wasn't so sure. Calling for "independent" monitoring of the agreement, she said that "we need more than regulations that look good on paper." She "expressed skepticism whether the agency would abide by the new requirements." Schey said that his Center for Human Rights and Constitutional Law would do the monitoring. "If they're not in compliance," he promised, "we will be knock-ing at the courthouse door fairly early."[35]

4 Congress Intervenes

1997-2002

After the second Flores settlement agreement was signed in 1997, litigation challenging the conditions of federal detention of child migrants ceased for a while. This was not because migration slowed; in fact, until 2005, there was no significant change in the number of unauthorized non-Mexican citizens apprehended by the border patrol.[1] The number of Central American migrants remained steady, despite the cessation of fighting in the civil wars in El Salvador and Guatemala. Unlike the Central Americans, Mexican adults and children were almost never detained; when they were apprehended, they were simply escorted to the border and allowed to depart with no formal judicial process. That procedure could not be followed with Central Americans, because even if they arrived at the U.S. border by walking through Mexico, they had no right to return to Mexico. If they had no basis for remaining in the United States, they remained in INS legal custody (either in a secure facility or in the physical custody of a relative or an institutional sponsor) until deported to their own country by plane, escorted by INS officers. The controversy was muted, therefore, not because there were no non-Mexican migrant children or because INS always released such children promptly,[2] but because the government did try to comply with the Flores agreement, and because challenging the instances of noncompliance was exceedingly difficult.

THE DIFFICULTY OF CHALLENGING NONCOMPLIANCE

One reason for the lack of public controversy was that the INS made significant efforts to comply with the new Flores agreement. It developed a manual with procedures to be followed. It also trained its officers on the new procedures. By 2001, the Department of Justice's Inspector General could describe the INS as having made "significant progress since signing the Flores agreement" although it found that there remained "deficiencies . . . that could have potentially serious consequences for the well-being" of the children. Specifically, the Inspector General reported that when a child had an undocumented parent in the United States who refused to risk coming forward, the INS continued to detain the child rather than release her to another acceptable sponsor. The Inspector General also found that thirty-four of fifty-seven secure facilities did not have procedures or facilities to separate nondelinquent migrant children from domestic juvenile delinquents and that in three of the eight INS districts the office reviewed, INS juvenile coordinators did not visit the detained children on a weekly basis as its new manual required. In addition, some INS facilities still shackled children while transporting them, in violation of INS policy.[3]

Because compliance with the Flores settlement and even with new INS policies was incomplete, however, individual cases of prolonged and apparently unfair detention occasionally burst into the public spotlight. One such case was the ordeal of Alfredo Lopez Sanchez, a sixteen-year-old boy who fled to the United States in 2001 from his home in Guatemala after brutal attacks by his own father. Once, he watched his father knock his mother to the ground, a blow that killed the baby strapped to her back. Sanchez was apprehended in Texas before he could locate a cousin in the United States. After being diagnosed with post-traumatic stress disorder, he spent eighteen months in detention, transferred eleven times to different shelters and jails. During this time, he was barely able to communicate with anyone, because he spoke only Mam, a native dialect, not Spanish or

English. INS officials refused to allow him to be sponsored when an undocumented relative declined to put himself at risk by coming forward.[4]

Schey was aware that there were instances in which the government was not in perfect compliance with the new agreement that he had negotiated, but he was also aware that he could neither expect perfection nor prove massive violations of the accord. As he put it in an interview,

> We never insisted on 100 percent compliance. And monitoring is difficult because they are apprehending [thousands of] children a year. . . . And so when you monitor you're only looking at a very, very small sample and then if you go in and start complaining, the government will always say . . . 'Mr. Schey is complaining about thirty kids, that's [a tiny fraction of the children in detention].' So monitoring is always difficult [even though we would argue that] there is no reason to believe that [the] experience [of the children with whom we randomly talked in the detention facilities] is any different from [others in detention on] the date upon which we agreed with the government that we could do an inspection.[5]

After hearing about several cases like Sanchez's, Schey did file a motion to enforce the Flores settlement,[6] but he withdrew it a year and a half later.[7]

ELIÁN GONZALEZ

On Thanksgiving Day, 1999, Elián González became the most famous unaccompanied immigrant child ever to enter the United States. His mother had fled Cuba on a raft, taking the five-year-old child with her. She and eleven others drowned en route, but fishermen found Elián clinging to an inner tube three miles off the coast of Florida. Florida officials released him to an uncle who lived in the state, but his Cuban father, supported by the Cuban government, wanted him returned. The uncle sought political asylum for the boy, but the INS took the position that his father was the one who should make decisions for him, and therefore he should be returned to Cuba. Until June 2000, a legal battle raged in the courts. Hundreds of angry Cuban-American protesters demonstrated and blocked access to the port of Miami. Vice-President Al Gore broke with the administration to support a bill in Congress to allow the child to remain in the United States until the litigation ended.[8] Some in Congress

The seizure of Elián González.

tried to promote a law to grant U.S. citizenship to the boy, but others resisted. Senator Dianne Feinstein (D–CA) said, "I don't believe our role . . . is to impose ourselves in a decision that should rightfully be made by [his] father."[9]

In April 2000, the nation was stunned to see a front-page photograph of INS agents in combat gear pointing a semiautomatic rifle at Elián and one of his relatives during a predawn raid. (The photo later won a Pulitzer prize). Massive demonstrations and counter-demonstrations followed.[10] The raid became a matter of intense jockeying by politicians, with Senator Orrin Hatch, chair of the Judiciary Committee, issuing a subpoena to Attorney General Janet Reno for the documents that led to it. The ranking Democrat on the committee, Patrick Leahy, called the subpoenas a political "ploy," because polls showed that most Americans wanted Elián reunited with his father, and Senator Feinstein called Hatch's action a "witch hunt."[11] Meanwhile, the boy remained in INS custody until the Supreme Court declined to decide the dispute, and he was returned to Cuba on June 28, 2000. His custody was not typical, however. Because of the national and international publicity about the case, the U.S. government had allowed his Cuban father, Juan Miguel González, to come to the United States while custody litigation that would decide the boy's fate moved through the courts.[12] For three months, Elián and his father were housed in comfortable surroundings at Carmichael Farm, part of the Wye River Plantation in Maryland.[13]

SENATOR FEINSTEIN

The Elián Gonzalez case had caught the interest of Senator Feinstein. Even while he was living with his uncle, news reports had contrasted Elián's living arrangements in the United States with those of "more than a thousand unaccompanied [migrant] children [who] were locked up in juvenile jails while U.S. officials decided what to do with them" because the INS had access to only about five hundred beds in nonprofit shelters, group homes or foster care. In 1999, the INS had taken 5,644 children into custody and had put 1283 of them into juvenile jails because it had no other place to house them.[14] Even two years later, reporters compared Elián's treatment with that of more typical child migrants, such as Edwin Muoz, whose parents abandoned him in Honduras when he was six, leaving him with a cousin who beat him until he walked to the United States, where he was arrested by the INS and jailed for six months with violent criminals.[15]

Six months after the INS raid in which Elián was taken into federal custody, Feinstein introduced her Unaccompanied Alien Child Protection Act in the Senate.[16] "We have been affected by the six-year-old shipwreck survivor from Cuba, Elián Gonzalez," she said. "His tragic story brought to light the plight of numerous other youngsters who find their way to the United States, unaccompanied by an adult and, in many cases, traumatized by the experiences provoking their flight."[17] Her bill would have created a new agency in the Justice Department, the Office of Children Services, separate from the INS, with responsibility for housing unaccompanied migrant children in shelters or foster care "rather than juvenile jails," and would have required "clear guidelines and uniformity" for the housing and care of children in the agency's custody.[18] Her bill would also have provided legal representation for the children so that they would

Senator Dianne Feinstein.

have a chance to argue that they had a legal right to remain in the United States rather than being deported.

In support of her bill, she noted that the INS had issued regulations pursuant to the Flores settlement three years earlier, but she asserted that the agency "regularly violates these regulations." She had learned from human rights organizations that "many of these children, some as young as four and five years old, are placed behind multiple layers of locked doors, surrounded by walls and barbed wire. They are strip searched, patted down, placed in solitary confinement for punishment, forced to wear prison uniforms and shackles, and are forbidden to keep personal objects. Often they have no one to speak with because of the language barrier." She cited several particular examples, such as the case of "Xaio Ling, a young girl from China who spoke no English," detained in the INS juvenile detention center in

Pennsylvania. She "slept in a small concrete cell, was subjected to humiliating strip searches, and forced to wear handcuffs. She was forbidden to keep any of her clothes or possessions and . . . was not allowed to laugh."[19]

The Senate did not act on Feinstein's bill in 2000 or in 2001, but as we shall see, Congress did pass a version of it in 2002, with dramatic consequences for the children whom the senator sought to protect.

THE WOMEN'S COMMISSION

Peter Schey and Dianne Feinstein were not alone in worrying about how the INS was treating children in its custody. In 1989, the International Rescue Committee, founded in 1933 at the suggestion of Albert Einstein to protect people living in Nazi Germany, created the Women's Commission for Refugee Women and Children, later renamed the Women's Refugee Commission. The Commission soon hired a young lawyer named Wendy Young. Young had grown up in upstate New York. In the 1970s, when she was in high school, the government had detained Haitian refugees in a facility near her home. Young had become aware of this when her French teacher visited them to teach English, and she started to wonder why Haitians were incarcerated in her vicinity. As a Williams College student, she had spent her junior year as a United Nations intern in Vienna, and after graduating in 1983, she had taught English for two years in Japan. Returning to the United States, she had earned a law degree and a master's degree in international relations at American University, worked briefly for a policy organization dealing with refugee issues, and then became a staff lawyer at La Raza, which focused on the rights of Latin Americans in the United States.[20] In 1998, she had co-authored a significant article arguing, among other concerns, that children should have special protections, including guardians ad litem and attorneys, in immigration court proceedings, and that the location of detention centers in remote areas, far from legal resources, made it difficult for children to be represented.[21] As one of her first assignments at the Women's Commission, where she was made the Director of Government Programs, Young investigated the conditions of INS confinement of unaccompanied minors, and as Senator Feinstein's bill gained traction, she kept the senator's office informed of what she was learning.[22] In 2002 the Commission published her 43-page report on her findings.[23]

Young and others who worked with her visited eight detention facilities among the ninety where the INS paid county officials to house migrant children, although officials refused access to four others. She discovered that because attorneys for detained children lacked the resources to challenge INS violations of the Flores agreement, "compliance with Flores was largely self-initiated and self-monitored, a function INS has performed inadequately." Although the Flores agreement required that children be released to responsible adults or placed in foster care, shelters, or other minimally restrictive settings, a third of the children had been assigned to "prisons designed for the incarceration of youthful offenders" for "anywhere from a few days to more than a year." The INS justified these placements based on an exception built into the Flores settlement, which said that it could use secure facilities, rather than less restrictive ones, when there was an emergency (such as a natural disaster) or an "influx." The agreement defined an influx as a situation in which the INS had already placed 130 children in non-secure settings. Schey had agreed to this number because in 1997, that was the number of shelter beds available to INS, but since then, INS had expanded its capacity to 500 shelter beds. By 2002, there were always more than 130 children in foster care and shelters and therefore, as Young put it, "a perpetual state of influx."

The Flores agreement required migrant children to be kept separate from delinquent children, but Young found that the terms of the agreement had never been communicated to the county officials who ran the juvenile halls and who were receiving upwards of $135 per day per child from INS. The environments were therefore "harsh and punitive." The children typically had to wear prison uniforms. In the San Diego facility, there was no natural light. Children were locked into cells at night. The male guard who oversaw the girls' wing could see the girls' showers and toilets through a plate glass window ten feet from his control station, and the female guard could see into the toilets and showers in the boys' wing. Fewer than half the children had attorneys, and the attorneys for those who did have one were often not notified ahead of time, as required by the settlement, that INS was about to transfer their young clients to other, more remote facilities. Language barriers and the counties' lack of planning for long-term detention made educational programs impossible or inaccessible. In some facilities, the children were shackled when taken to the medical clinic, and at one facility, they were subjected to strip searches and frequently to pepper spray.[24]

THE HOMELAND SECURITY ACT

Senator Feinstein had persevered throughout 2001 and 2002 in pressing to divest INS of the responsibility for custody of children.[25] In 2002, the senator found a legislative "vehicle" to which she could attach a version of her proposal. Shortly after the terrorist attacks of September 11, 2001, Congress began to consider the Homeland Security Act, which it passed in 2002. This law abolished the INS and transferred its functions to three new agencies in a new Department of Homeland Security (DHS). All three eventually would come to play a role in the detention of children. The new U.S. Customs and Border Protection (CBP) included the Border Patrol, which policed the border other than at the official ports of entry such as airports and land crossings, and the Office of Field Operations (OFO), which staffed the ports of entry and stopped persons trying to pass through them without valid entry documents. Immigration and Customs Enforcement (ICE) was in charge of arresting undocumented persons in the interior of the country; maintaining detention centers; and representing the DHS when adults or children appeared before Department of Justice immigration judges for decisions about whether or not they would be deported. The third new agency, U.S. Citizenship and Immigration Services (USCIS), was the "benefits" agency; it was in charge of naturalizations, of processing applications for lawful resident status (green cards), and of considering applications for asylum for individuals who had not first been apprehended by CBP or ICE. But Senator Feinstein persuaded her colleagues to include a special provision relating to "unaccompanied alien children," who now got their own acronym: "UACs." None of the three new agencies in DHS would be responsible for caring for or housing UACs; instead, after apprehension and a short processing period of at most three days, they would be transferred to the Office of Refugee Resettlement (ORR) in the Department of Health and Human Services.[26]

Every year for decades, in communities across the nation, the United States had been resettling tens of thousands of refugees who had been displaced by wars and the threat of persecution. Large numbers had been families of "boat people" who had fled from the North Vietnamese takeover of South Vietnam; many others had been Jewish refugees from persecution in the Soviet Union or post-Soviet Russia. After the State Department and the INS had approved refugee visas for them and flown them to the United States, ORR had taken responsibility for finding them new homes in the United States and providing them with social services until they could get back on their feet. In other words, instead of being in the custody of an agency like the former INS, which continued to incarcerate adults, the UACs would be taken care of by an agency with a mission to protect its wards, one that had considerable experience with foster homes and other placements for children. Furthermore, as one of the agencies that absorbed some of the duties of INS, ORR would be bound by the Flores agreement.[27] The statute specified, however, that ORR could not release a child on his own recognizance.[28] As a result, UACs who could not be placed with relatives or in foster homes would continue to be housed in institutional settings.

The Homeland Security Act affected only which agency had temporary custody of children who were detained, not the children's ultimate fates. The transfer of jurisdiction from INS to ORR offered the hope that more children would be placed in comfortable, non-restrictive settings rather than in juvenile jails, but in any event, the children's right to remain in the United States would be temporary, lasting only until an immigration judge decided whether or not they had this right on a permanent basis. In most cases, that would depend on whether or not the judge concluded that they were eligible for asylum.

5 Asylum

1980–1997

Months or occasionally years could elapse from the time a child was apprehended (either after having crossed the border or, less frequently, after asking for protection at a port of entry) until he or she had a hearing before an immigration judge. Undocumented migrants, whether children or adults, could get out of custody more quickly by agreeing to allow the Immigration and Naturalization Service (INS), or later, Immigration and Customs Enforcement (ICE), to deport them to their country of citizenship. Why would someone who had been caught by the authorities want to remain in custody, either in a jail or a foster home, rather than return home?

The answer is that while some individuals would eventually be ordered deported by an immigration judge, others could qualify to remain indefinitely in the United States. The main reason why some could remain was the United States law of asylum.

ASYLUM BEFORE 1997

In 1980, thirteen years after the United States agreed to an international treaty protecting refugees,[1] Congress passed a domestic Refugee Act.[2] It included a provision under which a foreign national in the United States or at its border had a right to apply for asylum.[3] That person would, sooner or later, get a hearing to determine whether he or she qualified. A person could demonstrate eligibility for asylum by showing that he had a "well-founded fear" of being persecuted on account of race, religion, nationality, political opinion, or membership in a particular social group.[4] A person who had already been persecuted on one of these grounds was presumed to have a well-founded fear of being persecuted again. This statutory scheme left out many people who are often thought to be "refugees," including victims of floods and earthquakes and, importantly, most people who fled from civil wars or generalized lawlessness in their own countries. But the fact that someone had fled from a civil war such as those in El Salvador and Guatemala did not necessarily bar that person from winning asylum. A judge could drill down deeper. If, within the civil war, the person had been targeted because of a characteristic that fell within the statutory definition, he or she could still win asylum. For example, many civil wars are caused by religious, ethnic, or political divisions. An individual who was attacked or credibly threatened with violence on account of a characteristic identified in the statute, such as a noncombatant attacked during a civil war because he belonged to a dissident political party, could still prevail. Even a child such as Jenny Flores, fleeing a civil conflagration, might win asylum by showing that an army was threatening to kill her because political leaders assumed that her parents belonged to the "wrong" political party or were associated with a disfavored group (such as a labor union).

During the 1980s, the odds were very long against asylum for Salvadorans and Guatemalans, notwithstanding the wars destroying their nations. Although the right-wing governments in those countries allowed their militaries, as well as paramilitary death squads, to commit atrocities against those thought to oppose them, the Reagan administration supported the governments and viewed their opponents as Marxists. Between 1980 and 1990, nearly a million people from those two countries sought refuge in the United States. Many were arrested, put in detention, and pressured into agreeing to return voluntarily rather than seek asylum. Many others applied for asylum but were denied by immigration judges. In 1984, when the asylum approval rate for Iranians was 60 percent and for Poles, 40 percent, the rate of approval for Salvadorans and Guatemalans was less than 3 percent.[5] Gradually, however, as the public became more aware of atrocities in the region and elsewhere, and some immigration lawyers began to challenge immigration judges' decisions in the Board of Immigration Appeals[6] and in the federal courts, case law developed that interpreted the Refugee Act's asylum provisions in more expansive ways. For example, judges began to grant asylum to people who were brutalized not only by governments or armies but also by thugs whom the government could not or would not control,[7] to victims of violent animus on account of homosexuality,[8] and to girls who would be subjected to genital cutting by local cultural practices.[9] After decades of litigation, it also became possible for victims of domestic violence to win asylum if their own police forces would not protect them.[10] Families were also recognized as particular social groups, so children could win asylum if they were threatened by governments or uncontrollable gangs as a result of something that a relative had done (such as testifying against a gang member).[11]

Despite the emerging law, however, asylum was extremely difficult to obtain, even if a claim could be pigeonholed into one of the categories that the law accepted as valid. Persons seeking asylum had to file a lengthy federal application form,[12] following the directions on an instruction booklet that ran to fourteen pages of fine print.[13] The form and instructions encouraged them to submit any available supporting evidence including "newspaper articles, affidavits of witnesses or experts, medical and/or psychological records, doctors' statements, periodicals, journals, books, photographs, official documents, or personal statements" from witnesses or experts.[14] After submitting this information along with the form, an applicant who had been apprehended and either detained or released would be summoned to a hearing in immigration court.[15]

In theory, an applicant for asylum could prevail simply on the basis of her oral testimony to the immigration judge; in practice, it was nearly impossible to win a case without corroborating evidence of the violence or threats to which the applicant had been subjected. But newly arrived asylum seekers rarely brought such evidence with them while fleeing violence in their home countries and often lacked either knowledge of how to obtain it or the necessary financial resources. Many of them did not understand that an "affidavit" was a sworn statement, and provided only handwritten, unsworn supporting statements that a judge could decide not to believe.[16] Others were reluctant to seek supporting documents through relatives at home for fear that doing so would put the relatives in danger. Few applicants had lawyers, because lawyers usually charged more than $10,000 to handle an immigration court case, and pro bono lawyers such as Carlos Holguín were in short supply.

Many adult asylum applicants were kept in detention until their hearing dates came up. Some were allowed release if they could post a cash bond, but many for whom bond was authorized could not raise the money. Winning an asylum case was especially difficult for detained applicants. From within a detention center, they had limited ability to make telephone calls or to access legal information, and even after the Internet became a standard method of communication and research beginning in 1995, access to internet facilities in detention centers was often nonexistent. Also, because most ICE detention centers were located far from cities, and lawyers could not afford to spend a day in travel each time they needed a private consultation with a client, detained clients were less likely to have legal representation than those who were not behind bars.

Children who were released to relatives and foster homes had additional problems in applying for asylum. Because of their age, many did not know that asylum was possible, and others were unable to understand how to complete the forms. Like many adults who had fled from war-torn regions or from violence directed at them personally, the children were often so traumatized by their experiences back home, and by the dangers and hardships they had faced on the journey to the U.S. border, that they were unable to think about the future, much less deal with forms and evidence. In addition, they were busy adjusting to new homes and caretakers.[17]

Those who remained in juvenile detention because no suitable placement could be located or who were deemed by ICE to be flight risks or dangers to themselves or others had the most difficult challenges of all. Like children who were released pending their hearings, they were often traumatized before they even reached the United States. A 1990 survey, conducted with INS approval, of the mental health of 133 randomly selected migrant children in three detention centers found that on average, they had experienced three traumatic events such as physical or sexual assaults, encounters with dead bodies, or kidnappings in their home countries, and three more such events en route to the United States. The same researchers administered psychological tests to sixty of the children and found that 18 percent of them suffered from post-traumatic stress disorder and 38 percent of them suffered from depression.[18] Incarceration apparently deepened their distress. Numerous studies of children who are incarcerated pending trial for juvenile offenses have found that detention "has a profoundly negative impact on young people's mental and physical well-being."[19] Experts estimated that at least a third of American children incarcerated for delinquent behavior suffered from depression that began after they were incarcerated.[20]

In addition, children who were confined to secure facilities, either by the INS or later by the Office of Refugee Resettlement, were often unable to obtain legal counsel because they had no money to pay for such assistance. In addition, those facilities were "in remote locations that lack immigrant communities and readily accessible legal and social services."[21]

ASYLUM AFTER 1997: EXPEDITED REMOVAL BEGINS

In the early 1990s, asylum became much more controversial than it had been in the decade after Congress passed the Refugee Act. In 1992, William Slattery was the New York district director of the INS. Slattery, an ex-Marine, had risen through the ranks, starting in Texas as a member of the Border Patrol. In New York, he was troubled because more than ten thousand foreign nationals who arrived at Kennedy Airport that year would be able to remain in the United States for more than a year by claiming asylum. They could not be deported until they were interviewed to assess the credibility of their assertions, and although he jailed as many as he could, his office controlled only 190 beds in local jails. If released, asylum seekers were usually sheltered by family members or friends until INS officials with long backlogs of cases could hear their stories and assess their evidence, and many disappeared into the country without showing up for scheduled interviews or hearings. Slattery advocated an idea known as "summary exclusion" that Senator Alan Simpson (R–WY) had been pushing for years. He wanted Congress to permit cursory screening, at the airport, of everyone arriving without a visa or some other basis for entering the United States lawfully. Those who failed to prove in this quick test that they were genuine refugees—persons fleeing persecution on one of the five grounds listed in the law—would have to return home on the next plane. For them, there would be no interview by an asylum officer, no immigration court hearing, no appeal, and no judicial review. Only those who passed this first test would go on to the next stage or stages of the application process.[22]

Slattery's proposal achieved traction after horrific events that occurred the following year. Mir Aimal Kasi, a Pakistani national, had entered the United States with a visa in 1991 and applied for asylum. The backlog of asylum cases was so large that by early 1993, he had not yet been assigned a date for an INS interview. On President Bill Clinton's fifth day in office, he went to the CIA parking lot in Langley, Virginia, and shot five agency employees who were waiting at a stoplight. Two of them died.[23]

In September, 1992, another Pakistani, Ramzi Ahmed Yousef, flew into to Kennedy Airport, claimed to be an Iraqi, and asked for asylum. INS inspectors realized that he had no visa, but they could not detain him because they were short of jail space. During the next several months, he organized a plot to blow up the World Trade Center. In February 1993, his bomb failed to topple the building but did kill six people and injured hundreds.[24]

These terrorist attacks gave Slattery the opportunity he needed to push for summary exclusion. First in an interview with the *National Review*, then in other papers such as *Newsday*, the *Los Angeles Times*, and the *New York Times*, and finally in a much-watched production on the TV show *60 Minutes*, Slattery argued that "Congress must change the law" to allow him "to send most of them packing after a quick hearing at Kennedy. . . . The aliens have taken control. The third world has packed its bags and it's moving."[25]

Within days after these interviews appeared, a new incident kept asylum on the front pages. A Chinese freighter, the *Golden Venture*, carrying 286 Chinese passengers who were being smuggled into the United States, ran aground on a sandbar near New York City. Many of the passengers jumped into the ocean, and ten died in the effort to reach land. Most of the rest applied for asylum. Slattery insisted that they be detained, and although he lacked space to hold them in New York, they were sent to jails across the country. The arrival of so many undocumented persons in such a dramatic fashion, coming on top of the *60 Minutes* broadcast and numerous newspaper stories, caught the attention of key members of Congress.[26]

Despite the efforts of many members of Congress who supported Slattery's call for reform, no immigration reform legislation passed Congress in 1993 or 1994. Congress was preoccupied with President Clinton's efforts to pass major health care legislation. The INS successfully prevented more Chinese smugglers' ships from landing by turning them around at sea. Slattery was given more detention spaces in New York. Airline officials were trained to prevent persons with improper documentation from boarding planes bound for the United States. And in late 1994, David Martin, the INS's general counsel, found a way to eliminate the processing backlog that had allowed people who had arrived with visas and then claimed asylum to remain in the United States for more than a year before they could be interviewed.[27]

Everything changed with the election of 1994, when Republicans, running on the platform of a "Contract with America," swept into control of both houses of Congress. Senator Simpson replaced Senator Edward M. Kennedy (D–MA) as chair of the Subcommittee on Immigration, and he revived the idea of summary exclusion that he had first suggested in the early 1980s. His House counterpart, Rep. Lamar Smith (R–TX), was a similarly enthusiastic proponent of curtailing procedural protections for asylum-seekers, particularly those who arrived in the United States or at its borders without visas or other permission to enter.[28]

These two chairs drafted bills that passed both houses. The resulting law was signed by President Bill Clinton in September 1996, shortly before voters went to the polls to determine whether he would be re-elected.[29] In the years to come, the section on summary exclusion,[30] re-named "expedited removal" in the final version of the statute, would have an important impact on a large number of child migrants—not UACs, because DHS never applied expedited removal to them, but children who arrived along with a parent or other adult relative.

The new law provided that the attorney general could apply expedited removal procedures to certain categories of foreign nationals who had no valid travel documents (that is, a genuine passport and a visa if the person was from a country for which a visa was required). The attorney general could designate the categories of individuals to whom the expedited procedures would apply at his or her "sole and unreviewable discretion." If an individual fell within a designated category, it did not matter whether the person had already entered the United States, or was at an airport, seaport, or land border crossing. The only exceptions were for Cubans and for individuals who could prove that they had been physically present in the United States continuously for two years before an official found that they did not have proper documentation.

If expedited removal applied, the foreign national did not have the right to have an immigration judge decide whether there was a basis for remaining in the United States. Instead, the individual could be deported forthwith. A person who had arrived by air and had been found by the airport inspectors not to have the proper documents could simply be kept in the airport and put on the next return flight (and the airline that brought him or her would have to swallow the cost). If expedited removal was to be applied to people other than Canadians or Mexicans apprehended at land borders or in the interior of the country, however, such immediate deportation was impractical. A flight would have to be arranged, and as a practical matter, it could not take place until enough deportees from that country could be aggregated to make the cost of the flight worthwhile. Congress therefore prescribed "mandatory detention" for such individuals until they could be deported.

Congress recognized, however, that some of the individuals who arrived or entered without valid documents were genuine refugees fleeing from persecution. It provided a swift screening system to try to protect those individuals. If, when encountered by an INS agent (after 2003, a Customs and Border Protection or ICE agent), the migrant did not express a fear of returning home, detention and deportation would soon follow. If, however, the individual expressed a fear of returning home, that person would soon have a preliminary interview with an asylum officer (who, after 2003, was employed by U.S. Citizenship and Immigration Services). The statute specified that the interview was not to be the same searching interview that asylum officers gave to "affirmative" applicants for asylum—those who came forward voluntarily and applied before being apprehended by an agent. Instead, the purpose of the interview was to determine whether the individual had a "credible fear" of persecution. The new law defined "credible fear" to refer to a "significant possibility, taking into account the credibility of the statements made by the alien in support of the alien's claim and such other facts as are known to the officer" that the alien could later persuade an immigration judge that he or she warranted a grant of asylum.[31]

This procedure appeared to put two new obstacles in the way of asylum claims by those who arrived without documents. One obstacle was presented by their first encounter with a border agent; the other was the credible fear interview.

First, migrants would have to express to arresting officers or airport inspectors or border guards a fear of returning, and they had to do so without the officer mentioning the word "asylum," though the border agents were directed to state that "U.S. law provides protection to certain persons who face persecution, harm or torture upon return to their home country." The form that the INS prescribed for use by inspectors and border agents specified the four questions they should ask:

[1.] Why did you leave your home country or country of last residence?

[2.] Do you have any fear or concern about being returned to your home country or being removed from the United States?

[3.] Would you be harmed if you are returned to your home country or country of last residence?

[4.] Do you have any questions or is there anything else you wish to add?[32]

These somewhat redundant questions represent the federal government's effort to achieve four goals: to find out which newly arrived individuals were afraid to go home; to avoid encouraging false asylum applications by mentioning or describing the availability of asylum; to standardize the procedures, so that some border officers would not fail to ask about fear while others explained asylum in detail; and to limit the information that border agents, who were not trained in the nuances of asylum law, would try to collect. A response to the first question that suggested fear, or a positive response to the second or third question, would require the agent to pass the migrant along to an asylum officer for a credible fear interview. Agents were not to probe into the details of why an individual was afraid to return or to try to assess whether an expressed fear was genuine or reasonable. Those tasks would fall to the asylum officers, who had weekly trainings that covered how to interview migrants in depth and the legal grounds for asylum under the most recent regulations and court decisions.

Nevertheless, there were reasons why genuine asylum-seekers might fail to express fear at this stage and therefore face immediate deportation rather than going on to the next stage. First, in some cultures, people learn at an early age to be stoic and not to express fear even when they actually are afraid, and especially not to exhibit fear to strangers. Second, encounters with border agents often took place within minutes or hours of their arrival in the United States. At that time, travelers were often hungry and tired from a long voyage, disoriented by arrival in a new country, and, if they had been tortured or incarcerated by uniformed military or police officials at home, fearful of communicating with the uniformed American officers who were interrogating them. They invariably lacked lawyers at this stage, and many, perhaps most, did not speak English and had to use whatever interpreters the border agents were able to round up. At airports, the interpreters were sometimes personnel of the state-owned foreign air carriers on which the migrants had arrived, who were themselves employees of a persecuting government. Finally, the border agents did not always follow the prescribed procedures. In 2005, the United States Commission on International Religious Freedom, which Congress had created, published a study based on observations of border inspectors. It reported that many inspectors were not in fact informing people of the fact that the United States offered protection to persecution victims, and that this omission resulted in unwarranted removals:

> DHS regulations require immigration inspectors to follow a standard script informing each alien that (s)he may ask for protection if (s)he has a fear of returning home. In approximately half of inspections observed, inspectors failed to inform the alien of the information in that part of the script. Aliens who did receive this information were seven times more likely to be referred for a credible fear determination than those who were not.[33]

The Commission also found that in 15 percent of observed cases, arriving migrants who did express a fear of return were not in fact referred to asylum officers and that in more than half of those cases, the inspector filled out the form to reflect that the migrant did not express such a fear.[34]

The second new hurdle that those arriving without proper documents faced was the credible fear interview itself. In order to avoid deportation at this second stage, a migrant had to testify under oath and persuade an asylum officer that her testimony was credible and that there was a significant possibility that an immigration judge would later find that she was eligible for asylum. But in this interview, as in the border encounter, many migrants faced obstacles. They did not have lawyers, and indeed, the expedited removal statute did not provide them with a right to have a lawyer represent them at this stage, even if they or their families had enough money to hire one.[35] The interviewer was not uniformed, but the encounter took place in the coercive environments of the detention facilities in which they had been confined. These settings were described by the Commission as "suitable in the criminal justice system but . . . entirely inappropriate for asylum seekers fleeing persecution."[36] It also reported that a "substantial number" of individuals who abandoned their effort to seek asylum did so because of their conditions of detention.[37]

For migrants who had once before been deported, the hurdles were higher still. Instead of having to prove "credible fear," they would have to prove "reasonable fear," meaning that instead of having a "significant possibility" of proving a case based on past persecution, they would have to persuade an asylum officer that they had a "reasonable possibility of future persecution."[38] Furthermore, they could not win asylum. They could win "withholding of removal," preventing deportation, but only by proving to the immigration judge that it was more likely than not that they would be persecuted if deported. Unlike those who won asylum, such individuals could not have their spouses or minor children join them in the United States.[39]

When expedited removal began in 1997, the government lacked the staffing to apply it to all undocumented individuals encountered by border officials. From 1997 until 2004, therefore, it was implemented only at "ports of entry"—airports, seaports, and official land border crossings where border agents were permanently stationed. In August 2004, however, the Bush administration used the authority provided by the 1996 statute to extend expedited removal to many immigrants who crossed the border between ports of entry—that is, largely to those who waded or rafted across the Rio Grande. Specifically, the administration ordered that expedited removal would be used for foreign nationals other than Mexicans and Canadians who were apprehended within one hundred miles of the border and within fourteen days after their entry into the United States.[40] INS had decided in 1997 not to apply expedited removal to the unaccompanied children that it apprehended.[41] But as we shall see, in the years after 2004, and particularly after 2013, expedited removal became an increasingly important legal procedure for detaining and deporting Central American children who had fled with adult relatives to the United States, and who were therefore not "unaccompanied."

6 Hutto

2003–2007

In the 1980s and early 1990s, civil wars in El Salvador and Guatemala left nearly three hundred thousand people dead. Many survivors, including the young Jenny Flores, fled north. The two nations, as well as Honduras, had some of the highest levels of income inequality in the world, with large segments of the population living in extreme poverty.[1] These three Central American countries soon became known as the "Northern Triangle" nations. The return of peace left them with large numbers of young, unemployed men with neither educational or job opportunities.[2] Some had been guerrilla fighters; others had served governments or governmentally-sanctioned death squads. Large numbers had weapons. Groups of these men coalesced into criminal gangs.

Many analysts believe that U.S. immigration policy helped to transform the small gangs into two large, national criminal organizations. Tens of thousands of young Salvadoran men had fled violence by escaping to the United States. Some had committed crimes and been imprisoned, primarily in Los Angeles. During their incarceration, they formed the gang that became known as MS-13. A rival gang, which became known as Mara 18, consisted primarily of Mexicans also imprisoned in Los Angeles. By the early 2000s the United States had deported approximately twenty thousand of these criminals. Both sets of these men settled in the Northern Triangle, to which they brought American gang "styles" such as "tattoos, hand signs and the observance of street rules."[3] By 2005, the three countries already had "some of the highest murder rates in the world": 45.9 per 100,000 people in Honduras, 41.2 in El Salvador, and 34.7 in Guatemala, compared to 5.7 in the United States. In El Salvador, 60 percent of the murders were gang-related.[4] As we shall see, that level of violence would become even more extreme a few years later.

FLIGHT TO THE UNITED STATES: THE SPIKE (2004–2005)

Unsurprisingly, as the level of gang violence increased in Central America, a larger number of people fled to what they hoped would be safety in the United States. While the number of undocumented Mexicans arrested near the southwest border (85 percent of whom were returned to Mexico without formal proceedings)[5] decreased from FY 2000 to FY 2005,[6] the number of such arrests of non-Mexcans (primarily Central Americans) rose from 28,769 in FY 2000 to 65,911 in FY 2004 and then spiked, jumping to 154,995 in FY 2005.[7] Among those fleeing were nearly 19,000 children who were presumably placed in deportation proceedings in immigration court.[8] Some had arrived with parents or other adults, and some—perhaps 7000[9]—were unaccompanied.[10] Three-quarters of the children were from the Northern Triangle, but some came from as far away as China. Their average age was fifteen, the same age as that of Jenny Flores when she arrived, and 20 percent were fourteen or younger.[11]

Custody over unaccompanied children apprehended by the Border Patrol was transferred to the Office of Refugee Resettlement (ORR), as the Homeland Security Act required. On any particular day, ORR had responsibility for more than seven or eight hundred unaccompanied children.[12] About 70 percent were eventually released to adult sponsors until their cases could be heard, but even those who had to be placed in shelters, because no relative or other sponsor was available, were much better off than in Department of Homeland Security (DHS) detention. While in ORR custody, they received education, recreation, health care, and mental health assessments.[13]

At the time, Customs and Border Protection (CBP) had a guideline prohibiting it from holding a child in its short-term facilities for more than twenty-four hours, and the Flores agreement barred DHS from holding a child for more than three to five days. DHS had an internal policy of extending this holding time to five days if the child was "apprehended in an area without bed space . . . in an ORR-approved facility."[14] Most of the children were in fact transferred within three days to ORR custody, but as the number of undocumented migrant children increased, "lack of sufficient shelter space" sometimes led to extended detention in Border Patrol stations that were "ill-equipped to care for them"[15] or in Immigration and Customs Enforcement (ICE) facilities intended for adults. The DHS inspector general found in 2005 that more than a third of the children were held at CBP processing facilities for longer than the twenty-four hours permitted by the agency's guidelines, and that 12 percent were held by DHS for more than five days—some as long as 225 days—before placement in longer-term care.[16] However, as one authority noted at the time, "even seventy-two hours in jail-like conditions, without access to education and recreation, feels like an eternity and can have adverse mental health consequences."[17]

ACCOMPANIED CHILDREN

The sudden increase in the population of children seeking refuge in the United States in 2004 and 2005 included many who had fled together with adult family members. DHS knew what to do with the unaccompanied alien children, because the Homeland Security Act directed their transfer to the custody of ORR. But it was completely unprepared to deal with children who arrived with parents or other adults. Its partial solution was to house a small number of the families in a detention center known as Berks, which is discussed in more detail in chapter 11.

In the 1990s, the Immigration and Naturalization Service (INS) had converted a county nursing home in Leesport, Pennsylvania, in Berks County, into the Berks County Youth Center (later renamed the Berks

County Residential Center), a detention center for unaccompanied children, primarily Chinese boys and girls who had been smuggled into the United States. The facility had one wing with thirty-seven beds exclusively for unaccompanied minors who had not been charged with crimes, and a secure detention wing in which such children were housed together with American children from the county who had been charged with or convicted of crimes. The facility, particularly the secure wing, had come under stinging criticism from Human Rights Watch.[18]

In March 2001 the INS had converted the secure wing into a "family residential center" to house detained immigrant families. The entire facility was very small, accommodating only forty families. The residents were asylum applicants who had been put into expedited removal proceedings. They stayed for only two or three weeks, until they were found to have a credible fear of persecution, and then were released to community sponsors. In its new incarnation, the facility had a long corridor with posters and hanging plants, small bedrooms with four beds, and unlocked doors. Both children and adults had classes and daily outdoor time. Children under seven were allowed to sleep with their parents, though all residents were checked at night every fifteen minutes.[19]

But Berks was too small to accommodate the many families arriving in 2004 and 2005. DHS's first solution to the problem of its lack of capacity was to separate children from their parents, often without informing ORR about the separations.[20] According to the DHS inspector general's 2005 report,

> Juvenile aliens who were accompanied when originally apprehended can become unaccompanied because of a lack of appropriate detention facilities. In these situations, accompanied juveniles, regardless of age, are separated from their family members because longer-term facilities are not readily available to accommodate the family. Juveniles ranging from babies to teenagers are transported to facilities without their parents. Separating juveniles from their family increases the risk in housing a particularly vulnerable population. . . . During the time of our review, accompanied juveniles apprehended at [Kennedy Airport in New York] were separated from their families and were sent as unaccompanied juveniles to ORR facilities in Chicago, IL, Miami, FL, and Texas.[21]

The fact that DHS was separating children from their parents came to the attention of immigrant advocacy organizations such as the Women's

Refugee Commission, the Lutheran Immigration and Refugee Service, and the United States Conference of Catholic Bishops. They pressed the government to find a solution other than family separation.[22] Key members of the House of Representatives also disapproved of what DHS was doing. In its report accompanying the 2006 DHS appropriations bill, the House Committee on Appropriations expressed its concern about the separations. It observed that children arrested with their parents were not in fact unaccompanied, so they should not be put into ORR custody. Instead, it said that "the Committee expects DHS to release families or use alternatives to detention [including supervised release, in which the families would have to report periodically, in person, to ICE officials] whenever possible." It added, however, that "when detention of family units is necessary, the Committee directs DHS to use appropriate detention space to house them together."[23]

In 2005, in response to the spike in apprehensions near the border, the Bush administration decided on a new policy. It declined to accede to the House Appropriations Committee's wish that alternatives to detention should be used for undocumented families awaiting hearings "whenever possible." It announced an end to what its critics called a "catch and release" policy toward undocumented immigrants, most of whom were single adults, and ICE began building and renting hundreds of jail cells.[24] Because some of the female immigrants were arriving with their children, ICE arranged for the detention of those children along with their mothers. It contracted with the Corrections Corporation of America (CCA) to convert one of its private prisons for convicted adult criminals into a detention center for the immigrant families. The institution, in Taylor, Texas, thirty-four miles from Austin, was renamed the T. Don Hutto Family Detention Center, in honor of the corporation's co-founder, T. Don Hutto. DHS would later tell the immigrants' advocates that it had created the family jail in response to those advocates' complaints about separating families, and that they were very proud to have been able to keep families together.[25]

BARBARA HINES

In 2006, University of Texas Law School Professor Barbara Hines was running an immigration law clinic. She and her law students provided counseling and representation to immigrants living in Texas who had cases pending before DHS or the immigration court. The clinic suddenly began getting calls from women who were being detained, with their children, at a private prison under contract with ICE. At least 80 percent of the families were asylum applicants.[26] They had been arrested at or near the southern border. Some had been put into expedited removal proceedings because the Bush administration had recently extended that procedure to the border area, had asked for asylum, and had passed the credible fear screening, thereby avoiding immediate deportation. Others had been put into the regular asylum adjudication process but were also waiting for immigration court hearings. It would be weeks or months before their asylum applications could be evaluated by a judge. What surprised Hines was not the long wait for hearings, but what the mothers and children were going through at Hutto in the meantime. "We really weren't aware of conditions at Hutto until we started going out there to visit [the clients]," Hines said.[27] What she learned so shocked her that she could not simply represent the mothers in individual immigration cases. Within months, she found herself in the center of a legal and public relations storm, working with national human rights organizations on federal litigation to protect the incarcerated families.

Barbara Hines's parents had fled Hitler's Germany in 1936. When Hines was nine, the family landed in Brownsville, Texas, a border town. "My parents fell in love with the border," she recalls. In the 1940s and 50s, "there was this very fluid border. You went across the river every Sunday to eat, to have your hair done, to have your pictures framed. [But one Sunday,] the customs agent [on the bridge] asked my father, who had a German accent, 'where were you born?' and my father asked him 'where were *you* born?' At that, they detained us for inspection and our car was taken apart." Her parents' flight from Europe and that experience at the border might have influenced her decision to become an immigration lawyer, Hines said.[28]

When Hines was seventeen, her mother worried that she was "becoming too provincial in Brownsville" and suggested that she go to Mexico City for six months. There she focused on Latin American studies and became fluent in Spanish. In 1965, as the civil rights movement was in full swing, she began college at the University of Texas in Austin. During her

Barbara Hines, speaking at a protest.

undergraduate years, she learned that the university health center refused to give birth control pills to unmarried women, and she worked with a student group that lobbied the university to change its policy. Women in the community learned about the group and began asking how to obtain abortions. Group members referred them to doctors in Texas and Mexico who performed the procedure, which was then illegal in Texas, but they were afraid of prosecution so they contacted one of the only two female lawyers in Austin, Sarah Weddington. As a result, Weddington challenged the abortion law in the case *Roe v. Wade*,[29] making history when the Supreme Court declared early-term abortion to be a constitutional right.

After getting a law degree from the University of Texas, Hines began a job at the local legal aid office. One day, she reported, "someone said 'you speak Spanish' and handed me twenty or forty immigration cases, and my life changed. I had never heard of immigration law." As a result of that chance event, Hines became an immigration lawyer, first working with Mexicans who were seeking to become U.S. residents, and then, around the time that Schey began representing Jenny Flores, with Central American refugees. Hines moved from legal aid into private immigration practice, but after returning from a Fulbright fellowship in Argentina in 1996, she discovered that a group of law students had persuaded the dean at the law school to start an immigration clinic in which they could work on cases. She applied to direct the new clinic and was hired. For nine years, she and her students worked on a variety of immigration cases for individual low-income clients.[30]

What Hines learned from her clients at Hutto, and confirmed in December 2006, when she was finally allowed to tour the facility with the Women's Commission for Refugee Women and Children, was that hundreds of children, from all over the world, were confined with their parents in penitentiary-like conditions.[31] Most of the children were under 12.[32] None of the parents knew when their court hearings would be scheduled, and some families had been in Hutto for five months.

Hutto had changed very little in the process of conversion from a prison. Two fences, topped with rolls of razor wire (which an ICE spokesperson said was "for the safety of those that we have housed"),[33] surrounded the complex. Inside, the cells had beds with thin mattresses, a small sink, and an exposed toilet. Mothers and their small children under six lived in the same cell,[34] so the neither could leave when the other needed to use the toilet.[35] Children older than six were separated from their parents.[36] During the day, the parents and children were subjected to up to seven head counts, each lasting up to an hour,[37] during which they had to be in their cells rather than in a common area; this confined them to their cells for as much as twelve hours.[38] All detainees, including the children, had to wear prison garb and prison-issued underwear that was sometimes torn and sometimes stained;[39] even newborns had prison-issued onesies.[40] Hines learned that "you have fifteen minutes to eat. You have to finish your food and then go back to your cell, so you can imagine

A family cell in the L. Don Hutto Family Residential Center.

trying to get your two little children to eat and then have time to eat your-self. And that was told to us by our client who was seven months preg-nant."[41] Meals were "heavily based on American food" which parents said their children were unable to eat, and many mothers reported that their children were losing weight.[42] The laundry system could not keep up with the families' needs, so both parents and children had to wear dirty clothes, in which they slept, at least once a week.[43]

Because of what an assistant administrator of the facility called a "staff shortage,"[44] the children had only one hour of schooling a day, which con-sisted of "how to color" and, for older children, lessons about child devel-opment.[45] They could draw in the common area but were not allowed to take their pictures back to tape to their cell walls, and they were not allowed to have toys, stuffed animals, or writing equipment in their cells.[46] Children had to accompany their parents to interviews with their lawyers, subjecting the youngsters to the parents' horrific stories of rape and other torture in their homelands.[47] Hines and her students did bring crayons and markers to lawyer-client interviews to distract the children. But one child drew a picture of an American flag with the words "please help me" on one of the stripes, and a law student smuggled it out of the prison and into the hands of the press. After that, the students were barred from bringing the children any writing equipment.[48] Comic books and other reading materials mailed to the children by relatives had to be opened in front of guards and were confiscated and thrown away upon arrival.[49]

An emergency light was kept on all night, making it difficult for the children to sleep.[50] The children were wakened frequently at night by guards shining lights into the cells and were roused at 5:30 every morning. Visits were rare, because of the remoteness of the prison in rural Texas, but when they did occur, the parents and children could communicate with the visitors only by telephone, and by looking at them through Plexiglass.[51]

The prison had nurses but no resident doctor; a family practitioner visited once a week. Ill detainees had to wait days for treatment. Many mothers complained that their children had rashes; the medical staff prescribed water.[52] Children who disobeyed the staff were threatened with being taken away from their parents.[53]

Hines tried to interest the press in what was happening at Hutto, but without success. She then organized a demonstration at the prison, which was covered on local TV, but not nationally. Finally, she contacted the Women's Commission and reached Michelle Brané, who had succeeded Wendy Young.[54] ICE allowed Brané and Hines to tour Hutto in December 2006, and the Women's Commission began to work on a report on conditions in the prison; *Locking Up Family Values* was published three months later.[55] In addition, Hines connected with Vanita Gupta at the Racial Justice Project of the American Civil Liberties Union, an organization that would have the resources to bring a federal case against the prison. Hines's goal was to shut it down.[56]

On March 6, 2007, Hines and Gupta sued Michael Chertoff, President Bush's Secretary of Homeland Security, on behalf of Saule Bunikyte, a nine-year-old Lithuanian girl who had been at Hutto for nearly three months, and nine other incarcerated children, some as young as four.[57] In each case, the parents were asylum seekers who had already passed the credible fear screening. Saule and her mother and sister had been arrested by ICE in Illinois, where Saule had been attending elementary school.[58]

THE HUTTO LITIGATION

The ten related cases were randomly assigned to Judge Sam Sparks of the United States District Court for the Western District of Texas. Sparks was a conservative Democrat who had been appointed by President George H. W. Bush in 1991. As a practicing lawyer from 1965 until he joined the bench, he had tried hundreds of cases. He had taken a 50 percent pay cut to become a judge.[59] In 1994, he had upheld the University of Texas's use of affirmative action in its admissions decisions. That opinion was reversed by the Fifth Circuit, but Judge Sparks's view prevailed nine years later, in a different case, in the United States Supreme Court.[60] He claimed that the secret to successful judging was that "you just need experience, a sense of humor, and the ability to drink whisky to handle this job."[61]

The lawsuits claimed that "there is simply no justification for imprisoning children" whose families have been found by asylum officers to have a credible fear of persecution and that, in any event, ICE was violating the Flores agreement. Specifically, they pointed out that Flores required the government to release minors "without unnecessary delay" unless the detention was required to secure the child's appearance in court, or to prevent a harm to public safety. If detention was necessary, the child had to be placed in a "licensed program" and make "continuous" efforts toward release and family reunification. Furthermore, any detention had to take place in "the least restrictive setting appropriate to the minor's age" and a locked facility could be used only if the child had committed delinquent or violent acts or was a serious "escape risk." In addition, the settlement required suitable conditions of detention for any children who were incarcerated, including appropriate housing conditions and food, the right to wear their own clothing, medical care, education in several subjects, recreation, contact visits with non-detained family members, the right to receive mail, and a reasonable right of privacy.

The relief that the lawyers sought on behalf of the families was simple. They wanted the court to require ICE and the Hutto managers to comply with all of the provisions of the Flores settlement, "including but not limited to releasing [each child and her mother] under reasonable conditions of supervision" such as electronic ankle bracelets to ensure that ICE knew where they were. They would not object if the court required

Judge Sam Sparks.

the mothers to report to ICE periodically until their immigration court hearings took place.[62] Anticipating a problem that would become a national crisis twelve years later, Hines was aware that the court might agree to release the children, putting them in the custody of ORR, while keeping the parents in detention, thus separating families. So she explicitly told the court that if the parents had to choose between releasing children alone or keeping everyone together in detention, they would choose to remain together, although that concession may have doomed their chances of getting the court to close the detention center and release everyone.[63]

On the same day that she filed the complaint, Gupta also filed a motion for a temporary restraining order, seeking to prevent the government from punishing the plaintiffs for suing by taking the children away from their mothers and transferring them to ORR for placement in foster care. If the government removed the children from Hutto, leaving the parents behind, the government might then claim that the suit was "moot," that is, not suitable for decision by a judge because the children were no longer housed in the detention center they were complaining about. Gupta's concern was founded on the fact that a few weeks earlier, lawyers had sued ICE to complain about severe overcrowding at an adult detention center in California. Within a week after they filed their amended complaint in that case, the government had moved four of the five plaintiffs out of that facility. In addition, the threat of separation was in the air because Hutto guards had often threatened to separate children from their mothers in order to control the children's behavior, and the children lived in constant fear of such separation.[64]

Hines and Gupta also hoped, by filing the application for a restraining order, that Judge Sparks would provide an early indication of his attitude toward the lawsuit's claims.[65] Nevertheless, moving for a temporary restraining order, which the judge would have to decide quickly to assure that the children would not be moved, had two downsides. First, "judges do not like to be forced to decide momentous issues under the pressure of a request for an emergency order; naturally, under such circumstances they are less likely to alter the existing state of the law."[66] Second, if the judge concluded, under pressure, that the children didn't have a valid claim, he might stick to his opinion later in the litigation.

The risk that the government might try to moot the case, either by removing the children or by releasing the ten children with their parents, could have been avoided if the lawyers had filed the Hutto case as a class action, as Schey had done in Flores. But the children were already members of the class of children protected by the Flores settlement. Any attempt to create a new class would likely have prompted the court to transfer the whole matter to the court in California, which had continuing jurisdiction over enforcement of the settlement. If that happened, Hines and the ACLU would have lost control over the case to Schey, who represented the class, and they could not have made decisions on legal strategy. Two other factors influenced the decision to rely on the Flores settlement but not to try to enforce it in the California court. Hines had heard from

Carlos Holguín that Judge Robert Kelleher, by this time elderly, was no longer actively interested in the case, and because Hutto was in Texas, Gupta and Hines thought that the federal court in Austin would be more concerned than one in California about the families incarcerated there.[67]

To the lawyers' dismay, Judge Sparks denied their motion on the very day they filed it. To make matters worse, he poured cold water on one of their most important legal theories—that the Flores agreement required the prompt release of parents and children together. The settlement, he wrote in his order, "does not direct the release of a parent in custody or require the continued detention of minors until the simultaneous release of their parents can be obtained." In a footnote, he pointed out that under Flores, a child could be released to another responsible adult designated by the parent, while the parent remained incarcerated.[68] In other words, even if a child could not be kept in Hutto for a long period of time, ICE could legally remove the child from its mother and allow ORR to place the child with some other adult, a remedy that might well cause more psychological harm to the child than keeping her at Hutto with her mother.

But Judge Sparks was clearly troubled about the allegations that the facility was not suitable for children. He scheduled a hearing two weeks later, because Gupta had also asked the court to issue a preliminary injunction which, if granted, would require release of the ten families until the court could hold a full trial of the case. He asked the parties to file legal briefs. He also allowed them to present expert witnesses at the hearing. In addition, over ICE's objection, he ordered it to allow the plaintiffs' expert witness, Dr. Andrew Clark, the Medical Director of the Children and the Law Program at Massachusetts General Hospital in Boston, to tour Hutto in the presence of ICE representatives, and to question some of the detainees. But he limited the tour to three hours.[69]

In its brief, ICE emphasized that the purpose of creating Hutto was to promote "family unity" and to provide a "reduction in stress on both the parents and the children." Hutto, it said, was a "state-of-the-art" facility providing a "complete range of service, including educational and medical services . . . with five hours of core curriculum per day . . . and excellent medical care, . . . a pleasant environment for both adult and adolescent residents, [and] three dietitian-approved meals every day." In any event,

Vanita Gupta.

it contended, just as the judge had said in his order denying the restraining order, the Flores settlement "only covers 'minors' in immigration custody, not adults." Therefore, ICE argued, "the only solution that the Court could offer is a release of the Plaintiff [to ORR custody] which would result in her separation from the mother."[70] As we shall see, this argument, that the Flores agreement applied only to children, and not to their mothers, would become the crux of conflict between immigration advocates and the federal government for the next twelve years.

Gupta agreed that separating mothers and children was not desirable; in fact it would be "indelibly traumatic" for the children, but she disputed the government's interpretation of the Flores settlement. "The only way for plaintiff to be afforded her full rights under the settlement," she wrote, "is for her to be removed from Hutto with her mother—either released from custody under reasonable conditions of supervision, or transferred to a less restrictive, home-like environment that complies with Flores standards." Separation of children from parents would make the settlement "virtually meaningless."[71] She also disputed the government's claims about the suitability of Hutto for children by filing a copy of the Women's Commission's report on the facility, along with sworn statements from mothers. One mother wrote:

> I read . . . Mr. Moore's statement [filed by ICE, that] interior doors remain unlocked, facilitating freedom of movement. That is not true. We cannot leave our pod ever except to eat and go to rec and then we are lined up like inmates and escorted by a guard, we are not even allowed to touch the door, much less open it ourselves and at night we cannot leave our cell.[72]

Gupta also filed statements by psychologists who had read the statements that the lawyers had taken from incarcerated mothers but had been denied permission by ICE to tour the facility. They found "severe neglect and psychological maltreatment" of the children, and "lack of access to and delay in receiving adequate medical and dental care." One of them reported that

> Even the most minimal experience of imprisonment may cause needless frustration, anxiety, fear and depression [especially for those who have] endured severe traumatic events. . . . As a mandated reporter of suspected cases of child abuse [in New York], if I were to receive statements by parents and children similar to those I have read from Hutto Prison, I would be legally required to report such an institution to Child Protective Services that would lead to an investigation of child abuse.[73]

Judge Sparks held a hearing the day after Gupta filed her brief and the statements from the mothers and psychologists. He began on a sour note, indicating that he had not read the filings: "those of you who filed hundreds of pages thinking that I was going to stay up all night, run it off on the computer and read it, are grievously mistaken." It got worse for the plaintiffs after that. When Gupta brought up Flores, he asked whether it was her position "that as long as an illegal is in this country with a child. . . .

they cannot go to jail anymore, they get a free pass with their child?" Gupta replied that the parents and children could be placed in a Flores-compliant facility, but she was already being cornered by the judge. Everyone knew that there was no such facility, as Berks had very few beds and, while not as bad as Hutto, might itself be out of compliance with Flores. Gupta was quickly being pushed to give up her argument that Flores required release to a non-restrictive setting as soon as practicable.

Gupta persevered, seeing that she was getting nowhere by focusing on the remedy. Realizing that the judge had not read the documents that she'd filed, she took time to argue that in fact, Hutto was out of compliance with Flores, because it was not a licensed program for the care of children, but a jail in which everyone was at the mercy of the guards, and the conditions of detention didn't come close to those specified in the agreement.

The judge gave just as a hard a time to Victor Lawrence, the government's lawyer, as he had to Gupta. When Lawrence conceded that Hutto was unlicensed but said that when the Flores agreement was reached there was no such thing as a "Family Detention Center," the judge interrupted with "So what is the price of apples in Italy?" Lawrence continued to argue that Hutto was actually "family friendly," but when he saw that the judge was doubtful, because the facility was, at the very least, unlicensed, he retreated to the legal argument that Flores "is not supposed to apply to accompanied children because the family is already unified." At that point, both of the most contentious questions of interpreting the Flores agreement were out in the open— that Flores didn't apply to parents, and that it didn't apply to children who had crossed the border along with parents or other adults.

Then Gupta called her expert witness, Dr. Clark. Lawrence started to question Clark on his qualifications, perhaps to object to his being qualified as an expert, but as Dr. Clark started to reel them off, the judge interrupted, "OK, that's enough. Sometimes you want to fish for catfish, you catch a carp. The witness is qualified as an expert." Clark then testified that the children at Hutto "were likely to experience a high level of fear and even terror" and to perceive themselves as criminals because of the conditions there. He also concluded that there was a significant likelihood that the children would suffer "irreparable psychological injury" because both the children and their parents were in a "state of powerlessness." As an example of the terror that the children felt, he revealed that one twelve-year-old girl told him that she was frightened because "the officers frequently told the children that if they did not behave, they would be placed in an isolation or a cold room by themselves for twenty-four hours."

In cross-examination, Lawrence tried to discredit Dr. Clark by challenging his ability to reach his opinions after only a three-hour visit, but the judge pointed out that the three-hour limit was one that he had imposed and the brevity of the visit was not something that could be attributed to Dr. Clark.

Lawrence called some witnesses from ICE and Hutto. The administrator of Hutto testified that the facility was "friendly," but on Hines's cross-examination, conceded that Hutto was a work in progress and that they were "working on a plan of action" to comply with Flores. For example, just a few days earlier, they had begun to allow the children to wear ordinary clothing rather than uniforms, and although they were not offering detainees individual needs assessments as the agreement required, they were "looking at" how to meet that goal. Although the current policy did not permit the children to have toys in their rooms, updating the policy "will be the next thing that needs to be addressed."

Toward the end of the hearing, Judge Sparks took particular interest in the fact that Hutto administrators required children to be in the same room with their asylum-seeking parents when the parents were being interviewed by their lawyers. "I can't imagine that," he said. He asked the Hutto administrator, "And that rule still applies?" "Oh, yes," she said. "All right," Judge Sparks continued, "It best not apply tomorrow." Lawrence quickly assured him that the rule would immediately be changed. "Even in the penitentiary the lawyers can see their clients one-on-one and do not have to speak in front of their children," the judge added.

The judge was clearly troubled by what he had heard about the conditions at Hutto. "I can't believe what I've heard today that happened at Hutto since 2006, when it opened up," he said. And he wasn't convinced by the government's argument that the Flores settlement applied only to unaccompanied minors. He pointed out that if the government had wanted the settlement to apply only to unaccompanied minors, it could have written that into the settlement agreement, but that isn't what the agreement provided. "They're stuck with it, either bad lawyering or unanticipated events that come down the track."

But whether the Flores settlement gave a parent a right to be released with her child was much less clear to the judge, who increasingly saw the lawsuit as one in which the issue was only conditions of confinement, rather than possible release of the families:

> It appears to me that the government could well be within the settlement to start placing these children in foster homes that are licensed in the state of Texas or in youth facilities. . . . If they want to do that, they have the authority under the settlement to do it. And I want you [Ms. Gupta] to look in your hold cards because I'm not so sure that that's in the best interest of the children. . . . I really implore both sides not to take a battle-line position because that's only going to hurt the people that you [the government] are trying to represent and they [the ACLU] are trying to protect.[74]

THE OUTCOME

Judge Sparks' decision was no surprise, given what he'd said in a more off-the-cuff way at the hearing. He would not release the families, because the Flores decision provided rights only to the children, and the parents were not asking for their children to be separated from them. On the other hand, he was clearly troubled by the government's failure to comply with the conditions of confinement required by Flores. Hutto required that children be held only in licensed facilities. ICE conceded that Hutto was unlicensed, but it claimed that it had obtained an exemption to that requirement from a Texas agency.[75] But Judge Sparks noted that a license "subjects the facility to periodic health and safety evaluations by an outside regulatory body, while a state licensing exemption, by its very nature, removes that layer of oversight." Besides, under Flores, a licensed program had to be "non-secure," while Hutto was a locked and tightly controlled facility.

The judge tentatively concluded that Hutto was "not in compliance" with the many detailed requirements of Flores. The testimony at the hearing had shown that the accommodations and food were not suitable for children, that the medical care was inadequate (with only one doctor on site for eight hours a week for four hundred people), that Hutto was not providing the children with instruction in "science, social studies, math, reading, writing and physical education" as Flores required, and that individual counseling was not being offered as the agreement specified. He also found "most troubling" the guards' threats to separate children from their parents as a means of discipline, which he said "may well constitute mental abuse." But Hines and Gupta had put all of their eggs in the release basket, as that would have set a precedent for other families that would likely have led to Hutto's closing, and they had not asked for a preliminary injunction requiring specific reforms in the conditions of confinement. Since the judge was unwilling to order release, and nobody had proposed a specific list of reforms, all he could do was deny the request to free the parents and schedule a trial for several months in the future. The schedule offered the lawyers time to confer and to try to reach an agreed settlement.[76]

Meanwhile, fearing that it might lose the case if it went to trial, the government attempted the very ploy that Hines had worried about when she sought the temporary restraining order at the beginning of the case. It released all ten families who had sued, either on parole or by allowing them to post bond, and then filed a motion to dismiss the case on the ground that it had become moot. In the alternative, it asked the court to put the case on hold for six weeks and to order the parties to try to mediate the dispute.[77]

On behalf of two of the plaintiffs who had been released on parole, the ACLU lawyers pointed out that ICE could revoke the parole and reincarcerate them at any time. Judge Sparks agreed, and he denied the motion to dismiss. He also refused to postpone the trial date but he did encourage "reasonable negotiation."[78]

The lawyers agreed to negotiate, with the assistance of Andrew Austin, a magistrate judge appointed by Judge Sparks as a mediator. They spent four days hammering out terms. Hines and Gupta wanted, at the very least, a commitment that the government would consider releasing a family after thirty days in detention. The ICE lawyers insisted on waiting at least ninety days before being bound even to review a family's case for possible release. The final day of the mediation started one morning and continued until 4:00 the next morning. Worn down by the marathon, Hines and Gupta finally agreed to accept language providing that ICE had sole discretion regarding the release of the families, but that a family that had been held in Hutto for more than sixty days could request release and ICE would have to explain a refusal in writing. "One should not be mediating at 4:00 in the morning," Hines later reflected. "At 4:00 in the morning there are a lot of things you accept that you might not accept at a later date."[79] In addition, at that hour, "we weren't really thinking about [what might happen] down the road because we weren't contemplating any other family detention centers [for which] this would be the norm."[80]

At the end of the marathon negotiation, the lawyers signed an eighteen-page settlement agreement. Besides the sixty-day review provision, the agreement had a twelve-page checklist of improvements or policy changes that ICE had made since the suit started or promised to make within three months. These changes would include installing privacy curtains around showers and toilets, providing a bed (with thicker mattresses) for every occupant so that children would not have to sleep in their mothers' beds, allowing residents to decorate their rooms and to wear donated personal clothing, allowing children to have pens, crayons, paper, and toys in their rooms before 8:00 P.M., allowing children to sleep until 6:30 A.M. and longer on weekends, providing five hours of class time each day, turning off the lights at night, substituting self-check-ins for multiple head counts, and allowing parents to meet with lawyers without their children present. Judge Austin would visit Hutto three times to verify compliance. The agreement would expire in two years,[81] a provision that Hines and Gupta agreed to because at the end of that time, they could file a new lawsuit if necessary.

Hines and Gupta didn't obtain the release of any family, or even compliance with every provision of the Flores agreement. For example, ICE promised only to explore state licensing, and it didn't agree to close Hutto if a license could not be obtained, or to turn Hutto into a non-secure facility. The detailed educational curricula specified in Flores were not incorporated into the settlement. Gupta "didn't think the government would agree to close Hutto down, so the settlement was the next best option." But, she said, she didn't think that detention was appropriate for children. "The settlement forced the government to make tremendous changes, but these are still prison walls."[82]

7 The TVPRA

2007–2008

The Hutto settlement ended Barbara Hines's efforts to close the facility by court order, but she and others persevered by other means. She and Michelle Brané successfully urged Congressional committees to hold hearings on the detention of migrant families and children,[1] and cooperated with independent filmmakers who made a documentary film about the effort to close Hutto.[2] The University of Texas Law School's clinic also successfully petitioned the Inter-American Commission on Human Rights to visit Texas to interview former detainees and to study the treatment of the families held at Hutto.[3] Awakened to the need to control its contractors more carefully, Immigration and Customs Enforcement (ICE) began to draft national standards for the detention of migrant children.[4]

Meanwhile, the Women's Commission (by this time renamed the Women's Refugee Commission) had returned to the subject of the processing and custody of *unaccompanied* children (termed "unaccompanied alien children" in the Homeland Security Act and commonly referred to as UACs). In 2003, that Act had transferred responsibility for their care and custody from the Immigration and Naturalization Service (INS) to the Office of Refugee Resettlement (ORR). ORR was therefore responsible for placing the children appropriately and overseeing the foster homes, shelters, and juvenile institutions to which it entrusted them. But it was not so simple, in part because the number of UACs who were being apprehended kept rising. By FY 2008, approximately 10,000 UACs were being put into ORR's custody annually.[5]

MICHELLE BRANÉ

In 2007, the Women's Commission and the law firm of Orrick Herrington and Sutcliffe began a two-year study of how CBP and ORR were treating UACs. The study was headed by Michelle Brané, who had just completed the *Locking Up Family Values* report on Hutto.

Like Peter Schey and Barbara Hines, Brané seemed destined to become a refugee lawyer by virtue of the family in which she grew up. Her mother left Hungary for Argentina in 1944, when conditions were becoming very bad for Jews as well as for what she calls "mixed" families such as hers. There she met Brané's father, and after Michelle was born, the family moved to the United States so that her father could do a medical residency. The "dirty war" in Argentina, which targeted Jews, made returning too dangerous, stranding the family in the United States.[6] Growing up, Brané was exposed to bedtime stories about bribing Swiss border guards to escape the violence of war and to her parents' dinner conversations about their friends who were disappearing in Argentina.

During law school, Brané designed a law class for Spanish-speaking prison inmates, which included a lot of information about immigration. Her first job after law school was at a small immigration law firm in Washington, D.C., and then she worked for the INS as a legal clerk. After that, she did human rights work in Bosnia, and when she returned to the United States she ran a program for survivors of torture in immigration detention. Cumulatively, those experiences gave her the practical experience that she needed to land an immigration policy job at the Women's Refugee Commission.[7]

After finishing her report on the accompanied children in detention at Hutto, she and her staff turned their attention to the UACs. They visited thirty facilities that were funded by ORR (including foster care services,

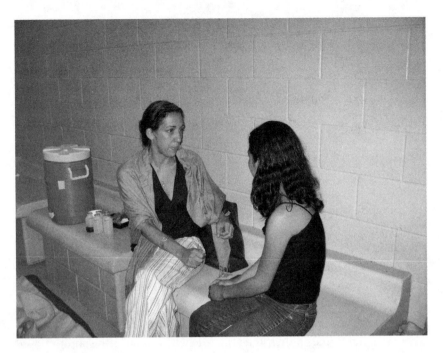

Michelle Brané, interviewing a refugee.

shelters, and juvenile detention centers), three border patrol holding facilities, and three ICE facilities. As they uncovered continuing problems,
they shared their findings with the United States Conference of Catholic
Bishops, which had long been concerned with UACs. It had been shelter-
ing UACs since the mid-1970s. The Archdiocese of Los Angeles had
accepted custody of two dozen unaccompanied children released by INS
in the late 1980s, while the Flores case was making its way through the
courts. In 1994, the Conference had created its Safe Passages program,
which had contracted with INS (and after 2003, with ORR) to provide
foster care services in state-licensed programs and to conduct home studies of prospective placements for some of the children who were being
released to family members.[8]

Both the Women's Refugee Commission and the bishops shared with
interested members of Congress what they were learning about the

adequacy of the government's care for the UACs in its custody. Two members of Congress in particular followed their work closely: Senator Feinstein, who had never lost interest in fair treatment for UACs despite her success in 2002 in transferring their care from INS to ORR; and Howard Berman (D–CA), an advocate of human rights in the House of Representatives.

Brané found that "the treatment of most unaccompanied children has greatly improved with the transfer of custody" from INS to ORR, that most of the UACs were "eventually" released to parents, and that most of the rest were "held in child-friendly shelter facilities or foster home placements." Nevertheless, the intent of the UAC provision in the Homeland Security Act providing for ORR custody, "which was to decouple prosecution from care, has not been fully realized. The roles of prosecutor and caretaker continue to be interwoven with the best interest of children."[9]

THE HALFWAY HOME REPORT

Brané discovered some problems arising from Customs and Border Protection (CBP)'s purportedly short-term detention of UACs for initial processing, some with the interface between CBP and ORR, and some that involved ORR's placement of and services to the children.

To begin with, both the Flores settlement and the government's procedures permitted CBP to hold the UACs that it apprehended for the first seventy-two hours, or for five days if there were no licensed program with space available in the apprehending CBP district. In principle, that period of time could have been used not only to learn the ages and nationalities of those who were apprehended, what documents they had with them, and who might take care of them in the United States, but also whether they were victims of sex or labor trafficking or feared persecution in their home countries. However, CBP lacked a screening mechanism to identify such children. The vast majority of the UACs it apprehended at that time were Mexicans, and most of the ninety thousand unaccompanied children apprehended in 2007 were simply sent back to Mexico without any screening.[10] As another report prepared at the same time explained,

These children are not officially entered into the immigration system. Instead, they are typically removed at the nearest port of entry by Customs and Border Protection within one business day and without an opportunity to appear before a judge or reunify with any family located in the United States. . . . Thus, even if those children are fleeing violence or persecution [in Mexico], in all likelihood they will be returned to their home country.[11]

For those from other countries who were arrested near the border, the conditions of confinement in the short-term border facilities were horrendous. The Women's Refugee Commission reported that the children were

> held in large, open cells that afford no rest or privacy. The cells consist of an open concrete room with concrete benches built into the wall. There is a half wall separating the main room from the toilet facilities. The front of the cell has a window, through which agents can watch the children held inside. The facilities we visited were exceedingly cold. . . . A Border Patrol agent acknowledged that the facilities are intentionally kept cold to keep the detainees docile. . . . Children may be mingled with non-relative adults. . . . Girls also reported being held in cells with adult males. . . . Like adults, children sleep on cold floors [and at one place we visited] received no blankets at all. When we asked why they had none, agents told us that the station used to provide them, but that the blankets became infested with bugs because the children were so dirty. . . . Many [children] told us that they were often very hungry. . . . There are no shower facilities or clean clothes. . . . [At one station] hospital gowns are used for children whose clothes are no longer wearable. . . . We heard . . . accounts in which Border Patrol waited until a [medical] situation developed into an emergency before providing appropriate care.[12]

That situation involved Carmen, who arrived in wet clothes, having crossed the river with her five-month old daughter Lily. "She requested something to keep the baby warm. . . . The agents refused. By morning Lily was turning blue." Finally the agents took them to the emergency room, with Carmen in shackles and deprived of any food. Lily was found to be suffering from hypothermia and had contracted pneumonia.[13]

Another concern with the Border Patrol, according to the report, was that it often violated the Flores settlement by holding children for longer than three to five days after identification as a UAC. Sixteen percent of them were not transferred to ORR custody within that time, and some were kept at border patrol stations or in county jails for "up to several weeks."[14] Despite many reports and lawsuits in the following decade, what Brané observed in 2009 could easily have described conditions in the border facilities in 2019.

The report also identified issues relating to the relationship between DHS and ORR. It asserted that at times, ICE did not want a child released to family members in the United States, so it classified the child as accompanied rather than unaccompanied.[15] Furthermore, in some areas of the country, it used children as "bait" to arrest undocumented relatives who came to pick them up.[16] This practice was, of course, one of the concerns that had motivated Schey and Holguín to bring the Flores case more than twenty years earlier, but it had not been banned by the settlement. Finally, ICE sometimes kept custody of adolescent children who had criminal convictions, although nothing in the Flores settlement carved out an exception that would have exempted ICE from the obligation to transfer the custody of these children to ORR for placement in a secure facility.[17]

The report was generally less critical of ORR, though it did express several concerns. The first was that ORR had given in to pressure from DHS to place most shelters in rural border areas, which made transfer from CBP custody easier but prevented the children from having easy access to medical, mental health, and legal services.[18] Mental health services were particularly in short supply in these areas, although "facility staff estimated that between 30 and 50 percent of children" needed them, up to 50 percent of the children were on psychiatric medications, and about 10 percent of the children were suicidal.[19] Second, as a result of a rapid increase in the number of UAC apprehensions, ORR facilities had become "larger and more institutional" over the years, with higher staff-to-child ratios, and more cameras and bars on doors and windows to facilitate monitoring, as well as more reliance than in previous years on "staff-secure" and secure facilities rather than therapeutic programs.[20] Finally, although ORR eventually managed to place about 60 percent of the children in its care with a relative or other adult sponsor, pending their hearings, it lacked the resources to do much follow-up and particularly did not attempt to connect the children with lawyers. As a result, many of those who were released in this way did not appear for their immigration hearings and were therefore issued deportation orders.[21]

A report issued at about the same time by the Inspector General of the ORR's parent agency, the Department of Health and Human Services, found that ORR was largely in compliance with important parts of the Flores settlement. Specifically, during a six-month period in 2006, 61 percent of the children were released to sponsors within, on average, thirty days—and most of those releases were to parents or other relatives.[22] Taking into account all children in ORR custody, the average stay in ORR-funded facilities was forty-five days.[23] But the Inspector General's staff only interviewed staff members and examined a sample of files; unlike the Women's Commission evaluators, they did not speak with any children, so they did not learn first-hand about the quality of care, either in CBP detention or in ORR custody.[24]

The Inspector General did, however, fault ORR for not having complete records regarding the quality of the services in the facilities where children were housed under its care. Fifty-six percent of the case files that it reviewed were missing at least one of the required assessments of the child's needs. Fifty-five percent lacked progress notes related to medical and mental health care, and 45 percent did not have case notes describing services associated with care, such as counseling notes and educational records. The Inspector General focused particularly on mental health records, because "facility staff stressed that most children experienced serious trauma during their journey to the United States or had mental health issues prior to their arrival."[25] Yet "75 percent of the sampled files lacked group counseling notes and 56 percent did not have individual counseling notes."[26] Furthermore, senior ORR officials indicated that "little oversight" occurred at the facilities in which children were placed, that only one federal field specialist conducted any oversight activities, and that nobody from ORR's staff routinely met with children in the facilities with which the agency had contracts.[27] Finally, the Inspector General faulted both DHS and ORR for their failure to coordinate. The two agencies had no agreement spelling out their respective responsibilities or procedures, and although DHS informed ORR about a child's age and country of origin when transferring a child, it did not convey medical or mental health information in its possession. For example, a child who had been in a car accident was transferred to an ORR facility needing follow-up treatment, but no medical information was provided.[28]

CONGRESS INTERVENES AGAIN

Representative Berman and Senator Feinstein were keeping track of the information that Brané and the DHS Inspector General amassed about the shortcomings of federal agencies in dealing with UACs. In 2005 and again in 2007, Feinstein introduced a bill that she termed the "Unaccompanied Alien Children Protection Act." The bill would have required the Secretary of Health and Human Services to promulgate standards for the detention of children in ORR custody and to notify the children of those standards in their native languages. It would also have authorized the ORR director to appoint "trained child advocates" for children in ORR care and to "ensure, to the extent practicable" that children in DHS or ORR custody, other than those from Mexico (who could still be repatriated without formal process) had competent immigration lawyers. However, the United States would not have been obligated to pay for such lawyers, which makes it difficult to understand how the ORR director could have managed to carry out that task.[29]

Senator Feinstein's bill was not enacted, but an opening for further protection of UACs arose in 2008, when the Trafficking Victims Protection Act of 2000 was due to be reviewed and reauthorized. The offices of Representative Berman, Senator Feinstein, and staff members of the relevant committees in both houses of Congress worked with the Women's Commission, the Conference of Catholic Bishops, the law firm of Holland and Knight,[30] and other organizations to incorporate features that they wanted into the reauthorization bill. Not all UACs were trafficked, but a substantial fraction were, and many others fled to the United States to flee persecution. Therefore the reauthorization bill seemed like a reasonable legislative "vehicle" to carry into law new protections for victims of persecution as well as for those who were the victims of sex or labor trafficking.

As 2008 drew toward a close, the NGOs negotiated energetically with Congressional staff members and administration officials to work into the legislation as many protections for migrant children as possible. Although the legislation had the word "trafficking" in it, and most of the child-protective protections in both the original 2000 bill and the 2008 reauthorization bill pertained to children who were smuggled into the United States by labor traffickers or sex traffickers, the NGOs persuaded key members of

Congress that children who were victims of persecution deserved federal protection for the same reason that trafficked children did. "Not all of [what we proposed was taken by Congress, but we got] as much of that language as could be relevant to protecting kids from trafficking as we could," Brané reported. "[We wanted every UAC] to be transferred to ORR within seventy-two hours. [But they excluded from that protection] the Mexican kids, and the reason for that was that they [both ORR and the staff of the House immigration subcommittee] were concerned that with the Mexican kids it would be too many kids"—perhaps one hundred thousand a year including the Mexicans, though those might have been only twenty thousand individuals who were sent back across the border and then found a way to cross over again.[31] Although the advocates did not achieve ORR care and custody for the Mexican children, they did win a partial victory even for them.

The William Wilberforce Trafficking Victims Protection Reauthorization Act (TVPRA), named in honor of a nineteenth century British abolitionist, was enacted unanimously in both houses of Congress and was signed by President George W. Bush at the end of 2008. The new law made several changes to existing practice. To begin with, Mexican children would no longer always be returned immediately to Mexico without any formal proceedings. The new law required that instead, they would instead be screened to determine whether they were trafficking victims or had a credible fear of persecution.[32] If they met one of those criteria, they would be given the same procedural rights as children from other countries.[33] (The extent to which DHS complied with the screening requirement for Mexican children was, however, later criticized in a United Nations report).[34] Although screening was not required for children from other countries, a few months after the statute was passed, DHS instituted such screening for all UACs apprehended at or near the border.[35]

The Act codified and therefore made permanent a DHS policy[36] that prevented CBP or ICE from putting UACs in expedited removal. Thus children would not be asked the "four questions," negative answers to which would result in immediate deportation. Mexican UACs who, after screening, were likely to have been trafficked or at risk of persecution, and all UACs from other countries, would eventually be given the opportunity to prove to an asylum officer or an immigration judge that they had a valid basis for asylum or some other right to remain in the United States.

Building on the Flores decision, CBP was required to transfer UACs to ORR custody within seventy-two hours, eliminating Flores's five-day exception for instances when no nearby licensed shelter had space available. There would also no longer be an exception for children charged with certain crimes.[37]

The act provided that once the transfer was made from DHS to ORR, the child had to be "promptly placed in the least restrictive setting that is in the best interest of the child."[38] Thus, for the first time, a "best interest of the child" standard, common in family law such as custody determinations, was imported into immigration law. The act further specified that if a suitable family member was not available to provide care, the child could be placed in a shelter, but that a child could not be put into a secure facility without a determination that the child was a danger to self or others or was charged with a criminal offense. Even then, the case of a child consigned to a secure facility had to be reviewed at least monthly.

The act also made an important change in the procedures for adjudicating asylum claims by UACs. Until its passage, the process for UACs was the same as for adults. UACs who were apprehended by the CBP or ICE and then sought asylum were eventually scheduled for adversarial hearings before immigration judges, because only asylum applicants who self-identified and sought asylum before being apprehended were allowed to have non-adversarial interviews with a DHS asylum officer who had authority to grant asylum without ever sending the case to a judge. A hearing in immigration court could be quite challenging for a child, particularly one who didn't have legal representation. In such a hearing, an ICE attorney cross-examines the asylum applicant, probing for inconsistencies or gaps in the narrative that would shed doubt on the credibility of the story that the applicant is telling. The ICE attorney can also make a legal argument as to why asylum should not be granted.

The act provided that UACs who applied for asylum would in the first instance be interviewed by asylum officers, as if they had applied before apprehension. No ICE attorney would be present, and although the asylum officer would question the child, the officer's duty was to make a fair judgment, not to seek to undermine the claim. In addition, asylum officers, unlike immigration judges, received frequent special training on how to interview children.[39] As in affirmative cases filed by adults, however, a child who was not granted asylum by an asylum officer would have a second chance to present her application to an immigration judge, in a formal hearing, and the immigration court system subsequently adopted guidelines urging judges hearing such cases not to wear robes, to allow a child to have a toy while testifying, and to "employ child-sensitive questioning."[40]

A second procedural change involved the statute of limitations for asylum claims. The 1996 immigration law that introduced expedited removal also provided that an asylum application could not be filed by a person who had entered the United States more than a year earlier, unless the person met one of two exceptions. The TVPRA created an additional exception to this one-year deadline for UACs.[41]

Finally, the act addressed the issue of representation for UACs, though it did not go any further than Senator Feinstein had proposed in 2005. It directed the Departments of Justice and Homeland Security to "ensure" that custodians for UACs receive legal orientation presentations and to "ensure to the greatest extent practicable" that the children have counsel.[42] No funds were provided, however, to pay for legal representation, so families would have to pay for lawyers or somehow find pro bono volunteers or institutions.

President Bush signed the bill into law on December 23, 2008. In less than a month, he would be out of office, and it would fall to the new President, Barack Obama, to implement the law and to formulate a new administration policy regarding child migrants.

8 Artesia

2009–2014

While the American Civil Liberties Union (ACLU) and the government were litigating and then settling the Hutto case, Immigration and Customs Enforcement (ICE) began drafting what became its Family Residential Standards. Chastened by the Hutto experience, ICE did not want to allow its private contractors, who had little or no experience in child welfare, to decide for themselves the quality of life for children and parents detained in their facilities. To develop standards, ICE consulted with medical, psychological, and educational experts and offered to include concerned NGOs in the process.[1] Some NGOs declined to participate because they believed that children should never be held in immigration detention, but others negotiated with ICE over the content of the standards, attempting to make conditions better for children at Hutto, Berks, and any future family detention centers.[2] ICE incorporated some of the suggestions from NGOs into the standards, which it issued in late 2007.[3] Implementation of the standards and of the Hutto settlement resulted in significant reforms to the conditions of confinement at Hutto and also at the much smaller family detention center in Berks County, Pennsylvania. Nevertheless, the

115

standards disappointed many child welfare advocates. Dr. Dora Schriro, who had served as the Director of the Departments of Corrections of Arizona and Missouri,[4] later noted that

> the standards, premised upon adult corrections case law for pre-trial defendants, were adopted largely intact after limited input outside of the government. Detainees were permitted only a few personal possessions; movement in the facility and on the grounds was restricted; and access to counsel curtailed. The standards were also advisory, with limited provision to impose sanctions and only a few penalties for non-compliance in place. ICE delegated the operation and the monitoring of the family facilities to others. Without checks and balances in place, Berks and Hutto usually received favorable reviews. Inspections were announced and always conducted during business hours. Final reports were frequently pending for months and final scores were routinely adjusted by facility operators and ICE administrators. Penalties were rarely imposed and contracts never cancelled. . . .[5]

Andrew Austin, the magistrate judge appointed by Judge Sam Sparks to monitor Hutto, seemed to agree: "Although the use of this facility to hold families is not a violation of the settlement agreement, it seems fundamentally wrong to house children and their noncriminal parents this way. We can do better."[6]

The Hutto settlement also called for ICE to attempt to license Hutto as a child care facility. Although Texas did license child welfare facilities, its child welfare agency believed that it had no authority to license institutions in which parents would also be housed. For a while, ICE did try to persuade the state to create a special license for Hutto, but nothing came of these efforts.[7]

While it was negotiating to create the family detention standards, ICE was requesting bids to build three additional family detention centers to house six hundred individuals in addition to the approximately five hundred at Hutto and Berks. The centers would have to provide schooling and recreational opportunities for the children but would be "designed to prevent escapes." The ACLU and other NGOs criticized the plan because even with improved conditions of confinement, the whole idea was a "penal model" applied to children, when alternatives to detention, such as ankle monitoring of their parents, would suffice. But an ICE spokeswoman defended the building of the new jails, saying that "family detention has had the desired impact. We don't see as many families coming across the border. The automatic pass is no longer there."[8]

Eight months after President Barack Obama took office, Janet Napolitano, his Secretary of Homeland Security, hired Schriro as an advisor. Schriro immediately began a study of ICE's detention facilities, including inspections of twenty-five of the most problematic venues. In August 2009, Napolitano hired Schriro as the first director of ICE's Office of Detention Policy and Planning and announced that Hutto would cease to be a family detention center.[9] The families who had remained there and sought asylum or other immigration relief were either released pending their hearings or, if they seemed to be flight risks, transferred to the small family detention center at Berks, Pennsylvania. ICE deported the rest of them.[10] Schriro quickly wrote a report that recommended that migrant families should usually be released until hearings could be held. Detention should be reserved, Schriro suggested, for situations in which the government had reason to believe that the migrant was dangerous or would not appear at a hearing.[11]

Schriro held the director's job for only about a month before becoming New York City's Corrections Commissioner.[12] The Obama administration's determination not to maintain a large detention center for migrant families with children lasted longer than a month but turned out to be temporary as well.

THE NORTHERN TRIANGLE: VIOLENCE ESCALATES

The increasing violence in Honduras, El Salvador, and Guatemala, which had prompted a spike in the number of refugees seeking safety in the United States in 2005, became much worse in the years after 2010. MS-13 and Mara 18 slowly attracted more adherents from local, smaller gangs, eventually becoming the region's largest gangs. By 2017, the two gangs had perhaps 60,000 members in El Salvador alone, and many others in the two other Northern Triangle countries.[13] After 2005, MS-13 in El Salvador and Honduras became organized into neighborhood "clicas," which were in turn grouped into "programas" under each country's national gang leadership, the "ranfla."[14] Sometimes, gang members murdered members of rival gangs in struggles over territorial control, but they thrived mostly by extorting residents of the villages they controlled, killing any members of the public who refused to pay the "impuesto de guerra" (war tax) or who complained to police.[15] By 2016, MS-13 was extorting 70 percent of business enterprises in Salvadoran territory it controlled, which consisted of 247 of the nation's municipalities.[16] Because the gangs had become national in scope, they were able to track down anyone who fled to a different part of the country. They recruited boys as young as six.[17] If a boy did not join he was threatened with harm or death, and if he did join he was compelled to engage in violent acts as part of initiation into a lifelong commitment.[18] Initiation sometimes required shooting a passerby and leaving the body in the street.[19] Desertion after initiation was severely punished.[20]

Girls living in gang-controlled neighborhoods were often raped and tortured to demonstrate that their bodies belonged to the gang. Sometimes their dismembered bodies were left in public places to demonstrate the gang's "dominance of the area and to instill fear in the community." In other instances, they simply disappeared, and their bodies were later discovered in secret graves. Boys and men were controlled by threatening sexual violence against their sisters, daughters, and wives. Teenage girls were kidnapped by gang members and repeatedly gang-raped; their families were threatened if they disclosed the abuse to which they had been subjected. In addition, "in many cases a gang member approaches a girl and tells her that she will become his girlfriend, and if the girl refuses, the gang member threatens to sexually assault her or to harm or kill members of her family." After the girl submits, she is considered the property of the gang member and is punished by death if she ever consorts with another man, even if the gang member is in prison.[21] In Guatemala, domestic violence was a leading cause of the murder of women. 665 women were murdered in Guatemala in 2005, and the majority of those murders "were marked by rape, torture and mutilation." At least a third of the murders were committed by husbands and boyfriends. Cases were rarely prosecuted "due to poor police work and a lack of forensic evidence."[22]

In the early years of the twenty-first century, "the gangs established control over slum areas in big cities" in all three countries. Terroristic acts and mass murders persuaded shopkeepers to submit to extortion. The governments of all three countries experimented for several years with "iron fist" crackdowns against gang violence, but these programs backfired as gang members were concentrated in jails where they taught each other more sophisticated extortion techniques and obtained new recruits, and from which they ran their criminal operations.[23] In 2012, the government of El Salvador tried a different approach. It brokered a truce between the two main gangs, MS-13 and Mara 18, and provided less restrictive facilities for imprisoned gang leaders. Homicide rates dropped precipitously, but the truce broke down in 2014, in part because of a lack of public support. When it ended, the gangs became even more powerful, as the competing political parties counted on them to round up votes in the territories they controlled.[24]

Extortion was the lifeblood of the gang operations (augmented by drug trafficking in Honduras). The gangs could not extort their victims successfully, however, unless they killed those who resisted. The homicide rate rose steadily. In El Salvador, 692 transportation workers were killed between 2011 and 2016, while in Guatemala, 498 bus drivers, 158 ticket inspectors, and 191 passengers were murdered between 2009 and 2011. The populace was so poor, and the number of people dividing the spoils of extortion was so large, that gang members did not become wealthy as a result of their crimes. But that did not matter to the victims for, as one of them explained, "if they've established a daily payment of $1 and you miss two weeks, they may kill you for it. It is no relief that it is a poor man's mafia."[25]

In 2005, observers had already become alarmed by the annual murder rate in Honduras: 46 homicides per 100,000 inhabitants. By 2012, this rate had nearly doubled, to 90.4.[26] But El Salvador soon surpassed it, with a murder rate of 104 homicides per 100,000 people, earning the country the title of "murder capital of the world," with the highest murder rate for any country not at war.[27] Unsurprisingly, the unprecedented level of peacetime violence in the Northern Triangle prompted many people, including both unaccompanied children and families that included children, to flee to the United States, just as Jenny Flores had gone north to escape the civil wars of the 1980s. Some Central Americans pursued surreptitious entry to the United States because they lived in poverty and hoped for better economic circumstances,[28] but a large proportion of those who attempted to migrate from the Northern Triangle, particularly women and children, were fleeing the violent conditions in their countries.

In two lengthy reports based on confidential interviews with mothers and children who fled, 94 percent of whom were being held in U.S. detention facilities when interviewed, the United Nations documented the specific reasons for their flight. The women, more than a third of whom had fled with one or more of their children, described "being raped, assaulted, extorted, and threatened by members of criminal armed groups, including gangs and drug cartels. Eighty-five percent of the women described living in neighborhoods under the control of maras [gangs]."[29] More than two thirds had unsuccessfully tried to find safety in their own countries. Sixty percent had reported attacks and sexual assaults to the police, but none of them had received protection. In fact, the police had been the abusers of 10 percent of the women. The experience of Norma was typical. She lived in a neighborhood controlled by Mara 18. Despite being married to a police officer, she had to pay extortion money every two weeks. Gunfights erupted frequently. Fifteen days before she fled, a boy was murdered and left in the street near her house. Then, four gang members abducted her. They took her to a nearby cemetery where they tied her hands and stuffed her mouth. Then three of them took turns raping her. She contracted a sexually transmitted disease. Her husband filed a report, which made things worse. The gang threatened her until she left the country.[30] Like Norma, 62 percent of the women had seen dead bodies in their neighborhoods.[31]

Another woman, Gloria, found the body of her thirteen-year-old grandson, who had been abducted. The gang had tied his hands and feet and cut off his head. Although Gloria then fled to another city in Honduras to escape the gang, she received continuing threats to her own life. Nelly, also from Honduras, was the aunt of a boy who was being recruited by Mara 18. He was murdered because he refused to join. Nelly reported the murder, but the police passed the report to the gang, forcing her to flee.[32]

Some of the women had fled from abusive husbands or partners after being unable to receive help from the police. They "detailed instances of violent physical abuse, including: beatings with hands, a baseball bat, and other weapons; kicking; being thrown against walls and the ground." Several of the women reported threats to kill their children if they tried to leave a relationship.[33]

The United Nations' second report, on the 404 unaccompanied children interviewed by its investigators, was equally horrifying. Sixty-six percent of those from El Salvador had fled because of violence by organized armed criminals. Maritza, for example, had been approached by a gang member who said he "liked" her, which meant that he would eventually rape her. "In El Salvador," she said, "they take young girls, rape them and throw them in plastic bags." Alfonso lived in a neighborhood that was controlled by MS-13, but which Mara 18 contested. The Mara 18 members had killed the two police officers who protected Alfonso's school and had also murdered two of his schoolmates. They believed that one of his friends was affiliated with MS-13 and threatened that if he went to school, he would be killed. Alfonso's friend didn't take the threat seriously and was murdered, wearing his school uniform. Then they made a similar threat to Alfonso, causing him to flee his country.

Honduran children told similar stories. Forty-four percent of the Honduran children had been victims of violence or of threats of violence by gangs, and 24 percent had been victims of violence in their own homes.[34] Kevin's grandmother advised him to leave, because if he did not, one gang or the other would shoot him. A twelve-year-old Honduran girl fled, at the urging of her mother and grandmother, because the gang members in her town "rape girls and get them pregnant. The gang got five girls pregnant, and there were other girls who disappeared and their families never heard from them again."[35]

Many reports by non-governmental organizations confirmed the escalating violence in the Northern Triangle countries and the effect of gang and domestic violence on emigration. The Women's Refugee Commission was able to hold fourteen focus groups with 146 unaccompanied children, ages ten to seventeen, who were in federal shelters or foster care under the custody of the Office of Refugee Resettlement (ORR). (Customs and Border Protection [CBP] did not allow any interviews with children in its custody.) More than 77 percent reported fleeing because of violence in their countries. Most longed to return home but said that they could not do so without facing certain death. One girl said she had been afraid to take a bus because Honduran gangs were burning buses full of people when the drivers did not meet an extortion request. Another had found a chopped-up body on her doorstep.[36]

Kids In Need of Defense (KIND) reported on sixty interviews with its migrant children clients from the Northern Triangle. It reported that "gangs use sexual violence to control the behavior of women and girls; for example, gang members frequently use rape to punish women and girls suspected of reporting gang activity to the police." Gang members have "raped and tortured girls and left their bodies in public places to demonstrate their dominance and instill fear in the community." For example, Lydia was fourteen when gang members abducted and raped her. Her mother called the police and identified the perpetrators. They went to jail briefly, and Lydia discovered that she was pregnant. When the men were released, they threatened to kill Lydia. She and her mother moved to another town, but the gang members followed them there and continued to threaten Lydia until she fled the country.[37] When Nancy was twelve, gang members raped and murdered her sister because she would not carry drugs for the gang. The family was afraid to report the identity of the murderer to the police because an elderly neighbor had recently been killed for reporting a gang murder that she had witnessed. A few years later, Nancy and her boyfriend were both shot because the boyfriend refused to pay extortion money. The boyfriend died. Nancy recovered but fled after being threatened by gang members who feared that she would report who had killed him.[38] A follow-up report by KIND noted that a new case of sexual violence was reported in Guatemala every forty-six minutes and that 64 percent of the victims were children, but that the total number of incidents was likely much higher because most sexual assaults are unreported. It quoted a Salvadoran police officer who said that "women and children don't migrate because of gender violence; they migrate because the state is unable to protect them from that violence."[39]

Doctors Without Borders surveyed 467 randomly selected Central American migrants in medical facilities that the organization supports in Mexico. Its findings, which were not limited to children, were consistent with those of the other studies. Fifty-six percent of the Salvadorans had a relative who had died due to violence within the previous two years.[40]

The United Nations study and the other reports recognized that not every family or child arriving in the United States from a Northern Triangle country was motivated to migrate by fear of gangs or domestic abusers. Some came to escape crushing poverty or because they hoped to earn money that they could send to relatives at home, or to reunite with relatives who had already settled in the United States, with or without authorization. But the reports and studies showed that fear of violence accounted for much of the increase in the number of Central American children and families seeking to enter the United States starting in 2011.[41]

THE SURGE

The Women's Refugee Commission saw it coming. "Beginning as early as October 2011" it observed an "unprecedented increase in the number of unaccompanied alien children (UACs) [arriving] from the Central American countries of Guatemala, El Salvador and Honduras. It noted that during the first six months of fiscal year 2012 (that is from October 2011 through April 2012), U.S. immigration agents apprehended "almost double the number of children apprehended in previous years."[42] Commission staff tried to warn ORR of a coming crisis, to which it would have to respond by preparing more shelter space and foster care. "The numbers of [unaccompanied] kids are going up," Michelle Brané told them. "'You guys need more shelters.'" But "they weren't really responding. You could see they started going up sort of a little bit in 2011 and then in 2012 they doubled and then they ... started doubling every year. ... Things in Central America were getting worse. ... They were very slow to respond. And so when the numbers doubled again ... they were overwhelmed and they couldn't move the kids out of the border patrol stations fast enough and that is why you [had] this crisis."[43]

The numbers of child migrants didn't quite double from year to year, but there was a very rapid increase. It soon became known in the United States as a "surge."[44] There was a dramatic, sudden increase in CBP apprehensions of Central American children, both unaccompanied[45] and accompanied by adults.[46] From FY 2011 to FY 2014, as violence increased in the Northern Triangle, the annual total number of children and their family members who were apprehended by CBP increased from about 20,000 to nearly 140,000.[47]

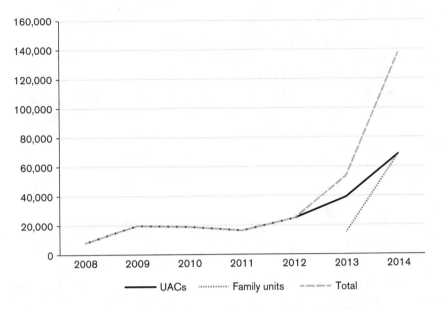

Unaccompanied child and family units apprehensions, and totals of those apprehensions, by year. DHS did not separately collect data on family unit apprehensions until FY 2013 when the number of such apprehensions started to become significant.

UNACCOMPANIED MINORS

Just as the Women's Commission had warned in 2011 and 2012 when it began to see the number of UACs rising, by 2014 both CBP and ORR were overwhelmed. In FY 2012, the Department of Homeland Security (DHS) had sent only 13,625 children to ORR as the Trafficking Victims Protection Reauthorization Act (TVPRA) required, but the following year, that number nearly doubled, to 24,668, and in FY 2014, it more than doubled again, to 57,496.[48] Almost all of these children were from Northern Triangle countries.[49] Neither CBP nor ORR had sufficient bed space or other facilities for them. As early as June 2012,

> the vast majority [of children interviewed about their time in CBP custody] reported receiving inadequate food and water, being denied blankets despite

holding rooms being kept at frigid temperatures and having no access to bathing facilities [after crossing the Mexican desert and the river]. Many of them could not accurately say how long they were in holding cells as the lights were constantly on and there were no windows.... One child described how the children organized themselves to sleep in shifts because there was not enough room in the holding cell for all of them to lie down. Pregnant girls reported that they did not receive adequate medical attention or food.[50]

In 2013 and 2014, with so many children arriving at once, the situation in the CBP holding cells apparently became much worse. In June 2014, five NGOs filed a complaint with the DHS Inspector General based on interviews with 116 UACs who had been released to ORR custody, in which the children described their experiences while temporarily in CBP facilities. A quarter of the children reported physical abuse "including sexual assault, beatings, and the use of stress positions." Seventy percent reported that they were held for longer than the seventy-two hour limit imposed by the TVPRA. They consistently reported "being held in unsanitary, over-crowded and freezing cold cells" and having to sleep on the floor with the lights on. More than 80 percent said that they had been denied adequate food and water. Children who had experienced sexual violence in their home countries or while traveling through Mexico said that they had been humiliated "by having to use filthy restrooms in full view of other detainees and security cameras." Thirty percent said that CBP officials had confiscated their money and other belongings and had never returned them.[51] The NGOs also noted that between 2009 and 2011, various organizations had filed seventy-five complaints about conditions in CBP holding facilities with the agency's oversight authority but had never received a response. The American Immigration Council had reported that 97 percent of 809 abuse complaints filed against Border Patrol agents resulted in the classification of "no action taken."[52]

The Inspector General responded two months later, stating that it had investigated sixteen of the 116 cases identified by the five organizations and that "we were unable to substantiate any of the allegations." Furthermore, he said, "we conducted 57 unannounced site visits to 41 CBP locations [and] did not observe misconduct or inappropriate conduct by DHS employees." The Inspector General did note that not all UACs were being transferred to ORR within seventy-two hours, but it blamed ORR, which was in a different federal department, for what it said was the lack of "availability of appropriate [ORR] housing." The cold temperatures could not be avoided because "in some facilities, DHS employees cannot adjust thermostats" and, in any event, "in all facilities with UACs, disposable blankets or cloth blankets were available."[53]

The NGOs deemed the Inspector General's investigation to have been a "perfunctory process [resulting in] little information about how or why it is reaching its conclusions" and said that they were continuing to receive "reports from other children of verbal and physical abuse and poor health conditions" at CBP centers.[54] In June, two ACLU staff members were allowed to visit the "operations center" in two CBP facilities from which they observed "appalling conditions" in the cells:

> The stark reality is that Border Patrol packs children as young as 5 or 6 into over-crowded cells that are bare except for a single open toilet and a large cooler of water. The agents who showed us the facilities acknowledged that the children are only allowed outside for approximately 20 minutes a day for recreation and exercise. Thus for more than 23 hours every day, the children are locked in cells in conditions that mirror the harshest deprivations imposed on the most dangerous criminals: they take their meals in the cell, sleep on the concrete floor of the cell, and use the open communal toilet in the cell. They have nothing to do to pass the time except to stare out of cell windows and at each other hour after hour [and officials] stated that as few as 30% of the children in its custody are transferred within the 72 hours required by law because of the lack of space at ORR shelters.[55]

In an interview with National Public Radio, the CBP Commissioner himself acknowledged the validity of the children's complaints about conditions in CBP detention, calling them "spot on" and attributing the poor situation to the sudden influx of UACs:

> Sleeping on a concrete floor is not anything any of us wanted to see, and to see a room the size of this office with 40 or 50 kids lying on the floor, covered in a blanket, waiting two and three and four days to be actually moved to a better facility, I know that we were overwhelmed. . . . I watch[ed] those Border Patrol agents trying to microwave burritos for 150 or

Children in CBP custody in 2014.

200 people until the microwave broke. We had to gear up pretty quickly. . . . I did not see, other than several complaints of offensive language, I didn't see complaints of assault or use of force . . . but I think the complaints about the facility are spot-on . . . I don't disagree with those complaints at all.[56]

Like CBP, ORR was not able to keep up with the influx. As early as 2012, it had to place arriving children in "surge" facilities rather than in the shelters that the agency had used for years. It leased quarters for the children at Lackland Air Force Base in Texas, which "looked and felt like an emergency hurricane shelter with cots for beds and portable furniture . . . [guarded by] uniformed local law enforcement agents."[57] Conditions were even worse at the International Education Services (IES) Emergency Shelter, where children spent "an average of two to four weeks, and some as long as two months" before ORR found family members or foster families for them. At IES, all activities were in a gym, and "the girls went outside only to walk to their sleeping cabins and the boys never left the gym [and slept and ate there]." They never had "even an opportunity to talk to family since their arrival," because IES did not have sufficient staff capacity to do counseling or help them locate family members.[58] Federal officials quickly opened "emergency shelters" all over San Antonio. A spokeswoman for the governor of Texas said, "We're seeing emergency shelters becoming more and more of a norm because they just don't have a plan, either to stop this at the country of origin or to handle this once the children are here."[59]

By 2014, when the numbers of child arrivals was much greater than in 2012, ORR had to scramble even more for emergency housing. It had managed to close its shelter at Lackland Air Force Base, but it had to use the base once again,[60] and also to lease space for more than a thousand children at Fort Sill, Oklahoma,[61] and Naval Base Ventura County in California.[62] With so many children in its care, and more on the way, ORR had to find ways to reduce the time spent in temporary shelters from an average of sixty-one days in FY 2013. It reportedly did so—and cut the wait time to an average of thirty-five days—by loosening the eligibility standards for sponsorship in a private home.[63]

Inevitably, ORR made some errors under the pressure of so many sudden arrivals. The Justice Department indicted members of a ring of human traffickers for forcing UACs, under threat of physical harm or death, to work in deplorable conditions on an egg farm in Ohio. The indictments provoked a Congressional investigation of ORR's procedures for screening sponsors with whom UACs were placed. A Senate subcommittee concluded that ORR had not taken "sufficient steps" to screen "alleged distant relatives or family friends," or to verify an alleged relationship with a UAC, which had resulted in placement of the children with sponsors who "were collecting multiple, unrelated children. The subcommittee identified thirteen other cases with "serious trafficking indicators."[64]

Bad as the situation became for Central American UACs, it may well have been worse for Mexican children, primarily boys, who crossed the border alone. Many, and probably most, of those children did not have valid claims for asylum or any other valid basis for remaining in the United States. Most of the boys wanted to stay in the United States to be "better providers [or to] achieve economic success."[65] Even for boys with economic motivations, however, many were "at risk of becoming victims of sex or labor trafficking" because "employers and 'sex tourists' within the United States lure women, boys and girls especially into sexual servitude or forced labor with false job offers."[66] Children who had actually been trafficked could qualify for special visas to remain in the United States for up to four years.[67] For girls, the reason for flight to the United States was more likely than for boys to be the "desire to escape domestic abuse and sexual violence."[68] In 2014, the Board of Immigration Appeals ruled that domestic abuse could justify an application for asylum.[69]

But because Mexican UACs were so numerous, Mexicans had been left out of the TVPRA's mandate for transfer to ORR pending resolution of any claims they might have for U.S. residence. Instead, the TVPRA provided that CBP would screen them, and only those found by CBP officers to have been trafficked or to be at risk of persecution in Mexico would be sent into ORR's custody. The rest would be returned to Mexico immediately, with no further immigration processing.

A seventy-two-page study commissioned by Appleseed and developed by thirty-two lawyers and legal assistants at four law firms concluded that CBP's screening of Mexican children was perfunctory and inadequate. Although the TVPRA had required all personnel who had contact with the Mexican children to have "specialized training" to help them identify those who were at risk and might therefore be able to remain in the United States, the study found that CBP officers in fact received no training on this process at all, much less specialized training. They were simply given a form with three questions, similar to those for all undocumented border-crossers, such as "Do you have any fear or concern about being returned to your home country or being removed from the United States?" The form had no questions about trafficking that a child might be exposed to upon being returned. In addition, children were interviewed in an open area, within earshot of detained adults, by officers sitting at a row of metal desks. Thus neither the questions nor the environment was likely to prompt children to reveal sensitive information about abuse. Although a second form given to the CBP officers stated that no child could be allowed to return to Mexico without first being given notice of their rights, such as the right to call a family member and the right to representation by a lawyer, three-quarters of the Mexican children interviewed by Appleseed stated that they had not been informed of their rights. Many were simply told that they were returning to Mexico.[70]

PUBLIC AND POLITICAL REACTION TO THE SURGE

Before the influx of families and unaccompanied minors became apparent, the Obama administration had supported legislation to provide a path to citizenship for eleven million undocumented immigrants in the United States, and it had created an administrative program, called Deferred Action for Childhood Arrivals (DACA), to grant temporary relief from deportation to certain undocumented people who had been brought by their parents to the United States before they were sixteen years old and before June 2007. To be eligible for DACA, an immigrant had to be a high school graduate or in school, had to be under the age of thirty-one on June 15, 2012, and had to be free of serious criminal convictions.[71]

The public had strongly supported these initiatives, but as a result of "media images of the porous southern border" and "a tide of children making the perilous journey," immigration became the "number 1 national problem" according to a Gallup poll. Forty-one percent of Americans said that the overall number of immigrants should be decreased, while only 22 percent thought it should be increased. A slight majority said that "the legal process for dealing with Central American children who cross the border illegally should be accelerated, even if that means that some children who are eligible for asylum are deported."[72] Support for immigration reform in Congress dropped by five percentage points.[73]

Politicians who opposed increased immigration were "gleeful at the shift" in public opinion.[74] Those who wanted to reduce public support for the Democratic administration blamed President Obama for the surge, some of them suggesting that Central American children had headed for the United States because the administration had created the DACA program.[75] The president of the National Border Patrol Council claimed that "smuggling cartels are using the surge of illegal immigrant children as a smoke screen to distract the Border Patrol, leaving gaps in security that the gangs then use to slip more drugs or known criminals into the country."[76] Representative Candice Miller (R–MI), chair of the House Subcommittee on Border and Maritime Security, said that "this humanitarian crisis can be laid directly at the feet of President Obama as a result of his DACA policy."[77] Susana Martinez of New Mexico, the country's only Latina governor, blamed the president.[78] Senator Lindsey Graham (R–SC) said, "we have to send them back because if you don't, you're going to incentivize people throughout that part of the world to keep sending their children here."[79] Michael McCaul (R–TX), the Chair of the House of Representatives Committee on Homeland Security, called a hearing at which he said that violence in Central America was not new "but what is new is a series of Executive actions by the administration to grant immigration benefits to children outside the purview of the law."[80] Rep. Mike Rogers (R–AL) asked Secretary of Homeland Security Jeh Johnson, "Why aren't we putting them on a bus like we normally do and send them back down to Guatemala?"[81]

The governor of Texas, Rick Perry, called on the administration to "rescind policies that serve as a magnet to encourage illegal immigration." Apparently unaware that TVPRA was a statute, not an Obama administration policy, he specifically suggested ending "DHS policies . . . that prohibit the agency from immediately deporting UACs [from countries other than Mexico] back to their country of origin." He claimed that "the power of boots on the ground I don't think can be overstated. [If President Obama had deployed 1,000 National Guard troops to the border and trained an additional 3,000 Border Patrol agents in 2009 or 2010 there would not have been] this great influx of young people coming in."[82] Senator Jeff Flake (R–AZ) was very aware that the TVPRA was a statute and not merely a policy, because he had opposed it as a member of Congress in 2007, and now he sought to change it "to ensure that these unaccompanied minors are sent home without delay."[83]

ARTESIA

The Obama administration feared that because of the surge, Congress would not pass the immigration reform bill that it had championed, and that the public would oppose relief for DACA and his planned expansion of it to the parents of DACA-eligible children.[84] It therefore did not to try to rally public support for humanitarian protection of children and families fleeing for their lives from gangs and domestic violence. Instead, it joined in the chorus of those who saw these migrants as gate-crashers rather than refugees.

Former Secretary of State Hillary Clinton, asked about the large number of children among the migrants, acknowledged that many children were fleeing from an "exponential increase in violence, drug trafficking, the drug cartels," and that "it may be safer" for them in the United States, but said nevertheless that "they should be sent back as soon as it can be determined who the responsible adults in their families are."[85] Vice President Joe Biden predicted that most of them would be removed: "We're going to send the vast majority of you back. . . . Once an individual's case is fully heard, and if he or she does not qualify for asylum, he or she will be removed from the United States and returned home. Everyone should know that. We expect many of the recent immigrants—migrants I should say—to fall into this category. My guess is a vast majority, and they will be going home."[86] Cecilia Muñoz, the director of the White House's Domestic Policy Council, said that "the vast majority of these cases probably will result in return to their countries of origin," and Esther Olavarria, the DHS Deputy Assistant Secretary for Policy, said that "the children allowed to remain would be few in number."[87]

The administration requested Congress to appropriate $3.7 billion in emergency funds to deal with the influx, with half of that money to go to ORR for the care of the UACs—a request that Congress ignored.[88] It also prioritized the deportation cases of recently arrived UACs and families in detention on the dockets of the immigration courts, so that the recent arrivals could either be deported quickly (with the UACs spending less time in shelters or foster care) or, if found eligible for asylum, begin normal lives. But the administration's most dramatic response to the increased number of people crossing the border was to reinstitute family detention for the first time since it had closed Hutto five years earlier. On June 24, 2014, DHS Secretary Jeh Johnson told a House committee that DHS was constructing a new "temporary" facility "to house and expedite the removal of adults with children."[89] Three days later, ICE opened a "family" detention center in a building that had formerly been used for a law enforcement training center in Artesia, New Mexico, a town so remote that it was more than a four-hour drive from Albuquerque or Santa Fe. The building was large enough to house more than six hundred people at a time,[90] and it was surrounded by two barbed wire and razor wire fences.[91] The average age of the children incarcerated in Artesia was six.[92] Though officially called the Artesia Family Residential Center, it actually housed only mothers and children, as fathers were detained elsewhere.[93]

Conditions at Artesia were not as bad as they had been at Hutto before Barbara Hines and Vanita Gupta brought suit, but the term "Family Residential Center" hardly conveyed what went on inside. The Detention Watch Network reported, based on reports from lawyers who were eventually able to meet with mothers incarcerated in Artesia, that many of the children were losing weight rapidly, and every mother the lawyers saw "is forced to sneak food under her shirt or in her pants for her children to eat later." No educational services were provided for the children, in violation of the Flores settlement and ICE guidelines. Children taken to the medical clinic were routinely given water rather than medication, and in July 2014, chicken pox caused the facility to be quarantined.[94] Women were allowed one five-minute phone call a day, but if children misbehaved, everyone lost access to phones.[95] Two lawyers who were able to see the residential quarters later wrote:

> We saw babies in diapers tottering around the facility's dirt paths and exhausted young children and mothers waiting in line for lunch in the sweltering heat. We saw two boys, about 7 years old, walking with a trash can, picking up garbage and dirty diapers off the floor. Every mother we spoke with expressed concern that their children were suffering from dietary problems due to malnutrition and depression, including diarrhea, loss of appetite, and/or severe weight loss.[96]

In an effort to satisfy the White House expectation that most of the families would be deported, DHS invoked the expedited removal procedures created by the 1996 law. When the families were apprehended, either at an official border crossing station where they asked for asylum, or shortly after crossing the border, CBP officers were supposed to ask them four specified questions to determine whether they were afraid to return. If they did not answer in the affirmative, they were processed for immediate deportation, without going to Artesia. Nobody knows how many genuine refugees were deported in this manner, either because the agents failed to ask the questions or because the person answering the questions did not understand them. However, there was reason for concern, because, as noted in chapter 5, the United States Commission on International Religious Freedom (USCIRF) reported that agents did not always ask the four questions and did not always record the answers correctly. In 2005, USCIRF had reported that "in more than half of the interviews observed . . . officers failed to read the required information advising the non-citizen to ask for protection without delay if s/he feared return" and that in 15 percent of the cases it observed, "asylum seekers who expressed a fear of return were removed without referral [for a credible fear interview] and in nearly half of those cases, the files indicated that the asylum seeker had not expressed any fear."[97] CBP had thereafter declined to accept USCIRF's recommendation that it videotape all interviews in which the fear questions were supposed to be asked.

In 2014 and 2015, USCIRF returned to the border but was able to observe only five interviews of migrants. Even in this small sample, it found "several examples of non-compliance with required procedures," including failure to record an answer correctly.[98]

The families who were sent to Artesia had passed this initial CBP hurdle. But before sending them to Artesia, CBP entered orders of removal against them, orders that would be suspended until asylum officers determined whether or not they had "credible fear" of returning to their homeland. As one immigration lawyer explained, "the removal order's ability to be immediately executed electrifies every interaction for the noncitizen. A single misunderstanding, a single bad translation, or a single inattentive government official could result in deportation."[99]

The administration apparently believed that creating expedited immigration court calendars for deportation hearings was not enough to show the public that it had a grip on what commentators now called an immigration crisis. Unaccompanied children were protected by the TVPRA from being jailed under harsh conditions and from expedited removal. The TVPRA also granted them the right to have their claims assessed first by asylum officers in office interviews, rather than by judges in formal, adversary immigration court hearings. So there was little that the administration could do to speed their deportation. But for accompanied children, those who had come to or crossed the border with an adult, rapid processing at Artesia would accelerate their deportation, and the Obama administration hoped that incarceration itself would deter more families from trying to come to the United States. On the day that Artesia opened, a "senior DHS official" explained to the press that "the goal [of the new jail] is to process the immigrants and have them deported within 10 to 15

days to send a message to their home countries that there are consequences for illegal immigration."[100]

It almost worked. Artesia was so remote from any city that there were
no immigration lawyers within three hours of the facility, and therefore
nobody to help prepare the mothers for their credible fear interviews.
Before Artesia opened 77 percent of noncitizens had been found to have
credible fear and had almost always been released on bond or parole,
often with ankle bracelet monitors, to live with relatives until their court
hearings could be scheduled. But among women who had credible fear
interviews with asylum officers at Artesia during its first ten days, the rate
at which the officers found credible fear dropped to 38 percent.[101] And the
families that did pass the credible fear stage of the process faced detention
rather than release until a court could hear their cases.

THE LAWYERS

But if the Obama administration was counting on the remoteness of
Artesia to cycle the women and children rapidly through CBP processing,
unsuccessful attempts to establish credible fear, and rapid deportation,
they didn't reckon with the determination and ingenuity of America's
immigration lawyers, many of whom were members of the American
Immigration Lawyers Association (AILA), which linked them together
through the Internet. A few days after Artesia opened, more than a dozen
volunteer lawyers descended on the facility, and one of them, Christina
Brown, began to organize them.[102]

ICE was reluctant to let anyone know the names of the women and
children who were incarcerated, and although ICE could not prevent a
woman from seeing a lawyer who already was her representative, the lawyers arriving at Artesia had not been retained by the people they wanted
to serve. However, some of the lawyers were from the National Immigration
Law Center, the organization that Carlos Holguín had been with when he
won the *Orantes-Hernandez* class action on behalf of detained Salvadoran
migrants.[103] As a result of the settlement of that case, signed in the 1980s,
they had a right to visit with detained Salvadoran migrants, wherever they
were being held. This provided the first opening to see many of the women

at Artesia.[104] The women were not allowed to send messages to the outside world, but once other women, including new arrivals, knew that lawyers were waiting in the lawyers' trailer that ICE had provided to the volunteers, they smuggled out notes—"papelitos"—on scraps of paper hidden in the bra straps and underwear of the represented women who were allowed to meet with the lawyers. Sometimes the scraps were passed to lawyers in bathroom stalls, or hidden in the palm of a handshake. The papelitos had their name and location, along with an indication that they desired representation.[105]

Among the early volunteers at Artesia were two immigration lawyers, Laura Lichter and Stephen Manning, who decided that no woman should fail the credible fear test and be deported simply because she was unrepresented. The women, they believed, were entitled by law to have lawyers help them give truthful, detailed answers to the questions they were asked in the credible fear interviews, answers that would help the asylum officers realize that they qualified for asylum because they had been persecuted for their political opinions or, more commonly, their membership in a particular group.

Both of these lawyers were leaders of AILA; Lichter had been president of the organization, and Manning was a member of its board. In cooperation with the American Immigration Council, an NGO based in Washington, DC, they organized the Pro Bono Project, with a unique vision and structure. They realized that few if any volunteers could afford to remain at Artesia for more than a few days, and therefore they could not see cases through from start to end. So they called for volunteers to come for three, five, or seven days, and Manning, who was technologically adept, created an online, password-protected case management system through which a volunteer could record what he or she did for each client. A volunteer who arrived a few days later could pick up where the original lawyer had left off. In addition, volunteers who had to return home and volunteers who could not go to Artesia at all could work remotely on cases through the system. Manning's cloud-based system also included documentary resources that the lawyers could file in their clients' cases, such as affidavits from political scientists who had studied the gang violence in each country in the Northern Triangle.

Lawyers were screened and provided with readings by AILA before they arrived, and upon arrival at Artesia they took a crash course on asylum law and the database technology.[106] Day after day, the volunteers worked in their trailer from 7:00 A.M. to 7:00 P.M. Near closing time, they would email ICE a list of the women they wanted brought to them the next day. Then they convened at the Artesia Chamber of Commerce for a meeting that would last until the wee hours, at which they reviewed the day's credible fear interviews and prepared strategy for the following day.[107] The project lasted for twenty-one weeks, during which 235 volunteers traveled to Artesia for this grueling work. Within two months, so many of the women were found to have credible fear that the rate of deportations had fallen by 97 percent.[108] In mid-November 2014, the mayor of Artesia reported that in the previous six weeks, only twenty-eight people held in the facility had been deported.[109]

"On-the-ground, the strategy was to win cases to prove the lie behind the Vice President's judgment [that few of the Central American migrants qualified for asylum]," Manning wrote. "If we could disprove it, then we could create the space to prove why family detention was utterly misguided and wrong."[110] Avoiding rapid deportations by establishing "credible fear" got the volunteers only part way to that goal. They also had to help the women win asylum from immigration judges, a much slower and more deliberate process that would have to be handled primarily by the remote lawyers, working out of their own offices. But while the project operated, fifteen of the women's cases were heard by judges, and the project's lawyers won fourteen of them.[111]

ICE released those fourteen women with their children, but for the rest of the families, the findings of credible fear meant only that they avoided immediate deportation, which carried a significant risk of death.[112] Most had to remain in detention until their claims for asylum or other relief could be heard by immigration judges. Some were eligible to be released on bond, but DHS opposed this, claiming that release posed a national security risk. DHS told immigration judges that unless the families remained in detention, more families would try to migrate to the United States, threatening the security of the country.[113] As a result, the judges set unaffordable bonds, some as high as $20,000 to $30,000, and the women and children remained in detention, month after month.[114]

The government closed Artesia in mid-December 2014, but not because the volunteers had persuaded it that incarcerating Central American families who were fleeing violence was pointless. Instead, the Obama administration had decided to detain such families on a much grander scale.

9 Karnes and Dilley

2014–2016

The Artesia family detention center had 650 beds.[1] Even before it closed in December 2014, the Department of Homeland Security (DHS) opened a larger family jail, the Karnes County Residential Center in Karnes City, about an hour's drive from San Antonio and two hours from Austin. Karnes was an adult male prison that an Immigration and Customs Enforcement (ICE) contractor spruced up slightly for families by August 1, when the first children arrived. Despite the renaming, it continued "to operate [like a prison,] on a rigid schedule with set times for meals and lights on and out, frequent head counts and room checks throughout the day and night," and the guards were "ill-equipped to interact appropriately with mothers and children, many of whom are trauma victims seeking asylum."[2] The other jail, the South Texas Family Residential Center, was located in the small, remote town of Dilley, about two hours south of San Antonio. Built largely of locked, interconnected trailers, it opened at the end of 2014. Together these two facilities, which became known both inside and outside of government circles simply as Karnes and Dilley, would be able to house 3600 mothers and their children, including many Artesia detainees who were moved there as Artesia closed.[3] Karnes was operated by the GEO Group, one of the largest private prison companies in the United States. Dilley was run by the Corrections Corporation of America (CCA, renamed CoreCivic in 2016), the nation's largest for-profit prison company, which had owned and operated Hutto when it had housed migrant families.[4] The detention of families with children was just a small part of the business of the two companies, which by 2017 operated 170 prisons and immigrant detention centers.[5]

DENISE GILMAN

Barbara Hines, who had discovered the inappropriate conditions at Hutto, was in the process of retiring just as Karnes opened, but she was passing the mantle of immigration clinic director at the University of Texas in Austin to her successor, Denise Gilman. Like Hines, Gilman had spent her childhood in Texas and had often traveled with her family to Mexico. Although none of her ancestors were Latin American, "part of my family culture is bi-national" as a result of that cross-border travel, she said.[6]

Sometime in the mid-1980s, as a summer was beginning, Barbara Hines had been overloaded with work. "My friend Sharon sent me a post-card," Hines recalled. "It said, 'I'm on my way to Spain, but the daughter of someone I teach with needs a summer job.' Denise arrived to talk to me just as I had to run out of the office because my son had a bloody nose and a broken tooth. I asked, 'Do you speak Spanish?' She said she did. I hired her on the spot. Then she worked for me every summer while she was in college at Northwestern University."[7]

After finishing Columbia Law School, Gilman returned to Texas to clerk for Judge Thomas Reavley on the U.S. Court of Appeals for the Fifth Circuit.[8] Then she worked for the Inter-American Commission for Human Rights (IACHR), a body of the Organization of American States in which the United States participates, and for the Lawyers Committee for Human Rights (later renamed Human Rights First). After six years in those organizations, in which she had focused on human rights in Latin America, she wanted to change directions and concentrate on U.S. law and to litigate in U.S. courts. "Immigration was the logical place to go with my human rights background," she recalled. "And I'd had that summer job in college working for Barbara Hines, so I had that connection to immigration law."[9]

Denise Gilman.

After two years in an immigration law teaching fellowship at Georgetown University, she returned to Texas in 2007, this time to work with Hines once again. The two worked together in the University of Texas's immigration law clinic from 2007 until Gilman became the clinic's director when Hines retired in 2014. Gilman began getting calls from relatives of people incarcerated at Karnes almost as soon as it opened, and within a week, she and Hines went together to see the facility. When Hines walked in she experienced a flashback to Hutto. "I can't believe this," she recalls feeling. "I'm going to suffer from PTSD."[10]

KARNES

In the summer of 2014, Hines and Gilman and the clinic students began visiting families at Karnes. They asked for help from the American Immigration Lawyers Association but were unable to obtain it. "The AILA people did not want to come to Karnes," Hines recalled. "[They said] 'We're focused on Artesia and we don't have the resources.'" Finally the law firm of Akin Gump sent a young lawyer, Lauren Connell, to help for two or three months, and Hines and Gilman recruited others from within Texas.[11] Their recruits included lawyers from a small non-profit organiza- tion known as the Refugee and Immigrant Center for Education and Legal Services, which was known by its acronym RAICES, a word that means "roots" in Spanish.[12] RAICES eventually took over representation of the families at Karnes. It invented a name for a program that would include both its own staff and the small group of local lawyers with whom the RAICES staff lawyers were working: the Karnes Pro Bono Project.

Hines and Gilman went repeatedly to Karnes for several purposes. They prepared the women for credible fear interviews, and when a woman was adjudicated to have credible fear, they represented those who were eligible to be released on bond,[13] asking for reasonable bond amounts to be set. They also began documenting conditions at Karnes (as Hines had done at Hutto) for possible litigation or press attention. Within two months, Gilman's clinic submitted to the IACHR the first of several reports documenting what she and other advocates called "grave rights violations" at Karnes.[14] This report asserted that what was happening at Karnes violated United Nations human rights standards in several ways:

- It objected to the whole idea of detaining the families, noting that the IACHR had said that for immigrants, pre-trial detention is an exceptional measure and that the guidelines issued by the United Nations High Commissioner for Refugees (UNHCR) included a strong presumption against detaining asylum-seekers, who constituted nearly the entire population of Karnes.

- It complained about the arbitrary denial of release on bond to the families at Karnes. Specifically, ICE had the statutory authority to release a family on bond of at least $1500, but ICE claimed that every woman and child at Karnes had to be detained on the ground that each one of them posed a danger to national security. The women had a right, which was difficult to invoke without a lawyer, to have their bond decisions "redetermined" by an immigration judge, but ICE made that same argument to oppose release on bond, or to set a very high bond, in virtually every redetermination case. ICE's claim was based on a 2003 decision by Attorney General John Ashcroft, known as the "D- J-opinion," in which he had ruled that "national security" justified refusing bond to Haitians trying to come to the United States because granting them bond would "encourage further surges."[15] ICE claimed the same need for deterrence of future migrants who were fleeing violence in Central America. As a result, many families had to remain locked up on Karnes for months.

- It noted that ICE had imposed numerous barriers to counsel for the families. There were no group "know your rights" presentations to the women when the facility opened. The location of the facility, two hours from Austin, made it difficult for lawyers to go there. The women were mostly poor and could not afford private lawyers, and the community had very few lawyers willing to take on pro bono immigration cases. When a pro bono lawyer was available, ICE imposed "strict access rules," such as limiting the number of clients they could see on each visit and making them wait for up to two hours before being allowed to see a client.

- Like Hutto, the facility looked and felt like a prison. Residents were locked in. The walls were cinderblock, and the interior doors were heavy and loud when slammed closed. The staff was male-dominated and not trained in the care of women and children, especially those fleeing from traumatic experiences. Only very limited medical and mental health services were available. Children were "written up" for running, laughing loudly, or playing too much, and guards threatened to separate them from their mothers. As at Hutto, there were frequent body counts. Children were not allowed toys in their rooms. Infants were not allowed to crawl on the floor.

- The Flores settlement provided that children could be detained only in a facility that was licensed as a residential facility for children. Karnes was not licensed. Flores also imposed standards for recreation and education and counseling, which the facility was not honoring.

In the months that followed, many other studies and reports echoed what the law clinic had observed. The American Academy of Pediatrics reported that "visits to family detention centers in 2015 and 2016 by pediatric and mental health advocates revealed discrepancies between the standards outlined by ICE and the actual services provided, including inadequate or inappropriate immunizations, delayed medical care, inadequate education services, and limited mental health services."[16] Lawyers from Human Rights First who visited Karnes noted that "children do not want to eat, they are clingier and more aggressive, cry frequently, and are

fearful. Women spoke tearfully of their own anxiety, feelings of despera-
tion, and confusion over the legal process, and confirmed the doctors' concerns that being held in detention was re-traumatizing."[17] Dr. Satsuki
Ina, a psychotherapist who had been born behind barbed wire in a
Japanese-American internment camp, visited Karnes and reported that

> I certainly never expected to see other families incarcerated just as my own
> family had been 73 years ago. . . . [When I was a child], we too lived in a
> constant state of fear and anxiety, never knowing what our fate would be.
> We too were forced to share our living space with strangers, line up for
> meals, share public latrines, respond to roll call and adjust to ever-changing
> rules and regulations with the eyes of the guards constantly trained on us.[18]

The American Bar Association's Commission on Immigration stated that
"the conditions are not adequate for the care of young children and their
mothers, some of whom are nursing, and there have been incidents of
sexual abuse within the facilities."[19] The reference to sexual abuse was
explained by the Inter-American Commission in a 2015 report, which
criticized several conditions of confinement at Karnes and noted that the
allegations about the guards, which GEO disputed,[20] "include removing
women detainees from their cells late in the evening or early in the morning to engage in sexual acts; calling women their 'girlfriends,' and using
their respective power over these women to request sexual favors in
exchange for money and/or promises of assistance with their immigration
cases or upon release; and kissing and groping women in front of other
detainees, including children."[21] Human Rights Watch criticized ICE for
holding women and children for ten months or longer by requiring bond
payments of up to $7500, amounts that the women could not produce.[22]
The American Immigration Council sent DHS's Office of Civil Rights and
Civil Liberties complaints regarding ten children who had escaped from
terror in the Northern Triangle, only to be re-traumatized in family detention.[23] The Lutheran Immigration and Refugee Service, teaming up with
the Women's Refugee Commission, released a report noting that

> like at Hutto, mothers reported several incidents of inadequate access to
> medical and mental health care, ranging from an inability to access any
> services to lack of adequate treatment. Reports include responding to
> diarrhea and other stomach issues with only an instruction to drink more

water, lack of treatment for fevers and similar conditions, and more. Mental health care is limited at both facilities despite the high prevalence of a history of trauma and sexual violence in detainees' home countries. Moreover, both Karnes and Artesia primarily rely upon male mental health care providers, which may leave women who have been sexually assaulted by men unwilling or unable to share their stories.[24]

The most important critique of detention at Karnes came from Luis H. Zayas, the dean of the School of Social Work at the University of Texas, in what became known as the Zayas declaration. Shortly after Karnes opened, he met with ten families there to assess their mental health status. The twenty-three children of these families ranged in age from two to seventeen. Most had been in Karnes for two to three weeks. Several of the mothers and teenaged daughters had been sexually abused by gangs in the Northern Triangle. Some of the younger children had seen "cadavers on the street." After some days in "intensely cold" CBP detention, where women, girls, and younger children were kept together in a room with "a toilet used by everyone that was exposed to the view of everyone in the cell," they were moved to Karnes. There, they were ordered around by employees who were "mean," "rude," and "bullies." If an adolescent was found in her mother's room, she was threatened with penalties. The younger children, Zayas found, had "high levels of anxiety," particularly "fear of losing their mother," while the mothers and adolescents "showed mostly signs of depression with such vegetative signs as lack of sleep, loss of appetite and weight loss, and hopelessness." The children exhibited "regression or arrests in their development and major psychiatric disorders." For example, an infant who had been weaned had reverted to breastfeeding. Several children had nightmares. Three teenagers had "major depressive disorders." Zayas concluded that the traumas these mothers and children had experienced "will require years of mental health services." He cited literature that children living even briefly in detention experienced "stresses [that] affect neural or brain development." These children often later became alcoholic or showed suicidal tendencies or provocative behavior toward the police, resulting in "suicide by cop." He concluded that "untold harm is being inflicted on these children by the trauma of detention" and that "some of these effects will be long lasting, and very likely permanent."[25]

In March 2015, some of the mothers imprisoned in Karnes began a hunger strike to protest the length and conditions of their detention. ICE was able to break the strike, however, by putting some of the families in solitary confinement and by threatening mothers that reduced brain functioning caused by the lack of nutrition would affect their ability to care for their children, causing them to lose custody.[26] Within a month, the strike had ended.[27]

DILLEY

In at least two respects, Dilley, which opened a few months later, was even worse than Karnes. Hines and Gilman were able, over time, to organize the legal communities in Austin and San Antonio to provide a good deal of representation to the Karnes residents. Instead of passing along cases, week after week, to different lawyers, as at Artesia, the local attorneys, including some from nonprofit organizations who worked without charging fees and others who were paid by detainees' families, were able to take on clients for the duration of their confinement. Dilley, on the other hand, was so remote that it was impossible for immigration lawyers to represent clients on a long-term basis. Even a single trip from a metropolitan center would take a lawyer an entire day.

In addition, privacy at Dilley was worse than at Karnes. According to Gilman, who had been allowed to tour both facilities, each cell at Karnes has four bunk beds and a private bathroom with a door. The housing at Dilley consisted of trailers, each of which had beds for more than one family, as well as a couch, a television, and a phone, but no bathroom or other private area. Children from one family were therefore housed in the same quarters as adults from other families, just as Jenny Flores had been housed with unrelated adults in the Mardi Gras Hotel. (This intermingling of adults and unrelated children would not be allowed in a licensed child care facility). To change clothing in the living area, adults or children had to pull a curtain around themselves; to use a bathroom they had to go outside of the living area and down a hallway.[28]

The families were reportedly awakened by middle-of-the-night bed checks, and the wait for medical care could "exceed five hours," after which the staff nurses "prescribe[d] a mixture of honey and water for a wide variety of ailments."[29] When children misbehaved, they were sent with their mothers to solitary confinement for several hours in a "cold room."[30]

Those confined at Dilley were also concerned about the water. Fracking in other areas of Texas produced "millions of gallons of contaminated wastewater" that was trucked to the town of Dilley and dumped into abandoned wells that were "repurposed as 'disposals' for the toxic mix."[31] The officers and medical staff reportedly drank bottled water,[32] and volunteer lawyers were also cautioned to drink only bottled water, but the mothers and children had to drink tap water.[33]

THE HOLDING FACILITIES AT THE BORDER

Despite the terrible conditions at Karnes and Dilley, most mothers were initially relieved to arrive there after several days in the CBP's processing stations at the border. Just before Karnes opened, the National Immigrant Justice Center, the American Civil Liberties Union (ACLU), and other organizations filed with DHS a lengthy complaint about abuses of unaccompanied children, including beatings, death threats, and sexual assaults, in border facilities,[34] and while the CBP Commissioner himself acknowledged that conditions in those stations were unsatisfactory, the Department took no action. Thereafter, the ACLU filed a request seeking DHS records of complaints of child abuse by CBP agents. The Department stonewalled, but an ACLU lawsuit under the Freedom of Information Act (FOIA) eventually forced the disclosure of 30,000 pages of relevant records, which, according to the ACLU, showed "a pattern of intimidation, harassment, physical abuse, refusal of medical services, and improper deportation" over a five-year period, from 2009 to 2014.[35] Because the surge in arrivals of *accompanied* children began only toward the end of that period, the report did not explicitly discuss treatment of the family groups. However, other reports by mothers, before and after these dates, confirmed that while in CBP custody with their children, they experienced many of the same issues.[36]

The complaints uncovered through the FOIA request included dragging apprehended children on the ground, thereby bruising and cutting them; kicking and punching them; tightening handcuffs excessively, cutting off circulation; and using tasers on children. Once the children were taken into detention at the border, they were put into holding cells. One such cell was described by a DHS inspector as a filthy room with "no trash receptacles [and] body fluids on the walls and floors, along with used sanitary napkins and used toilet paper containing feces on the floor."[37] Some children reported being denied solid food for days. A teenaged mother described being denied milk for her baby for two days and then being given milk that smelled bad and made her daughter sick.

The descriptions by mothers of treatment in CBP facilities in the years after the ACLU published its report revealed that little had changed. The mothers described shivering during their entire stay of one to eight days in the "ice box," being given frozen sandwiches and spoiled burritos to eat and foul-smelling water to drink, being denied the use of toothbrushes or showers, being kicked by female officers, being deprived of needed antibiotics, having to use dirty toilets that flooded periodically and lacked toilet paper, and trying to sleep on concrete floors while shivering under aluminum foil blankets.[38] CBP does not generally allow photographs to be taken in its facilities, but in 2016, a few such photographs were ordered released by a federal judge and they have been posted on several websites.[39] CBP released a few others in 2018 to show the conditions in its holding cells during the *previous* (Obama) administration, as well as a few pictures of then-current conditions.[40]

R. I. L- R- V. JOHNSON

By December, 2014, the government was opposing the release of almost all of the Karnes detainees, relying in case after case on Attorney General Ashcroft's 2003 D- J- opinion, mentioned above. Over time, it became increasingly time-consuming and difficult to obtain release of families held in Karnes. Arguments in each individual bond hearing took hours, often with negative results. Repeatedly, ICE lawyers justified keeping families in detention at least in part through the need to discourage other families, still in Central America, from trying to come to the United States. The government was clearly going to use the same argument to prevent release of the families that it would soon detain at Dilley. At Karnes, much of the burden of arguing for bond fell on Gilman. She believed that it was unfair to keep families confined at Karnes in order to send a message to families who were still in the Northern Triangle.

By January, 2015, she'd had enough of making that argument again and again. "The families were so distraught, facing indefinite detention," she recalls. "There were not enough snacks for the kids, there were no toys, there were huge deficiencies in the medical staff, they were doing regular intrusive body counts where they had to line up and they would come in the middle of the night and shine flashlights . . . and the families [were] feeling like they were never going to get out."[41] The time had come for a frontal assault on the government's policy. She persuaded the ACLU to bring a class action to challenge the use of deterrence of others (a concept known to lawyers as "general deterrence") as a rationale for detention. General deterrence had long been regarded as a legitimate policy to deter crime. For example, long sentences for armed robbery could be justified by the need to discourage robbers. But general deterrence by incarceration had never been applied outside of the criminal law.

Eight Karnes residents who had passed the credible fear test therefore became plaintiffs in the class action of *R. I. L- R-* (the initials of the first plaintiff) *v. Jeh Johnson*, the Secretary of Homeland Security, seeking an injunction to prevent ICE from relying on general deterrence to keep them locked up. The ACLU could have sued in Texas, where Karnes was located, but it had the option of suing in the District of Columbia, DHS's headquarters, and it chose the latter option rather than having the case ultimately decided by the appeals court in the much more conservative Fifth Circuit, which included Texas. The government tried several tactics to avoid a decision. It released the eight named plaintiffs and then claimed that the case was moot, just as it had done in the Hutto case. It claimed that the plaintiffs could only sue by seeking individual writs of habeas corpus, not by a class action for an injunction. It claimed that it did not really have a policy of invoking general deterrence because no such policy had been reduced to writing. It claimed that the suit was fruitless because the government would keep the families locked up for other reasons, even if it couldn't rely on general deterrence. It opposed allowing the suit to become a class action, claiming that various reasons against release

applied with different weights to each family, so the cases were not sufficiently alike.

The case was assigned to Judge James Boasberg, who quickly batted
away of all of these technical arguments. The government therefore had to
justify its claim of national security, and it couldn't just rely on a vague
catchphrase. As the judge put it, "incantation of the magic words 'national
security' without further substantiation is simply not enough to justify significant deprivations of liberty." So the government's lawyers cited a study
by Jonathan Hiskey, a Vanderbilt University scholar, who had written a
report on why people migrated from Central America.[42] The lawyers
claimed that this paper showed that "detention is especially crucial in
instances of mass migration." But in fact the paper never mentioned
detention, and the ACLU supplied a statement from its author who
reported that the government's lawyers had missed the point of the paper.
"DHS ignore[s] the report's central finding," he told the court, "namely,
the critical role that crime victimization in Central America plays in causing citizens of these countries to consider emigration as a viable, albeit
extremely dangerous, life choice."

Judge Boasberg therefore found that the need for general deterrence
was unproved and, in any event, legally unprecedented outside of criminal
law.[43] Six weeks after the case was filed, he granted a preliminary injunction against its invocation.[44] The government moved for reconsideration
of that decision, arguing that the government had a strong security interest in using family detention to deter illegal mass migration.[45] Perhaps
anticipating that the judge would not change his mind, the government
notified the court that it was changing its policy, and that it would "discon-
tinue, at this time, invoking deterrence as a factor in custody determinations in all cases involving families" although it "maintains its position . . .
that application of that policy was lawful at the time and would be lawful
in the future if reinstated."[46] Having secured the policy change they
sought, Gilman and the ACLU agreed to terminate the case and to dissolve the preliminary injunction, and the government agreed that the lawyers for the plaintiffs could move to reinstate the injunction if the government subsequently began once again to invoke deterrence as the basis for
family detention.[47]

THE FLORES CASE, RESURRECTED

The R.I. L- R- case and the Johnson statement solved one problem for the families in detention; the government could not rely on general deterrence to keep them incarcerated. But it did not improve the conditions of confinement in the CBP facilities or in Karnes or Dilley, and it did not prevent the government from setting high bonds or denying parole to the families, so long as it did not try to justify its actions by reference to deterring the migration of others. ICE continued to prevent release by setting high bonds and claiming that the mothers were flight risks. "For a while it was either $7,500 or $10,000," Gilman recalls. "That's not really individualized. They were still trying to deter."[48]

Gilman realized that still more litigation would be required to get the families out of detention. She considered filing a new lawsuit in Texas, as Hines had done in the Hutto case, because that is where the families were incarcerated. But the case could well have been assigned to Judge Sam Sparks, as he was already familiar with family detention issues, and she knew that Judge Sparks cared about detention conditions but was reluctant to order anyone released. In addition, a case in Texas could have been appealed to the conservative Fifth Circuit court on which she had clerked. After conferring with allies, she decided that the best bet would be to revive the dormant-but-never-dismissed Flores case in Los Angeles. Litigating there would mean that Peter Schey and Carlos Holguín, rather than the teams that had brought the Hutto and R.I. L- R- cases, would determine the strategy and conduct any new settlement negotiations with the government, but giving up control of the case seemed justified by keeping it out of the Fifth Circuit. In addition, Gilman could keep a hand in the case, because she would be the Texas anchor, collecting sworn declarations from the jailed mothers and from expert witnesses such as Dean Zayas.[49]

And so, on February 2, 2015, Schey filed a motion to enforce the Flores settlement in the very court in which, thirty years earlier, he had brought suit on behalf of Jenny Flores. The motion was accompanied by fifty-three exhibits. Some were statements by experts about the harm to children from detention, but most were sworn declarations, handwritten in Spanish with English translations, that Holguín, Hines, and Gilman, along with lawyers in Pennsylvania, had collected from women detained in Artesia, Karnes, Dilley, and Berks. The declarations explained the threats or violence from which the women fled and described the conditions of their treatment in border patrol facilities and in long-term detention and their inability to obtain release through reasonable bond conditions.

The new motion was based on the claim that the government was violating three parts of the 1997 settlement. First, by setting high bonds and, in effect, not releasing most families, the government was failing to honor its commitment to minimize the detention of children. Second, the government was detaining the children in locked, unlicensed jails rather than honoring its commitment to house juveniles, except those who posed dangers to the community or were flight risks, only in non-secure, licensed child care facilities. Finally, the conditions in the border patrol processing stations exposed children to "cold, overcrowding, inadequate food and drink, sleep deprivation, and poor sanitation."[50]

Judge Robert Kelleher had died in 2012 at the age of ninety-nine, the oldest federal judge in the nation.[51] The clerk of the court reassigned the case to Judge Dolly Gee. Based on her biography, Schey could hardly have hoped for a judge more likely to be sympathetic to his arguments.

Judge Gee's great-great-grandfather had been a Chinese immigrant who worked on the transcontinental railroad in the late 1800s. As a result of the Chinese Exclusion Act of 1882, however, he was barred from reentering the United States after a trip to China. Gee's grandfather immigrated in the 1930s. He owned a factory in Brooklyn that made soy sauce and pickled cabbage. Her father joined the Navy during World War II, became an aerospace engineer, and worked on the space shuttle. Gee's mother had also immigrated from China. She had been a teacher, but because her English was poor, she had to settle for being a seamstress in the United States. She refused to teach her daughter to sew, because she wanted her to have an education and a better life.[52] By observing her mother's working conditions Gee "decided at an early age that I wanted to do some type of work that would help address some of the inequities I saw as a child."[53]

Gee graduated from UCLA in 1981 and continued there for law school. After clerking for a federal district judge, she joined a private Los Angeles law firm, where she represented labor unions. She chose that work because

Judge Dolly Gee.

she was "inspired by an urge to reform the exploitative conditions" under which her mother had labored.[54] She also worked to oppose government efforts to end affirmative action. She rose to become the firm's managing partner.[55] President Bill Clinton nominated her to the bench in 1999, but the Senate failed to act on her nomination. Ten years later, President Barack Obama renominated her, and she was finally confirmed on New Year's Eve in 2009.[56]

The government made a two-pronged attack on Schey's motion to enforce the Flores agreement. First, it argued that the motion should be denied because, it claimed, while the Flores settlement barred the long-term detention of unaccompanied children, it didn't apply at all to children who arrived in the presence of a related adult such as a parent or aunt. The government had to acknowledge that the settlement's wording provided, in a definitional section, that the term "minor" as used in the agreement "shall apply to any person under the age of eighteen years who is detained" and that, according to the agreement, whenever a minor was not released to a parent or other adult relative, the minor had to be placed in a program that was licensed by a state agency to provide residential services for dependent children. But it argued that in 1997, neither party could foresee the influx of families nor the "need" for family detention centers, so "the parties simply did not contemplate at the time that the Agreement would apply to . . . the housing of families."

The agreement's definition of a minor was only meant to clarify "who would be treated as a child and who would be treated as an adult," not to imply that all minors would have to be released to related adults or licensed facilities. In addition, the licensing provisions of the agreement should not apply to family detention, because in 1997, nobody could have contemplated the existence of such facilities. Also, if the provisions of the agreement did apply to family facilities, ICE would be in "substantial compliance" with the agreement, despite the lack of licensing, because "ICE family residential centers are operated in strict compliance with ICE family residential standards." As for conditions in the CBP holding facilities, children remained in them for "an extremely short period of time," and CBP's hold rooms "are designed to have sufficient space and the appropriate number of toilets. . . . There are no trash cans in the rooms for safety reasons . . . medical care is available . . . the rooms are well-lit at all times . . . [and] CBP also provides Mylar blankets which provide the most hygienic solution for temperature control. . . . The need to ensure sanitary conditions leads to water that may taste different than that to which individuals from another country are accustomed, and blankets that seem sterile."[57]

The government evidently thought it might not persuade Judge Gee that the word "minor" didn't encompass all minors. So at the same time that it filed its opposition to the motion, it filed a request to the judge to modify the Flores agreement on the ground that it was "no longer equitable."[58] The agreement, it claimed was no longer equitable because family migration had markedly increased in recent years, and also because the 1997 Flores agreement was inconsistent with the 2008 Trafficking Victims Protection Reauthorization Act (TVPRA). As examples, the government noted that Flores required transfer of a child to a licensed facility within five days, whereas the TVPRA required transfer within three days. Flores permitted transfer of certain unaccompanied children (those who posed dangers) to secure Immigration and Naturalization Service facilities, but the TVPRA required all unaccompanied children to be transferred to Office of Refugee Resettlement custody.[59] Unfortunately for the government, the TVPRA imposed *more* limits on what the government could do than the Flores agreement did, so it was possible for DHS to comply with Flores without violating the TVPRA.

The plaintiffs' lawyers replied by emphasizing an argument that would have been very familiar to Justice Antonin Scalia, who often focused in his decisions on the actual text of legal documents. The Agreement defined minors as all persons under the age of eighteen, and several sections of it, which applied only to UACs, specifically referenced the subset of unaccompanied minors.[60] As for the claim that conditions in the CBP facilities were humane, they called the judge's attention to the many testimonials by families that had been through those processing stations and said that the evidence in those declarations "is simply too voluminous and disturbing to brush aside on the weight of defendants' general protestation to the contrary."[61]

On April 24, 2015, Judge Gee held a hearing on the motion to enforce the settlement. Holguín argued for the mothers in detention; the government was represented by Leon Fresco. Fresco had for many years been an advocate for immigrants, often on a pro bono basis, at the law firm of Holland & Knight, and when Chuck Schumer (D–NY) became chair of the Senate Immigration Subcommittee, Fresco had become his staff director.[62] But after the failure of Schumer's effort to enact comprehensive immigration reform (which passed the Senate in 2013 but was dead on arrival in the Republican-controlled House of Representatives), Fresco had joined the administration as the Deputy Assistant Attorney General in charge of immigration litigation. He had some qualms about handling

Leon Fresco.

litigation against immigrants, including asylum-seekers, but he reasoned that "you need people who would do the job in the way that was the most palatable. It doesn't make sense to give these jobs to the most enforcement-oriented people."[63] When Schey filed his motion, Fresco decided that he himself would lead the government's defense of family detention. "There is a perception that the government has endless resources," he explained. "This was an incredibly important case. I [would] either [have] to reassign a lot of people, or I had to take it on".[64]

Fresco thereby put himself in the position of having to make a legal argument to justify a policy with which he personally disagreed. "As a policy matter, in my ideal world every [parent who passed a credible fear interview] would have electronic monitoring and you wouldn't need detention," he said. But

> nobody asked me what I thought about ankle monitors. I was told, 'Shut up. You're the lawyer. It's not your job to get involved with policy.' Given the way the administration wanted to go, there were only three options: release without monitoring, family separation, or family detention. So under those choices, I was fine with arguing for detention, because release was politically untenable [and] I had no problem defending [the administration's position] because I thought the [Flores] settlement only pertained to [unaccompanied] minors.[65]

Before the hearing even started, Judge Gee sent the parties a copy of a twenty-two-page tentative order that she had written, siding entirely with the mothers. The tentative ruling announced squarely that "The agreement encompasses accompanied minors," adding that the language defining "minor" in the agreement was unambiguous. The tentative order said, as well, that the government had materially breached the agreement. Although the agreement said nothing about releasing parents, the tentative ruling noted, the government had been releasing family members together for years, ever since President Obama had closed Hutto. "The parties intended," her tentative opinion added, "to allow for the release of the accompanying parent, so long as the release does not create a flight risk or safety risk." Therefore "defendants must release an accompanying parent as long as doing so would not create a flight risk or a safety risk." In addition, "the fact that the family residential centers cannot be licensed by an appropriate state agency simply means that, under the Agreement, class members cannot be housed in these facilities, except [for a few days] as permitted by the Agreement." Citing the Zayas declaration, the tentative decision stated that "secure confinement [such as at Karnes and Dilley] can inflict long-lasting psychological, developmental, and physical harm on children regardless of other conditions." Finally, crediting the statements of the mothers about the conditions of the CBP facilities, the tentative decision concluded that the government had "wholly failed" to provide "safe and sanitary" holding facilities as the Flores agreement required. And according to the tentative ruling, Judge Gee saw "no change in circumstances warranting modification" of the Flores settlement.[66]

THE HEARING

Fresco was handed the tentative order as he entered the courtroom and barely had time to scan it. When he did, he realized that Judge Gee was already disposed to support the plaintiffs. He knew that he would have an uphill battle to change the judge's mind.

Within minutes after the hearing started, Judge Gee asked Fresco the central question in the case: if the Flores settlement wasn't intended to cover accompanied minors, "why in your stipulated settlement agreement did you not limit it to 'unaccompanied minors'?"

"Because in 1997 . . . we were not engaging in family detentions," Fresco replied. "Nobody knew about that concept." Besides, he argued, family detention was necessary because without it, smugglers could bring children "across the border in an attempt to avoid detention by representing themselves as a family unit."

In that case, asked the judge, "why in the world didn't you seek to modify the agreement or promulgate regulations that would deal with the situation?"

Fresco replied that the government didn't need to, because it had opened the small Berks family facility in 2001 and "we got no lawsuits from the plaintiff. . . . So we have operated family residential facilities. Their legality has not been questioned even in the [Hutto] case."

But the issue, the judge pointed out, was that even if family detention was permitted for a short time under the agreement, the question was which minors were being detained and "for how long." The agreement had put a five-day limit on the detention of children in secure, unlicensed facilities except for children who posed dangers to the community or were flight risks. Then the judge revealed her conclusion: "This is a contract," she said. "What you're asking me to do is to unilaterally modify the agreement, and that I cannot do."

Seeing that he was going to lose, Fresco tried to salvage the case. He asked the judge to "at least not issue the order, and let us try to figure out some way that could work, you know, to satisfy some of the concerns of the plaintiffs."

Holguín hadn't spoken up to this point, but the judge asked him about the fact that although Berks had been in operation for thirteen years, he hadn't sued to prevent the detention of families there. He replied with a series of distinctions between Berks and the Texas jails. Berks was very small. Unlike Karnes and Dilley, it was not a secure facility. Berks did have a state license. The average period of family detention at Berks was only a week or two (compared to a longer average in Texas, up to ten months for some families). In addition, there had been a suit over Hutto.

Fresco said that one of the affidavits filed by the plantiffs stated that Berks actually was a secure facility, and he was willing to accept that as a fact for purposes of the case he was arguing. Nobody had complained about the noncompliance of that "secure" facility with Flores for thirteen years, he noted. But Judge Gee suggested that by contrast, the Texas facilities involved "wholesale" violations.

As the hearing drew to a close, Judge Gee gave the lawyers thirty days to meet and discuss her tentative ruling. She permitted them to keep copies, but asked that "you not share it with anyone or publicize it in any way."[67] Nevertheless, her tentative order leaked almost instantly. Within four days, Bryan Johnson, a New York lawyer who, as a consultant to Schey, knew that the tentative ruling was supposed to be secret, provided it to Franco Ordonez, a McClatchy reporter, who published it immediately, after which it was described in other media.[68] Two days later, Schey and Holguín circulated a detailed summary of what Gee intended to order to immigration advocates, so that he could obtain "input" from them on "our next steps."[69]

To reinforce the secrecy of the settlement negotiations that were continuing, Judge Gee reminded the lawyers in writing not to inform the press of her tentative ruling (although it had already leaked), and then she formally entered a gag order regarding the discussions among the lawyers about how to settle the case.[70] Johnson signed the gag order but then leaked a second document—a settlement proposal that Schey made to Fresco—and Gee ordered him to show cause why he should not be held in contempt of court and reported to his state bar for disciplinary proceedings. Schey promptly fired Johnson as a consultant. Johnson later accepted responsibility for the leak, explaining that he had disagreed with the proposal and felt "ethically obligated" to defend his clients, and Gee required him only to do seventy-five hours of community service.[71]

Schey and Fresco tried to negotiate a final order that they would jointly offer to Gee. After several weeks of discussions both with the immigration advocacy community and with Fresco, Schey offered a proposal that he said was a "fair compromise." He suggested that the apprehended children "and their accompanying parents" could be held for processing for twenty-four hours "after which they will be released on their own recognizance or on parole without being required to post a parole bond," unless they presented a "substantial flight risk." In that event, they could be required to report periodically to ICE, and in "exceptional and unusual cases" in which that would not be sufficient, they could be fitted with electronic GPS location monitors. If ICE believed that a parent was a danger to herself, her child or others, ICE could hold the family for seven days but would have to release the family after that "if the danger is not substantiated" and explained in writing, subject to judicial review. Schey's proposal also would have required CBP to upgrade conditions at its processing stations, for example, by keeping the temperature between seventy and seventy-four degrees, providing toys, books and recreational equipment to the children, providing families with free or low-cost telephones, giving families potable drinking water, darkening the sleeping areas at night, and providing mattresses.[72]

Schey suggested that the government should accept his proposal because "a court ruling would be highly publicized and send a public message that DHS has not treated Flores class members (immigrant children) lawfully, and in fact has detained them illegally under pretty deplorable conditions." He also argued that if DHS appealed a ruling by Judge Gee "the likelihood of success ... is low."[73]

Fresco countered that the government should at least be able to detain, until full hearings, families that had not been found to have credible fear— about 15 percent of the families who had been interviewed by asylum officers at that time. Some of these families couldn't be deported promptly, despite the officers' findings, because they were pursuing other legal claims or because the government was having trouble obtaining travel documents for them from their home countries.[74] Schey did not accept this proposal, perhaps because he believed that no child should be kept in detention for more than a few days, or perhaps because some of the advocacy groups supporting Schey's position took that view, and Schey could not accept a proposal that did not command the support of all of his allies.

Meanwhile, advocacy organizations kept up the pressure. They circulated a *New York Times* editorial calling for an end to mass immigration detention, "particularly of families."[75] They urged members of Congress to visit Karnes and Dilley. A group of eight House members did so. While they were at Dilley, the mothers and children launched a protest against confinement, chanting their desire for "libertad."[76] Despite ICE rules against photography in the detention center, a staffer for one of the members of Congress used a cell phone to film the demonstration, then posted the video on YouTube.[77] Shortly thereafter, 136 Democratic members of the House of Representatives, including minority leader Nancy Pelosi, signed a letter to Secretary Johnson complaining that DHS "has not fully grasped the serious harm" being inflicted on the families and calling on him to "end the use of family detention."[78]

As the negotiations between Schey and Fresco seemed less and less likely to meet with success, and pressure on the government grew (from the press and politicians as well as from the likelihood that Judge Gee would eventually issue her order), the government made a final attempt to prevent what it regarded as a disastrous loss in court. Secretary Johnson announced in a press release (which satisfied almost nobody)[79] that it would "offer release with an appropriate monetary bond or other condition of release to families at residential centers who are successful in stating a case of credible or reasonable fear of persecution in their home countries" and would "conduct credible fear and reasonable fear interviews within a reasonable timeframe."[80] The government then filed a copy of its press release with Judge Gee, claiming that its unilateral change of policy should cause her to rule in its favor and not issue her tentative order.[81]

THE JUDGE DECIDES

Not surprisingly, the negotiations between Schey and Fresco failed,[82] forcing Judge Gee to issue an order and opinion. She did so on July 24, 2015. Her order was little changed from the tentative decision she had written months before. She batted away the government's claim that Secretary Johnson's press release changed anything, saying that "defendants could easily revert to the former challenged policy as abruptly as they adopted the new one."[83] She granted Schey's motion to enforce the agreement and denied the government's motion to amend it. She ordered the government to release the accompanied children, preferably to a parent, "including a parent who . . . was apprehended" with the child. She ordered the government not to detain the children in unlicensed or secure facilities, except as permitted in unusual instances by the Flores settlement. She specifically ordered that accompanying parents be released along with their children, unless the parent posed a significant flight or security risk. Addressing the complaints about conditions in the border stations, she ordered the government to consult with Schey and to propose standards for safe and sanitary conditions. And she ordered that all of this be done within ninety days. Finally, she gave the government two weeks to respond in writing, if it so desired, to her order.[84]

The families had won. Karnes and Dilley could not be used to house families, because they would be unable to get licenses, and even if they did, the mothers and children would have to be released within days of being incarcerated there, as the Flores settlement required.

That might have been the end of the matter. But it was not. Years of additional litigation followed.

10 Litigation Proliferates

2015–2016

The Obama administration would not take "no" for an answer. It remained committed to family detention as a deterrent to more family migration. But after its loss in the R.I. L- R- case and Secretary Jeh Johnson's pledge not to rely on a theory of "general deterrence," its lawyers could no longer claim deterrence as justification for detention. It needed a new strategy.

RECONSIDERATION

The government lawyers' first move was to make creative use of Judge Dolly Gee's invitation to respond to her order. Instead of either stating that the government would comply, or sitting down with Peter Schey to discuss improving conditions in the border facilities, or even asking the court for additional time to come into compliance, it tried to reargue its case and persuade the judge to withdraw her order. Specifically, it requested that Gee reconsider her ruling. It wanted her to take account of changes that Immigration and Customs Enforcement (ICE) had made since she held her hearing a few months earlier. It also said that it could not conduct credible fear interviews and release families as quickly as her proposed order required.

The government's new brief said that ICE was "transitioning the facilities [from long term detention centers] into processing centers," so that it could "release those found eligible to apply for relief or protection within an average of approximately 20 days." The twenty-day period, rather than the five days required by the Flores settlement, was needed to "conduct background checks, provide health screenings and immunizations, screen individuals for a credible fear or reasonable fear . . . and release individuals who [pass credible or reasonable fear screening] under reasonable conditions." The judge's order would require ICE to release some families who had no plausible basis for remaining in the United States.

The government also asked Judge Gee to reconsider her ruling that the Flores agreement applied to accompanied as well as unaccompanied minors. It reiterated the argument that it previously made that "the parties did not consider family detention" in 1997 because family detention did not exist then. As for the order to develop new standards for the Customs and Border Protection (CBP) holding stations, it said that the many sworn statements that Schey had submitted from mothers were merely "anecdotal declarations" that should be outweighed by governmental assurances that the border facilities were safe and sanitary. Furthermore, the government brief claimed, government lawyers had "no opportunity to cross examine" any of the mothers who filed those statements. And although all the declarations concerned the border stations in the Rio Grande Valley, Judge Gee had gone overboard in requiring CBP to come up with standards for all of its holding facilities nationwide.[1]

In response, Peter Schey dismissed most of the government's brief as a "rehash." He also pointed out that the Department of Homeland Security (DHS)'s proposal to release families within an "average" of twenty days could still leave some families in long-term detention. He noted that the only reason that it took twenty days to screen mothers in credible fear interviews was that DHS had not assigned enough officers to perform the screenings, and, in addition, DHS's own internal memos showed that DHS did not have to put the mothers into expedited removal proceedings. It could simply release them until they were summoned to hearings. As for medical care, the sworn declarations from mothers showed that families were far worse off with the substandard medical care they received in Karnes and Dilley than with what they would receive in the communities of their relatives. Schey also pointed out that GEO, which operated Karnes, had recently boasted to its shareholders that it planned to double the capacity of that facility and therefore earn more profit; this was evidence that ICE was not planning to comply with the judge's order.[2]

Judge Gee was not pleased by the government's brief. She signaled her displeasure with its repetition of arguments she had already rejected by beginning her opinion with a biting quotation from Mahatma Gandhi: "An error does not become truth by reason of multiplied propagation, nor does truth become error because nobody sees it." Gandhi's concerns about "multiplied propagation" were reflected in one of the court's rules, which barred the repetition of arguments in motions for reconsideration. Therefore, she wrote, "defendants' reheated and repackaged arguments are improper." Judge Gee then acknowledged that the government had issued press releases announcing new policies that could result in shorter periods of detention, but she noted that those policies did not include "the complete cessation of detention of accompanied minors in secure, unlicensed facilities." And the government's claims that release of the families would lead to another migrant influx were "speculative at best and, at worst, fear mongering."

Nevertheless, she was troubled by the government's explanation that it needed up to twenty days to conduct credible fear and reasonable fear interviews while the families were still in confinement, so that it could rapidly deport detained asylum applicants who had scant chances of winning their cases before an immigration judge. Giving the government a bit of the relief from her order that it had sought, she seized upon the clause in the Flores settlement agreement that provided an exception to the five-day limit on confining migrant children in unlicensed secure facilities. The exception provided that the five-day period could be extended "in the event of an emergency or influx of minors," in which case the children had to be released from such facilities "as expeditiously as possible." The agreement defined an influx as a situation in which the government had more than 130 minors eligible for placement in a licensed program, a level that had been exceeded annually for many years. Therefore, she wrote, "if 20 days is as fast as Defendants . . . can possibly go in screening family members for reasonable or credible fear," the settlement agreement permitted twenty days of detention. Turning to the border facilities, she acknowledged that the sworn declarations of the women pertained only to stations in the Rio Grande Valley, but she also said that the government had failed to contradict "the deplorable conditions" that the women had described in those stations. Although the government claimed that it wanted to cross-examine the women who had written the statements, it "had multiple opportunities to request an evidentiary hearing before the Court ruled" and it had not done so. "It is too late for a second bite at the apple." And "to the extent that any Border Patrol station is out of compliance with the Agreement, those stations must comply."

She concluded her decision by confirming her order that the government had to comply with the Flores agreement, beginning on October 23, 2015 (two months hence), but with the leeway to detain families for up to twenty days in unlicensed, secure facilities where necessary, due to an "influx." She accepted the government's argument that it could take that long to conduct credible fear interviews and other processing. Her order included a sentence that would later engender much controversy: "To comply with Paragraph 14 of the Agreement [which specified that minors released from confinement should ideally be released to 'a parent'] . . . a [child's] accompanying parent shall be released" with the child, unless an individualized determination found that the parent was a threat or a flight risk that could not be mitigated by imposing a bond or monitoring requirement.[3]

DHS was nothing if not tenacious. On September 18, 2015, it set into motion two different efforts to obtain authority to keep migrant families incarcerated for long periods despite Judge Gee's ruling. Because the Flores settlement permitted holding children in licensed, non-secure facilities, it began a process of trying to license Dilley and Karnes (leaving until later the problem posed by their being locked). And it appealed Judge Gee's decision.

GRASSROOTS LEADERSHIP AND RAICES

While the legality of family detention was being contested in Judge Gee's courtroom in Los Angeles, the advocates in Texas were stepping up their local activities.

Robert Libal and Cristina Parker.

A key player in what followed was Grassroots Leadership, an organization based in Austin. The organization had been founded in Tennessee in 1980 as a training center for building social justice organizations. During the 1980s and 1990s, it had sponsored community advocacy against the privatization of governmental functions. It had increasingly focused on the private prison industry and specifically on the use of private prisons for immigration detention. By the time Hutto opened in 2006, the organization had moved its headquarters to Austin, Texas.[4]

Grassroots Leadership's communications director, Cristina Parker, was good at organizing demonstrations and attracting press attention. In 2006, Grassroots Leadership had organized the first demonstration and vigil at Hutto, and for months it had conducted weekly demonstrations there.

In 2014, the organization's executive director, Robert Libal, began to hear rumors that ICE was going to use Karnes to detain asylum-seeking families and that, in fact, ICE and the GEO Group, which owned and operated the facility, were seeking to double its capacity from six to twelve hundred beds. The expansion would require approval from the local county's Board of Commissioners, so Libal organized local opposition to that approval. Immigration activists believed that migrant families should not be incarcerated, and some local residents sided with them because they expected that immigrants who eventually were released would settle in their communities. Still others opposed it because, after hearing allegations of sexual abuse and nutritional deprivation at the facility, they expected that the county would face lawsuits and that taxpayers would have to pay to defend it. Other residents supported the expansion because more of them would be hired to work in the detention center. After the county's attorney assured commissioners that the county would have immunity from liability, and that most released immigrants settled out of the state, they approved the expansion by 3–2, a closer division than Libal had expected.[5]

While the expansion controversy simmered, Libal also brought attention to the plight by the families in Karnes by holding a rally, as it had done at Hutto, and by alerting the press to some of the families' plights. In particular, he brought press attention to Nayely Bermudez Beltran, a seven-year-old girl who, with her mother, had fled El Salvador and been put into Karnes. Nayely had a life-threatening malignant brain tumor, which had been operated on unsuccessfully in El Salvador. She needed urgent medical attention. Her mother had passed a credible fear interview, and a hospital in Austin had agreed to re-evaluate her and was poised to offer treatment for free. But ICE refused to release the family from Karnes. After several weeks of pressure from Grassroots Leadership and from the girl's attorney, ICE finally did release her.[6] When Dilley opened, Grassroots Leadership began a public opposition campaign there as well. It organized a demonstration with more than five hundred protesters at the site. While Grassroots Leadership engaged the public, RAICES continued to represent the families incarcerated in Karnes. The key player at RAICES was a young lawyer, Manoj Govindaiah. Govindaiah was the son of two immigrants from India. His father, a doctor, had come to the United States in the late 1960s, when, because of a doctor shortage, it was easy for Indian doctors to obtain visas. His mother, a psychiatrist, had come a few years later. Govindaiah had a large family, with fifty-four first cousins, most of whom lived in India, so as a child he frequently

Manoj Govindaiah.

traveled internationally. After studying economic development in college, he taught English to adults in China, where he discovered that most of his students, who were doctors and engineers, wanted to improve their English by working abroad, but were considering Canada, New Zealand, and Ireland, and not the United States, having concluded that it was too difficult to obtain a U.S. visa. He started wondering why it was so difficult for these young professionals, when it had been so easy for his father thirty years earlier. His curiosity about U.S. immigration law provoked his desire to go to law school.

He expected to have a career in immigration policy, but his first job was with a small nonprofit organization near St. Louis, which did individual representation for immigrants in rural Illinois. "We were basically traveling three to four days a week and staying in a lot of Motel 6s in the middle of nowhere and eating a lot of crappy food," he recalled. He liked the work but after about eighteen months he got a job with the National Immigrant Justice Center in Chicago, working with unaccompanied children. After another job working at the Southern Poverty Law Center in its Miami office, he settled in San Antonio for the job with RAICES, first working with unaccompanied minors and then, in 2015, becoming the director for family detention issues and of the Karnes Pro Bono Project that Gilman had originally organized.[7]

He was in communication with the American Immigration Lawyers Association and the American Immigration Council, which had set up the computerized tag-team system through which hundreds of volunteer lawyers had represented the Artesia detainees. During 2015 those two organizations, together with RAICES and the Catholic Legal Immigration Network, set up the CARA Pro Bono Family Immigration Project, named for the initials of the four founding organizations,[8] and both Govindaiah's lawyers and their counterparts at Dilley began using the case management database that Stephen Manning had created for Artesia.[9]

In the fall of 2015, Govindaiah, Libal, and Hines began hearing rumors that the prison companies that operated Karnes and Dilley were applying to the Texas Department of Family and Protective Services (DFPS) for licenses, despite the fact that several years earlier the Department had concluded that it lacked state regulatory authority to license a family jail such as Hutto. This was obviously an attempt, instigated by DHS, to get out from under the impact of Judge Gee's ruling. Under the Flores agreement, children (and therefore families) could be detained indefinitely in a non-secure facility licensed for the care of dependent children.

THE EMERGENCY RULE

The opening shot was fired on September 2, 2015. Without notice to anyone or any public hearing, DFPS adopted an "emergency rule." The rule provided that its normal standards for a childcare facility could be waived in order to grant a license to a "family residential center" operated under a contract with ICE. Specifically, the emergency regulation stated that for such a facility, it would waive the state's minimum standards for how many people could be housed in one room, the state's limitation on children sharing bedrooms with adults, and the state's limitations on children of the opposite gender sharing a bedroom.[10] These proposed changes in the state's normal standards resulted not from the Department's internal analysis, according to Robert Doggett, a lawyer at Texas RioGrande Legal Aid (TRLA), which soon sued DFPS on behalf of Grassroots Leadership and several incarcerated mothers. The waivers resulted from agreements between ICE and the prison corporations, which did not want to spend the money to expand the facilities.[11]

The immigrants' advocates could be expected to oppose a regulation allowing Karnes and Dilley to be licensed, but the fact that the prison corporations were able to get the state agency to adopt this rule in secret, without notice to the public, was the red flag waving in front of a bull. The advocates could hardly wait to get to court. In this case, because they needed to reverse the actions of a state agency, they would have to head to a state court rather than back to Judge Gee. It took a few weeks, however, before Libal, who is not a lawyer, could secure a lawyer who would handle the case, obtain retainers from families that would join as plaintiffs, obtain sworn statements about what was happening in the detention centers, and collect expert affidavits and other litigation documents. Meanwhile, GEO lost no time. It quickly filed a license application for Karnes under the emergency regulation.

TRLA, a statewide agency providing services to low-income individuals, agreed to litigate the case. Doggett, the TRLA lawyer in charge of the litigation, discovered from internal DFPS documents, as the suit progressed, that DFPS had not wanted to license the family detention centers, but that "pressure was brought to bear on the Governor, and the Governor finally made a phone call or two, or his staff did, over to the department head."[12] On October 26, Doggett brought suit in the district court for Travis County on behalf of Grassroots Leadership and some detainees, asking for temporary and permanent injunctions against the licensing. The complaint pointed out that DFPS had itself suggested after the Hutto case (when it said that Hutto was "exempt" from licensing) that Texas statutes did not give DFPS authority to license family facilities as childcare centers, to license prisons as childcare centers, or to license residential childcare facilities that did not actually offer twenty-four-hour a day childcare. Doggett also attacked the emergency rule on the ground that there was no actual emergency.[13]

The case was assigned to Judge Karin Crump. Once again, the immigrants' advocates had reason to be pleased with the judge they drew for the litigation. Judge Crump was a graduate of St. Mary's University School of Law in San Antonio. As a student there, she had taken the civil justice clinic. She later said that the clinic "gave me the opportunity to meet members of our community who were going through the hardest times of their lives, who were truly desperate to have a voice and who otherwise wouldn't have had that voice, with matters that were . . . life altering—their children, their homes and their livelihoods."[14] By chance, as a clinic student, she had advocated for the wellbeing of children who had escaped traumatic violence, including burning with an iron, in their homes.[15] Four days after the suit was filed, she granted a short-term temporary restraining order,[16] halting the licensing, and she scheduled a hearing less than two weeks later to determine whether it should be continued.

JUDGE CRUMP'S FIRST HEARING

Judge Crump began the hearing by asking DFPS why it had issued an emergency rule rather than going through the ordinary process of seeking public input through comments. Pat Tulinski, an Assistant Attorney General of Texas, candidly admitted what the problem was: if members of the public made comments "they have to be specifically addressed [and] I assume they'll be substantial."

"But isn't that the point of having a process?" the judge asked.

A sequence of temporary emergency rules and longer-term rules is "a bit of a sausage making process," Tulinski conceded.

Doggett put Libal on the stand. He testified that his organization would have wanted to comment on the regulations but was not allowed to do so because there was no opportunity for public input. Tulinski cross-examined him: "Is it your position that you should have been able to comment?"

"We have already provided comments," Libal said. "We sent a letter along with 140 other organizations . . . and have received no response."

"Well, that's understandable," Tulinski said, "because there is no process for comments, [but] do you plan on filing comments tomorrow" in response to the Department's invitation for the public to comment on a permanent regulation?

"Today is the first time I've heard anything about the permanent rule," Libal said.

"Oh, so you didn't see the rule published in the Texas Register?"

"No. Is it published yet?"

"It'll be published tomorrow. I'm sorry, my fault," Tulinski said.

Doggett wanted the judge to hear testimony from Dean Zayas about harm to the children. Tulinski objected, suggesting that the judge should uphold the emergency procedure without first hearing any evidence about jail conditions. Judge Crump nevertheless allowed Zayas to testify. He explained to the judge that Karnes was like a prison and nothing like a childcare facility, and that the waiver of the rules proposed by the emergency regulation could be harmful to the children. For example, if children were sleeping in the same room with unrelated adults, "we would be concerned with issues of nudity and exposure of personal habits." He also stated that he didn't see anything in the rule that would actually protect children.

During closing arguments, Judge Crump asked Tulinski, if it was so important for DFPS to license the facilities, and do so quickly, why the agency didn't simply grant a license but require that the facilities meet normal state standards, rather than waiving those standards. The real answer was that the state didn't have the political clout to force ICE or the prison corporations to pay what it would take to upgrade the facilities. Tulinski would have been embarrassed to admit that reason. She replied, "I don't know . . . there is always room for improvement . . . but they've done the best they can under these circumstances. [So] let's get some kind of oversight in place." To which Doggett replied, "I think the real reason . . . is because those facilities can't meet [the State's] minimum standards."[17]

A week later, Judge Crump temporarily enjoined the emergency rule, stating that it "does not address an actual emergency," and she scheduled a trial for the following May, several months later.[18]

THE PERMANENT RULE

The preamble to the DFPS's emergency rule mentioned Judge Gee's decision in the Flores case. It didn't claim, nor could it have, that Judge Gee required the state to license the family detention centers, but Gee's order, issued a month before the emergency rule was published, was likely the impetus. Pursuant to Gee's order, after October 23, 2015, families who had been incarcerated for more than twenty days would have to be released if the facilities could not be licensed. They would have to be made "nonsecure" as well, but little attention was paid to that part of Judge Gee's order, because if they could not be licensed, it did not matter that they were locked.

October 23 came and went. That weekend, hundreds of families were released from Karnes and Dilley, and ICE began a practice of releasing, within twenty days, families in which the mother had passed the credible fear test—the vast majority of families, as a result of the work of Govindaiah and the CARA project.

But GEO and the Corrections Corporation of America (CCA), which owned Dilley, did not give up. The judge had temporarily enjoined the emergency rule but had not barred DFPS from going ahead with a permanent rule. On November 13, the day after Judge Crump's hearing, it published its licensing regulation as a proposed permanent rule, rather than an emergency rule, and it invited public comment.[19] In response, DFPS received 1460 responses, but it noted that most of them were "standardized" emails that opposed licensing.[20] The agency also held a public hearing, at which forty-five people spoke. Nearly all of the comments opposed the regulation that would allow licensing; two people, including a representative of the Karnes management, supported licensing.[21]

DFPS published its responses to the comments, agreeing with the two commenters who said that licensing would "ensure the safety and wellbeing" of children. As to the comments opposing licensure or opposing the waiver of normal childcare standards, the agency said that licensing would bring to bear a "host" of requirements to protect the health and safety of the children.

To its credit, DFPS then addressed, as best it could, the very specific criticisms that the commenters had leveled at the rule.

- To the criticism that Karnes and Dilley were really privately owned prisons, not childcare centers, and that they had locked doors, limited access to telephones and charges for using them, discipline and harsh consequences for children's misbehavior and threats to remove children from mothers if complaints were made, it replied that "DFPS has concluded that the FRCs (family residential centers) and their staff are providing childcare. The purpose of licensure is to ensure compliance with the standards for the provision of such care."

- To the criticism that the risk of psychological harm is acute for immigrants who have fled persecution, abuse, and trauma, and that infants living in detention centers have problem with brain development and social functioning, it replied that "it is more protective of the children in the FRCs for DFPS to exercise its oversight than to abdicate its responsibility based on the notion that the centers are harmful."

- To the critique that living conditions were inadequate, it replied that "to the extent the living conditions relate to the practices of the federal government or its contractors with respect to adults in the FRCs, they are outside DFPS's scope of authority."

- To the comment that the FRCs did not comply with the standards of the Federal Prison Rape Elimination Act, and that staff misconduct regarding abuse and sexual assault had not been adequately addressed, it said that compliance with that law was "outside DFPS's scope" and that licensing "would address some of the concerns regarding staff."

- To the complaint that the Flores settlement required not only that children be placed in state-licensed facilities but that the facilities had to be non-secure, it replied that its role was to oversee the care of children, "not to determine whether the facility is secure."

- To the claim that state law provided no authority for the new regulation, and that in fact licensing FRCs would violate state juvenile detention laws, which required adjudication by a court before children could be incarcerated and prohibited the secure detention of children under the age of ten, it replied that the Texas statutes did not govern federal facilities.[22]

In response to the comments, DFPS did make one change in the regulation it had proposed, however. It modified the waivers to its normal standards and required that the bedroom floor space had to be at least sixty square feet per child,[23] that a child could share a bedroom with adults only "if the bedroom is being shared in order to allow a child to remain with the child's parent," and that children from different families who were over the age of six and members of the opposite gender could not share bedrooms.[24] The ban on children sharing bedrooms with adults did not actually bar children from living with unrelated adults as well as their own mothers, so long as the purpose of allowing the children to live with adults was to keep the children together with the mothers.[25]

JUDGE CRUMP'S SECOND HEARING

Having gone through the rulemaking process by responding to the public comments, DFPS promulgated the regulation as amended. It then moved quickly to accept license applications for Karnes and Dilley. Doggett started drafting a challenge to its validity. He was preparing to file it during the first week of May 2016, having understood from testimony given to the Health and Human Services Committee of the Texas Senate that the license would be granted in late May.[26] But DFPS granted a six-month license to Karnes on Friday, April 29,[27] two working days before Doggett was ready with his papers.[28]

Nevertheless, Doggett quickly challenged the licensing law in Judge Crump's court.[29] His main arguments were that Texas statutes did not give DFPS any authority to license family detention facilities as childcare centers, and that detaining children in such a facility was actually inconsistent with a Texas law that provided that a child "who has been taken into custody and is being held solely for deportation out of the United States, may not be detained for any period of time in a secure detention facility or secure correctional facility, regardless of whether the facility is publicly or privately operated."[30] He also asked for a restraining order "to prevent DFPS from taking any further action to implement" its new regulation until a final judgment in the case.[31] The very next day, Judge Crump granted the restraining order.[32] She specifically ordered DFPS not to license Dilley.

A week later, she held the hearing that she had scheduled the previous November. At the outset, Judge Crump once again went to the heart of the matter, asking the State's lead lawyer on the case, Nichole Bunker-Henderson, to explain the agency's "ability to create a rule that directly contradicts the Family Code's prohibition against detaining minors" in secure facilities. Bunker-Henderson replied that "simply because the doors are locked at the front, that doesn't mean that it's a secured facility." Judge Crump declared that she was "a little surprised" by this argument, because Karnes and Dilley had constantly been referred to as secured facilities. DFPS might have lost the case right there, but it slogged on for several hours and 322 pages of transcript. DFPS's lawyer argued that the fact that the facility had a "gate" didn't necessarily mean that it was secured, because, as opposed to conditions in a real prison, the children could walk around within the facility without being escorted by a guard. She argued that the children in Karnes and Dilley weren't held "solely for deportation out of the United States," and therefore the state prohibition didn't apply, because some of them were eventually found to be eligible for asylum and then released.[33] It argued that licensing improved conditions for the children, because after Karnes had applied for its license, DFPS did background checks on its employees, and "five or so people have actually been fired" because they had "something so bad" in their background that posed "a threat to these children."

Because Doggett was asking the court to enter an injunction against the licensing, he had the burden of proving—and the opportunity to present evidence to prove—that children would be harmed if the facilities could lawfully be licensed. Of course the premise of such proof, unstated by any of the lawyers, was that if the facilities were not licensed, then ICE would continue to release the families after twenty days, as it had been doing since October 23, when Judge Gee's order took effect. To prove harm from continued detention, Doggett subpoenaed several of the mothers who had joined Grassroots as plaintiffs in the suit. One of them testified that at Dilley

> my daughter's gotten sick. She's been depressed. . . . She's refusing to eat. She doesn't want to go to school. . . . She keeps asking me . . . mommy, if we're running away from evil in our country, why is it that we get here and we are in this jail? Is it that people here are bad like they are down in Guatemala? I don't know how to answer her. . . . They don't really let us sleep. People [that work there] are coming into the room where we sleep. They slam doors. People traipse through it, every night. [The people in the room with us are] from a different country. The water . . . tastes awful. . . .

My daughter refuses to drink from that [fountain so she] limits herself to drinking soda. If one has money one can buy bottled water. . . . When the children have fever or they're vomiting [they say at the medical clinic] 'oh give them water.' And it's the water that is making those children ill because of the amount of chlorine in it.

The testimony of the other mothers was similar, except that one of the mothers testified that the other, unrelated adult with whom she was sharing a room "opened the door when my daughter was in the bathroom and caught my daughter naked in there on three occasions. . . . She started making fun of her about how her private parts looked . . . and on another occasion she went up and touched her on her private parts. . . . It made my daughter very scared."

At the end of the hearing, Judge Crump continued her temporary restraining order for two weeks and required a further hearing at that time. She also asked about the water at Dilley, based on what she had heard. A lawyer for the CCA, which had intervened in the case, told her that "it's city water" that "is tested every year" and that "my administrator drinks it often." He said "I've had it before. It's not the same as Houston water. I'll just leave it at that [but] we find these allegations false and offensive." Nevertheless, the judge insisted on having a water report when the hearing resumed.[34]

Doggett brought several new witnesses to Judge Crump's third hearing, which was held two weeks later. Laura Guerra-Cardus, a physician who was serving as the associate director of the Children's Defense Fund's Texas branch, testified that licensing would amount to state certification that the children in Karnes and Dilley were safe when in fact they were not. She said that research on what happened to the children in the Japanese-American internment camps during World War II, as well as reports from mothers released from Dilley and Karnes, showed that the older children "regressed to childlike states" and experienced hair loss, weight loss, and psychiatric disorders. Zayas also testified. He discussed the long-term psychological and physical damage being done to the children as a result of seeing that their parents were disempowered and unable to protect them, because the guards, who "insulted, degraded, and threatened" their mothers, had all the power in the institution.

At 11:45, the judge interrupted the hearing to note that the hearing was likely to go on all day, but the temporary restraining order that she had

Laura Guerra-Cardus.

previously entered would expire at 12:29 and she did not have authority to extend it. So she asked the state's lawyer if he would agree to extending it for the rest of the day, and not issue a license to Dilley before she could hear all of the evidence and decide what to do. "I don't think that we can agree to extend the TRO," he said. As 12:29 approached, however, the judge noted that the interim assistant commissioner for licensing was in the court. She asked the court to consult with his client and to state on the record that even if the judge did not enter a new order during the day, no license would be issued before 5:00. The lawyer understood the pressure he was under. "We're not agreeing to continue the injunction in any way," he said, but "I can tell you that we are not [going] to issue the license through, you know, 5:00 P.M. today."

During the afternoon, Wesley Lee, a CCA representative, testified about the quality of accommodations and services at Dilley—three hot meals a day, six sets of clothing, a refrigerator, sink, and TV in each "apartment complex," medical services provided by a division of ICE, classrooms, a library with computer stations and 24,000 books, mostly in Spanish, and three recreation areas. He also stated that he'd had the water tested, and it met the state's standards. Doggett's cross-examination revealed that typically, four families were assigned to each bedroom. When Doggett asked him the purpose of the chain-link fence around the facility, he said "I can't really tell you why they put the fence up there other than to keep those families safe and secure." He testified that nobody had ever escaped from Dilley, but that if there were an escape, law enforcement would do a search.

As the hearing closed, the lawyers for the state tried to play the usual mootness card. ICE had released from the Texas facilities all of the mothers who had originally been plaintiffs (though some might have been transferred to the Berks facility in Pennsylvania), and although Doggett therefore had added a few more plaintiffs a few days before the hearing, DFPS claimed that they would soon be released as well, so "their interest would be over with in a week or so."

Judge Crump was doubtful about this tactic. "If CCA continues to release every time a plaintiff files a claim . . . to avoid there being an interest at the time of trial, then we have a problem," she said. And Doggett pointed out that ICE sometimes picked up people who had been released and sent them right back to Dilley or Karnes, an echo of the reasoning that had led Judge Sam Sparks to deny the mootness claim in the Hutto case.

At the end of thirteen hours of testimony, Judge Crump went right back to where she had been at the beginning. "I'm going to enter a temporary injunction" until a full trial in September, she said, to replace the expiring temporary restraining order. "The rule at issue allows ICE to house immigrant children . . . in secure detention facilities despite the prohibition" in the Texas law. "And I do find that [Karnes and Dilley] are secure." She added that she believed that DFPS also lacked any legislative authority to create family residential centers.[35]

The September trial never took place. DFPS and Doggett agreed that Judge Crump could decide the case on the basis of documents and briefs that they submitted, which largely rehashed the points they had made during the hearing that led to the temporary injunction. On December 2, she entered a final judgment in the case. She declared that DFPS's permanent rule "runs counter" to the laws of Texas and is therefore "invalid."[36] She did not explicitly address the license that had already been granted to

Karnes, but Libal pointed out that the judgment "invalidates the Karnes license, because it was issued under an invalid regulation."[37] DFPS did not renew Karnes's six-month license when it expired, although for years thereafter, Karnes continued to display the expired license at the entryway to the facility.[38] Meanwhile, the DFPS appealed.

The case actually produced a modest benefit for the incarcerated families. While it was proceeding, the Karnes administrators reduced to four the number of occupants per bedroom, to conform with the permanent rule that DFPS had promulgated. After Judge Crump ruled, the lower room occupancy limit remained in place.[39]

THE TEXAS LEGISLATURE

GEO wouldn't give up. It received $55 million per year from ICE to operate Karnes, so it had a great deal at stake.[40] Judge Crump's decision was based on the rule's inconsistency with state law, so while DFPS was appealing the decision, GEO rushed to the Texas state legislature to get the law changed. Both houses of the legislature had Republican majorities, and the state's governor was Republican, so the prospects of passage were good. GEO drafted a bill, SB 1018, to allow DFPS licensing. It wasn't difficult to obtain support from many state legislators. GEO had contributed $193,000 to some of their political campaigns since 2013.[41] "I've known the lady who is their lobbyist for a long time," Rep. John Raney said. "That's where the legislation came from. We don't make things up. People bring things to us and ask us to help."[42]

The opponents of licensing prepared to testify against the bill, but they also organized a public protest. They set up a small daycare center outside of the governor's office in the State Capitol, with a sign saying "why don't you license this?"[43]

The Texas Senate held a public hearing, at which "dozens of people" testified against the bill, and only four, three of whom were GEO employees, supported it.[44] The Texas Pediatric Society expressed its opposition. Dr. Guerra-Cardus was also among the opponents; she reminded senators that state licensing was not necessary for the detention centers to operate, and that the state could continue to investigate any allegations of mistreatment or abuse, even without licensing. She urged that "the only reason that licensing is being sought is to get the ability to prolong the stay of children and women in these facilities."[45]

But the bill's opponents had little political clout. The only thing that senators were worried about was whether allowing DFPS to license the facilities would result in more lawsuits against the agency or against the state, which would at the least cost money. So they amended the bill before approving it in committee, tacking on provisions to prevent lawsuits against the state.[46]

On May 9, 2017, the Senate passed the bill on a party-line vote, 20–11. All of the Republicans voted for it.[47] The bill then moved to the Texas House. The Texas legislature is in session for only a few months. Under the rules of its House, no bill could be considered unless it was approved by a committee by May 23. The process of amending the bill to immunize the state from suits had taken so much time that its opponents needed only to prevent a committee vote for two weeks. The bill was referred to the House Committee on State Affairs, chaired by Rep. Byron Cook.

This assignment was a lucky break for the opponents of licensing. Cook, a rancher, was regarded by *Texas Monthly* as the one of the ten best members of the legislature, known for his moderation.[48] Nevertheless, the pressure that GEO put on Cook was intense. According to Cheasty Anderson of the Children's Defense Fund, industry representatives were in the Capitol every day with eight-by-ten glossy pictures showing the playgrounds and other attractive features of the detention centers. "One legislative aide [told me], they keep showing me these pictures but it's like they don't even notice there are no kids in them, just shiny things."[49]

Representative Cook bottled up the bill in his committee. May 23 came and went, and the bill finally died. A Democratic state senator called it a "good death."[50]

THE NINTH CIRCUIT: ROUND THREE

The United States Court of Appeals for the Ninth Circuit, in San Francisco, had last heard the Flores case in 1991, when it had ruled, en banc, that undocumented children had a right to a hearing to determine whether they should be released to an unrelated adult sponsor. That was the decision that the Supreme Court had reversed on the assumption that compliance with agreed shelter care standards was "good enough." In 2016, a generation later, it was presented with another issue in the same case: whether Judge Gee had been correct in ruling that pursuant to the Flores settlement, families could not be detained in facilities like Karnes and Dilley for more than twenty days, even during a migration "influx."

The Department of Justice filed an eighty-five-page brief. All but five pages of it restated the arguments that it had made to Judge Gee: that the Flores agreement must have pertained only to unaccompanied minors, and not to children entering with adults, because back in 1997, the INS wasn't detaining families, and undocumented families weren't even crossing the border in significant numbers. The brief hinted at the importance of reversing Judge Gee's decision for the purpose of general deterrence, without using that phrase. The family detention centers, it said, "are an essential component of an integrated response designed to signal to potential illegal entrants" that they will be deported if they don't have meritorious claims. Furthermore, it argued, the small family detention center at Berks had been in operation since 2001, and Hutto had operated from 2006 to 2009, and although Schey represented the class of children in the Flores case, he hadn't objected to detention in either of those facilities.

Then, in five pages at the very end of its brief, the government took issue with the part of Judge Gee's order in which she had decreed that a mother should be released from family detention along with her child, after credible fear had been established, unless the mother presented a danger to others or a significant flight risk. "There is simply no provision in the [Flores] Agreement that addresses the treatment of parents at all," it stated. Judge Gee had based that part of her order on the part of the settlement that gave to children a "preferential right of release to a parent." But, argued the Justice Department, "it is not plausible that the parties could have intended for the Agreement to speak to a situation where a child and parent are in immigration detention together," because such detention did not exist at the time.[51]

Schey responded, as expected, that the settlement unambiguously applied to "all minors" who are detained, and that the government had produced no evidence to suggest that the word "all" as used in the agreement meant anything but "all." Noting the hint about deterrence of other migrants in the government's brief, he reminded the court that after the R. I. L- R- case, DHS Secretary Jeh Johnson had claimed to have abandoned that rationale, and that the government could not constitutionally "punish innocent class members to deter future unidentified family units." With respect to the coda in the government's brief, suggesting that Judge Gee should not have ordered the release of the mothers along with the children, Schey simply ignored the issue. This might have been a tactical decision, not wanting to call attention to the government's challenge to this secondary, though nevertheless extremely important, part of her ruling. Or perhaps Schey had no interest in securing release of the mothers or agreed with the government that Judge Gee had overstepped her authority.[52]

But in its reply brief, the government pounced. On the third page, it argued that "even if the Agreement is interpreted to include accompanied minors, the Agreement cannot reasonably be read to govern the release of a parent with whom an accompanied minor is detained." The clause of the agreement giving preferential right of release pertained to release "'to" a parent, not "with a parent," the brief noted, suggesting that such releases were to be made only to parents who were not in custody with the child in question.[53]

The case was assigned to a panel consisting of Ronald Gould, a Clinton appointee, Andrew Hurwitz, an Obama appointee, and Michael Melloy, a senior judge who had been appointed by George W. Bush to the Eighth Circuit Court of Appeals, and who was serving temporarily in the Ninth Circuit. Once again, Schey and Leon Fresco squared off. Judge Hurwitz, who presided over the oral argument and asked most of the questions, began the proceedings by announcing that there were two distinct issues: whether the agreement applied to accompanied minors, and whether Judge Gee had improperly included adults in her release order. Turning to the first point, he immediately signaled to Fresco that he thought that Judge Gee had correctly interpreted the settlement to apply to all minors. Fresco restated his arguments, but he could not persuade the judge. "On the face of the agreement," Judge Hurwitz said, "it sure seems to apply to all minors."

Then the judge asked Fresco, "assuming that you win" on the second issue in the case, and we hold that the agreement does not contemplate the release of parents along with their children, would that resolve the issue? Fresco replied that the agreement included a paragraph stating that when the INS determined that continued detention of the child was in the child's safety interest, the minor could be kept in detention. Judge Hurwitz followed up: "Do you read the agreement as saying that when the minor's safety would be better served by being with the parent," the minor may be kept in detention? Fresco replied, "I read the judge's order as saying that when the minor's safety is not served, you have to release the parent too."

"Assuming that you win on that (second) issue," the judge continued, "doesn't that solve your problem?" Fresco answered, "Yes, your Honor. Assuming that the court rules that we don't have to release the parent, and we can keep the minor with the parent, because that is in the safety interest of the minor, instead of releasing that minor into an uncertain environment [that could include an adult who was a trafficker] . . . that resolves the issue from the government's perspective."

In stating that the safety of the children was the government's concern, Fresco was subtly offering Schey a settlement, in open court. DHS would keep families in detention for more than a few days only if releasing them would put them in harm's way—for instance, if there was reason to believe that the adult to whom the child would be released was a trafficker. In other situations, the whole family would be released. A settlement along those lines "was exactly what I wanted," Fresco recalled.[54] But Schey did not pick up on Fresco's hint, perhaps for the same reasons he had been unable to negotiate a settlement with Fresco during the two months before Judge Gee had decided the case. He may have regarded himself as the spokesman for a coalition of advocates who had not authorized him to compromise in court.

When it was Schey's turn, Judge Hurwitz continued to focus on the issue of whether the mothers had to be released along with the children. "The order says that the parent shall be released with the [minor], but that's not what the settlement agreement says." Schey was unable to persuade the judge that anything in the settlement warranted Judge Gee in ordering parental release. He might have seized upon Fresco's apparent concession that the only condition warranting detention of a mother was when her release presented a concern for the safety of the child, because Judge Gee's order itself made an exception to parental release when the parent posed a danger to others. Schey instead made a big concession of his own: "If a child had an uncle or an auntie or a grandmother here . . .

under the settlement, you could have the mother stay in custody, and you could have the child released to the [relative]. But if . . . the only option is to [release the child with the apprehended parent]. . . . "

His point trailed off, but the damage had been done: mothers could be kept in detention, and their children could be separated from them and sent to live with other adults. Schey added, "The only legitimate concern we have is where the detention of the mother is used to block the release of the child." This stance was consistent with Schey's view of himself as an advocate for migrant children, whether or not they were apprehended with parents. It was also consistent with the fact that as a formal matter, the class he represented was a class of children, not families. But it ignored the interest of children in being with their parents, and it took no account of the psychological harm to children that separating children from their parents, even if they went to live with "an uncle or an auntie," could cause.[55] And although putting separated children in shelters or foster care rather than with relatives might not have been on Schey's mind, his concession set the stage for the separation of parents from their children during the Trump administration two years later.

Given how Judge Hurwitz appeared to view the case before the argument even started, and how the argument went, the opinion, released in July 2016, was no surprise. It split the difference, ruling for Schey on the first issue and for the government on the second. "The settlement unambiguously applies both to accompanied and unaccompanied minors, but does not create affirmative release rights for parents," the court said. It cited both the "plain language" of the agreement and the Hutto decision's conclusion to support its first conclusion. It also said that "the government has not explained" a basis for distinguishing accompanied and unaccompanied children. "[M]inors who arrive with their parents are as desirous of education and recreation, and as averse to strip searches, as those who come alone." With respect to the fact that the settlement agreement indicated that the best custodian for a released child was the child's parent, that "does not mean that the government must also make a parent available; it simply means that, if available, a parent is the first choice."[56] Round three for the children . . . but not for their mothers.

The appellate opinion opened the possibility that children could be released into Office of Refugee Resettlement (ORR) custody within twenty days, and then either placed with some responsible adult (another relative, a foster parent), or housed in a licensed shelter, while their mothers were transferred to adult detention centers, to be held for months or years while they awaited court hearings, decisions, and the outcome of appeals on their asylum claims. That outcome could serve the government's unstated goal of deterring other families from fleeing to the United States. On the other hand, separating children from their mothers for periods of indefinite duration would be traumatic for all family members, as well as costly for taxpayers.

The court's decision would likely have been the same even if Schey had advocated more strongly for the release of the mothers. Probably only a compromise agreement between Schey and Fresco could have affected the outcome. Judge Hurwitz, who seemed to be the only member of the panel actively engaged in the argument, appeared to have made up his mind about the case before Fresco and Schey even got up to argue. And it is likely that nobody—not Fresco, or Schey, or the judges on the court—believed that the government would actually separate family members. From 2009, when it closed Hutto, until 2014, when it opened Artesia, and ever since October 23, 2015, whenever a family had passed the credible fear test, the Obama administration had released family members together. In addition, whenever there had not been sufficient bed space available in the family detention centers, the administration had simply given families summonses to appear in immigration court, fitted the adults with ankle monitors, and let them leave the border processing facilities to live with friends or relatives until their court dates.

THE TEXAS COURT OF APPEALS

The bill to allow DFPS to license Karnes and Dilley had died in the Texas legislature. But the licensing litigation remained very much alive. DFPS had appealed Judge Crump's decision to an intermediate court of appeals in Texas, a court below that state's supreme court. In December 2018, two years after Judge Crump ruled that the state could not license the jails, the appellate court overturned her ruling. The court did not rule on whether such licensing was permitted by Texas law. Instead, it held that the mothers of the children incarcerated in Karnes and Dilley did not have standing to challenge DFPS's licensing authority because the length of incarceration of their children was "traceable to federal immigration policy" rather than state licensing of the facilities. In addition, it said, long-term detention of the children in Karnes and Dilley was "speculative" because ICE might choose to release them or to move them to another state.[57]

Grassroots Leadership sought *en banc* review in the appeals court that reversed Judge Crump, a prelude to a possible appeal to the Texas Supreme Court.[58] If its appellate ruling is not reversed by the intermediate court, the Texas Supreme Court, or the Texas legislature, DFPS could license Karnes and Dilley, although it cannot do so until all appeals in the litigation have been completed.[59] Licensing would force Grassroots Leadership or the incarcerated families to argue, on grounds less clear-cut than the unlicensed state of the jails, that long-term detention of children in those facilities violates the Flores settlement. In later litigation, for example, perhaps in the Flores case, parents of the incarcerated children might argue that those jails are not "non-secure" or that a jail is not actually a "program . . . licensed to provide residential services for dependent children" as required by the Flores agreement.[60]

In the fall of 2016, neither the Ninth Circuit's decision nor fact that an appeal of the licensing case was pending in Texas seemed to matter, because the next federal administration was likely to abandon family detention altogether. By the time the court rendered its decision, Hillary Clinton was certain to be nominated as the Democratic presidential candidate. Clinton had pledged on her campaign website that she would "end family detention for parents and children who arrive at our border in desperate situations and close private immigrant detention centers."[61] On the campaign trail she said that she would "close the family detention centers opened by the Obama administration in 2014,"[62] explaining that "I don't think we should put children and vulnerable people into big detention facilities because I think they're at risk. I think that their physical and mental health are at risk."[63] She had advocated for "giving such migrants support and representation" and had criticized the fact that the detention facilities were "run by private companies."[64] And on the day of the court's decision, national polls showed Clinton substantially ahead of the putative Republican nominee, Donald Trump, 46 percent to 41 percent.[65]

11 Berks

1998–2018

The incarceration of mothers and children in Artesia, Karnes, and Dilley, and the litigation over detention in those facilities, received considerable press attention. Meanwhile, a parallel struggle was underway in rural Pennsylvania, with much less media coverage, over family detention in the Berks County Residential Center, known to immigration advocates and government lawyers simply as "Berks." Compared to the family detention centers in Texas, Berks was "out of the spotlight, in part because of its size and distance from the border."[1] Sixty miles northwest of Philadelphia, Berks differed from the other family detention centers in that it had been in existence for much longer, was much smaller, was licensed by the state in which it was located, and was less like a prison than its Texas and New Mexico counterparts. Also, until 2015 it held relatively few occupants for longer than two or three weeks.

But Berks generated controversy twice. Criticism was first leveled at it between 1998 and 2001, when the Immigration and Naturalization Service (INS) used it only to house children, not families. Between 2001 and 2015, when the government used it only for short-term family detention, it was not much in the public eye. But in 2014 and especially after September 2015, when long-term family detention in Texas ended by court order, Berks again became a focus of legal and political controversy.

THE EARLY YEARS

The site consists of several buildings centered around a former retirement home, which the county government originally acquired to use as a detention center for local juvenile offenders and neglected and abused children. It began to house migrant children in October 1998, five years before the Homeland Security Act entrusted unaccompanied migrant children to the care of the Office of Refugee Resettlement (ORR). As noted in chapter 6, INS then began to use a renovated wing of the former retirement home to incarcerate some of the unaccompanied children in its custody. Most of the children at Berks between 1998 and 2001 were Chinese.[2] Conditions for those children quickly came under criticism.

A few months after Berks became a detention center for those migrant children, Human Rights Watch conducted an inspection of the two residential buildings in which the INS housed them through a contract with the county. The two buildings were similar in some ways. Children in both buildings were punished by having to perform exhausting pushups (as many as four hunred in a day), sometimes because they did not understand English-language orders. In neither building were the children told anything about possible legal rights or representation.

But the two buildings differed in other respects. Two-thirds of the INS detaineees lived in a building with carpeting, comfortable furniture, television, games, and two classrooms. The others were placed in the secure facility, which was surrounded by a fifteen-foot razor wire fence, to which they had been brought in handcuffs and leg irons, They had been strip-searched upon entry. In that building, the children were denied their personal possessions, and lived in cells with "concrete walls, ceiling and floor, completely bare except for bedding and a Bible."[3] They "were not allowed to laugh, often told not to talk, and were even required to ask staff for permission to scratch their nose."[4] They had to use toilet stalls with no doors, and the staff supervised their showers. The placement of children in the secure building, as opposed to the carpeted building, appeared, at least to Human Rights Watch, to be arbitrary.

In March 2001, the INS converted Berks into its first family detention center, where "as many as 40 mothers, fathers and children from Albania to Yugoslavia" could "stay together while their claims for asylum are processed."[5] The INS did a lot to make the living conditions humane. The facility had couches, a pool table, televisions, and toys. Children over the age of seven had daily lessons. The adults had "life skills classes, where they learn everything from basic American hygiene to opening a checking account." Nevertheless, the Berks detainees were anything but comfortable. "I need to leave, and we cannot leave," said a Rwandan father who was awaiting his immigration court hearing. Because of his political activism, he had been beaten four times in his home country and had survived the killing of all but three members of his family. "There is always someone watching me. I am still in prison, and I'm not sure why."[6] Life in detention was regimented, with chores, meals at set times, no seconds without permission, phone calls costing $2 per minute, and bed checks at night every fifteen minutes.[7]

After it toured Hutto, the Women's Refugee Commission visited Berks in 2007. By this time, the facility's detainees were mostly Latin Americans who had been apprehended near the border, but the facility had asylum-seekers from several other continents. The Commission found that although many of the children were depressed, a condition exacerbated by threats of separation from their parents if they disobeyed the rules, conditions were far better than at Hutto.[8] The better conditions, and the relatively short periods of detention for the few families confined there—only about seventeen in April 2014[9]—kept Berks from being a focus of protest.

BRIDGET CAMBRIA AND CAROL ANNE DONOHOE

Everything changed when President Obama decided, in June 2014, to detain asylum-seeking migrant families indefinitely, to the extent possible, in response to the perceived "surge" of asylum-seekers from the Northern

Carol Ann Donohoe and Bridget Cambria.

Triangle. At about the same time that Artesia opened, Immigration and Customs Enforcement (ICE) filled Berks with families. Bridget Cambria, an immigration lawyer in Reading, Pennsylvania, not far from Berks, received a call from a former colleague in Boston, who had been asked to represent a woman being detained at Berks. She went to the facility and discovered that it was at capacity, which by then had grown to about ninety beds. Fathers, mothers, and children all needed lawyers. Seeing a greater need for representation than she and her partner Jacquelyn Kline could handle, Cambria called her friend Carol Anne Donohoe, who also had an immigration practice in Reading. The lawyers discovered that most of the parents had already passed credible fear interviews, suggesting that their cases might well be meritorious. "We didn't want them to go unrepresented," Donohoe later said. "So pretty much from that day on we were the ones who represented them. There were [a few other] attorneys here and there, but that became our lives."[10]

Both women had arrived at that point in their professional lives through unusual routes. Cambria had gone to Albright College in Reading, with a major in criminology and a minor in psychology. She took a job as a counselor at Berks in 2002 or 2003, expecting to use the skills she had been taught. But the job wasn't what she'd imagined: She spent her time counting residents and standing guard while they showered or went to class. "A counselor counsels," she said. "A guard guards. I was guarding."[11]

In the course of her employment at Berks, she saw

> dozens of kids who were amazing, and there was absolutely no reason for them to be treated like prisoners, which is what they were. They lined up every day, they were counted, there were no legal services [and] they absolutely had no idea why they were there or how long they were going to be there [and] very little access to communication with family. Half of my coworkers were there to help children, and the other half thought 'we're correctional officers and my job is to make these kids' lives a living hell. . . . ' They saw them as animals. . . . I saw kids get restrained all the time in the immigration unit. If they didn't like a child they would provoke them so that they could take them to the ground [and then send them to a] clank, clank jail cell. I never saw lawyers. There were kids . . . who were there for three years. . . . I also had a lot of trouble in the facility [because I gave the children the phone numbers of lawyers or agencies that might help them] so I would get ratted on by other co-workers.[12]

So Cambria eventually decided to resign and to go back to school. The children asked her to become a lawyer so that she could help them with their cases.[13] In her exit interview, "my boss told me not to become one of those assholes that helps these kids. You don't swear in an exit interview and I thought it was strange for my boss to do that."[14] Rejecting the boss's advice, Cambria went to law school. She returned to Reading as an immigration lawyer.

Carol Ann Donohoe had planned to be an environmental scientist and had obtained a master's degree in that field. But after a divorce, she found herself living with two small children in rural Pennsylvania, where there wasn't much environmental science work to be done. She took a job teaching at the juvenile detention center, where some of her students were undocumented children. "I would actually get to know the immigrant kids

better than the [juvenile offenders] from Reading" because they would be
detained for longer times. And then one day

> This one kid came in, and I was doing an intake and [he didn't know where
> he was]. He said 'the only thing I know is yesterday I was in court with my
> family in Oregon or Utah, one of those places, and now I'm here.' [And I real-
> ized] this teenage kid has no idea where 'here' means. And I started walking
> back to my desk and I said in my head, 'I've got to go to law school.' And at the
> age of forty-six I went to law school. That triggered me to go . . . and when I
> graduated in 2010 I opened a [solo immigration] practice here.[15]

Donohoe's immigration practice did not involve Berks. In fact, for about
three years, she never set foot in the facility, until she took a tour there in
April 2014 and saw that only about seventeen people were housed there.
She did not realize, of course, that she was witnessing the end of an era,
and that within months, she would hear from Cambria, return to Berks,
and see that it was almost overflowing with families needing legal assistance. A year later, along with Cambria and Kline, she would be awarded
the Pennsylvania Bar's 2015 Pro Bono Award for representing more than
two hundred asylum-seeking families who had been detained in Berks.[16]

THE LICENSING BATTLE
IN PENNSYLVANIA: 2015-2018

Although many of the accompanied migrant children arrived at the border with their mothers, some came with fathers. Artesia, Karnes, and
Dilley were equipped only to incarcerate women and children, but since
2001, Berks had always had both mothers and fathers as detainees. For
nearly a year, Cambria and Donohoe simply represented as many of the
parents and children as they could, in individual cases in which their clients sought release on bond or other relief. But by the spring of 2015,
when ICE began negotiations with the county to renovate Berks in order
to double its capacity,[17] they began to think about whether systematic
pressure on the institution could result in ending family detention there.

First they encouraged Human Rights First to request a visit to the facility. After several visits between June and August, and interviews with
twenty-three families who had been detained there for periods ranging

from a few weeks to more than a year, the organization issued its report.[18] It acknowledged that Berks had a "less severe appearance" than Karnes or Dilley and that "the scenic landscape and availability of limited activities for children might be positive." But it reported, consistent with the prior conclusions of Dr. Zayas and others, that the very fact of incarceration, particularly long-term detention, was harmful to the mental health of children, and it observed that the recently released children exhibited symptoms of depression, behavioral regression, and anxiety. A prominent pediatrician who visited Berks with Human Rights First "observed significant stress and symptoms of mental health conditions in the group [of former detainees] with whom we met."[19]

In addition, although the families interviewed by the Human Rights First delegation did not have many complaints about the physical medical care, the mental health services appeared inadequate. The pediatrician on the delegation noted that Berks lacked "any formal, evidence-based validated tools for screening or monitoring children and families, raising serious concerns about the care that detained families with compounded histories of trauma receive." Human Rights First also reported that the facility lacked Spanish-speaking mental health staff, though most of the detainees were Spanish-speaking.[20] In addition, the staff's practice of entering each room every fifteen minutes at night and shining a flashlight on each person, which Berks personnel said was required by Pennsylvania law, caused some of the children to become afraid of the staff and to suffer recurring nightmares.[21]

In a later investigation. Human Rights First obtained the written complaints that mothers (all of them asylum-seekers) had made about their children's health, and the responses of ICE personnel at Berks. It found that parents who expressed concerns about their children's medical problems were advised by ICE personnel to waive their rights and agree to deportation. For example, one mother wrote:

> My daughter has been having diarrhea for about three weeks now but they did not give us any medication, not even serum. With every passing day her behavior is getting worse and the psychologist just tells me to be patient. I need you to give me adequate medication and that you give me the opportunity to take my case outside of here. I am not a criminal. You gave the opportunity to other persons that have been deported to leave, why did you not give it to me. It has been more than four months that I have been detained.

ICE responded: "Thank you! You may dissolve [sic] your case at any time and return to your country. Please use the medical department in reference to health related issues."[22]

As was the case for Karnes and Dilley, an attack on the detention of children at Berks would depend on the application of the Flores settlement,[23] which provided that children[24] could not be held in immigration detention for more than five days unless placed in a licensed program, and it defined a licensed program as one "that is licensed by an appropriate State agency to provide residential, group, or foster care services for dependent children." The settlement agreement also specified that all facilities operated by licensed programs "shall be non-secure as required under state law."[25] From long before it was a family immigration detention center, Berks had been licensed by Pennsylvania for the care of dependent children. Therefore, a challenge to the incarceration of children at Berks would have to be based on one of three premises: (a) that the existing license did not permit the detention of adults as well as children, (b) that Pennsylvania should revoke (or fail to renew) the Berks license because of conditions at the facility, or (c) that even if Berks was appropriately licensed and the license continued in effect, children could not be detained in Department of Homeland Security (DHS) custody there because the facility was in fact "secure."

The first move in what became an epic licensing battle consisted of a letter to Governor Tom Wolf and to the director of the licensing agency, the Department of Public Welfare, from a New York immigration attorney, Bryan Johnson (the same Bryan Johnson who later became a consultant to Peter Schey and was punished by Judge Dolly Gee for leaking information about settlement negotiations).[26] Johnson argued that Berks was a secure facility, as described by Pennsylvania law; that is, one "from which voluntary egress is prohibited,"[27] and that state law prohibited the placement of children younger than ten in such facilities. In addition, children under ten could not be detained even in non-secure shelter care unless they were dependent or delinquent, and none of the migrant children in Berks who were under ten, some of whom were babies, had been determined to be dependent or delinquent. Johnson therefore asked for Berks' license to be revoked.[28] On the same day, a Philadelphia lawyer sent a similar letter to Pennsylvania's attorney general, on behalf of Cambria and

Donohoe, in which they asked not only for revocation of the license but also for an investigation into whether charges of false imprisonment should be brought against Berks officials.[29]

The Deputy Secretary of the Department of Public Welfare, Jay Bausch, replied that Berks "was in substantial compliance with regulatory requirements and met all conditions for licensing" and that it was "not operating as a secure care facility and has no locks preventing resident children or their families from gaining egress."[30] Johnson wrote back, saying that "there are numerous locks, in addition to guards, preventing children and families from leaving." He also pointed out that the facility's website stated that it was governed by ICE's Family Residential Standards, which provided that detainees could not be released without permission from ICE and authorized physical force, including the use of steel batons, to prevent children or families from escaping.[31]

Bausch did not reply to this letter, but Johnson wrote a third letter, concentrating on his original argument that the state had no authority to license a facility for detaining children who were neither dependent nor delinquent. He argued that "even assuming that [Berks] somehow stripped all locks from every door," the licensing would still be unlawful because state legislation authorized the detention of only three classes of children: children who had been adjudicated to be delinquent, those alleged to be delinquent, and those who had been declared dependent— but the migrant children in Berks fit none of those descriptions. He again called for the license to be revoked.[32] Governor Wolf's chief counsel replied summarily to Johnson that the Department of Public Welfare had inspected the facility and found "no evidence" that it was "non-compliant with state licensing requirements." She did not address any of Johnson's legal arguments.[33]

Nevertheless, problems at Berks were becoming an embarrassment to the state. A few months earlier, Daniel Sharkey, a Berks guard, had been charged with having sex with a nineteen-year-old Honduran woman who had been detained with her three-year-old son.[34] He had offered help with her immigration case in exchange for her supposed "consent." Sharkey's offense was discovered because he and the woman were observed by a seven-year-old girl who had been sexually abused in her own country. When the girl exhibited signs of new trauma, her mother took her to the

Berks psychologist, who eventually persuaded the girl to draw a picture of what she had seen.[35] (Sharkey later pleaded guilty and was given a sentence of six to twenty-three months plus three years of probation; he had to register as a sex offender for fifteen years).[36]

Three days before the governor's chief counsel had written Johnson her "no evidence" letter, the *Guardian* published its own study of conditions at Berks, based on interviews with former detainees. In addition to the charge against Sharkey, the Guardian described a three-year-old girl who was vomiting blood and was advised by Berks medical staff to "drink more water," a mother with children as young as three restricted overnight to something like solitary confinement, and ten children at the facility who had mental illnesses. It quoted Cambria, who noted that some of the children had been detained at Berks for more than a year.[37]

In July, the American Immigration Lawyers Association issued a press release documenting ten cases of medical neglect of detainees in the ICE family facilities. Two of them concerned children at Berks. One was "Iliana," who was detained for nine months and suffered from severe headaches and blackouts. ICE refused to release her from the facility on parole even when a doctor determined that she was legally blind as a result of glaucoma. Finally, after several months, she was diagnosed with Chiari malformation, a condition in which the brain tissue is not fully covered. She was released when she had additional dental issues, requiring the removal of five teeth. The other Berks detainee was "Maria," who fell unconscious on a bathroom floor and was told to drink water rather than being sent for tests. Her daughter, "Flor," was probably the girl described briefly in the Guardian article. She vomited blood for three days but was never sent for testing or treatment. She wasn't able to eat, and when her mother requested yogurt for her, she was told that she needed a prescription for special food. A Berks doctor said that she did not need the medication that her outside doctor had prescribed. Maria and Flor were released after Maria's lawyer called an outside doctor who telephoned the state child abuse hotline, after they had been detained for eleven months.[38] The stories of these two families were reported the next day in the *Philadelphia Inquirer*.[39]

ICE exacerbated these problems the following month, immediately after Judge Gee ruled that ICE would no longer be able to detain children for more than twenty days at Karnes or Dilley. At that point, "ICE began transferring families from the Texas family detention facilities" to Berks after they had been in Texas for twenty days, in order to keep them in "prolonged detention," because Berks had a state license.[40] Even more Texas families were transferred immediately after October 23, 2015, when Judge Gee's order took final effect. Cambria's clients came to include Steven A., age six, who suffered from *Molluscum contagiosum*, a contagious skin conditions that caused itching rashes all over his body. When his mother asked for medical help, ICE advised her to withdraw her immigration claims and accept deportation to El Salvador. Steven occasionally simulated self-asphyxiation. Several others had medical or mental health problems, such as six-year-old Jefferson A., who had extremely low body weight as a result of malnutrition and who exhibited defiance, outbursts, and aggression.[41]

Unlike Karnes and Dilley, Berks had always housed some fathers as well as mothers. The event that Donohoe thinks finally got the attention of the Pennsylvania authorities[42] was her complaint on October 16, 2015, that an eight-year-old girl at Berks was made to sleep in a room with unrelated teenage and adult males and that "detainees use a shared bathroom with no door, only a short curtain."[43] A few days later, Donohoe and Cambria's law partner Kline were at last able to get a personal meeting with Ted Dallas, Pennsylvania's Secretary of Human Services. They explained that refugees were being kept in long-term detention, and that the facility was secure, in violation of the Flores settlement and Pennsylvania law. They showed him a picture of the shirt onto which their three-year-old client had vomited blood and a picture of a baby who had been incarcerated in Berks at the age of eleven days. They argued that an agency within his department had no authority to license a facility that incarcerated children who were neither dependent nor delinquent. And they pointed out that ICE was using Pennsylvania's license as precedent for trying to license family detention centers in Texas.[44]

The next day,[45] Dallas informed Berks that it was not operating in compliance with its license to provide residential treatment for court-adjudicated children and that if it continued to "provide services to families rather than children" the state "does not intend to renew [the license] when it expires on Feb. 21, 2016."[46] (Two weeks later, the Department did issue a license, but this turned out to be a clerical error, and the Department rescinded it eight days later).[47] After Berks affirmed that it intended to continue to serve as a family detention center, the state followed through with its threat and notified the county that it was not renewing the license. Simultaneously, it denied a pending request from the county to double the number of beds in the facility.[48]

But as in Texas, this first round was just the beginning. Perhaps because approximately fifty county employees worked at Berks,[49] the county appealed to the Bureau of Hearings and Appeals, a unit within the Department of Human Services with the authority to review licensing denials by other components of the Department. The appeal was assigned to an administrative law judge, David A. Dudley. Cambria and Donohoe filed a petition to intervene on behalf of the children so that they could file additional evidence, but Judge Dudley rejected it on the ground that the Department of Human Services adequately represented the interests of the incarcerated children. The advocates appealed to state court, but the Department of Human Services advised them that the case would move faster if they withdrew that appeal, and they reluctantly acquiesced (though, as it turned out, the case would drag on for years anyway).

The Department and the county filed briefs, and an oral hearing was held "in the basement of a building," with a "folding table, folding chairs."[50] Because Donohoe had withdrawn her petition to intervene, Cambria and Donohoe could only observe. The county argued that "the Department's decision was based on outside pressures on the Department, and not on any statutory violations" by Berks, and that because the state had known for years that Berks was housing family detainees of DHS, it was too late to revoke its license on that basis.[51]

While the county's appeal was pending, its lawyers went to state court, seeking to enjoin the Department from stopping the facility from operating while the appeal was pending. The state and the county agreed on an interim freeze: Berks could continue to operate without a new license, but it could not expand its capacity. Because Judge Dudley had rejected the children's petition to intervene in the case, Cambria and Donohoe could not object to the agreement.

Six months after the hearing, Judge Dudley ruled in favor of the county. Berks "housed family units from the initial day it was licensed," he wrote, and it reasonably relied on annual licensing over a fifteen year period to renovate and expand the facility. Therefore "the Department is estopped from revoking" its license. In addition, although the Department also argued that Berks was not really a child residential facility and was therefore not eligible for a license, Judge Dudley opined that its argument was unconvincing because "the Department cannot revoke something which it has no authority to grant in the first place."[52]

Donohoe was livid. "[That's like saying] 'okay, we found a meth lab in your basement, we never had a problem with the meth lab before' so we can't close you down now," she reflected.[53]

The Department of Human Services asked Judge Dudley to reconsider his decision. The Bureau of Hearings and Appeals agreed to reconsider, but before anything else happened, Secretary Dallas asked his deputy, Cathy Utz, to decide the matter.[54] Months later (two years after the Department had notified Berks that it was not renewing the license), Utz canceled Dudley's order on the ground that he had not addressed the evidence or some of the arguments made by the Department, or even determined whether Berks was eligible for any kind of license from the Department. She ordered a new hearing in the case.[55]

Meanwhile, Cambria and Donohoe had formed a new nonprofit organization, Aldea, to advocate for the interests of families detained at Berks.[56] With the help of Elizabeth Simpson and David Bennion of the National Immigration Project, they made a second effort to intervene in the case, this time on behalf of Aldea. They put their petition in a binder, along with about three hundred pages of evidentiary exhibits, and Fedexed it to the Bureau of Hearings and Appeals. Bureau officials claimed not to have received it, so in an abundance of caution the attorneys Fedexed another copy and called to make sure that this second copy had arrived. The lawyers had a Fedex receipt showing that it had been signed for, but in a phone call, a Bureau employee at first claimed that this second copy had never arrived. When Donohoe pointed out that they had a signed Fedex receipt for their submission, the clerk finally said, "oh, you mean the binder, oh yeah, we got that." But Judge Dudley denied the petition to intervene, claiming that the second copy that the Bureau admitted receiving had arrived after the deadline for submissions. The children's lawyers appealed that denial to state court, and this time, they did not intend to withdraw their appeal.

What is at stake in this long licensing battle? First, if Berks ultimately loses its license, perhaps the state could bar the county from allowing children to be confined in the facility. But even that isn't certain. The county might argue that its contract with ICE is sufficient to permit it to detain migrant children there, and that Pennsylvania can't interfere with a federal contract, or that while a state license is needed for anyone who wants to house delinquent or neglected children, no state law requires such a license for housing family units. Judge Dudley raised this possibility at the end of his decision, writing that "It is unclear in the hearing record . . . whether [Berks] is a facility for which licensure is required."[57] In 2016, the Sheller Center for Social Justice at Temple University's School of Law wrote an opinion noting that "although there is no express statutory grant of authority to [the Department of Human Services] to issue a cease-and-desist order," it "implicitly has the authority to ensure the safety of all children in child care facilities . . . by requiring that they be licensed [and closing them down if they lack one]."[58] It cited a decision by a Pennsylvania trial court allowing the Department to order a church to cease operating a preschool without a license.[59]

But a later court might distinguish the Berks situation by the fact that the county was merely leasing the facility to a federal agency, or by the fact that the church in the precedent case was operating a program that was only for otherwise-unsupervised children, while at Berks, adult family members were largely responsible for their children. Furthermore, depending on what administration is in power in Harrisburg at the time that the licensing issue is eventually resolved, the state government might choose not to try to shut down the facility even if it lacked a license. In fact, Governor Tom Wolf's administration said that "regardless of any action on the part of the state, the federal government continues to operate the facility because the center is run by Berks County in a direct contract with the federal government."[60]

More important, the licensing battle is significant because Judge Gee's 2015 order makes it clear that the Flores settlement prohibits keeping children for long terms in unlicensed facilities, and ICE has abided by that decision in Karnes and Dilley, though an appellate court decision in Texas may eventually enable that state to license those facilities.[61] So if the license is ultimately denied to Berks, ICE might give up on keeping children there for longer than the Flores agreement permits.

On the other hand, the licensing question is unimportant for Flores purposes if a jail for migrant families is a "secure" facility. With limited exceptions, such as those for children who present a public danger, the Flores settlement bars holding children for more than twenty days except in a "non-secure" facility even if it is licensed. ICE continues to detain children for longer than twenty days in Berks, apparently claiming that it is non-secure as well as being licensed. Therefore, the question of whether Berks is in fact "secure" or "non-secure" is of equal importance.

Furthermore, a decision that Berks is "non-secure" as ICE claims may set a precedent for Karnes and Dilley—if the Texas courts allow that state's agency to license them—and for any new family jails that the federal government builds in a state that grant licenses for similar facilities. At present, Karnes and Dilley are clearly "secure." For example, they have high cement walls, nighttime illumination of the entire area, internal locks, and prohibitions on children leaving their rooms at night. In addition, they have double-gated sally ports so that escapes are not possible when vehicles enter or exit, and when a truck is too long to fit between the two gates, an guard armed with a shotgun is posted at the outer gate.[62] But if Texas licenses that facility and ICE sought to comply with Flores, those security features could be altered. Suppose, for example, the outer walls were removed and the front door was unlocked, but an armed guard stood outside the jail ready to arrest any child who tried to leave. Or suppose the guard did not stand outside the door, but any child who escaped and was apprehended was then deemed a flight risk and moved to a truly secure facility?

That issue is complicated. The Flores settlement did not define a non-secure facility. It stated that all facilities operated by licensed programs "shall be non-secure as required under state law," apparently leaving it to state law to describe what "non-secure" means.[63] Pennsylvania law defined "secure care" for "delinquent and alleged delinquent" children as a setting from which voluntary egress is prohibited through one of the following mechanisms:

(i) Egress from the building, or a portion of the building, is prohibited through internal locks within the building or exterior locks.

(ii) Egress from the premises is prohibited through secure fencing around the perimeter of the building.[64]

That definition doesn't purport to apply to children who have not been alleged to be delinquent. In addition, for years, there has been disagreement about even the most basic fact: whether the children at Berks are physically locked in. Bryan Johnson's first letter claimed that the facility was "locked," and plaintiffs' attorney Jacquelyn Kline stated at a Berks County Commissioners Meeting that "when I go there, I've personally had to be let out of the facility."[65] But this fact is disputed by the ICE and by the County Commissioners.[66] The children's advocates have also argued that regardless of the lock issue, the facility is "secure" because children are not free to leave; they may be restrained if they try to leave; they will be hunted down if they "escape"; and they are subjected by guards to round-the-clock observation and regimentation.[67]

They also point out that the building is surrounded by signs saying "No Trespassing Secure Property" (although those signs could mean only that visitors are not permitted without permission), and that while arguing the Flores enforcement case before Judge Gee, DHS's attorney Leon Fresco had stated that "there is no dispute that Berks has been operating since 2001 as a secure family residential facility."[68] But ICE continues to maintain that Berks is not secure.[69]

If a licensed facility can be deemed "non-secure" by leaving its front door unlocked and arresting any child who leaves, all three baby jails eventually may be able to incarcerate children for years without violating the Flores agreement. Who could definitively determine whether Berks (or a newly licensed and remodeled Karnes or Dilley) is "secure" or "non-secure"? Judge Gee, if Schey were then to ask her to enforce the Flores agreement.

While Donohoe and Cambria were trying to prevent Berks from holding children in long-term detention by attacking its license, a new problem emerged. Some families in expedited removal proceedings in Texas had been found to lack credible fear and sent to Berks so that they could be held there for as long as necessary until ICE could arrange the necessary documents and transportation to deport them, rather than releasing them per Judge Gee's order. Some of them claimed that their credible fear interviews had been conducted in a rush during a period of unusual understaffing in the asylum office, resulting in inaccurate rejections of their claims. The transfers of these families to Pennsylvania resulted in the Castro case.

THE CASTRO CASE: 2016–2018

In the first week of October 2015, after Judge Gee decided that families could not be detained for more than twenty days but shortly before her order became effective, something changed at Berks. ICE began releasing the families after only about two weeks, rather than after long periods of detention.[70] The reason for this sudden change in policy, according to Donohoe and Cambria, was apparently to make room for certain families nearing their twenty-day limit at Karnes and Dilley—families that had received final orders of deportation, but who couldn't be deported immediately (e.g., because no aircraft was available, or because travel documents had to be obtained). ICE "had to get rid of them," Cambria recalled.[71] ICE believed that it could transfer them from Texas to the licensed Berks facility and keep them there for as long as necessary until deportation could be effected.

According to Donohoe, many of the families were transferred from Texas to Pennsylvania "in the middle of the night" without being told where they were going. "Some were falsely told that they were going to be reunited with their families." Several children were ill; one was rushed to the hospital upon arrival in Pennsylvania. Donohoe reported that over the next few weeks, "nearly every young child I interviewed at the Berks facility had a fever or a throat infection. In addition, there was a chicken pox outbreak."[72]

Donohoe and Cambria looked into the cases of these families and discovered that they had received credible fear interviews "at a time where even the asylum office itself admitted that their interviews were poorly done."[73] In one such case, Donohoe recalled, the asylum officer had asked a woman who had only two years of schooling a question as vague as "have you ever had any problems or conversations with anyone at any time?" and then wrote down that the answer was "no."[74] Because these families had failed credible fear interviews, they had never had the chance to present their claims for asylum in full hearings before immigration judges, and they had never had any kind of judicial review in a regular federal court.

For a while, Donahoe and Cambria worked night and day to prevent deportations. They reviewed every detainee's file and in many cases found procedural or other errors that government officials had made. They filed petitions and appeals to try to reverse the deportation orders and obtain new asylum officer interviews. "We were up every night trying to stop deportations," Donohoe recalled. We were "literally stopping deportations as people were getting on the plane, and turning around the vans," Cambria added.[75]

Unable to persuade the government to reopen many of these cases, and aware that the families could be deported at any time, the lawyers asked the ACLU to partner with them in emergency federal litigation to try to force some kind of review of the adequacy of their initial credible fear interviews. The ACLU eventually filed federal habeas corpus cases for thirty-five families, which were consolidated into a single lawsuit that became known as the Castro litigation. Donohoe, Cambria, and Kline worked with the parents to compile declarations describing their cases, which the ACLU then filed in the court proceedings.[76]

The ancient writ of habeas corpus, which predates even the Magna Carta, has been given a modern form and limited by statute, but it remains deeply enshrined in American law. Under certain circumstances, the writ authorizes persons who are detained or imprisoned to seek a judicial inquiry as to the legality of the process through which they came to be held in custody. For example, criminal defendants who have exhausted their appeals in state court are entitled to use habeas corpus to seek federal court review of alleged violations, during the state court proceedings, of their federal constitutional rights. The Supreme Court has also ruled that detainees incarcerated at Guantanamo Bay can challenge the legality of their detentions by using the writ to obtain federal court review.[77]

Marta Rodriguez,[78] a Salvadoran, was one of the habeas corpus petitioners, along with her two young daughters. She had a fourth grade education. In her home town, she had gone to the wake of a family friend.

Suddenly, three male members of the Mara 18 gang opened fire, shooting at several other male attendees. She was close to the shooters. She knew one of them by name and saw the faces of the others. She was also present at the scene of the crime when the police arrived, though she did not tell them who did the shooting. She knew that neighbors had been killed for reporting criminals to the police, and her own brother had been killed by gang violence. Two days later, a gang member came to her home and said that the gang would kill her if she reported the shooters to anyone. She fled to the United States with her daughters and sought asylum. She was given a credible fear interview while incarcerated in Texas. She explained in her habeas corpus petition that the interview was flawed. She and the interpreter had trouble understanding each other. The asylum officer told her to keep her answers short to aid in communication, which made her nervous and confused. The asylum officer kept asking her whether the gang member who delivered the threat called her by name, but he never asked her where the threat took place; had he done so, he would have realized that it occurred at her own house, showing that the gang member had already identified her. If a lawyer had been present with her in the interview, the lawyer could have requested follow-up questions to make the story clear. The asylum officer determined that she lacked credible fear, and she was sent to Berks to await deportation.

Delma Cruz, also a Salvadoran national, was in her mid-twenties when she fled to the United States with her six-year-old son. She had moved in with a man when she was nineteen, but while they lived together he often raped her violently, as well as punching her. Once, he had pushed her into a wall so hard that she suffered a concussion. On another occasion he knocked her to the floor while she was seven months pregnant. He told her the she belonged to him and would not let her leave the house. She finally left him, but he went to the house where she was living, locked her in a room, and raped her. Shortly after that, gang members came to her house and demanded money. They held her at knifepoint on one occasion and threatened to kill her and her son if she did not pay. After fleeing to the United States and seeking asylum, she was taken into custody and interviewed by a male asylum officer in a small room. She was not able to consult with a lawyer before the interview. According to her petition, she was afraid to tell this man, who asked "rapid fire questions," about the

sexual violence to which she had been subjected. At the end of the interview, the asylum officer called in her son and asked who he was afraid of.
Her son said, "you." The asylum officer decided that she was telling the
truth but denied her a finding of credible fear. In violation of the statutory
requirement[79] that officers provide written analyses of their denials, he
did not provide any reasoning. Like Rodriguez and the thirty-three other
petitioners, Cruz was transferred to Berks to be deported.[80]

The fundamental problem in the Castro litigation was that in 1996,
when Congress created the expedited removal process, it had also severely
limited both legal representation and judicial review in cases initiated by
the government through that process. Lawyers were not permitted to represent clients in credible fear interviews. If an asylum officer determined
after the interview that the asylum-seeker did not have credible fear, the
asylum applicant could appeal a day or two later to an immigration judge,
but no lawyer was allowed to represent a client in that appeal either. If the
immigration judge affirmed the asylum officer, the asylum-seeker would
be deported, never having had any review by a member of the judicial
branch of government. Congress had emphatically provided that "no court
may enter declaratory, injunctive or other equitable relief in any action
pertaining to an order to exclude an alien in accordance with [the expedited removal procedure.]"[81] It had created exceptions only to allow
habeas corpus petitions for persons who claimed to be citizens or permanent residents, or who could prove that they had previously been granted
refugee status.[82] This seemed to bar judicial review of the adequacy of the
credible fear interviews that DHS had provided to Rodriguez, Cruz, and
the others who had been sent to Berks to await deportation.

The case was assigned to Judge Paul S. Diamond. The judge had been
a Philadelphia prosecutor for six years and had then spent nearly twenty
years in corporate law firms before being appointed to the federal bench
by President George W. Bush.[83] In his Senate confirmation hearings, he
indicated that he would be extremely reluctant to declare an act of
Congress unconstitutional: "It seems to me," he said, "that a statute comes
to the court with an overwhelming presumption of constitutionality and
courts should strike down acts of the legislature only in the rarest circumstance when something is palpably, obviously in violation of the
Constitution, and that should be very rare indeed."[84]

Recognizing that the language of the 1996 law seemed to prevent the court from exercising what normally would be its jurisdiction in habeas corpus cases, the ACLU's main argument[85] was that the jurisdiction-stripping statute violated the "Suspension Clause" of the Constitution, which provides that "The Privilege of the Writ of Habeas Corpus shall not be suspended, unless when in Cases of Rebellion or Invasion that public Safety may require it."[86] The ACLU argued that if alleged foreign terrorists seized abroad and brought to Guantanamo Bay had habeas corpus rights, people apprehended on U.S. soil, or who had sought asylum at an official entry point and been brought to a U.S. detention center, should also have such rights.[87]

In his decision, Judge Diamond acknowledged that "absent judicial review, the chance of mistake and unfairness increases," but he decided that Congress had prohibited him from reviewing the fairness of credible fear interviews and that its jurisdiction-stripping law did not violate the Suspension Clause. He distinguished the Guantanamo detainees by noting that their detentions could "last a generation or more," whereas an asylum-seeker's detention "is necessarily brief" because she and her children would soon be deported. He acknowledged that "those fleeing persecution or torture have a substantial interest in the rigor and fairness of the process," but he decided that the government had an even stronger interest in its "need for expedition" and its "need to deter foreign nationals from undertaking dangerous border crossings." He therefore dismissed the case.[88]

The ACLU appealed to the Court of Appeals for the Third Circuit, which encompassed Pennsylvania, and the case was assigned to a panel presided over by Judge David Brooks Smith. Like Judge Diamond, Smith had begun his career as a Pennsylvania prosecutor and had served for a year as the District Attorney of Blair County. Then he had served for four years as a state court judge before being appointed to the federal bench by President Ronald Reagan in 1988.[89] The other members of the panel were Patty Shwartz, who had been appointed by President Barack Obama, and Thomas Hardiman, appointed by President George W. Bush.

Judge Smith wrote the court's opinion. Like Judge Diamond, he noted that the expedited removal procedure "is fraught with risk of arbitrary, mistaken, or discriminatory behavior," but this was no justification for disregarding the jurisdictional limitation that Congress had imposed on the courts. Furthermore, he agreed with Judge Diamond that the law that prevented the court from considering the cases of the asylum-seekers did not violate the Suspension Clause. His reasoning different somewhat from Diamond's, even though he reached the same result. For Smith and the Third Circuit panel, the key fact was not the brevity of the period during which the asylum-seekers would remain detained, but the brevity of their presence on American soil before being apprehended. Smith quoted a side comment made by Supreme Court in 1982[90] to the effect that a foreign national "seeking initial admission to the United States [at its border] requests a privilege and has no constitutional rights regarding his application." The Castro petitioners "were each apprehended within hours or surreptitiously entering the United States," Smith wrote, so we think it appropriate to treat them as 'aliens seeking admission.'" Therefore, they cannot claim constitutional rights under the Suspension Clause.[91]

Judge Hardiman agreed with the result but not the reasoning. He did not think that the Supreme Court's language quoted by the court was controlling, because that case did not deal with habeas corpus rights and the Court's language was merely dicta. But he distinguished the Guantanamo detainees because they faced indefinite detention, while the detainees in Berks were trying to avoid the release from detention that would be an incident of deportation.[92]

The ACLU sought review in the Supreme Court, but the Court declined to consider the case.[93] Nevertheless, Cambria and Donohoe did not give up. While the federal court litigation chugged along, they successfully filed petitions in the Berks County Court for declarations that the children who had been petitioners in the Castro case "could not be reunified with their fathers due to abuse, neglect or abandonment, and that it would not be in the child's best interest to be returned to his or her country of origin." This finding enabled the lawyers to file petitions to DHS to grant them status as "Special Immigrant Juveniles." As such, they could apply for green cards—that is, status as permanent residents.[94] But there was a more-than-two-year wait for the green cards, because Congress had set a limit on the number that were available in any given year. During those years, the government had kept the children and their parents detained in Berks.

THE LAWYERS PERSEVERE

Sixty minutes after the Supreme Court declined to review the Third Circuit's decision in the Castro case, lawyers recruited by Cambria and Donohoe filed a class action seeking habeas corpus relief for children who had been found by the county court judges to have been abused, neglected, or abandoned by their fathers and who had pending petitions for special immigrant juvenile status . . . and for their mothers as well. The case was assigned randomly to Judge Lawrence Stengel, who, like Judge Diamond, had been appointed by President George W. Bush. Judge Stengel granted the mothers a temporary restraining order, barring the government from deporting the families or transferring them to detention centers outside of Pennsylvania.

Of course the federal government's lawyers saw this as a circumvention of the Castro decision, and they expected that Judge Diamond would agree with them that his earlier ruling should not be subverted. They asked the court to transfer the case to Judge Diamond, on the ground that it was related to the Castro case that he had decided as well as to another individual habeas case that had been originally filed with another judge and transferred to Judge Diamond.[95] Judge Stengel transferred the case, and within two weeks, Judge Diamond dissolved Judge Stengel's restraining order, leaving the government free to deport the families. He wrote he was denying their request for relief "as an effort to relitigate" Castro, and that that the plaintiffs "have no greater chance of success here than petitioner did in Castro." In fact, he wrote, there is "no chance that Plaintiffs will succeed on the merits" of their claim.[96]

Undaunted, Cambria and Donohoe, assisted by the law firm of Pepper, Hamilton, went back to the Court of Appeals for the Third Circuit. This time, a different panel was assigned to the case, and the key member, who wrote the opinion, was Judge Cheryl Krause, an appointee of President Barack Obama, who had devoted "a large part of her private practice to pro bono civil litigation and representing indigent criminal defendants."[97] Before joining the bench, she had also successfully brought a class action against the Philadelphia school system on behalf of children with autism who were being transferred without proper procedures from school to school.[98] The other members of the panel were Thomas Ambro, an appointee of President Bill Clinton, and Anthony Scirica, an appointee of President Ronald Reagan.

Judge Krause wrote the court's opinion in this case, known as *Osorio-Martinez*, which reversed Judge Diamond's denial of an injunction. She held that Congress's denial of federal court jurisdiction to hear the claims of these children was an unconstitutional suspension of the writ of habeas corpus. She distinguished the Castro case, saying that these children "have satisfied rigorous eligibility criteria" for special immigrant visa status, "denoting them as wards of the state." They therefore stood "much closer to lawful permanent residents than to aliens present in the United States for a few hours before their apprehension." They were, she wrote "a hair's breadth" from being able to become lawful permanent residents "pending only the availability of immigrant visas." Their visas were imminent, given the fact that the waiting line was two years long and the children had already been waiting for nearly that length of time. The court therefore ordered Judge Diamond to consider their assertions that their credible fear interviews had been inadequate, and it restrained the government from deporting them while the case was pending.[99] In a footnote, it hinted that although only the children had a right to habeas corpus review, because of the pending visa applications, the trial court should consider releasing the mothers along with the children until the children's rights could be fully decided.[100]

Cambria and Donohoe were thrilled. The Third Circuit's decision contributed to a string of successes they'd had, working one by one with about fifty families who had been denied credible fear and who had expected to be deported from Berks. They had prevented the deportation of all but fourteen of those fifty families.

But by June, 2018, when the Third Circuit rendered its decision, the Trump administration was in the midst of a long, determined campaign to undo the Flores agreement and alter the standards for granting asylum so that it could deport asylum-seeking children and families—and most other migrants—as quickly as possible.

12 Trump

2017–2019

Donald Trump's presidential campaign loudly proclaimed his desire to restrict immigration. He began the announcement of his candidacy in 2015 by saying that Mexican immigrants are "bringing drugs. They're bringing crime. They're rapists [and] it's coming from all over South and Latin America, and it's coming probably—probably—from the Middle East." Later in the same speech, he promised that "I will build a great, great wall on our Southern border. And I will have Mexico pay for that wall."[1]

A few months later, at a campaign rally in South Carolina, he released a statement saying, "Donald J. Trump is calling for a total and complete shutdown of Muslims entering the United States until our country's representatives can figure out what the hell is going on."[2] Later, he called on Gonzalo Curiel, an Indiana-born federal judge, to recuse himself from a case involving Trump University, because Curiel's parents were Mexican and Curiel was proud of his Mexican heritage.[3]

Encouraged by remarks such as these, the Center for Immigration Studies, a nonprofit organization that favored restrictions on immigration, quietly developed proposals for "79 immigration actions the next president can take" without Congressional action to reduce the "historically high percentage of immigrants among our population, raising serious questions about assimilation and integration of migrant popula-tions." The organization recognized that "these roll-backs" were unlikely to occur "in the event a Democrat takes the White House."[4] But many of the organization's ideas were welcomed by what became the Trump administration.

THE WAR ON IMMIGRANTS BEGINS

Shortly after Trump was elected, his transition team pulled together a working group of Republican Capitol Hill staffers, such as aides to Senators Jeff Sessions and Chuck Grassley, as well as a few people from outside government, to write new policies to discourage immigration and deport undocumented immigrants. Many members of this group would be appointed to positions in the Department of Homeland Security (DHS) after Trump was inaugurated. The group came up with several ideas for discouraging the migration of families and children from Central America, including making asylum more difficult to achieve, prosecuting parents as human traffickers, and separating migrant parents from their children (an idea that the administration at first shelved).[5]

Given his campaign statements, it was not very surprising that the Trump administration opened with a volley of actions to discourage immi-gration and accelerate deportations. A week after taking office, the new president issued an executive order barring the entry of all nationals of seven majority-Muslim nations for at least ninety days. He also suspended the admission of all refugees for 120 days, cut the FY 2017 annual refugee admission quota that President Obama had established from 110,000 to 50,000, and indefinitely suspended the admission of any Syrians, not-withstanding the humanitarian crisis occasioned by the Syrian civil war raging at the time.[6] Another clause in the president's order directed the Secretary of State to prioritize refugee admissions, once they resumed, "on the basis of religious-based persecution for persons of minority religions in their countries," which was "widely described as a special provision for Christian refugees from predominantly Muslim countries."[7]

The so-called "travel ban" created chaos at the nation's airports because it was applied to people who were in flight when the President signed it.

Airport protests, press characterization of the order as a "Muslim ban," and court challenges (which were successful until the president twice modified his order to make it less restrictive) made headlines for weeks. Because of the intense focus on that issue, the public was less aware of two other immigration-related executive orders that President Trump signed at virtually the same time, and that his new Secretary of Homeland Security, John Kelly, sought to implement with directives of his own.

One of these orders repealed the Obama administration's priorities for deportation. From November 2014, until Trump upended the plan, Immigration and Customs Enforcement (ICE) had directed its officials to spend the agency's finite enforcement resources on arresting and deporting foreign nationals who had been convicted of serious crimes, who were security threats, or who were apprehended shortly after crossing the border. The new order transformed many more undocumented foreign nationals into priorities for deportation; in other words, it eliminated the hierarchy of priorities.[8] That policy change did not target children in particular, but as *TIME* showed in an article on its effects, the "surge of arrests" that followed caused some American children to be deprived of a law-abiding parent, and the fear of suddenly losing a parent put "constant, extreme levels of psychological stress" on children in millions of households.[9]

In addition, the President's order directed DHS officials to seek the deportation of any foreign national charged with "any" criminal offense "where such charge has not been resolved" and any such person who had ever committed an act that constituted a chargeable criminal offense, even if no police official had charged the commission of a crime. An ICE agent who saw a foreign national jaywalking could initiate deportation proceedings against her. The order also requested ICE to seek to hire 10,000 additional officers.[10]

The president's other order addressed "border security and immigration enforcement." It announced the policy of the executive branch to seek "the immediate construction of a physical wall on the southern border" and defined the wall to mean a "contiguous and impassable physical barrier." It directed DHS to "allocate all legally available resources to immediately construct . . . facilities to detain aliens at or near the land border with Mexico."[11]

The border security order also instructed DHS to detain undocumented aliens who are apprehended, terminating what Trump called "the practice commonly known as 'catch and release,' whereby aliens are routinely released" on bond or parole.[12] ICE already had about 40,000 people in detention at any given time; the order anticipated far more incarceration of people who had not been convicted of crimes. Within days, DHS changed its training manual for asylum officers who conducted credible fear interviews of asylum seekers, deleting the sentence that said "After a positive credible fear determination, Immigration and Customs Enforcement (ICE) may exercise discretion to parole the alien out of detention."[13] This deletion did not itself end parole for individuals who passed credible fear interviews, because the government did not yet have enough jail space to house all such people, but it presaged that in the future, passing credible fear might not be a basis for release.

The order also asked DHS to arrange for migrants who arrived without visas to be "returned to the territory from which they came" until they could have immigration court hearings. Since Central Americans almost always arrived by crossing through Mexico, this meant that they should be detained in Mexico, although that would require the cooperation of the Mexican government, perhaps in exchange for financial support from the United States. And it directed the Secretary of DHS to apply expedited removal "in his sole and unreviewable discretion" not only to undocumented persons who were apprehended near the border, but to "any such persons, wherever found."[14]

The President's executive orders did not explicitly deal with child migrants, although several of the new policies, such as the abolition of President Obama's priorities for deportation, could affect children as well as adults. But one section of Secretary Kelly's implementing memorandum anticipated a significant change directed at unaccompanied children. Kelly noted that under current practice, unaccompanied children retained that designation, and the special benefits that the Trafficking Victims Protection Reauthorization Act (TVPRA) conferred on them (such as the right to have their asylum claims adjudicated by asylum officers rather than immigration judges) even after being placed by the Office of Refugee Resettlement (ORR) with a parent in the United States who could care for the child. He directed his department to "establish standardized review procedures to confirm that alien children who are initially determined to be unaccompanied . . . continue to fall with the statutory definition."[15] In other words, the memorandum contemplated that if the unaccompanied child was placed with by ORR with a parent in the United States, DHS could deny her the procedural protections of the TVPRA. Secretary Kelly estimated that as many as 60 percent of unaccompanied migrant children could be redefined as no longer unaccompanied as a result of his memo.[16]

The three executive orders that President Trump issued immediately after taking office avoided resolving the most visible immigration issue that the end of the Obama administration had left in limbo: the fate of 800,000 undocumented migrants who had been brought by their parents to the United States when they were still children. In 2012, President Obama had created a program of Deferred Action for Childhood Arrivals (DACA), assuring them that, so long as he was President, those who registered would not be deported. But he did not have the power to bind his successor, and Trump's announcement of his candidacy for president had included a promise that if elected, "I will immediately terminate President Obama's illegal executive order on immigration, immediately." Trump didn't actually follow through on that pledge until September 2017, when he announced that he was phasing out the program over six months.[17] (The United States Court of Appeals for the Ninth Circuit later affirmed a preliminary injunction that temporarily halted the rescission of the program.[18] The Trump administration sought Supreme Court review. The Court eventually agreed to consider the issue during its 2019–2020 term.[19]

PROSECUTION OF PARENTS DURING TRUMP'S
FIRST YEAR

In 1985, undocumented relatives of unaccompanied children such as Jenny Flores were afraid to come forward to obtain the release of the children because they were afraid that they themselves would be arrested and deported. Children therefore remained in jail when they could have been housed with parents or other adult relatives and gone to school while awaiting their immigration court hearings. Peter Schey brought the Flores case to fix this problem by permitting release of migrant children to relatives other than their parents. In later years, this problem largely disappeared for unaccompanied children thanks to the Flores settlement, the

Homeland Security Act's assigning ORR to place children with relatives, and administration policies under which relatives who took in undocumented migrant children "would usually not be arrested, even if they were undocumented, unless they had committed a crime" unrelated to their immigration status.[20]

Early in 2017, following the guidance of the working group that the Trump transition team had suggested,[21] Secretary Kelly reversed that lenient policy, and his department began to arrest the parents. If a mother had paid a smuggler to bring her child over the border, the government might prosecute her for "alien smuggling," even though the alien in question was her own child. If the government could not prove that the parent had paid a smuggler, it might prosecute her for immigration-related crimes, such as the felony of having entered the United States after a previous deportation. Even when it did not prosecute parents, ICE began arresting them and detaining them for deportation. Michelle Brané of the Women's Refugee Commission denounced the practice as "punishing parents for trying to save their children's lives." DHS officials acknowledged that many of the children were fleeing violence in Central America,[22] but Secretary Kelly defended the new policy as a measure to "put human smugglers out of business" and "end the flow of illegal migration."[23] Between late June and late August 2017, more than four hundred parents and other guardians were arrested, although most were charged with immigration offenses rather than smuggling.[24]

CANCELLATION OF THE FAMILY CASE MANAGEMENT PROGRAM

One of the government's most frequent justifications for detaining families with children, in both the Bush and Obama administrations, was the claim that if released pending immigration court hearings, many of the mothers and children did not appear for those hearings. Secretary Kelly claimed that migrants "are highly likely to abscond and fail to attend their removal hearings."[25] Therefore, they had to be imprisoned until those hearings could be held. Secretary Kelly's claim was embellished by President Trump, who said that migrants who are not detained "never come back" for their hearings "or very rarely. It's the rare person who comes back."[26]

Neither of those claims was supported even by the government's own reported statistics and methods of calculation. Ingrid Eagly and Steven Shafer's analysis, using the government's numbers and methods, showed an *in absentia* order of removal rate of 34 percent for FY 2008–18.[27] But Eagly and Shafer also demonstrated that the Justice Department's calculations were flawed. First, the government had failed to consider pending cases in which a non-detained migrant had shown up in court for all preliminary rounds of adjudication, or cases in which such a migrant did appear in court and the judge closed the case without either ordering deportation or granting relief (for example, cases in which the migrant could not be deported because she had a valid, temporary right to remain in the United States). Taking those cases into account, the *in absentia* rate was only 17 percent.[28] Second, the government failed to take into account that about 14 percent of *in absentia* removal orders were later vacated and the cases reopened.[29]

The government's statistics also did not incorporate the fact that non-detained asylum seekers in general, and asylum-seeking families in particular, had very high rates of appearing in court. For asylum seekers, the rate of *in absentia* deportation orders was only 6 percent.[30] For families seeking asylum after being released from one of the family detention centers, including those who did not have counsel, it was only 4 percent.[31]

In 2016, the Obama administration had undertaken an initiative to maximize the likelihood that families who were released from detention would show up in court. It had given a contract to the GEO Group (ironically, one of the nation's leading owners and managers of private prisons, including Karnes) to operate a "family case management program," through which asylum-seeking families released from the family detention centers were provided with social workers who helped them to apply for housing and welfare benefits and enroll the children in school. The social workers also kept the mothers informed of the time and place of their required court hearings. The cost of the system was $38 per day for each family, compared to $319 per person housed in a family detention center.[32]

The program was successful, not only in helping the families adjust to life in the United States but in getting them to court. 99.3 percent of the participants (including more than a dozen who were deported) attended their court appearances, and 99 percent attended all of their appointments with ICE officers.[33] But in June 2017, after the program had worked with more than two thousand family participants, the new administration abruptly terminated the GEO contract and ended the program. Although cynics might contend that the administration did not want statistics showing that detention wasn't necessary, the administration's justification was that it could save money by instead fitting the released women with ankle monitors and requiring frequent visits to ICE offices. The cost of that procedure was only about $7 per day, though the women complained that the monitors bruised their legs and contributed to "social ostracism."[34]

ATTEMPTS TO PREVENT DETAINED IMMIGRANTS FROM BEING INFORMED ABOUT RIGHTS

Similarly, the Trump administration tried to end a program, begun under President George W. Bush, that provided federal funding to enable detained migrants, including families with children, to learn about their rights under the immigration laws. The Department of Justice had been providing grants to the Vera Institute, which parceled out the money to many non-governmental organizations, so that organizations could enter detention centers and give hour-long "Legal Orientation Programs" (informally called "Know Your Rights" meetings) to about 53,000 migrants a year, most of whom had no lawyers. The organizations were not funded to offer representation to the migrants, but just providing basic information had value in enabling the migrants to make decisions about what to do. The Department itself had found that the program saved $18 million per year for taxpayers by reducing wasted time in immigration court.[35] But in April 2018, Attorney General Sessions decided to suspend the grants, ostensibly to audit the cost-efficiency of the program.[36] After intense negative reaction from members of the Senate Appropriations Committee, Sessions was forced to reverse his decision and keep the program open until a review could be completed.[37]

NEW PRINCIPLES AND "LOOPHOLES" RHETORIC

In October 2017, the White House sent House and Senate Leaders a set of "Immigration Principles and Policies" that expressed its desire to make major changes in policy, some of which would require new legislation, to discourage immigration and facilitate deportation. It justified many of these changes by characterizing features of the Flores agreement and the TVPRA as "loopholes in current law" that "create a dramatic pull factor for additional illegal immigration."[38]

In this document, the President called on Congress to terminate the Flores agreement and to amend the TVPRA. He particularly asked that undocumented children no longer be allowed to have their asylum claims decided by asylum officers rather than immigration judges, advocated that parole authority, which was being used to release families from detention, be limited to "appropriate" cases, and asked that special immigrant juvenile visas be granted only to children who had been abandoned or neglected by both parents, rather than by only one parent. He also indicated his desire, while not specifying details, to expand expedited removal to cover more migrants.

To the extent that repealing protections for children required Congressional action, Trump was unsuccessful, but he frequently increased the political pressure on Congress by equating the "loopholes" with crimes committed by some MS-13 gang members in the United States. For example, in his 2018 State of the Union message he called on Congress "to finally close the deadly loopholes that have allowed MS-13 and other criminal gangs to break into our country." Evidently referring to the particular legislation he sought in his "Principles and Policies," he added, "We have proposed new legislation that will fix our immigration laws, and support our ICE and Border Patrol Agents, so that this cannot ever happen again."[39]

The President would eventually select, as head of Customs and Border Protection (CBP), a man who shared his tendency to see young Central American males as MS-13 members, or at least potential MS-13 members. Mark Morgan, who in 2019 became acting director of the agency, told Fox News earlier in the year: "I've walked up to these individuals that are so-called minors, seventeen or under, and I've looked at their eyes and I've said, 'that is a soon-to-be MS-13 gang member, it's unequivocal.'"[40]

SHUTTING THE GATES AT THE SOUTHERN BORDER

Most asylum-seekers from Central American crossed the Mexico-United States border surreptitiously, often with the help of smugglers. Some were never apprehended. Some, especially those with children, turned themselves in to the first border patrol agent they could find. Others were apprehended by border patrol agents. But a third of the asylum-seekers from Central America sought to avail themselves of their right, under U.S. law, to approach an immigration agent at a border crossing and request asylum, without committing even the misdemeanor of unlawful entry.

As early as the summer of 2016, during the last year of the Obama administration, human rights organizations began to hear reports that at some of the border crossings between the United States and Mexico, CBP officers had been giving Central American asylum-seekers "various forms of misinformation" and "telling them [falsely] that they could not apply for asylum" or that they had to apply for asylum in Mexico before they could apply to U.S. officials.[41]

Just before President Trump was inaugurated, several organizations, including the American Immigration Council, the ACLU, and the Women's Refugee Commission, complained to the DHS Office for Civil Rights and Civil Liberties and to the agency's Inspector General about these rejections of asylum seekers.[42] Immediately after the president's three initial executive orders were published, they wrote, lawyers for immigrants noticed "a marked shift in the conduct of some CBP officers," who "reportedly made a range of statements [to migrants seeking asylum at the border] to the effect that the United States is no longer granting asylum." One of them reportedly said "Trump says we don't have to let you in," while another said "you can't just show up here." Other officers told the migrants that they needed visas or that "the U.S. is not processing asylum for people from your country anymore." In some cases they reportedly used physical force to turn families away.[43]

By the spring of 2018, the trickle of reports of CBP officers closing the borders to asylum seekers had become a raging river. At "several cities along the border," asylum seekers were being "turned away and told to return later," the Washington Post revealed. The administration threatened prosecution of asylum seekers who crossed the border illegally and advised them to go to official border posts, but then refused to allow them to apply at those posts. In its defense, CBP said that the border posts were at capacity and couldn't process more migrants. "We want to treat the people humanely," a supervisor said, but "it's not humane to simply pile people up on top of each other."[44] U.S. newspapers and televised news showed pictures of migrants roasting in long lines, in the hot sun, and sleeping for days on pieces of cardboard on the bridges approaching the border.[45] Some people simply gave up after waiting for weeks.[46] Congressman Beto O'Rourke, who represented a border district, criticized CBP for "lack[ing] the desire to find additional capacity to handle fluctuations in asylum applications."[47] But whether the CBP border posts were really at capacity was hotly disputed.[48]

DHS's inspector general later stated that although the government was encouraging migrants to come to ports of entry, "CBP was regulating the flow of asylum-seekers at ports of entry through 'metering' [and that] a CBP official reported that the backlogs created by these competing directives likely resulted in additional illegal border crossings."[49] Metering severely limited the refugees' access to lawful ports of entry. For example, in September 2018, there were days in which the CBP officials at the Nogales port of entry did not admit a single foreign national.[50] The metering policy drove the migrants "into the hands of the . . . smuggling cartels" that offered surreptitious entry across the Rio Grande.[51]

DHS faced yet another federal lawsuit as a result of CBP's actions. In *Al Otro Lado v. Nielsen*, a refugee assistance organization based at the border in San Diego and Tijuana charged that DHS was using threats, intimidation, false information, and processing slowdowns to deter or prevent migrants from applying for asylum.[52] The case was destined to last for years because of procedural issues raised by the government, including a (successful) motion to transfer the case from Los Angeles to San Diego[53] and an (unsuccessful) attempt to moot the case by allowing the individual plaintiffs to apply for asylum.[54]

In August 2018, the court in San Diego dismissed part of the case—the claim that the government had an unwritten "policy" to reject asylum seekers at the border—on the ground that the plaintiffs hadn't produced plausible evidence of a "policy" as opposed to individual unlawful actions of some particular CBP officers. But it allowed them to amend their complaint if they could plausibly suggest evidence of a federal policy, an invitation that the plaintiffs quickly accepted.[55] The amended complaint cited, among other things, a presidential tweet that might bolster their evidence of a government policy. The tweet tended to show that what President Trump really wanted was to end asylum processing altogether: "We cannot allow all of these people to invade our Country. When somebody comes in, we must immediately, with no Judges or Court Cases, bring them back from where they came."[56]

By October 2018, reports surfaced to the effect that Mexican agents were blocking asylum-seekers at the Mexican ends of some of the bridges, so that they could not even approach U.S. immigration officials to ask to be processed. Some Mexican agents reportedly asked for bribes of $500 per person to allow adults or their children onto a bridge. Other Mexican officials apprehended and deported Central American migrants if they lacked Mexican travel documents. Jennifer Harbury, a Texas RioGrande Legal Aid lawyer, complained to the Inter-American Commission on Human Rights that Mexican agents had told her that their intervention had resulted from pressure from the Trump administration.[57] At the crossings between Tijuana and San Diego, on the other hand, a more orderly system prevailed, through which asylum-seekers were given a number and told to wait for weeks in Mexico, checking each day to see whether CBP officials had reached their number.[58] But this system required them to remain at risk from extortion and violence in Tijuana, "where police abuses against migrants are rampant and homicides are at an all-time high."[59]

The bottleneck at the legal border crossings worsened in the late fall of 2018, when it became clear to people fleeing from Central America that they were safer traveling in caravans than going alone, and that the routes to Tijuana were less hazardous than the routes to border crossings further east. Refugees piled up in Tijuana and were told to wait in a shelter near a sports center. The shelter "assumed the squalor of an overwhelmed refugee camp"[60] until a larger shelter was opened further from the border. Tijuana's mayor estimated that three thousand migrants were already in his city, and that if half of the migrants in the caravans headed there, it might be six months before U.S. officials would interview them.[61]

Al Otro Lado persevered with its litigation, adding new plaintiffs and renewing its claim that the government had adopted a "pattern or practice," of metering, in order to deny asylum-seekers access to the official border crossings. The government vigorously argued that the court should dismiss the case, but in an 84-page opinion, the court at last concluded that public statements by the president and several Secretaries of Homeland Security plausibly showed that the government had adopted a "policy" of turning people back at the gates. It refused to dismiss the case.[62]

It is not irrational for the United States to suggest that Mexico share some of the burden of caring for refugees from Central America. But most of those who flee the violence of the Northern Triangle do not want to apply for asylum in Mexico, even though they share a common language with Mexicans. They know that migrants in Mexico are frequently kidnapped and murdered, that the Mexican asylum system is already "overtaxed," and that its process for dealing with asylum-seekers is "deeply flawed."[63]

FAMILY SEPARATIONS

Until 2017, with two exceptions, the federal government had tried, largely successfully, to prevent the separation of undocumented children from adult relatives with whom they had arrived. In the mid-1980s, children arriving without adults, like Jenny Flores, might be separated from relatives when held in Immigration and Naturalization Service (INS) facilities such as the Mardi Gras Hotel, but there were no family jails. So until Hutto opened, when whole families arrived and sought asylum, the mothers and children were usually released together, even if the fathers were sent into detention.[64] After Hutto closed, families were again released together, and after Artesia opened, families were either jailed together or released together.

One exception in which a substantial number of family separations occurred involved Haitian asylum-seekers who arrived in large numbers in 1992 and were sent to a refugee camp at the U.S. naval base in Guantanamo Bay, Cuba. There, despite an official policy of keeping families together, many children were separated from their parents and reclassified as "unaccompanied" minors. American employees who worked at the camp blamed the separations on "chaos" and "inadvertent errors in record keeping" as well as "cultural differences between Haitians and U.S. officials that caused confusion about whether a group of relatives was a family or not." On the other hand, some officials who tried to reunite separated families said that "they faced opposition from INS officers" who wanted to limit the number of migrants who would eventually enter the United States. One official said that some of the INS officers "looked at them [the Haitians] as numbers and not as people."[65] Some separated children were left behind when their parents were deported, and some suffered abuse in the camp. An American worker saw a teenager handcuffed to a chair and left in the sun because he had removed his identity bracelet. At least one girl, who later went to Boston, was raped in the camp.[66]

The other exceptional circumstance in which parents and children were often separated occurred during the spike of family arrivals in 2004–05, when Berks was at capacity and families were separated simply because DHS did not want to release them and had no way to keep them together. This early separation practice, described in chapter 6, ended when Hutto opened.

Although neither the Bush nor the Obama administration implemented a deliberate policy of family separation, the possibility was used to justify long-term family detention. "We could let families go or split them up," Gary Mead, ICE's assistant director for detention and removal, told the *Los Angeles Times* in 2007. "Hutto became very important," he said, "in avoiding separations."[67]

When detention in Karnes and Dilley was challenged in the 2015 motion to enforce the Flores settlement, the government argued that if it couldn't detain families together, it "would essentially be forced to separate [apprehended] parents from their children and transfer those children to [ORR]."[68] Similarly, while arguing to Judge Dolly Gee in the spring of 2015, Leon Fresco warned that if court limited the number of weeks during which the government could keep children in detention, the administration might decide to separate the children from their parents so that the parents could be incarcerated until their hearings took place.[69] The Ninth Circuit's subsequent ruling to the effect that the Flores settlement afforded rights only to children and not to their parents made it possible for the government to follow through on that threat of separation. But Fresco had good reason to doubt that the Obama administration actually would separate families. In 2014, an interagency group had met several times in the situation room at the White House to discuss what to do about the increased numbers of Central Americans coming across the border. Officials had concluded that separation was a bad idea. As Cecilia

Muñoz, the director of Obama's Domestic Policy Council, recalled, "the morality of it was clear—that's not who we were."[70]

For the Trump administration, the morality was less clear. Stephen Miller, the president's senior policy advisor, pushed to begin separating families to deter Central American migration, although, in principle, the decision in *R. I. L- R-* would preclude deterrence from being successfully articulated as the justification. Instead, Miller argued, "law enforcement" should be cited in support of the practice. "No one is exempt from immigration law," he told the *New York Times*.[71] Later, Attorney General Jeff Sessions would embellish that argument with a Biblical citation. After evangelical leaders objected to what became the administration's separation policy, Sessions explained that "Having children does not give you immunity. . . . I would cite you to the Apostle Paul and his clear and wise command in Romans 13 to obey the laws of the government, because God has ordained them for the purpose of order."[72]

The first hint of a policy change occurred only days after Trump's inauguration. John Lafferty, DHS's asylum director, privately told asylum officers in early February 2017 that DHS might have to hold parents in detention while sending their children to ORR custody. In March, DHS Secretary John Kelly told CNN that he was considering family separations for the purpose of deterrence.[73] Senator Heidi Heitkamp (D–ND) took notice. In a hearing the next month, she asked Kelly whether the agency was really going to separate family members.

"Not routinely," he answered.

"If you thought the child was endangered, that's the only circumstance to which you would separate," Heitkamp asked.

"Can't imagine doing it otherwise," Kelly replied.[74]

But by the summer of 2017, Kelly had left DHS to become the president's chief of staff, and his hand-picked successor, Kirstjen Nielsen, was directing the agency. To test the efficacy of splitting up families as a deterrent to migration, DHS quietly began separating families at the border in Texas. It made no announcement that it was doing so, perhaps judging either that word would not reach the American public or that if it did, Americans would not care.

But the experiment did not escape the notice of immigrants' advocates. As early as December 11, 2017, the American Immigration Council, the Women's

Refugee Commission, RAICES, and other organizations complained to the acting inspector general of DHS that it had "identified 155 cases of family separation at the border involving parents and children as of late October 2017,"[75] too many to have been occasioned by accident or by rogue officers.

A lawsuit soon followed. In early February 2018, "long before most of the rest of the world was aware that thousands of children were being separated from their families at the border," the ACLU filed a class action, *Ms. L v. ICE*, in federal court in San Diego. Ms. L, whose name was withheld for privacy reasons, was a thirty-nine-year old Congolese woman who feared imminent death. (Catholics had organized large anti-government demonstrations in the Congo, and some had been killed by security forces, but it was not clear whether she was involved in the demonstrations). With her seven-year-old daughter, she hid in a church until they could flee the country. They made their way to Mexico, and on October 1, 2017, they presented themselves at the official border crossing in San Ysidro, California, seeking asylum. At first, they were detained together, but four days later, immigration officials forcibly separated mother and child. Ms. L could hear her daughter screaming from the next room that she wanted to stay with her mother. But the mother, who was found by an asylum officer to have credible fear of persecution, was kept in detention in San Diego, while her daughter was transferred to ORR custody and housed in a shelter for "unaccompanied" minors in Chicago.[76]

Notably, while the ACLU's suit claimed that family separations were unlawful and even a violation of the due process clause of the Constitution, unless there were some justification for them (such as threatened harm to the child from being with the parent), it did not seek to prevent family detention. It explicitly stated that the government must "at a minimum detain [family members] together."[77] After four months, under "orders from up top," ICE abruptly released Ms. L, perhaps to try to render the case moot or perhaps because the family's plight had received national publicity, though her daughter remained in ORR custody.[78]

The case was assigned to Judge Dana Sabraw, the son of an American soldier who fell in love with and married a Japanese woman while stationed abroad during the Korean War. Prejudice at the time made it hard for a mixed-race family, especially one with a Japanese woman, to find housing in California, but the family was able to settle in Sacramento. Sabraw attended San Diego State University and the University of the Pacific's law school in Sacramento, and in his final year of law school he met his future wife. He joined a law firm in Santa Barbara, but the couple moved to San Diego where his wife had more career opportunities. In the San Diego office of Baker & McKenzie, one of the largest law firms in the world, Sabraw rose from associate to partner. He left the firm when Governor Pete Wilson appointed him to a state court, and in 2003, President George W. Bush appointed him as a federal district judge. He was known both for his even temperament and for not making snap decisions.[79]

A week after releasing Ms. L., the government asked the court to dismiss the case, claiming that it had become moot, a ploy that was unlikely to succeed and in fact did not. ICE also told the court that "ICE has no family separation policy for ulterior law enforcement purposes, and considers each case on the facts available at the time a placement decision must be made. In addition, such a policy would be antithetical to the child welfare values of ORR."[80] It also argued that the if case was not moot, it should be dismissed anyway because, based on a balance of the government's interests and the families' interests, Ms. L and other asylum-seekers had no constitutional right to remain with their children. "The interests of immigration detainees in being detained with their children is far outweighed by the government's interest in protecting children from smugglers and human traffickers"[81] by deterring migration.

True to his reputation, Judge Sabraw did not reach a snap judgment. Weeks passed. Meanwhile, the Trump administration gave the ACLU's position a huge boost by announcing a formal separations policy. The new program was rolled out slowly, as if to suggest that it came not from Stephen Miller, Trump, or DHS Secretary Nielsen, but was being pushed on the administration from the more junior officials responsible for immigration enforcement. By mid-April, more than seven hundred children, more than a hundred of them under the age of four, had been taken in the previous six months from adults who said they were their parents.[82]

On April 23, the heads of ICE, CBP, and United States Citizenship and Immigration Services (USCIS) sent a joint memorandum to Nielsen urging a "zero tolerance" measure under which all parents who were apprehended after crossing the border without presenting themselves at an official border crossing would be prosecuted. Prosecution was possible because in 1929, Senator Coleman Livingston Blease of South Carolina, a white supremacist, had persuaded Congress to make crossing the border without permission a misdemeanor.[83] Prosecution of border-crossers would necessitate family separation, because the parents would be held in jails for criminal defendants until trial, and unlike Karnes and Dilley, those jails had no facilities for children. The joint memorandum was leaked to the press. Lee Gelernt, the ACLU attorney handling the Ms. L case, quickly responded that the prosecutions would make "children as young as 2 and 3 years old pawns in a cruel public policy experiment."[84] Michelle Brané referred to forcing mothers to elect between agreeing to return home or abandoning their children "a horrific 'Sophie's Choice' for a mom."[85] Amnesty International called it torture, as defined by international and U.S. law.[86] Meanwhile, DHS officials continued to tell Congress that "we do not currently have a policy of separating women and children."[87]

That would soon change. During a cabinet meeting on May 9, in front of all of the other heads of departments, the president engaged in a "lengthy tirade" against DHS Secretary Nielsen, berating her for a "lack of progress toward sealing the country's borders." Trump reportedly was furious that "officials in the department were resisting his direction that parents be separated from their children," a policy he had been pushing "for weeks." Nielsen denied a report that she was "miserable" in her job and had drafted a letter of resignation.[88] Instead of resigning, she quickly joined the separation bandwagon.

But it was Attorney General Sessions who broke the news of a new official policy of separating families. In early April, he had announced a "zero tolerance" policy, directing Justice Department personnel to prosecute anyone who committed the misdemeanor of unlawful border crossing.[89] Whether the policy would apply to mothers with children was not clear at that time. In a speech to prosecutors early in May, however, Sessions said

> If you cross this border unlawfully, then we will prosecute you. It's that simple. If you smuggle illegal aliens across our border, then we will prosecute you. If you are smuggling a child, then we will prosecute you and that child will be separated from you as required by law.[90]

Within two weeks after that announcement, the government separated from their mothers an additional 658 children, as many children as those

US Border Guards Separating Parents and Children
Your Tax Dollars at Work

Family separation editorial cartoon, 2018.

taken from mothers in the previous seven months.[91] A rash of press accounts followed, including personal stories of mothers who were plaintiffs in the Ms. L case.[92] Senator Patrick Leahy (D–VT) took the floor of the Senate to say that "there is simply no way to sanitize the cruelty of this policy. . . . Who here would defend such an abhorrent practice if it were happening in Russia?"[93]

Meanwhile, Judge Sabraw was becoming increasingly concerned about the separations. In a court hearing in May, he asked the Justice Department's lawyer, Sarah Fabian, whether parents "just fall into a black hole" with no way to reunite with their children unless they hire lawyers. He could not have been heartened by Fabian's response that the government did not try to reunite the families.[94] Finally, as the public was becoming increasingly aware of the issue, the judge acted. He denied the government's motion to dismiss the plaintiffs' claim, in the Ms. L. case, that family separations violated the due process clause of the Constitution. He wrote that the government's conduct, as alleged in the plaintiff's complaint, was "brutal, offensive, and fails to comport with traditional notions of fair play and decency [and it] shocks the conscience and violates Plaintiffs' right to family integrity."[95]

Although the judge's order kept the case alive, it did not require an immediate end to family separations. The judge was somewhat hesitant to issue an injunction, because "the case has developed in the media, but the recent events are not in the record before the court."[96]

The judge was right about the media. Widespread condemnation of the president's policy resulted from the publicity about the mounting number of separations,[97] the apparent fraud and cruelty through which the policy was being administered,[98] and Trump's admission that the purpose of the policy was to pressure Congressional Democrats to agree to build a wall.[99] Ordinary Americans were so outraged that a Facebook page started by a Bay Area couple raised more than $20 million for RAICES within ten days—more than forty times what the organization had raised during all of 2017.[100] Conservatives who often supported the president began to distance themselves from the policy. The U.S. Conference of Catholic Bishops and the Southern Baptist Convention denounced it, as did Franklin Graham, the son of Rev. Billy Graham.[101] Pope Francis called it immoral.[102] Behind closed doors, the president's daughter Ivanka asked him to abandon it.[103] Seventeen states sued the federal government.[104] International condemnation rained down on the president as well, from the U.N. High Commissioner for Human Rights, the U.N. High Commissioner for Refugees, and the prime ministers of such U.S. allies as Canada and Great Britain.[105] Finally, in a rare break with the Trump administration, thirteen Republican Senators asked that the policy be suspended.[106]

The day after the Republican senators acted, Trump "caved to enormous political pressure" and signed an order ending the separation policy, couching his concession as "Affording Congress an Opportunity to Address Family Separation." He blamed both the other branches of government for ostensibly having forced him to separate families: "It is unfortunate," he wrote, "that Congress's failure to act and court orders have put the Administration in the position of separating alien families."[107] His order tasked the military to provide DHS with new family detention centers and the Justice Department with trying anew to undo the Flores agreement, but it did nothing to try to reunify the two thousand families that had already been separated.[108] In fact, a spokesman for the Department of

Health and Human Services (HHS) said that the White House had made a decision that "there will not be a grandfathering of existing cases."[109] The HHS spokesman may have known a fact that was not yet public: that reunification would be extremely difficult because the government had no electronic records connecting the children, who were in ORR custody, with the parents, who were in ICE custody, and caseworkers would have to "sift by hand through the files of all of the nearly 12,000 migrant children in HHS custody to figure out which ones had arrived with parents, where the adults were jailed, and how to put the families back together."[110] Although DHS announced that it shared a "central database" with ORR that included location information for separated parents and their children, the DHS inspector general "found no evidence that such a database existed."[111]

The reunification problem, therefore, fell into the lap of Judge Sabraw, whose task had been made much easier by the president's reversal. The government could hardly now protest or appeal an order to ban further separations, making it easy for him to enjoin the practice. He also certified the Ms. L case as a class action and authorized the ACLU to represent the class. He enjoined future separations of families "absent a determination that the parent is unfit or presents a danger to the child, unless the parent affirmatively, knowingly, and voluntarily declines to be reunited with the child in DHS custody."

As to reunification, he was incensed that the government did not plan to do anything to connect the separated children with their parents. He noted that the government keeps track of property that it takes from people in criminal and immigration proceedings, but it did not keep track of where it put the children who were removed from their parents, and it had already deported some of the parents without their children. He described the anguish of the separated parents, the mental health consequences for the children, and the suicide of a parent after being separated from his wife and three-year-old child. He also ordered the government to reunify all children under the age of five with their parents within fourteen days, and all children over the age of five within thirty days. He ordered the government to put all of the children in telephonic communication with their parents within ten days and he barred the deportation of any parent without that parent's child.[112]

The government had great difficulty meeting Judge Sabraw's deadlines because HHS had not electronically distinguished between unaccompanied children and children who were deemed unaccompanied as a result of being separated from their parents at the border or while in ICE custody. DHS missed several court deadlines.[113] But within a month, it had reunified most of the thousands of children who had been separated, though 711 children remained separated, including more than four hundred whose parents had been deported without their children. By the beginning of fall 2018, that number had declined to two hundred.[114] At that point, the government planned to deport about one thousand reunified families where an asylum officer had found that the parent lacked credible fear—but nobody had evaluated whether the child had an independent claim for asylum.[115] In addition, some of the parents claimed that their credible fear interviews had not been properly conducted, because their children had just been taken away from them and they were suffering from extreme trauma when they were interviewed. They filed yet another lawsuit, *Dora v. Sessions*,[116] which the federal government quickly settled by agreeing to new interviews for a thousand parents.[117]

In November 2018, the cost of caring for the separated children and reuniting them with their mothers became clear. It exceeded $80 million, about $30,000 per child.[118] The costs continued to rise, because even five months after the administration ended its separation policy, 140 children remained in custody. These included the children of ninety-nine parents who had been deported and did not want their children returned to them because their home countries were too dangerous.[119] Three months later, the inspector general of DHS revealed that ICE had separated thousands of additional children and never reported them to Judge Sabraw,[120] prompting additional litigation by the ACLU.[121] In the course of that litigation, ICE revealed that it had separated an additional 245 families after the President had ordered an end to family separation. It claimed that in some cases, the adult family member had a criminal record, and was thus a danger to the child, but it turned out that some of those criminal records were for minor or old offenses, such as a twenty-year-old nonviolent robbery conviction or possession of a small amount of marijuana.[122]

In the summer of 2019, the government revealed that family separations continued to take place. By this time, ICE had taken more than 900 migrant children away from their families after the President had issued his executive order ending them. Nearly half of them had been under the age of 10, and 185 of them had been 5 or younger. ICE claimed that it had continued to separate children only when the accompanying adult posed a risk to the child or when the adult appeared to be someone other than a parent. But the ACLU filed court documents showing that ICE had justified some of the separations not only for minor or very old criminal convictions but also for "reasons as minor as a parent not changing a baby's diaper or having a traffic citation for driving without a license" or because the accompanying adult was a sibling or aunt rather than a parent.[123]

ATTEMPT TO MODIFY JUDGE GEE'S 2015 ORDER

Trump's executive order ending the family separations implored Congress to address immigration issues, but it was unrealistic to think that Congress could do so. Congress had been deadlocked on immigration legislation since 2008, when it had passed the TVPRA. In 2013, the Senate had overcome a filibuster threat and passed a bipartisan comprehensive immigration reform bill by a vote of 68–32. But in 2014, the House Republican Majority Leader Eric Cantor lost a primary election to David Brat, a candidate opposed to immigration reform, and the influx of Central Americans at the southern border became national news. The Republican-controlled House of Representatives never took up the Senate-passed bill, and it died.[124] Since then the possibility of a filibuster in a closely-divided Senate had discouraged any significant effort to change the immigration laws in either direction, so Trump's repeated calls to close the "loopholes" of the TVPRA and the Flores agreement went unheeded.

In the absence of Congressional action, Judge Sabraw's order appeared to put the administration in a hard place. It did not want to release migrant families. But as a result of the court's ruling and the President's own executive order, DHS could not separate families, and because of Judge Gee's order enforcing the Flores settlement, ICE could not keep the children in jail for more than twenty days. The executive order required the Justice Department to try once again to persuade Judge Gee to alter her ruling, a mission that was unlikely to succeed but that would enable the President to blame a judge for the continued influx of migrant families.

So the Justice Department dutifully went back to Judge Gee seeking what it called "limited relief." Specifically, it wanted to be allowed indefinitely to detain families in Karnes and Dilley, and perhaps other facilities to be constructed in the future, notwithstanding the lack of state licensing.

Judge Gee quickly denied what she called a "thinly veiled motion for reconsideration," both because it violated the court's rule that barred repeated attempts to obtain the same result, and because the government could not prove, as it claimed, that her 2015 decision had been the cause of additional border crossings by migrant families. "Any number of factors" could be motivating the families, she wrote, "including civil strife, economic degradation, and fear of death." In fact, Manoj Govandaiah had demonstrated that of 5177 families detained in Karnes to whom RAICES had provided legal assistance over the course of a year, five thousand had received positive credible fear determinations, tending to show that fear, not the judge's previous decision, was driving the migration.

The judge also challenged the government's claim that "families frequently fail to appear at the required proceedings," citing the article by Professor Ingrid Eagly and her colleagues that showed that 86 percent of released family detainees attended their immigration court hearings and that 96 percent of those with asylum applications went to court as required.[125] She concluded by labeling the government's effort "a cynical attempt . . . to shift responsibility to the Judiciary for over 20 years of Congressional inaction and ill-considered Executive action that have led to the current stalemate."[126]

FAMILY SEPARATIONS, REVISITED

In August 2018, nearly thirteen thousand family members were apprehended near the southern border, a monthly number that would increase to more than eighty-eight thousand by the following May.[127] Large groups of one hundred or more migrants were reportedly turning themselves in to agents and asking for asylum. Overwhelmed, and running out of space in Dilley and Karnes, ICE began dropping of "busloads" of families at church shelters, some with ankle bracelets, others only with notices to appear in court, because ICE was running out of the bracelets. An ICE spokesperson blamed the Flores agreement's limitations on detention.[128]

The Trump administration's response was to consider re-starting family separations. This time, Trump's advisors, led by Stephen Miller, advocated something they called "binary choice." Instead of simply separating the families at the border, and prosecuting the parents, they would jail the families for twenty days, as permitted by Judge Gee's 2015 order. At the end of that time, they would tell the mothers that they could either remain in jail with their children indefinitely, or let the government take their children from them and put them in an ORR shelter or place them with a foster family. The choice would be theirs.[129]

The government faced several practical obstacles to implementing the plan. For example, until it opened a new family jail, it lacked space to house indefinitely families that chose detention,[130] and ORR was so short on shelter space that it was frantically building and expanding a tent city to house unaccompanied minors.[131] In addition, the computer systems of DHS and ORR still lacked compatibility, so it would be difficult for the two agencies to keep track of which children belonged to which parents, and where the parents and children were located at any given time.

There was also a knotty issue as to whether the parents could be forced to choose between detention and separation consistent with the orders in the Flores and Ms. L. cases. Could the government lawfully threaten family separation in order to pressure mothers into waiving the rights of their children, under Flores, not to be jailed for more than twenty days? The issue had first arisen during the April 2015 hearing before Judge Gee on the plaintiffs' motion to enforce the Flores agreement so as to bar long-term detention in Karnes and Dilley. The judge asked Carlos Holguín, who was arguing for the plaintiffs, "Does the [Flores] agreement as it stands allow for an accommodation to either a minor or a parent who wishes to remain in the facility?" Holguin replied, "A class member is entitled to waive those rights. . . . Mothers and parents speak for children all the time."[132] Holguín's statement did not address a coerced waiver under threat of family separation. But the waiver issue arose again, in both the Ms. L case and the Flores cases.

On June 26, Judge Sabraw questioned Lee Gelernt, the ACLU attorney who was arguing against forced separation, about the effect of ordering the government not to separate families. If he prohibited the separations, would the children then be jailed with their parents for only twenty days? Or would Flores require release after that? Gelernt was well aware that the Ninth Circuit had held that Flores afforded no rights to parents; they could be kept in jail. He may have been concerned that if he insisted that *children* be released at the twenty-day mark, without their mothers, he would himself be supporting family separation, and the judge might have wondered why he should bother entering an injunction that prevented separation for only twenty days. Gelernt responded that Flores "doesn't take away the parent's right to make decisions for the child. . . . [So the parent can] waive the Flores right to release at the 19th day." He added that "because the government can and does release parents who are not a flight risk or a danger, especially the parents who have passed the initial asylum screening interview, I don't think Flores is an impediment" to the entry of an injunction barring the separations.[133]

In other words, Gelernt cited the government's *present* practice of releasing those who passed credible fear interviews to fight the judge's hypothetical question. He ignored the more difficult problem of whether the mothers could be compelled to waive their children's rights to release under the agreement if, in the future, the government adopted a policy of keeping all of the mothers in jail until their hearings. He therefore skillfully avoided the issue of whether a waiver of a child's Flores rights could be coerced by a threat of separation. Judge Sabraw, too, avoided being too specific about that issue in the order that he entered after the hearing. He enjoined the government from detaining mothers in DHS custody "without and apart from their children, absent a determination that the parent is unfit or presents a danger to the child, unless the parent affirmatively, knowingly, and voluntarily declines to be reunited with the child in DHS custody."[134] He did not address what he meant by "voluntarily."

After both the president and Judge Sabraw had ordered an end to family separations, the government claimed that it couldn't comply with both his order in the Ms. L case and Judge Gee's order in the Flores case. That was the basis for its request for Judge Gee to reverse her interpretation of the Flores settlement. The government also sent Judge Gee a document that it called a "Notice of Compliance," which appeared to be a notice of noncompliance, stating that "the Government will not separate families but [it will] detain families together during the pendency of immigration proceedings."[135]

Judge Gee was as unimpressed by the "Notice of Compliance" as she was by the government's new request for her to change her mind about the Flores settlement. "Absolutely nothing prevents Defendants from reconsidering their current blanket policy of family detention and reinstating prosecutorial discretion [to release families on bond or parole]," she wrote.[136] But then she added that "all parties admit that these parents may also affirmatively waive their children's rights to prompt release and placement in state-licensed facilities. . . . Given the situation arising from Defendants' earlier family separation policy, detained parents may choose to exercise their Ms. L right to reunification or to stand on their children's Flores rights. Defendants may not make this choice for them."[137]

That statement was a little ambiguous. Did she mean to say only that a mother could decide to stay in jail with her children if, for example, she had no place else to go and preferred that the government house and feed her family until her hearing took place? Or did she mean also to imply that the government could force her to choose between staying in jail with her children and being separated from them, excluding a third possible outcome—the one most likely to be chosen by a mother—being released with her children? It seems likely, in view of her discussion of prosecutorial discretion and her statement that the government could "not make this choice for them" that she meant to allow only a truly voluntary waiver of her children's Flores rights, not one that was compelled by the threat of separation.

The day after Judge Gee wrote her decision in Los Angeles, at yet another hearing in San Diego in the Ms. L case, the government seized on that ambiguous language. A government lawyer told Judge Sabraw that Judge Gee had "explained that the parent could waive this Flores right." Therefore, the government would

> interpret your order to permit us to provide families detained together with one of two options. First, the . . . parent would be able to waive the child's Flores rights so the child could stay with the parent [in detention]. The second option the government can give, Your Honor, is that the family, through the parent, can agree to release the child to ORR custody, in which case the family would be separated, but with the parent's consent, as Your Honor has

allowed. . . . In neither case would the parent be able to use this court's order, together with the Flores court's order, to bootstrap a right to release.[138]

Then the government's lawyer explained what could happen if Judge Sabraw did not agree that such a coerced waiver was permissible: "If we are forced to release parents . . . we will need to pursue immediate appeal."

This was a moment of high drama. Judge Sabraw turned to Gelernt, who had to choose between defending an appeal before the Ninth Circuit, which already had ruled that parents had no right to release under Flores, or consenting to the government's interpretation. He chose the latter course. "We don't disagree," he said. "If the parent wants to waive their Flores rights and keep their child with them in family detention or waive Your Honor's ruling and [accept separation] the parent has that right, so we agree with the government's ruling."[139]

Why did Gelernt make a concession that could tempt the Trump administration, in the future, to force mothers to make a "binary choice" between separation and long term detention for their children? "Our judge was a very conservative Republican," Gelernt said. "It took a lot to get him to rule for us on separations. What was critical was that he said a hundred times that this [case] was not about detention or release. He was adamant that he wasn't going to interfere with family detention" and an enforced waiver by the mothers of one right or the other was the only way that a right to be released wouldn't inevitably have resulted from requiring the government to comply with both the Flores and the Ms. L. court orders. Besides, Gelernt said, the public was much less likely to be outraged over separations if the alternative was to release every family, and Trump might have backtracked on his executive order. In addition, the ACLU could well have lost on appeal, because of the Ninth Circuit's holding that parents had no rights under the Flores agreement.[140]

Three days later, Gelernt and the government lawyers filed a joint statement agreeing that DHS could "require" parents to select remaining in custody with their children, thus waiving the children's right to release, or waiving their right under Ms. L not to be separated from their children. But the agreed statement went further, and provided that if the parent didn't choose either option, she would be "deemed to have temporarily waived the child's release rights [until she decides]."[141] Judge Sabraw signed an order to that effect a month later.[142] Thus the government could indeed "make this [waiver] choice for them," notwithstanding Judge Gee's ruling. The *Washington Post* predicted that the judge's order would eventually set up "a new court fight, one that will test Homeland Security's risible insistence that the new policy would 'satisfy the basic purpose' of the Flores agreement."[143]

The public uproar over family separations died down after the president ordered them halted and Judge Sabraw required reunification. The public barely noticed that the Trump administration was working to separate parents from children in two other ways:

- The president announced in January 2018 that by September 2019 he would end temporary protected status (TPS) for 200,000 Salvadorans who had been living in the United States since 2001. TPS is a program of protection against deportation for several years that is sometimes but not always given by U.S. presidents to groups of people who were already in the United States when disaster struck their countries. The Salvadorans had been allowed to remain after a devastating earthquake in their country. During that time, they had made new lives, and they had borne 200,000 children who were U.S. citizens.[144] The children, who attended American schools and had never been to El Salvador, could not be deported, so the deportation of their parents would deprive them of financial support and require them to live with relatives, if they had any, or with foster parents.[145] At about the same time, the President ordered an end to TPS for 59,000 Haitians who had been in the United States when a terrible earthquake hit Haiti in 2010.[146] Like so many of President Trump's other actions against foreign nationals, the order ending TPS for the Salvadorans and Haitians was challenged in a lawsuit, *Ramos v. Nielsen*, and was also blocked, at least temporarily, by a federal judge.[147]

- Trump also cancelled President Obama's effort[148] to protect from deportation the parents of children who had been saved from deportation under the DACA program, which had been kept in force by a court order until the Supreme Court decided the fate of the DACA-eligible children. That decision meant that if Congress or the courts ever gave the children who had registered for DACA the opportunity to remain in the United States indefinitely, their parents could be deported without them.

OVERTURNING FLORES BY REGULATION

The efforts to keep families in jail by threatening separation if they did not consent would amount to an indirect attack on Flores, in contrast to the administration's unsuccessful direct attack when it asked Judge Gee to reinterpret the settlement. Perhaps fearing renewed public backlash if it announced a new family separation policy, the Trump administration opted for yet another attempt to erase the Flores case indirectly. Unable to get rid of the settlement by persuading Judge Gee to change her mind, and with no prospect that Congress would override the Flores settlement by statute, the administration decided to try to eliminate it simply by writing a regulation.

The importance of this regulation to the Trump administration can hardly be overstated. Stephen Miller, the President's principal immigration policy advisor, made this clear when he berated Ronald D. Vitello, the acting ICE director: "You ought to be working on this regulation all day every day," he shouted in a meeting. "It should be the first thought you have when you wake up. And it should be the last thought you have before you go to bed. And sometimes you shouldn't go to bed."[149] On April 5, 2019, when ICE had still not issued a final regulation, Trump withdrew his nomination of Vitello as director of ICE.[150]

The settlement itself provided that it would expire "45 days following defendants' publication of final regulations implementing the Agreement," but "notwithstanding the foregoing, the INS shall continue to house the general population of minors in INS custody in facilities that are state-licensed for the care of dependent minors."[151] In September 2018, the government published a proposed regulation to "parallel the relevant and substantive terms of the Flores Settlement Agreement [and therefore] terminate [it]."[152] Members of the public submitted more than 95,000 comments.[153]

In August 2019, the government brushed aside most of the comments and issued a final regulation.[154] The regulation did away with the requirement that children could be held for more than twenty days only in a "state-licensed" facility. It provided, instead, that if a state in which a family jail was located does not license such facilities, "DHS will employ an outside entity [with auditing experience] to ensure that the facility complies with family residential standards established by ICE and that meet the requirements for licensing under the [settlement agreement]."[155] Therefore, the government could bypass the state licensing requirement. Through an intermediary of its choice, ICE would not need a license from Texas to approve Dilley and any other privately operated family jails established there or elsewhere.

It could detain families there until their cases were finally decided by the immigration judges and all appeals had been exhausted, a process that could take two years or more if a case was appealed to a U.S. Court of Appeal. In addition, to "parallel" the Flores agreement's requirement that such facilities be "non-secure," the regulation deemed a facility to be "non-secure" if "egress from a portion of the facility's building is not prohibited through internal locks within the building or external locks and egress from the facility's premises is not prohibited through secure fencing around the perimeter."[156] In its announcement of the final rule, DHS stated that it would remove the locks from its family jails but warned that leaving the premises would have "significant immigration consequences."[157]

Other aspects of the regulation did incorporate many of the educational, recreational, and other requirements of the Flores settlement for children in custody. ICE already had crafted, at Karnes and Dilley, more tolerable environments for children than Hutto had ever provided, though mental-health experts continued to assert that detention caused "long-lasting harm on their well-being, safety, and development."[158] The estimated cost of the additional detention that the regulation would require might be as high as $12.9 billion, mostly for the cost of housing thousands of families for long periods of time, though DHS claims that the costs actually can't be estimated because they depend on the number of arriving families.[159]

Even while reviewing the tens of thousands of public comments, the administration took another major step in the direction of keeping asylum-seekers, including families, in detention. A little-known provision of the immigration law authorized the Attorney General of the United States to "review . . . determinations in immigration proceedings . . . and perform such other acts as the Attorney General deems necessary for carrying out his duties" in connection with immigration.[160] He could "certify" to himself any case involving a policy decision by the Board of Immigration Appeals and then decide that case himself. In 2005, the Board had decided that immigration judges could release, after payment of bond, a migrant who had passed the credible fear test. The Attorney General certified to himself a case in which an immigration judge had granted bond, and in April 2019, in the *M- S-* case, he overruled the 2005 precedent, depriving immigration judges of that authority.[161] Adult asylum seekers faced detention without the prospect of release on bond, and if the administration could succeed in nullifying the Flores agreement by regulation, families found by DHS to have a credible fear of persecution would also have to remain in jail for as long as it would take to have their asylum cases decided (including all appeals). In July 2019, a federal judge in a case known as *Padilla* issued a temporary injunction against the new policy of denying bond hearings to otherwise eligible asylum-seekers who had received favorable credible fear determinations.[162] Soon afterward, the temporary injunction was partially lifted by the Court of Appeals, but the court continued in force the requirement to provide bond hearings to detained migrants who had passed the credible fear test.[163]

Peter Schey returned to court to challenge the regulation.[164] His task was not exceedingly difficult. The whole purpose of the settlement was to keep children out of long-term detention, but the government itself had stated that the purpose of the new regulation was to "detain the family unit together as a family by placing them at an appropriate [family detention center] during their immigration proceedings." Far from "implementing" the Flores agreement, therefore, the regulation effectively abrogated it. Furthermore, the 2001 amendment to the settlement explicitly provided that the requirement of housing children only in "state-licensed" child-care facilities would outlast even a regulation implementing the agreement.[165]

The government had attempted to justify the regulation by arguing that it was simply modifying the Flores agreement "to reflect changes in circumstances and accumulated agency experience."[166] But Judge Gee entered a permanent injunction against its enforcement of the regulation. She noted that it was inconsistent with the settlement agreement in at least three ways. First, she pointed out that it limited the categories of adults to whose care a child could be released under the terms of the settlement, omitting, for example, an adult designated by a parent as capable and willing to care for a child. Second, she noted that "the new regulatory definition of 'licensed facility' would effectively authorize DHS to place [children] in ICE detention facilities that are not monitored by state authorities, but are instead audited by entities handpicked by DHS to ensure compliance with the family residential standards *established by ICE*" (emphasis in original). This was inconsistent, she stated, because "the purpose of the licensing provision is to provide [children] regular and comprehensive oversight by an independent child welfare agency." Finally, she took note of the regulation's incorporation of a new definition of a "non-secure" facility. "In Kafkaesque fashion," she wrote, "the regulation declare[s] that [Karnes and Dilley] are non-secure (and always have been), regardless of whether they are or ever have been, in fact, non-secure. . . . No part of this regulatory provision bars ICE officials from arresting class members who attempt to leave ICE facilities," although she had previously ruled that a "non-secure" facility was one in which "individuals are not held in custody." She pointed out that "the history of this case is replete with findings of [the government's] non-compliance with the Agreement," and she concluded that that government officials "cannot simply impose their will by [eliminating the Flores] consent degree's most basic tenets. That violates the rule of law. And that the Court cannot permit."[167]

Given the administration's commitment to detaining children and President Trump's frequent demands that the Flores settlement agreement be terminated, Judge Gee's decision seemed likely to be appealed to the Ninth Circuit and eventually to land on the docket of the Supreme Court, which had last considered an aspect of the very same case in 1993.

RESTRICTING ASYLUM

All of the battles over detention and family separations dealt with the front end of the process: that is, what would happen to asylum-seeking unaccompanied children and to families with children in the period between their arrival in the United States and an eventual final decision of an immigration court (following any appeals). Perhaps sensing that it would lose the battle to deter migration by jailing the migrants for long periods of time, the Trump administration tried a different tactic. If it could restrict asylum so that few if any of the migrant children or their parents could be granted that status at the back end of the process, perhaps word would get back to their homelands that deportation was inevitable, and people would submit to human rights violations in their own countries rather than attempting entry into the United States.

Most of the children and families seeking asylum from the Northern Triangle countries of Central America were fleeing violence from family members or domestic partners, gang members, or both. This is not surprising, as studies have consistently reported high rates of violence against women and children in those countries. KIND and the Women's Refugee Commission cited studies showing that "more than half of all Salvadoran women reported experiencing some form of violence, and a quarter have been victims of sexual or physical abuse," and 22 percent of women in Honduras "had experienced intimate partner violence" during a recent year, according to a study by the Honduran National Institute of Statistics.[168]

In some cases, the women suffer abuse at the hands of a parent or stepparent, rather than a husband or boyfriend. The experience of Cecilia Ulloa, who turned herself in to a Border Patrol agent immediately after crossing the Rio Grande, is representative:

> She handed [the agent] her Honduran identification cared. Cecilia Ulloa was 25. Darwin, her son, was 13. The math took a moment to sink in, and Ulloa appeared to recognize a familiar look of confusion.
>
> 'My stepfather,' she said. 'It started when I was 10.'
>
> After a decade in prison for rape, her stepfather was free now, stalking them, blaming her for ruining his life, Ulloa said. 'He's going to kill us.'
>
> Police in Honduras had told her there was nothing they could do, she said, so she and her son left for the United States. They wanted asylum.[169]

The law provides for asylum to a person with a well-founded fear of persecution on account of the person's membership in a "particular social group."[170] Gradually, over the years, the interpretation of the term "social group" had evolved. By 2000, it had come to include, for example, women and girls threatened by tribal customs with genital cutting,[171] gays and lesbians persecuted for their sexual orientation,[172] and Jews threatened by thugs whom a government was unable to control.[173]

Between 2000 and 2014, many victims of domestic violence had won asylum, either from asylum officers or from immigration judges. Others had lost and had been ordered deported. The law was in flux. But finally, in 2014, the Board of Immigration Appeals had held, in a precedential decision known as *A- R- C- G-*, that "married women in Guatemala who are unable to leave their relationship can constitute a cognizable social group that forms the basis of a claim for asylum."[174] As a result, women from

Central America or elsewhere claiming asylum because of domestic violence began to win their cases at much higher rates than before. Cases of flight from gang violence remained challenging, because when a gang threatened a person with death only to extort money from that person or to force that person to join the gang, many adjudicators did not regard the threatened individual as a member of any group or the threat as one "on account of" such membership. Even so, some asylum applicants who had fled gangs had succeeded, particularly if they had been targeted by a gang because the gang was retaliating for the actions of the victim's close relative, and therefore the victim was a member of a social group consisting of his family.

In June 2018, in the midst of national furor over the family separation policy, Attorney General Sessions invoked his "self-certification" power to overturn the four-year-old *A- R- C- G-* decision of the Board of Immigration Appeals. He reversed the Board's grant of asylum to a victim of what he said was "vile abuse . . . at the hands of her ex-husband," characterizing domestic violence as "private criminal activity." Victims of such violence, he wrote, "must establish membership in a particular and socially distinct group that exists independently of the alleged underlying harm, demonstrate that their persecutors harmed them on account of their membership in that group rather than for personal reasons, and establish that government protection from such harm in their home country is so lacking that their persecutors' actions can be attributed to the government." Applying this standard, he concluded that "generally, claims by aliens pertaining to domestic violence or gang violence perpetrated by nongovernmental actors will not qualify for asylum." Perhaps attempting to prevent courts from reviewing his decision, he added in a footnote that "few such claims would satisfy the legal standard to determine whether an alien has a credible fear of persecution."[175] If followed, the footnote would mean that DHS asylum officers would deny credible fear findings to victims of domestic or gang violence, and they would be deported immediately, without the possibility of review by a federal Court of Appeals.

The decision had immediate impact, destroying the hopes of women such as Blanca from Honduras. She had been raped, and her attacker had broken her child's arm. Her sister was also raped, her breast was cut off, and she was eventually murdered. The Honduran police would not take action. Her chances of winning asylum were dashed by the Attorney General's action.[176] Many other Central Americans lost their cases as a result of Sessions' decision; the grant rate for asylum seekers from Northern Triangle countries fell from 24 percent in the first five months of 2018 to 14 percent between June and November.[177]

A month later, officials at DHS acted on the Attorney General's footnote, and essentially directed asylum officers to stop finding credible fear in domestic violence and gang violence cases. "Few gang-based or domestic violence claims involving particular social groups defined by the members' vulnerability to harm may merit a grant of asylum or refugee status—or pass the 'significant possibility' test in credible-fear screenings," the order provided."[178]

Immigration advocates could not appeal Sessions's ruling, because he had remanded Ms. A- B-'s case to the immigration judge (who would be sure to deny it), and appeals to federal courts can only be taken from final decisions of the administrative body, the Board of Immigration Appeals. But the ACLU and the Center for Gender and Refugee Studies at Hastings Law School launched an indirect attack on the ruling by seeking an injunction against the implementation of the decision, in credible fear decisions, by DHS asylum officers.[179] In *Grace v. Sessions*, brought in the federal district court in Washington, D.C., they argued that "there is simply no legal basis in immigration law for the extraordinary new rule against [domestic and gang violence] claims. Rather, like all other credible fear claims, those relating to domestic violence or gang harms are entitled to individualized fact-specific consideration under the established general standards."[180] The court agreed. It issued a 107-page opinion concluding that a "categorical ban on domestic violence and gang-related claims" was "arbitrary" and "contrary to the individualized analysis required" by the Immigration and Nationality Act. It entered a permanent injunction prohibiting the government from applying the Attorney General's reasoning to expedited removal cases.[181] The government promptly appealed, arguing that the district court lacked jurisdiction to review the Attorney General's interpretation of asylum law and that even if the court did have jurisdiction, the Attorney General's interpretation of the asylum law was correct.[182]

Because the district court's jurisdiction extended only to expedited removal decisions and not to decisions that immigration judges made when finally deciding asylum cases, the *Grace* decision left up in the air the question of what those judges should do after hearing all the evidence in domestic violence cases. The Justice Department sent them a formal guidance memo stating that "the decision applies only to the credible fear interview. It has no effect on the conduct of [deportation] hearings."[183] The court's reasoning, however, was equally applicable to final asylum decisions and seemed likely to influence courts of appeal that reviewed any appeals from immigration court decisions that purported to rely on the Attorney General's decision in A- B-.

Violence or threats of violence from gangs were also a major reason why both adults and children fled from Northern Triangle countries. Little authority existed for the proposition that a migrant could be eligible for asylum simply because she had a well-founded fear of persecution by gangs. Nevertheless, it had become well established that a nuclear family was a "social group." Therefore, a child could win asylum if threatened with death because his father had refused to pay extortion money to a gang such as MS-13. The father could not get asylum on that basis, but the child was at risk on account of being a member of the social group consisting of his nuclear family. In one of the earliest cases based on this idea, MS-13 members threatened to kill the asylum applicant because his uncle had testified in court against the gang. The U.S. Court of Appeals for the Fourth Circuit overturned a denial of asylum by the Board of Immigration Appeals, noting that "we can conceive of few groups more readily identifiable than the family."[184] In that case, the family relationship was an uncle and nephew, not even as close as a parent and child.

Using the same device that it invoked to terminate asylum for domestic-violence victims, the Trump administration determined also to try to end asylum based on gang threats to family members. The Attorney General certified to himself a case in which a Mexican drug cartel had threatened a man because his father had refused to sell drugs out of his store. The Board of Immigration Appeals had denied asylum to the man, but along the way it had accepted DHS's concession that a family constituted a social group. Attorney General William Barr, who had succeeded Attorney General Sessions, proclaimed that the Board could not simply accept the government's concession: "An applicant must establish that his specific family group is defined with sufficient particularity and is socially distinct in his society. In the ordinary case, a family group will not meet that standard, because it will not have the kind of identifying characteristics that render the family socially distinct within the society in question."[185] This ruling, if followed by asylum officers and immigration judges, would deny asylum to thousands of applicants who had been wounded or threatened by gangs, but like the A- B- decision, it was sure to be challenged in federal courts.

UNACCOMPANIED CHILDREN TURNING EIGHTEEN

The administration focused its attention on restricting the rights of unaccompanied minors as well as of children in family groups. Under the TVPRA, the cases of unaccompanied children were required to be adjudicated, in the first instance, by DHS asylum officers rather than immigration judges. If the asylum officer rejected the application, an immigration judge would make an independent evaluation of the asylum claim. Many advocates for migrant children believed that children's claims were more likely to be granted by asylum officers than by immigration judges. Unlike immigration judges, asylum officers received weekly training not only on the law but also on how to interview applicants (including children) with sensitivity and due regard for their age. In addition, an interview by an asylum officer was not adversarial, while in immigration court, an ICE attorney represents the government and usually seeks deportation. Finally, the TVPRA provided that unaccompanied children were not subject to expedited removal or the one-year deadline on filing asylum applications after arrival in the United States.[186]

The Homeland Security Act had defined an unaccompanied minor as a person under the age of eighteen. But when was that definition to be applied? In 2008, when the TVPRA was passed, the time between the arrival of an unaccompanied child and the adjudication of the claim was short, but by 2018, the immigration court had a backlog of more than 700,000 cases, and migrants who were not in detention could wait years to have their cases heard. Would an unaccompanied child who arrived before the age of eighteen but who turned eighteen before her case was heard be entitled to the protections of the TVPRA?

During the Obama administration, the Department of Homeland Security concluded that if a CBP or ICE official had decided that a person was an unaccompanied minor and that determination was "still in place" when the person applied for asylum, DHS's asylum officers would adjudicate the case "even if there appears to be evidence that the applicant may have turned 18."[187] Therefore, so long as DHS had granted, and neither DHS nor ORR had revoked, a child's status as an unaccompanied minor, DHS would decide the validity of an asylum application that was filed even after the applicant had turned eighteen.

In September 2017, the Trump administration began discussing a plan to apply expedited removal to unaccompanied children when they turned eighteen, to prevent those who failed the credible fear test from having either full-scale interviews by asylum officers or immigration court hearings, though administration lawyers resisted the plan because they believed that they could not successfully defend it in court.[188]

Instead of putting it into effect, the administration began to take less visible steps to restrict the rights of this group. A Justice Department lawyer opined that "an alien may lose certain protections of the TVPRA if the alien's status changes" and specifically that the right to an asylum interview by a DHS asylum officer was available only to children who applied for asylum before turning eighteen.[189] A few months later, the Board of Immigration Appeals ruled that unaccompanied children who filed asylum applications after they turned eighteen would not be entitled to interviews by asylum officers, even if DHS had never changed their official status. The Board dismissed the more lenient DHS policy guidance, which had never been withdrawn, because it had been written as an instruction to asylum officers and "was not embodied in a regulation."[190]

The Board's new policy is likely to be challenged in the courts.

Meanwhile, after the Board issued its decision, the Trump administration directed asylum officers also to "redetermine" the status of unaccompanied minors who turned 18, in order to deny them interviews by asylum officers.[191] The administration did so without permitting public input. This sudden change also provoked a lawsuit, *J.O.P. v. Dept. of Homeland Security*, and a federal judge issued a temporary order to DHS enjoining it from implementing its new policy.[192]

In addition, DHS instituted a practice of taking children out of ORR custody and putting them in adult ICE detention facilities on their eighteenth birthdays. On this issue, Congress had provided some guidance in the

TVPRA. The statute provided that when a child in the custody of ORR reached the age of eighteen, they could be transferred to the custody of DHS, but the Secretary of DHS "shall consider placement in the least restrictive setting available after taking into account the alien's danger to self, danger to the community, and risk of flight [and] shall be eligible to participate in alternative to detention programs" such as placement "with an individual or an organizational sponsor, or in a supervised group home."[193]

Representing several children whom ICE had put into adult detention facilities and denied bond or parole, without seriously considering them for placement in a less restrictive setting, the National Immigrant Justice Center in Chicago brought yet another federal class action lawsuit, the case of *Ramirez v. ICE*. ICE defended the suit by claiming that it used its "risk assessment" algorithm to judge where to place eighteen-year-olds transferred to its custody. But a judge enjoined ICE, finding that the risk assessment tool had been used only to decide in which adult detention facility to place the plaintiffs, not to consider alternatives that were less restrictive than detention.[194] A few months later, the court extended its ruling to the class of migrant children who were transferred to ICE from ORR custody.[195]

THE IMMIGRATION COURT SPEEDUP

Immigration judges had long complained, through their union spokesperson, that because indigent migrants had no right to appointed lawyers and because immigration courts had a shortage of judges and an increasing backlog, resulting in pressure to decide cases quickly, asylum hearings were "like holding death penalty cases in traffic court."[196]

In 2018, the Trump administration made it even less likely that asylum seekers would receive full and fair hearings. It changed the performance standards by which immigration judges were evaluated for promotion or possible transfer. This change was not specifically directed at children or families who sought asylum, but it would affect them as well as adults. Until the new policy went into effect, immigration judges could decide how much time to devote to hearing and weighing evidence in an asylum case. Many cases required more than one day of hearings, because the judges would advise asylum applicants appearing for the first time of the desirability of having legal representation and then give them time to obtain it. Once a hearing began, the presentation of evidence, and cross-examination of the applicant by an ICE attorney, could take several hours. Sometimes an immigration judge would ask an applicant to return with additional evidence or would run out of time at the end of a day and need to continue the case to another day. And like other judges, immigration judges sometimes took weeks to research the law, review the record, and reach a decision in a complex case. Due process is not usually instant justice.

The Trump administration amended the old standards, for the first time introducing "metrics" that would, in effect, force most judges to spend less time on each case. The new standards, which became effective on October 1, 2018, specified that judges could not earn "satisfactory" ratings unless they resolved at least seven hundred cases a year[197] and were reversed no more than 15 percent of the time by appellate bodies.[198] Performance of each judge would be monitored constantly through electronic systems and constantly available to the judge on a "performance dashboard."[199]

Judge Ashley Tabbador, the president of the National Association of Immigration Judges, the labor union representing the judges, denounced the speedup. "Asylum cases . . . often have hundreds of pages of supporting documents, hours of testimony, deliberation, the time to make a decision," she said. "All of that is allotted about two-and-a-half hours. Clearly, this is not justice." Judge Amiena Khan, the Association's vice-president, was even more blunt, stating that the metrics "seem like an attempt to turn judges from neutral arbiters into law enforcement agents enacting Trump administration policies."[200]

Department of Justice officials were apparently not pleased that the association's officers were criticizing the speedup and advocating the creation of an independent immigration court rather than one that was an arm of the department. The department initiated proceedings in the Department of Labor to decertify the association as a union, claiming that the judges were actually "management officials."[201]

Asylum claims of small children were especially unlikely to receive the attention they deserve. "It takes a long time to get the child to fully open up and explain why they might be here and what basis they may have for protection," said Wendy Young, president of Kids in Need of Defense (KIND).[202] The problem is exacerbated by the fact that the government does not provide legal representation for children against whom the government is seeking deportation orders, one of the subjects addressed in the concluding chapter.

THE PROCLAMATION

The president took another drastic step in an attempt to curtail asylum for Central American asylum-seekers. On November 9, 2018, he claimed that the large numbers of Central Americans entering the United States "who appear to have no lawful basis for admission into our country" constituted a "crisis" and that "members of family units pose particular challenges" because "the federal government lacks sufficient facilities to house families together." He therefore issued a proclamation that purported to suspend entry into the United States from Mexico, except at official border crossings. (Such entry was already a misdemeanor, but that hadn't stopped thousands of people from crossing the Rio Grande). The suspension was to last for ninety days, but it could be renewed at the end of that time. Referring to a regulation that the administration issued the same day, the proclamation added that people who entered the United States unlawfully through the southern border "will be ineligible to be granted asylum."[203] While Central Americans were explicitly the targets of this proclamation, it applied as well to people fleeing from persecution in other countries.

Simultaneously, the Departments of Homeland Security and Justice issued an "interim final" regulation, effective immediately, to implement the proclamation.[204] This regulation not only created a new bar to asylum for those who crossed the Rio Grande, but also changed the screening procedure for asylum seekers, including families, who were put into expedited removal proceedings. In FY 2018, people from the Northern Triangle had received positive credible fear determinations in 89 percent of their interviews with asylum officers.[205] In other words, DHS officials themselves thought that the vast majority of those Central Americans had a reasonable possibility of ultimately winning asylum. Two-thirds of them had crossed the border unlawfully.[206]

Under the proclamation and the new rule, as well as new guidance supplied to all asylum officers, their counterparts who arrived while the

President's proclamation was in effect would no longer have any chance of winning asylum, so they would not be given credible fear interviews. Instead, they would be given only "reasonable fear" interviews, in which they would have to meet a higher standard. They would have to show that there was a "reasonable" possibility rather than a "significant" possibility of winning in an immigration court hearing.[207] DHS expected that many fewer Central Americans would meet the higher standard. Only 45 percent rather than 89 percent of people who were screened for "reasonable fear" had met the higher standard in FY 2018.[208] Therefore half or more of the Central Americans who sought refuge in the United States by crossing the river, including children arriving with parents, could be deported immediately rather than being released to have court hearings.

The ACLU and other organizations knew in advance from press accounts that the regulation would be issued. On behalf of several organizations that helped to represent asylum seekers, the ACLU filed suit in a federal district court on the day that the regulation was published.[209]

This lawsuit, *East Bay Sanctuary Covenant v. Trump*, involved a thicket of seemingly conflicting laws. To justify the President's proclamation, the government relied on the same broad language in the law that it had cited to justify its travel bans on passengers from certain predominantly Muslim countries: a 1952 law that provides that

> whenever the President finds that the entry of . . . any class of aliens into the United States would be detrimental to the interests of the United States, he may by proclamation . . . suspend the entry [of that class of aliens] . . . or impose . . . any restrictions as he may deem to be appropriate.[210]

The proclamation by itself didn't stop anyone from getting asylum, but the regulation piggybacked on the proclamation by barring from asylum anyone who had entered the United States in violation of it. The government's justification for this bar was very general language in the immigration law that gave the Attorney General authority to "establish additional limitations and conditions [besides those in the law, such as bars against asylum for aggravated felons], consistent with" the asylum law "under which an alien shall be ineligible for asylum."[211] The "additional limitation," in this case, was that asylum was to be barred for anyone who entered the United States in a manner inconsistent with the proclamation.

The plaintiffs in the lawsuit argued that the regulation's bar on all those who crossed the border unlawfully was not "consistent with" the asylum law that Congress had passed in 1980, decades after the 1952 law. The 1980 law provided eligibility for any person who was physically present in the United States and who proved a "well-founded fear of persecution" on one of the five permitted grounds. In 1996, Congress had amended the language of the 1980 law, making it even more explicit. As amended, it stated that a person who "arrives in the United States (whether or not at a designated port of arrival . . .)" could apply for asylum.[212] The government's rebuttal was that the 1952 law was the more important one, but that even if the more specific and subsequent laws took precedence, thereby making the migrants "eligible" for asylum, some court cases had said the Attorney General had "discretion" to deny asylum to an eligible individual.[213] In the past, denials of asylum based on "discretion" had been very rare, and had only occurred in individual cases.[214] Whether the government had "discretion," in advance of any individual determinations, to deny asylum to thousands of otherwise eligible migrants, remained an open question.

The ACLU's East Bay suit also noted that although the proclamation asserted that its purpose was to encourage asylum seekers coming through Mexico to apply at ports of entry, the evidence collected for the Al Otro Lado lawsuit showed that the CBP had actually blocked those ports of entry. Asylum seekers trying to enter through the San Diego border crossing, for example, "are currently waiting an average of four to six weeks in Tijuana due to an alleged lack of CBP capacity," the East Bay lawsuit noted.[215]

In addition, the ACLU claimed that the regulation was invalid because it was issued without an opportunity for the public to comment on it, as is required for most regulations. The government had justified the elimination of the usual thirty-day "notice and comment" procedure by suggesting that thousands of migrants would have rushed into the country illegally to take advantage of the short comment period, but the ACLU claimed that the government had no proof for that asserted fear.[216]

Ten days after the ACLU filed the suit, the court preliminarily enjoined the government from enforcing the ban on asylum for those who crossed between ports of entry.[217] Trump denounced Judge Jon Tigar, who had entered the injunction, and had declined to stay his decision while it was being appealed calling him an "Obama judge" and threatening that he would file "a major complaint."[218] The government promptly appealed and asked the appellate court to stay Judge Tigar's order while the appeal was pending. A panel of the Court of Appeals for the Ninth Circuit, by a vote of 2–1, nevertheless declined to stay the injunction. It held that Congress had limited the President's discretion "by establishing a detailed scheme that the Executive must follow."[219] The government sought Supreme Court review of that decision, but that Court denied review by a vote of 5–4, with Chief Justice Roberts among the five justices who voted not to disturb the preliminary injunction.[220] The Ninth Circuit then scheduled an argument, on October 1, 2019, to help it to decide whether to sustain or overturn the injunction.

A similar lawsuit was filed in federal court in the District of Columbia by Human Rights First on behalf of individual migrants barred by the government's new rule. In August 2019, the court sided with the plaintiffs and took an action even more drastic than Judge Tigar's entry of a temporary injunction. It said that because the government's regulation was unlawful, the proper remedy was to nullify it, and that is precisely what the court did.[221]

THE THIRD COUNTRY TRANSIT RULE

Undaunted by losing in the Supreme Court, the administration tried to bar asylum-seekers entering the country from Mexico by employing a different tactic. In July 2019, it published a regulation, invoking the same type of "emergency" to avoid a prior period of public comment, that bars applications for asylum from anyone who had reached the United States from Mexico without first having applied for and been finally rejected for asylum in Mexico (or some other country while en route from their own nation). This regulation, which was immediately effective, went even further than the proclamation, because it bars those who sought asylum at official crossings as well as those who rafted or swam the Rio Grande. It applies to unaccompanied children as well as to families and single adults. It also applies not only to Latin Americans, but to Africans who initially flew to Brazil or Mexico, then entered the United States to seek asylum.[222]

The administration's legal justification was the same "additional limitations and conditions" authority it had used while trying to sustain the regulation that accompanied the President's proclamation, but it is subject to the same objection: that a "limitation" barring nearly all asylum-seekers coming from the south is not in fact "consistent" with the immigration statute. In particular, Congress had amended the law in 1996 to deal specifically with people who sought protection in the United States after transiting through other countries. It barred asylum for such individuals only if they had come through another country that had a "full and fair procedure" for making asylum determinations, and then only if the United States had negotiated a formal agreement with that country.[223] The United States had entered into such an agreement only with Canada.[224]

Also, Congress had explicitly dealt with the situation of asylum-seekers who had passed through other countries, without seeking asylum, on their way to the United States. It had barred them from asylum if they had been "firmly resettled" in that country of transit,[225] a provision that DHS had officially interpreted as requiring that they had received an offer of citizenship, permanent resident status, or some other type of permanent resettlement."[226] While the "firm resettlement" bar did not explicitly rule out another bar for something like fleeting transit, it did tend to show that Congress had considered the status of those coming through other countries and did not intend to prohibit asylum because a person had merely passed through another country.

On the day the new regulation went into effect, the ACLU filed yet another lawsuit. In that case, *East Bay Sanctuary Covenant v. Barr*, the government argued that "Nowhere . . . did Congress say that firm resettlement in a third country [or a safe third country agreement]—and nothing less—could be the sole ground for denying asylum to an alien based on actions in that third country."[227] But Judge Jon Tigar, who had enjoined the asylum bar in the first *East Bay* case, concluded that "the new categorical prohibition" on migrants entering from Mexico "fundamentally conflicts with the [the approach that] Congress took in enacting mandatory bars based on a safe option to resettle or pursue other relief in a third country." He concluded that once again, the government had acted inconsistently with the law, and he entered a preliminary injunction.[228] On appeal, the Court of Appeals for the Ninth Circuit made a strange decision. It agreed with Tigar that the government's rule was improper (at least because the government had not allowed public comment), and it upheld his injunction insofar as it applied to processing asylum applicants in the Ninth Circuit. But it also held that he had not cited enough evidence to justify nationwide application of the injunction.[229] Thus, the administration could bar asylum for most migrants coming through Mexico, because most of them crossed the Rio Grande into Texas, in the Fifth Circuit.[230] But it could not apply the illegally issued regulation to those who crossed the desert into Arizona or California, in the Ninth Circuit. A dissenting judge criticized this unequal application of federal law as a "split the baby" approach.[231] Lee Gelernt, the ACLU lawyer who had handled the family separations case and both East Bay cases, headed back to Judge Tigar's court with a new motion and additional evidence showing why the nationwide injunction that Tigar had entered was justified.

Along with RAICES, the CAIR Coalition (an organization that for years had recruited and counseled lawyers who represented migrants detained in Maryland and Virginia) brought a second suit challenging the new rule.[232] It was assigned to Judge Timothy Kelly, who was no "Obama judge"; he had been appointed by President Trump. Kelly denied the organizations' initial motion for an injunction against the new rule.[233] After the Ninth Circuit ruled that the government had improperly failed to allow public comment before the rule took effect, the two organizations renewed their effort, hoping to stop the policy from being applied in any state.

Meanwhile, the government was not satisfied to ban asylum only for migrants crossing from Mexico into Texas and New Mexico. It asked the Supreme Court to intervene and to suspend Judge Tigar's injunction to the extent that it had been sustained by the Ninth Circuit.[234]

In Judge Tigar's court, Gelernt's new motion succeeded. On September 9, 2019, Judge Tigar accepted the Ninth Circuit's invitation to justify a nationwide injunction with more proof that it was justified. In a new decision, based on evidence that Gelernt had filed, he reinstituted the nationwide injunction, noting that some of the plaintiff organizations had offices in Texas and represented asylum-seekers in circuits outside of the Ninth Circuit, and that asylum-seekers "move between jurisdictions" while their cases were pending. However, two days later, the Supreme Court granted the government's motion to stay the preliminary injunction and allowed the third country bar to go into effect for months or years while the case against the ban proceeds through a final decision and all appeals.[235]

A decision that ultimately upholds this ban on asylum applicants who enter through Mexico would spell the end of asylum for most people seeking that protection from the United States government. Asylum would still be available for Mexicans and for people who did not come across the southern border, such as people who flew to the United States from Europe with tourist or student visas and sought asylum after arrival. But it would doom the prospects for asylum for everyone fleeing the violence in Central America, including unaccompanied children.[236] The rapid deportation of tens of thousands of people resulting from application of the rule in the expedited removal process—which is specifically authorized by the rule—would also severely exacerbate the humanitarian crisis in Central America.

THE "REMAIN IN MEXICO" PLAN

Frustrated by court orders that blocked many of its efforts to prevent the long-term incarceration of Central American asylum-seekers, the administration negotiated at the end of 2018 with the newly elected Mexican president, Andrés Manuel López Obrador, for agreement on a plan called "Remain in Mexico." The Mexican foreign ministry announced that "certain" asylum applicants who had passed credible fear screening in the United States could be returned to Mexico to await their immigration court hearings, and that they would be allowed to work in Mexico.[237] The announcement was received skeptically on both sides of the border. With shelters in Mexican border cities already full, Tonatiuh Guillen, the director of Mexico's National Migration Institute, said that "we don't have the capacity to receive them."[238] In the United States, advocates expressed concern that migrants would be unsafe in Mexico, where some had already been murdered,[239] and experts suggested that the plan would be illegal. Professor Stephen Legomsky, who had been the USCIS chief counsel, said that "if a student in my class wrote [a paper justifying the legality of the Remain in Mexico plan], they'd get an F."[240]

The plan had three legal vulnerabilities. First, the section of the immigration law that arguably authorized the government to make some undocumented would-be immigrants wait in Mexico[241] appeared to exempt asylum-seekers.[242] Second, the plan would effectively deprive asylum-seekers waiting in Mexico of the opportunity to be assisted by lawyers as they prepared for immigration court hearings, even if they could afford to pay legal fees, because there are few if any American immigration lawyers in Mexico.[243] Third, the Refugee Act and the protocol to the international Refugee Convention, which the United States had ratified, barred sending any refugee to a country where that person's life or freedom would be in danger on account of one of the grounds that was a basis for asylum eligibility.[244] Mexico has become an extremely dangerous country, and some of the people the United States might require to wait there might be at risk on account of one of those grounds, but the plan did not require officials even to ask migrants whether they had anything to fear in Mexico.[245]

In January 2019, DHS changed the name of the new policy to "Migrant Protection Protocols" (MPP), perhaps the most ironic title that the agency could conjure, and it began forcing Central American asylum-seekers across the United States's southern border. The next month, it expanded the program to include families with children.[246] That day, the ACLU filed a lawsuit, seeking an order declaring the program to be unlawful,[247] and it followed up a week later by seeking a temporary injunction.[248] In April, a federal judge granted the injunction, preventing any further expulsions to Mexico while the suit was pending but not requiring it to bring back to the United States the hundreds of individuals and families that it had already forced across the border.[249] The government appealed to the Ninth Circuit. In May, it dissolved the temporary injunction, although two of the three judges intimated that when a different three-judge panel of the court considered the case fully in October (rather than deciding only whether a temporary injunction was appropriate), the court might strike down the MPP program.[250] In July 2019, while the appeal was pending, the union representing the nation's asylum officers took the unusual step of filing a brief in the case in which they argued that the MPP program "abandons our tradition of providing a safe haven to the persecuted."[251]

That decision cleared the way for the government to ramp up the temporary deportations to Mexico. By early October 2019, it had forced more

than forty thousand asylum-seekers back across the Mexican border, joining another twenty-six thousand asylum-seekers who, because of metering,
had never even gotten as far as a credible fear interview. These migrants
included more than sixteen thousand children, including nearly 500 babies
less than a year old. Most were sent to Tijuana and Ciudad Juárez, cities
where, reportedly, "gangs and drug cartels operate and migrants are often
kidnapped or robbed."[252] The migrants were told that they would have to
wait for months or years in Mexico, after which they would be allowed back
into the United States, under escort, for immigration court hearings. But
because they were south of the border, almost none of them were able to
obtain lawyers.[253] Mass graves of migrants have been found in the state of
Tamaulipas, just south of the Texas border, causing human rights activists
to regard a lengthy wait in northern Mexico as a "death sentence."[254]

Syracuse University's Transactional Records Access Clearinghouse of
migrants studied the cases of migrants who had been required to wait in
Mexico. It found that by the end of June 2019, only 1 percent of those
whose cases had been decided had been able to obtain lawyers, and only
1.3 percent of those with cases pending had counsel. In San Diego, "the two
legal aid organizations accepting clients in Tijuana are overwhelmed," and
although migrants waiting in Mexico were given lists of pro bono legal
services in the United States, a Honduran woman reported that she had
"called them all [and] no one wants to help me because I'm in Tijuana."[255]

Nevertheless, the U.S. government was also putting into place the
administrative machinery to increase the rate of these temporary deportations to Mexico to one thousand migrants per day.[256]

For its part, Mexico had promised that that the migrants who had to
wait there would have access to humanitarian support and work authorization, as well as health care and education.[257] This promise, along with
the claim that the asylum seekers would have access to attorneys, was
cited by the U.S. government in its argument to the Ninth Circuit as it
sought to dissolve the temporary injunction. But in fact, "Mexico has not
provided work authorization to asylum seekers in the MPP program, leaving tens of thousands stranded for prolonged periods, many with no way
to support themselves. Human Rights Watch reported that as of June, the
number of asylum seekers marooned in Ciudad Juarez already outnum-
bered the spaces available in free humanitarian shelters by 11 to 1." It iden-

tified several asylum-seeking migrants who had been sexually assaulted, robbed, or kidnapped while waiting in Mexico to be called for immigration court hearings in the United States.[258]

Human Rights First also investigated. It sent a team to interview the asylum-seekers waiting for hearings in Mexico and discovered "more than a hundred and ten reported cases of rape, kidnapping, sexual exploitation, assault, and other violent crimes" against them, though there were likely more such cases because most of the tens of thousands of migrants who had been forced across the border had not been interviewed.[259] Ironically, the government itself possessed volumes of evidence showing that Mexico was an extremely dangerous place for migrants, including reports from the United Nations High Commissioner for Refugees, Amnesty International, and Human Rights First. It introduced these reports in the case of *East Bay Sanctuary Covenant v. Barr,* seeking to persuade Judge Tigar that Mexico was trying to live up to its international obligations. Judge Tigar pointed out that the government's evidence "consists simply of an unbroken succession of humanitarian organizations explaining why the government's contention is ungrounded in reality."[260]

NEW HARDSHIPS FOR ASYLUM APPLICANTS

At the end of April 2019, the President announced three more policies to deter migrants from seeking asylum and to make life more difficult for those who did apply. He directed DHS to begin a rule-making process that would impose a fee for filing an asylum application and bar asylum applicants from obtaining authorization to work in the United States until claims were finally decided in their favor, even if hearings were delayed because of an inadequate supply of immigration judges rather than through any fault or tactic of the applicant. (The rule in effect since 1995 has been that if adjudication is delayed because the government could not process claims quickly enough, an asylum applicant could obtain a work permit 180 days after seeking asylum.) He also directed the immigration courts to decide all cases involving asylum claims within 180 days after the application was filed[261] (a virtual impossibility, given the court's backlog at the time of more than 900,000 cases).[262]

The promulgation of a final rule to carry out this Presidential order was likely to take months, because the government would have to seek public comment and respond to the comments, as in the case of the proposed rule to overturn the Flores settlement. After that, litigation would be inevitable. Most people who flee to the United States fearing for their lives have few resources and can't afford to pay filing fees, or to wait for years without being able to work.[263] The lack of exemptions for indigent individuals and families, particularly with respect to the fee for filing an application, might violate the due process clause of the Fifth Amendment.[264]

After complaining that asylum officers were making positive credible fear determinations too frequently,[265] the administration in 2019 also began "racing to implement a plan" to designate Border Patrol agents as asylum officers for the purpose of conducting credible fear interviews with both families and single adults at the border, immediately after the migrants arrived. These agents began to conduct credible fear interviews at Dilley in September 2019. "Theoretically, we could end up deporting [migrants] in two weeks, rather than two to five years," a Border Patrol official explained.[266] Human rights groups argued that law enforcement officers "are not suited to carry out sensitive, non-adversarial fear screenings," while the President's senior immigration advisor, Stephen Miller, pressed for the change precisely because he viewed asylum officers as "soft."[267] The legality of this plan was also doubtful, because the immigration law requires credible fear interviews to be conducted by DHS officials with training equivalent to that of asylum officers, who must undergo a six-week residential training course and thereafter participate in weekly trainings on human rights violations around the world.[268] Like so many other immigration restrictions of the Trump administration, the plan to have Border Patrol agents determine whether migrants legitimately feared persecution or torture was sure to be challenged in court.

NORTHERN TRIANGLE "ASYLUM COOPERATION" AGREEMENTS

As noted above, Congress amended the immigration law in 1996 to permit agreements with certain other countries that would require asylum-seekers who passed through those countries to seek asylum there rather than in the United States.[269] The law imposes only two standards for such agreements. The first is that the country to which the deportation occurs must be one in which the migrant's life or freedom would not be threatened on account of race, religion, nationality, political opinion, or membership in a particular social group. Although this standard seems at first blush similar to the standard for granting asylum in the United States, it is not the same. This part of the statute uses the same "threatened" language that appears in the standard for "withholding of removal."[270] The Supreme Court has held that the withholding of removal standard is much more difficult for a migrant to meet, as protection may be denied unless the migrant can prove a more than 50 percent likelihood of persecution, as opposed to a "well-founded fear" of persecution, requiring only a reasonable possibility, perhaps a 10 percent chance, that persecution would actually occur.[271] The second standard is that in the country to which the migrant is deported, she must have "access to a full and fair procedure for determining a claim to asylum or equivalent temporary protection."

Angry about the rising number of migrant apprehensions during the spring of 2019, President Trump threatened to impose high tariffs on Mexican exports to the United States if Mexico did not stem the flow of people fleeing from Central America. Faced with a threat that could wreck the nation's economy, Mexico's president agreed to reinforce its southern border and to allow a large expansion of the MPP program through which non-Mexican migrants who had arrived in the United States from Mexico would have to wait in that country until their immigration court cases were heard. This agreement caused President Trump to postpone but not withdraw the tariff threat, which remained subject to being "reinstated." The President intimated that the agreement with Mexico included a secret clause that provided that if those two measures proved insufficient to reduce migration through Mexico to levels acceptable to him, Mexico and the United States would sign a "safe third country agreement." At the same time, Vice-President Mike Pence claimed that the United States had already "reached" an agreement with Guatemala that would be implemented "if necessary."[272]

Pence's announcement presaged the signing, in rapid succession, of vaguely worded "asylum cooperation agreements" with all three Northern

Triangle countries, although not with Mexico, which continued to resist.[273] None of these agreements was titled a "safe third country" agreement, and the administration did not use that term in describing the agreements, perhaps in deference to the wishes of Northern Triangle countries' governments, or perhaps because the administration feared ridicule for asserting that these countries were "safe" for people who had just fled from them. Nor were the agreements framed as bars to asylum in the United States for Central American or other refugees. Instead, the agreements refer to "transfers" of migrants from the United States, and they do so in an oddly backhanded manner. For example, Article 3 of the agreement with El Salvador states that El Salvador "shall not return or remove a Protection Claimant [that is, an asylum applicant] referred by the United States under the terms of Article 4 to another country until an administratively final adjudication of the person's Protection Claim has been made," but Article 4 does not explicitly state under what conditions the United States will "transfer" a person to El Salvador, or even that it will engage in transfers. Instead, Article 4 says that El Salvador "shall examine [these cases] in accordance with its Protection Determination System, to determine the Protection Claim of any person who makes such claims after arriving at a port of entry, or crossing a border between ports of entry of the United States on or after the effective date of this agreement." Unlike the third country transit bar, these agreements exempt unaccompanied minors from "transfer," but, also unlike that bar, they do not require that a migrant who is being "transferred" pursuant to the agreement must have entered the United States across its southern border.

According to their terms, the agreements will be elaborated through further "standard operating procedures" that the countries will develop.[274] As of this writing, it is unclear whether those procedures will in any way narrow the sweeping language of the agreements themselves. If not, these agreements would appear to allow the United States to simply deport most of its asylum applicants to the Northern Triangle. Each agreement exempts nationals of the signing Central American country; for example, Guatemalans could not be "transferred" to Guatemala.[275] But Guatemalans seeking asylum in the United States could be "transferred" to Honduras, Hondurans to El Salvador, and Salvadorans to Guatemala. Furthermore, applicants from elsewhere in Latin America (such as political refugees from Venezuela or Cuba), from Africa, or from Asia who arrived in the United States by any means (on foot, by boat, or by plane) could be "transferred" to any of the Northern Triangle countries without having their claims heard in the United States. For example, an African family that flew from Nigeria to Mexico City and then made it to the United States could be "transferred" to El Salvador even though no member of the family had ever set foot in that country.

These agreements, which would consign asylum applicants to the most dangerous non-warring countries in the world,[276] may represent a "belt and suspenders" approach by the Trump administration as it sought to cut off asylum adjudication. Trump and other U.S. officials may have feared that the courts would ultimately strike down the bar to asylum for those who arrived between official ports of entry, the Remain in Mexico program, and the third country transit bar. But if those other efforts don't survive judicial scrutiny, the Northern Triangle agreements are equally unlikely to be sustained. Recall that the Immigration and Nationality Act assures asylum adjudication by U.S. authorities to any person arriving in the United States or at its border, excepting only those arriving from a country with which the U.S. has a valid safe third country agreement (Canada alone)[277] or those who have been firmly resettled elsewhere.

Despite U.S. efforts, some or all of these agreements may never be implemented because of court challenges in the United States or resistance within the countries in question. The agreement with Guatemala, for example, is apparently very unpopular there. President Jimmy Morales signed it just six months before his term of office was to end, reportedly so that he could seek a safe U.S. haven from President Trump after he loses his immunity from prosecution for corruption. Guatemala's incoming president has been critical of the accord, while stopping short of repudiating it.[278] If transfers of tens of thousands of migrants begin and are not halted by U.S. courts, the Northern Triangle's skeletal asylum adjudication systems will quickly be overwhelmed. Guatemala, for example, has only three people available to interview asylum applicants, and El Salvador has only one such officer.[279] The Trump administration's threats of tariffs and offers of modest foreign aid may have been enough to persuade Central

American leaders to agree to become countries of refuge, but the fact that tens of thousands families have fled from the region to seek safety in the United States suggests that outsourcing what the administration sees as its refugee problem may be more challenging than collecting signatures on cooperation agreements.

Conclusion

The Trump administration conceived its own unique solution to the problem of preventing the entry into the United States of the children and families fleeing from violence in Central America. Like prior administrations, it believed that long-term detention would deter migration. But it was stymied by Judge Gee's order in Flores, and in any event, it preferred total exclusion, if that were possible. Its threefold policy was to deter migrants from trying to travel to the United States, to keep them out if they tried to enter, and to deport them as quickly as possible if they managed to cross the border.

It adopted at least nine approaches to the task. First, it tried to prevent asylum seekers from seeking entry at border crossings. Either it deliberately slowed processing at Customs and Border Protection (CBP)-staffed land ports of entry or it declined to expand those posts so that they could accommodate the refugees from the Northern Triangle. As a result, long lines of refugees were forced to wait under dangerous conditions in Mexico. Second, it tried to undo the Flores settlement, in Congress, in court, and through a regulation. Third, it tried to separate families, using the children as pawns to discourage others from coming. Fourth, with the A- B- and L- E- A- cases, it overruled the A- R- C- G- opinion and decades of precedent, in an effort to deny asylum to victims of domestic violence and gang violence. Fifth, through a proclamation and accompanying regulation, it purported to bar asylum to any migrants who entered the United States without applying for asylum at the border crossings that it had blocked them from reaching. Sixth, it issued another regulation, to bar asylum to any non-Mexican who came through Mexico, even those who managed to apply at an official port of entry. Seventh, it forced thousands of asylum seekers to wait in Mexico for months or years before their claims are resolved by backlogged U.S. immigration courts. Eighth, it sought to deny bond hearings to detained migrants, including children, who were eligible for release on bond. And ninth, with threats of tariffs and other inducements, it persuaded the governments of the Northern Triangle countries to agree that their countries could become dumping grounds for the United States' asylum-seekers.

Each of the measures that the Trump administration adopted prompted litigation: the Al Otro Lado case, challenging the slow processing at the border crossings; a contempt motion in the Flores case itself, challenging the anti-Flores regulation; the Ms. L case, attacking the family separations; the Grace case, seeking to enjoin enforcement of the A- B- decision; the East Bay and O.A. cases, reacting to the barring of asylum for those who cross the Rio Grande; the second East Bay case, challenging the July 2019 regulation; and the Innovation Law Lab case, testing the legality of the Remain in Mexico plan, a motion in the Flores case, and the initiation of the Padilla case, seeking bond hearings for detained migrants; and the second East Bay case, challenging the regulation that would deny asylum to nearly everyone arriving from Mexico. Additionally, the Ramos case would at least temporarily prevent family separations resulting from the termination of Temporary Protectedff Status for Salvadorans and Haitians. The compacts with the Northern Triangle countries are bound to be the subjects of litigation as well.

Litigation often moves slowly, as the Flores case itself demonstrates. These cases, with their twists, turns, and appeals, may well outlive the Trump administration. Along with the other cases discussed in this book, such as Orantes, the Hutto litigation, the battles over licensing the baby jails in Texas and Pennsylvania, and the Osorio-Martinez case, as well as the legal community's support for individual families detained in Artesia, Karnes, and Dilley, they demonstrate that since the initiation of the Flores case in 1985, the number of immigration advocates willing to take on the United States government on behalf of migrant children has grown considerably. They also show that both the courts and Congress have frequently reined in efforts of successive administrations, both Democratic and Republican, that resulted or would have resulted in harsh conditions of confinement for migrant children, unfair procedures for adjudication of their cases, or improper denials of asylum.

But the work of the advocates, the legislature, and the courts is far from done. There have been many incremental reforms since the Flores case began, most of which are under sudden and sustained attack by the Trump administration. Even after that administration ends, and even if the status quo as of 2016 were restored, further progress toward a humanitarian response to the flight of children and families from violence abroad will be necessary.

UNACCOMPANIED MINORS

In recent years, most of the public controversy over the detention of migrant children has focused on the detention of those who arrived with adults and were subject to being jailed in Artesia, Dilley, Karnes, Berks, or new family detention centers that the Trump administration may build. Less criticism has focused on how the government deals with the unaccompanied children. There is good reason for this, because on the whole, the treatment of most unaccompanied children by the Office of Refugee Resettlement (ORR) has been relatively benign, and that good outcome could be traced to the Flores case.

As the population of migrants in ORR shelter care has increased, more concerns have been raised about inadequate medical care in some of the facilities as well as "thousands of sexual abuse allegations and reports of personal enrichment by some nonprofit operators."[1] But there have been no recent reports of makeshift jails like the Mardi Gras Motel, incarceration of unaccompanied children in rooms with unrelated adults, strip searches without cause, or deprivation of contact with lawyers. In the 1980s, the early stages of the Flores case called attention to the abuses of the Immigration and Naturalization Service (INS). The litigation also prompted the government to embody a series of required reforms in its contracts with institutions that would house migrant children, and to try to transfer responsibility for the children to the Community Relations Service.

Most importantly, the Flores case resulted in the 1997 settlement that assured a child's prompt release from detention into the least restrictive environment that could be arranged, given the needs of that child. The Homeland Security Act assigned custody of the children to ORR, an agency concerned with migrants' welfare. Once assigned the task, ORR made real efforts to place children with adult relatives or, if necessary, in acceptable foster care, and even when it had to house children in the equivalent of halfway houses, conditions there were not at all like prison environments. The Trafficking Victims Protection Reauthorization Act of 2008 (TVPRA) eventually followed, improving on the Homeland Security Act and the Flores agreement. After 1985, many lawyers and social workers became involved in protecting migrant children, but the initial achievement of Peter Schey and Carlos Holguín in obtaining the Flores agreement should not be overlooked.

This is not to say that all the problems involving unaccompanied minors have been solved. In addition to problems at particular ORR shelters, four other concerns have not been addressed sufficiently. Conditions during short term CBP custody seems still to be a problem. Threats to prosecute or deport undocumented relatives who would otherwise care for unaccompanied children, as well as a failure to anticipate a substantial increase in the number of such children in 2019, forced ORR to house many of those children in unregulated temporary detention centers, sometimes referred to as "tent cities". Fear that some undocumented family member will be identified, arrested, and deported has discouraged potential sponsors from coming forward, resulting in more children being confined for lengthy periods in ORR shelters. And children are deported despite possible eligibility for U.S. protection simply because they lack legal representation.

The CBP Processing Facilities

Complaints about the INS, and after 2003, CBP processing facilities at the border have continued ever since the Flores case was originally filed.[2]

In 2015, in response to an enforcement motion that Schey filed in the Flores case, Judge Dolly Gee had ruled that CBP "must comply" with the requirements of the Flores agreement in border facilities.[3] Convinced that CBP remained unresponsive to this order, Schey persisted, filing another motion in 2016, in which he asserted that children at the border stations in the Rio Grande Valley were still "forced to sleep in overcrowded cells on cold concrete floors with no mattresses or blankets, no change of clothes, no soap, towels or washing facilities, and entirely inadequate food and dirty drinking water." He accompanied his motion, as usual, with many sworn declarations from children who reported those conditions. He asked Judge Gee to appoint a special monitor to observe the conditions in the CBP holding facilities.[4]

The government denied the allegations and noted that the children were not available to be cross-examined about the poor conditions they alleged. Judge Gee gave DHS three months to take sworn depositions from any children who had filed the declarations. When the government's lawyers took no such action during that time, and only filed statements from senior officials describing CBP's policies, she held that the government had waived its right to interrogate the children, and that the record showed that the CBP policies were not actually being implemented. She found that in the Rio Grande Valley sector, CBP did not provide adequate access to food or clean water; that it did not have "safe and sanitary" facilities,[5] and that the stations lacked proper temperature control, causing the children to be unable to sleep.[6] She noted that the Flores agreement required sanitary conditions for the children. Based on the declarations that Schey had filed, she found that CBP was violating the agreement by its failure to provide "soap, towels, showers, dry clothing [and] toothbrushes" for the children in its Rio Grande Valley holding centers.[7] But she declined to order the appointment of an "independent" monitor as Schey had requested, instead telling DHS to appoint a monitor and promising to review the request for a more independent monitor in a year if there was still an issue.[8]

A year later, there was indeed still an issue. In May 2018, the ACLU published a forty-eight-page study, based on 30,000 pages of records it had obtained through a Freedom of Information Act request that CBP had first ignored but had then been forced to honor as a result of a still another lawsuit.[9] The study looked at the complaints of abuse and neglect that children had filed against CBP. It found that a quarter of them involved physical abuse including sexual assault, the use of stress positions, beatings, death threats, denials of necessary medical care, and inadequate food and water.[10]

The ACLU's data was based on several years of complaints, but Schey had to prove abuses, if they existed, after Judge Gee had appointed DHS to monitor itself. This he did. On July 16, 2018, he filed declarations showing that in recent weeks, children in CBP custody were kept hungry, were given frozen, green ham sandwiches that made them sick, had to drink water that smelled bad from a sink above the toilet, could not brush their teeth, were not allowed to shower for five days, had to use toilets that did not flush, and were kept in rooms so cold that the mylar blankets issued to them still left them shivering.[11] This time, Judge Gee had seen enough to warrant the appointment of an independent monitor, and she appointed Andrea Sheridan Ordin.[12] Ordin, then a partner in a large law firm, had been the third woman in the nation to be appointed as a United States Attorney. She was also the President of the Los Angeles County Bar Association.[13]

Judge Gee decreed that DHS would have to provide Ordin with detailed information about the food and liquid given to each child in CBP custody, the toiletries and towels provided, temperature readings in CBP facilities, whether the child was given a blanket and mattress if held overnight, and whether the child was notified of her rights under the Flores agreement. It also allowed her to inspect detention facilities without prior notice and to interview children and facility staff, and it required the government to pay Ordin at the rate of $250 per hour.[14] Undaunted, the Trump administration appealed this order,[15] though it ultimately dropped its objection to Ordin's appointment.[16]

It did pursue its appeal of Judge Gee's 2017 decision finding that DHS had failed to provide sanitary conditions in the Rio Grande Valley holding stations. A Justice Department lawyer told the judges of the Ninth Circuit that the Flores Agreement's requirement of "safe and sanitary" conditions for children did not mean that the children had to have such items as soap or toothbrushes, or that they could not be made to sleep on concrete floors. The judges were incredulous. "I find that inconceivable that the government would say that is safe and sanitary," Judge William Fletcher told the government's lawyer. "It's within everybody's understanding that if you

Inspector General's photograph of CBP overcrowding at the McAllen, Texas, station, 2019.

don't have a toothbrush, if you don't have soap, if you don't have a blanket, it's not safe and sanitary," added Judge A. Wallace Tashima, who as a boy had been held with other Japanese-Americans in a U.S. internment camp.[17] The appellate court dismissed the government's appeal.[18]

Meanwhile, the increasing number of child migrants in the spring of 2019 took CBP by surprise and overwhelmed its facilities. Lawyers reported that despite Gee's orders, at a station in Clint, Texas, "children as young as 7 and 8, many of them wearing clothes caked with snot and tears, are caring for infants they've just met. . . . Toddlers without diapers are relieving themselves in their pants. Teenage mothers are wearing clothes stained with breast milk. . . . They have no access to toothbrushes, tooth-paste or soap."[19]

Undaunted by the then-pending appeal of her 2017 order, Judge Gee also issued a new order in June, 2019, directing the government to report within two weeks on the steps it had taken to comply with her 2017 order.[20] Her order was based on 103 pages that Schey filed, filled with children's horrific descriptions of the conditions to which children were subjected during their recent detention by CBP.[21] Just three days later,

DHS's own Inspector General confirmed that its investigators had observed "serious overcrowding" of unaccompanied children and families at CBP holding facilities in the Rio Grande Valley and that "31 percent of the 2669 children in those facilities had been held longer than the 72 hours generally permitted under [government standards] and the Flores Agreement."[22]

Unregulated Detention Centers

In 1985, Jenny Flores's undocumented mother was afraid to claim custody of her because she feared being arrested, so Flores languished in jail until Peter Schey discovered her. Over the years, the fear of arrest abated, as the government dropped its policy of arresting and deporting sponsors. But the Trump administration re-instituted the policy, insisting on finger-printing every relative or other responsible adult who offered to sponsor an unaccompanied child so that the child could be released from an ORR shelter.[23] It also let it be known that any undocumented person who came forward as a sponsor could be prosecuted or deported. Although it was evident that this policy would deter many undocumented parents from revealing themselves, some did so anyway, and by October, 2018, "dozens of applicants who took the chance of applying to be sponsors have been arrested on immigration charges," leaving more children "stranded in fed-eral custody."[24]

All other members of prospective sponsors' households also had to be fingerprinted, and ORR was required to provide the fingerprints to ICE.[25] This further deterred sponsorship, and the predictable result was that ORR ran out of shelter space. In addition, an increased number of unac-companied children arrived in 2018. ORR had to respond to the "emer-gency" by constructing a vast "tent city" (the government's term for tents was "soft-sided facilities") on a military base in a remote area of a Texas desert. It was originally planned to hold 360 teenagers but by October 2018, fifteen hundred children were living in the tents, having been awak-ened and moved there from other facilities in the middle of the night because "they will be less likely to try to run away in the dark."[26]

Because the tent city was on a federal military base, it was not subject to the "regulations that other traditional migrant youth shelters [other than the family detention centers] must follow to maintain their state licensing." As a result, schooling was not provided.[27] Instead, children were "given workbooks but are not obligated to fill them out" and because the location was so remote "access to legal services at the tent city is also limited."[28] The sponsorship crisis caused by the fingerprint policy also caused the government to spend $775 per day to take care of each child, compared with $250 per day in an ORR shelter program.[29] Negative publicity and mounting costs eventually forced the administration to abandon the policy of fingerprinting household members other than a child's sponsor,[30] and in 2019, Congress prohibited DHS from initiating removal proceedings against anyone based on information shared by ORR except in rare instances.[31] ORR closed the Texas tent city, but at the same time expanded another unregulated "temporary shelter" on the Homestead Air Reserve Base in Florida because the population of unaccompanied migrants continued to expand.[32]

Like its tent city predecessor, Homestead was not subject to state child welfare rules, and conditions there quickly attracted criticism. Schey complained to Judge Gee at the end of May 2019 that "children are housed in prison-like conditions and unnecessarily incarcerated for up to several months without being determined to be flight risks or a danger to themselves or others."[33] As if to prove his point, five days later ORR announced that it had run out of funding for education and recreation at Homestead and other ORR shelters and was discontinuing such services, notwithstanding the requirements of the Flores settlement agreement.[34] Three weeks later, Congress passed emergency legislation to fund those ORR services, as well as to enable CBP to set up temporary facilities at border stations, but the Superintendent of the Miami-Dade public schools called the law a "stop-gap measure" and called for a long-term solution to avoid future crises in ORR facilities.[35]

The length of ORR detention at Homestead and elsewhere is also an issue, at least during peak periods. The Flores settlement agreement required the government to try to place unaccompanied children with family members as quickly as possible. For many years, ORR was able to place the vast majority of children in its custody within about a month, by reuniting them with parents, other close family members, or in some cases, more remote family members. But as fear of arrest spread through immigrant communities in 2018 and 2019, and fewer people came forward as sponsors, the proportion of children at Homestead and elsewhere who could not be placed promptly expanded. By June 2019, a third of all the children in ORR care had no identifiable sponsor, a much higher proportion than during the Obama years. These children faced the prospect of remaining in ORR custody for years, until either their immigration cases were finally resolved or they were transferred to ICE's adult detention centers upon reaching the age of 18.[36] Peter Schey had complained bitterly to Judge Gee about this violation of the agreement, particularly at Homestead. The government's lawyers acknowledged that many children at Homestead remained without sponsors, but it noted that in order to encourage sponsorship, it had in recent months relaxed its fingerprint requirements for potential sponsors and had ceased requiring ICE to confirm that a potential sponsor had legal status. It explained that it was dealing with "an unprecedented influx" of unaccompanied minors, and that Schey's "only proposed solution" (transferring children from Homestead to licensed child care facilities after they had been there for twenty days) would harm the children because it would "delay their release by interfering with the ongoing efforts [to place them with sponsors] of their case manager at Homestead."[37]

Representation

If a child of an indigent family is charged with a juvenile offense that could lead to her incarceration in a residential facility, the government must pay for an attorney to represent the child.[38] But no court case or statute requires the state to pay for an attorney for an indigent child whom the government is seeking to deport, even if that child faces possible torture or death as a consequence.[39]

Yet representation is the "single most important factor" in determining whether an unaccompanied child ultimately obtains relief from deportation in immigration court.[40] The Transactional Records Access Clearinghouse at Syracuse University studied data on more than twelve thousand cases of unaccompanied children whose fates were determined by immigration judges from FY 2012 through FY 2014. The rates at which the children were represented varied from 71 percent in 2012 to the much lower rates of 46 percent and 20 percent in FY 2013 and 2014, as the numbers of unaccompanied children rose dramatically. The disparity in success rates was even more striking than the changes in representation rates. Through the three-year period, 73 percent of the children who were represented were allowed to remain in the United States, compared with only 15 percent of the unrepresented children.[41]

The immigration court system takes the position that representation of unaccompanied children isn't necessary.[42] Assistant Chief Immigration Judge Jack Weil testified in a deposition as follows:

Q. What about children that are so young, that even if they receive the notice [of the hearing] and even if they're given an explanation by the judge, they're still not going to understand what's going on, right?

A. I have to do a case-by-case basis determination. I've taught immigration law literally to three-year-olds and four-year-olds. It takes a lot of time. It takes a lot of patience. They get it. It's not the most efficient, but it can be done.

Q. I understand that you think it can be done. Are you aware of any experts in child psychology or comparable experts who agree with the assessment that three- and four-year-olds can be taught immigration law?

A. I haven't read any studies one way or another.

Q. What about like a one-year-old?

A. I mean, I think there's a point that there has to be communication.[43]

Weil's suggestion that children could represent themselves in immigration court was ridiculed in several darkly hilarious videos showing children being questioned in mock immigration court hearings.[44]

For a time, the federal government attempted to provide representation to at least some children through the Justice Americorps program of the Department of Justice , but President Trump and Attorney General Sessions ended such assistance in 2017 by terminating the partnership between the Justice Department and Americorps.[45] Now, children as young as two have to defend themselves in immigration court, although in some cases local charities may provide them with legal representation.[46]

FAMILIES WITH CHILDREN

At least most unaccompanied children are not detained in jail-like settings for up to two years (which as of 2018 was the average time for between apprehension and an immigration court hearing).[47] Children who arrive with adults would receive much worse treatment, if parents are forced to waive their children's Flores rights under threat of family separation, or if the Flores settlement's ban on long-term detention of migrant children is undone by legislation or if higher courts reverse Judge Gee's injunction against the rule purporting to repeal the Flores settlement. The overwhelming weight of pediatric and psychiatric testimony and reporting warns that many of those thousands of children, growing up in jail, will suffer substantial long-term mental and emotional damage, and that their relationship with their mothers will be shattered as a result of the family being under the total control of guards, day in and day out.

An end to the protections of the Flores settlement, after all these years, is also a real possibility, particularly after the reconstitution of the Supreme Court with two conservative justices appointed by President Trump. While it's always risky to predict what the court will decide, the current Court might well either defer to DHS's claim that its regulation to repeal Flores actually "implements" it, or to a policy condoning coerced waivers. Or Texas might license jails for migrant families, and the Court might declare those facilities to be "non-secure" and compliant with the Flores agreement.[48] The government could use contractors to build more family jails; in fact, the Trump administration unsuccessfully asked Congress to add 960 beds to Dilley, which would have brought its capacity to nearly 3,500 people. In the spring of 2019, it had converted Karnes from a family detention center to an adult detention center, apparently because it was easier to deport single adults than to deport families. But by the fall, it planned to reopen Karnes as a family detention center.[49] Similarly, the Court might defer to the Attorney General's reinterpretation of asylum law in the A- B- case and deny asylum to nearly all mothers fleeing domestic violence and gang violence.[50] A law student who volunteered at Dilley for the entire summer of 2018 estimated to me that 80 to 90 percent of the mothers incarcerated there had experienced actual domestic violence, not just the threat of violence. The A- B- decision, if upheld, would mean that after a period of family imprisonment, the mothers and children will be deported to countries where their lives will be in danger. The MPP "Remain in Mexico" policy, as applied to families forced to fend for themselves south of the border for many months while they wait for asylum adjudication, also puts children in grave danger. So will the Trump administration's agreements with the Northern Triangle countries if they are ever implemented.

A BETTER SYSTEM

Those are the harsh outcomes that are possible. But a different outcome is also possible. Recall that as a presidential candidate, Hillary Clinton called for an end to family detention. A future president from either party might take up that mantle of reform.

What would humanitarian reform mean for the processing of migrating families? To begin with, it is worth noting that simply opening the borders to all who want to live in the United States is unrealistic, but that prioritizing admission for people fleeing persecution and torture (as well as for people seeking to reunite with close relatives, and those who bring special talents to the country) makes sense—and these categories of would-be immigrants are indeed already singled out for lawful immigration in the Immigration and Nationality Act. Given that some groups of people, such as those fleeing persecution, are to be admitted and others, such as those who want only to better their economic prospects, are not, the country has to have both sorting and deportation processes. And to be legitimate, these processes must be fair.

Because at times there are relatively large flows of migrants, particularly at the southern border, a system that did not rely on a vast prison network would likely require a streamlined process, such as credible fear interviews, to screen out those who have no possible legal basis for remaining in the United States, as well as some means of making it likely that families who are allowed to remain until they can prepare adequately for hearings will appear in court. Screening for family groups could take place at the border, rather than in an ICE jail, but each border processing center should be augmented and upgraded so that children and adults alike would have beds rather than floor space for those who have to stay overnight, clean water and hygienic supplies, appropriate temperature controls, and facilities in which legal representatives could, in private, prepare parents for the screening interviews, much as they do now at Karnes and Dilley.

The experience at Artesia, in which most families were deported before the lawyers arrived, but few were deported after they arrived, demonstrates the importance of making it possible for volunteer lawyers to help the parents to relate their stories cogently to an asylum officer. The screening interviews could take place by videoconference. Many are already conducted in that manner. Although DHS would continue to confirm the identities of arriving migrant children, and it could retain legal custody of them during a short processing period, the physical custody of children and families (as opposed to single adults) should be transferred to ORR immediately upon their arrival at a CBP facility. From that point on, ORR rather than CBP should be responsible for their safety, housing, physical needs, and medical care while CBP does its paperwork and asylum officers conduct credible fear interviews to screen out families with no plausible claim to present to an immigration judge. For decades, CBP has proved a poor caretaker for children, and it should be divested of that responsibility, just as it was divested of longer-term responsibility for UACs by the Homeland Security Act.

Parents who pass the screening interview should be released promptly, with their children, to await hearings. The government released most such families, in the years before Judge Gee limited the amount of time during which they could be detained, because it did not have jail space for all of them. The successful, well-received case management system that President Trump ended showed that families will show up for hearings to have their asylum claims heard, even if they might be ordered deported, if they are given support, including information on how to get to court. Not as good, but at slightly lower cost, the government could purchase many more ankle monitors.[51]

Both solutions are much more humane and much less costly than family detention. In the case of families with older children who had committed violent crimes, or who were determined, based on evidence, to be dangers to themselves or others, the parents might have to decide between entrusting the children to secure facilities maintained by ORR or staying together with them in a small detention facility, preferably a humane one that is more like Berks than like Dilley. The government should also continue the effort, commendably started by the Trump administration, to hire more immigration judges so that the average waiting time for a hearing is reduced from years to perhaps six months,[52] and until that occurs it should prioritize for hearings the cases of any families whose children remained confined.

Immigration judges and the members of the Board of Immigration Appeals should not remain employees of the Justice Department, subject to being transferred to undesirable locales or to other agencies if they render decisions that don't suit the Attorney General, and to having their decisions reversed when they don't accord with the President's political agenda.[53] Instead, Congress should create an independent immigration court system, and the existing immigration judges and BIA members should become trial and appellate judges of that new court.[54]

The Bush, Obama, and Trump administrations have all wanted to lock families up, not because they thought that these families would commit crimes or fail to appear for their court hearings,[55] but because they thought that stories of harsh treatment, filtering back to Central America, would deter families from trying to make the trip north. Even if legal,[56] deterrence doesn't work, at least for families desperate to escape from violence, or even from grinding poverty. Despite the widely publicized existence of the baby jails, the number of families apprehended by CBP near the Mexican border increased from 106,000 in FY 2017 to 160,000 in FY 2018.[57] The monthly number of family members apprehended by CBP near the southern border—most of whom were only too happy to turn themselves in to the first officer they could find—hit a record 84,491 in May, 2019.[58]

While these figures might be lower if Flores were overturned and the duration of family detention was longer, it seems doubtful that most families facing brutal violence or death would avoid migrating on that account. If the United States were to make a serious effort to reduce migration from the Northern Triangle, it would vastly increase the foreign aid directed to the region, rather than reducing or suspending it as the Trump administration has done.[59] A relatively modest increase in foreign aid to El Salvador during the Obama administration reduced gang violence to some degree, and Salvadoran migration to the United States reportedly fell before the Trump administration cut off the assistance.[60] Instead of building more jails, the United States government should provide massive assistance to relieve poverty, provide decent employment opportunities for young men who have nothing better to do than join violent extortion gangs, and assist the governments of Guatemala, Honduras and El Salvador to transform cultures in which many young men think of women as their property, beating and raping them to control their behavior.[61]

A further step would be to restore and expand the processing of U.S. refugee applications in the Central American countries, so that families could apply for refugee status without having to make a dangerous trip through Mexico and risk deportation. The Obama administration started a Central American Minors Program so that some children at risk in the Northern Triangle countries—those who had a parent with legal status in the United States—could have refugee claims considered at U.S. consulates in their own countries. More than three thousand children came to the United States safely as a result of this effort, either as refugees or as parolees, limited though it was.[62] The Trump administration canceled it.[63]

A humanitarian approach to the problem of fear-induced migration of children from the northern triangle countries would be far better than using the prospect of long periods of detention, or of being warehoused under poor and dangerous conditions in Mexico or Guatemala, to deter the children and their families from attempting the dangerous journey through Mexico. Human Rights First and other non-governmental organizations have published a comprehensive plan for addressing the "crisis" that is far superior to the punitive programs of administrations from Reagan through Trump.[64]

THE BIG PICTURE

The detention of child migrants, which has been the subject of this book, is a little horror story that is part of a much larger one. The United Nations estimates that the world has a record number of more than twenty-five million refugees, half of them under the age of eighteen.[65] Not all of those people would qualify as "refugees" within the meaning of the Convention on the Status of Refugees and its Protocol or the Refugee Act of the United

States; many have fled armed conflict or natural disasters rather than persecution, or gang violence, a category at the contested borderline of the type of harm for which asylum is offered under current U.S. law.[66] Nevertheless, many millions of children need protection, and with the notable exceptions of Canada and Spain, the gates of the developed world are closing in Europe, Australia, and elsewhere, as in the United States.[67]

Global warming will intensify displacement and suffering, as coastlines are flooded, devastating storms become more frequent, fertile land becomes dry, and island nations sink.[68] Indeed, the United States is already seeing the arrival of victims of climate change. Crops are failing in Guatemala and Honduras because those countries have become too warm, and people who are starving as a result have been heading for Texas, and then Florida, and other states, joining the tens of thousands fleeing from violence.[69] The World Bank has suggested that at least 1.4 million people could leave Mexico and Central America during the next thirty years because of agricultural failures.[70] Climate change will likely require the nations of the world at least to consider whether the Convention should be amended to encompass more categories of people, such as those who need to live in other nations because their own countries become uninhabitable.

Nobody expects the United States to solve the world refugee problem alone; the whole idea behind an international refugee convention was that the cooperation of all the nations was needed to solve what was, in 1951, a much smaller problem. But the United States can do its part, especially with respect to desperate people in nations quite close to its borders.

Perhaps surprisingly, given the misleading border "crisis" rhetoric regularly trumpeted by the Trump administration,[71] Americans have the political will to protect foreign nationals who are threatened with or who have been the victims of violence. Whatever Americans think about immigration in general,[72] they apparently strongly support the protection of refugees. A 2018 survey by Lake Research Partners, a professional polling company, for the Women's Refugee Commission found that 66 percent of voters think that it is important that the United States allow refugees to apply for asylum because they are providing safety for their children, that 70 percent think it important to allow refugees to seek asylum to escape rape or sexual violence, and that 66 percent opposed (53 percent strongly opposed) family jails.[73] Other polls show lower levels, but still majority support, for welcoming refugees fleeing violence and persecution abroad,[74] and particularly for welcoming Central American refugees.[75]

Neither Congress nor any president has yet translated public concern for refugees into a plan that would integrate families with children into the community while they are waiting for determinations on their claims for the protection of American law. That time may yet come. Meanwhile, dedicated lawyers like the advocates featured in this book will continue the struggle, initiated so long ago by Peter Schey and Carlos Holguín, to try to keep children from being locked up in America's baby jails.[76]

WHERE ARE THEY NOW?

Jenny Flores and Alma Cruz live in Southern California with children of their own.[77]

Epilogue

President Donald Trump and his staff did everything they could conceive of to deter, detain, expel, and exclude migrants who sought asylum in the United States. Many of the administration's initiatives were blocked by lower court decisions. One of those blocks—the preliminary injunction barring implementation of a rule that would have denied asylum to those who crossed the Mexican border in an irregular way—was sustained in December 2018 by a 5–4 vote of the Supreme Court.[1]

In late summer 2019, Trump eventually succeeded in putting into force a "third country transit" rule that requires sweeping exclusion of refugees.[2] As noted in chapter 12, a federal district court in California had enjoined enforcement of this new rule, which bars asylum for anyone who has crossed the Mexican border, even at an official port of entry, without first having applied and been rejected for asylum in Mexico or another country. The Ninth Circuit sustained the injunction, though limiting its effect to refugees who arrived from Mexico into its area of jurisdiction, California and Arizona. As this book was going to press in September 2019, the Supreme Court issued a stay of these decisions, thereby reinstating the third country transit rule.[3] It did so without stating any reasons. In dissent, Justices Sotomayor and Ginsberg reflected that "once again the

Executive Branch has issued a rule that seeks to upend longstanding practices regarding refugees who seek shelter from persecution."[4]

The third country transit rule is the most sweeping of all of the Trump
administration's restrictions on asylum adjudication and the most harmful to children who flee from violence in their own countries to seek refuge
in the United States. If the third country transit rule remains in force, it
will effectively gut the regime of protection that has operated for forty
years, ever since Congress enacted the Refugee Act of 1980. This wholesale destruction of the asylum system for both children and adults will
occur even if the courts ultimately strike down the metering practice, the
ban on asylum for people who cross the Rio Grande, the Remain in Mexico
policy, and the agreements with Central American governments. The tens
of thousands of refugees arriving at the U.S. border each month after
arduous trips through Mexico will be deported without due process or
judicial fairness. They will be put into expedited removal proceedings,
interviewed at the border most likely by border patrol agents deputized as
temporary asylum officers, and found to lack credible fear. It won't matter
how badly they were persecuted or whether the interviewer believes their
narratives. Normally, a person who satisfies the "credible fear" standard in
an interview is given a chance to seek asylum in a hearing before an immigration judge. The credible fear standard is a low screening standard, far
lower than the test of having to show a judge that the asylum applicant has
a well-founded fear of persecution. But because of the third country transit rule, refugees arriving from Mexico will be disqualified from making a
credible fear showing because they didn't seek first seek asylum in Mexico
or another country. They will not be heard to argue that the countries
through which they travelled are largely controlled by murderous gangs
(often the same gangs that persecuted them in their own countries) or
that those countries do not have functioning asylum adjudication systems
or the ability to provide safety even for their own citizens.

Many, perhaps most, will also be denied the opportunity to ask a judge
to grant them withholding of removal, which is not as advantageous as
asylum but would at least prevent their immediate deportation. To be
allowed a hearing for that claim, a migrant would have to pass the "reasonable fear" test by showing a reasonable possibility of being able to
prove to an immigration judge that persecution in the home country is

more likely than not. That "more likely than not" standard for obtaining withholding is a much higher standard than the "well-founded fear" standard for granting asylum. A refugee who arrives at the border with no legal representation and no documentary evidence of persecution—indeed, with little more than the shirt on her back—will therefore have a hard time passing the reasonable fear test, and not passing that test will result in prompt deportation.

If sustained, the third country transit rule will bar nearly everyone seeking asylum at the southern border, including families and unaccompanied minors. It will bar Africans and Asians who managed to get to Latin America en route to the United States. The only people who will not be barred are victims of trafficking who were involuntarily taken to the United States; Haitian, Cuban, or other Caribbean refugees who somehow evade the Coast Guard and arrive by boat rather than crossing the Mexican border; and people who are able to obtain tourist or student visas to fly to the United States. It is exceedingly difficult for someone who fears persecution to get a visa, because consular officers must interview all applicants and are directed to deny permission to anyone who seems likely to apply for asylum.[5]

It is possible, however, that the new rule will not remain in force indefinitely. It could yet be blocked in any of several ways:

- The Ninth Circuit, considering the merits of the nationwide preliminary injunction entered by Judge Tigar, could sustain the injunction, and the Supreme Court might decline to review such a decision or might affirm it.[6]

- Congress could override the rule or prohibit the administration from using any funds to enforce it.

- A new administration could repeal it.

- A federal judge in another district, deciding another case, could again enjoin the rule.[7] The government would surely ask the Supreme Court to stay that decision, too. But perhaps the Supreme Court granted the stay in the California case for a technical reason, not because it thought the third country transit rule was legal. For example, the Court may have concluded that the plaintiff organizations lacked standing to sue because no migrant had yet been barred when the ACLU filed suit.[8] Or the court may have been troubled by the fact that the Ninth Circuit rendered what looked like a compromise decision, applicable only to migrants arriving in two states. If so, another case, brought elsewhere by other plaintiffs, including people rejected under the new rule, might win in a different court and succeed in avoiding a Supreme Court stay.[9]

- It is not clear whether the U.S. government, after denials of asylum under the third country transit rule, will remove the applicants to Mexico (the most recent country of transit) or deport them to the countries from which they fled. If applicants are pushed through the border turnstiles into Mexico and the limited Mexican asylum system becomes deluged with asylum applicants who are being directed to apply there rather than in the United States, the Mexican government might summarily deny all those applications. Then, under the third country transit rule, these migrants would be free to reapply in the United States.[10] If, on the other hand, the United States deports asylum-seekers to their own countries, and many people are murdered there after being rejected for asylum by the United States simply because of having transited through Mexico, there might be a public outcry against the policy, which might alter the administration's calculus and persuade it to soften the rule.

Trump's primary backups, if the third country transit rule fails, are the agreements that the administration has signed with Northern Triangle countries, which are vague enough to allow the United States to park all its asylum-seekers in that part of the world; e.g., by sending all the Salvadoran refugees to Guatemala and all of the Guatemalan asylum-seekers to El Salvador. But it is one thing to sign a piece of paper and another to provide food and shelter for tens or hundreds of thousands of refugees. It seems unlikely that the populations of those countries, which have so many problems of their own, will happily tolerate hosting large numbers of refugees from neighboring or distant countries.

While the third country transit rule and the related exclusion policies remain in force, there may ironically be less detention of adults, families, and children, except for short holds at CBP facilities. If virtually every Central American migrant and many from other countries are deported after credible fear and reasonable fear denials at the border, there might be no reason to keep open the baby jails. However, a scenario in which the detention of children suddenly comes to a halt seems improbable. First, the third party transit rule is not retroactive to those who arrived before it was issued, so thousands of families are already in a queue for hearings.[11]

Second, the government cannot eliminate immigration court applications for withholding of removal, because that would violate U.S. treaty obligations under the Protocol to the Refugee Convention. While most interviews for "reasonable fear" will probably result in denials of the right to have applications for withholding of removal decided by an immigration court, some families are likely to pass the reasonable fear test, and they could be sent to family jails at least temporarily. They could be held at those jails for long periods if Judge Gee's rejection of the Flores regulation is overturned or stayed by the Supreme Court. In addition, the border facilities may continue to be overloaded. In that case, families might be sent to Dilley or Karnes for at least twenty days so that reasonable fear interviews can be held there. In fact, the government itself does not expect that its new exclusion policies will end its detention of families. After making thousands of families wait in Mexico for hearings, signing the first of the Central American agreements, and promulgating the third country transit rule, it announced that it was reopening Karnes as a family detention center after having used it for several months exclusively for adult detainees.[12]

Detention is traumatic and harmful, particularly for children, as the many mental-health and pediatric organizations and specialists have shown. But persecution, torture, and death are worse. By choking off asylum adjudication for large groups of persecuted migrants, irrespective of human rights and humanitarian concerns, the administration has adopted a policy of extreme but largely invisible cruelty, particularly to children. Deportations under the third country transit rule, the Remain in Mexico policy, and the warehousing agreements with Central America take place out of sight of television cameras in contrast to penning children in cages or separating them from their parents. The legal and political struggle over immigration policy, which for years has been a major national controversy, continues. But until there are major changes in policy, refugee children as well as adults will at best be jailed and at worst will be deported to countries where they will live in perpetual fear.

Important Laws and Lawsuits

LAWS

Immigration and Nationality Act (INA) A long statute compiling virtually all of the immigration laws passed by Congress.

Refugee Act of 1980 An amendment to the INA that created the right to seek asylum in the United States by applying while in the United States or at its border.

Illegal Immigrant Reform and Immigrant Responsibility Act of 1996 (IIRIRA) A set of amendments to the INA that, among other things, created an "expedited removal" procedure for undocumented persons apprehended at the border and the "credible fear" process for those in expedited removal who sought asylum.

Homeland Security Act of 2002 (HSA) Provides that unaccompanied alien children are to be transferred from the Department of Homeland Security to the Office of Refugee Resettlement in the Department of Health and Human Services until their claims for relief from deportation are resolved.

William Wilberforce Trafficking Victims Protection Reauthorization Act of 2008 (TVPRA) Requires transfer of custody of unaccompanied migrant children from Customs and Border Protection to the Office of Refugee Resettlement within three days, and mandates that their asylum claims should be heard in the first instance by asylum officers rather than immigration judges.

LAWSUITS

Cases brought by immigrants or immigrant organizations are referred to by their short names; the names of the government defendants change when political appointees are replaced while the cases move through the court system. Full citations to reported cases appear in the endnotes, associated with the opinions in question. Many documents, including court decisions, that are discussed in this book are not published in official court reporters, but they may be retrieved electronically from the records system of the court in question (in the case of federal records, PACER), using the docket numbers given in the endnotes.

A- B- (Matter of A- B-)   Case in which Attorney General Jeff Sessions overruled the A- R- C- G- decision and barred asylum for most victims of domestic violence and gang violence.

Al Otro Lado   Suit to prohibit DHS from refusing to allow migrants, including families, from seeking asylum at official ports of entry along the United States–Mexico border.

Appeal of Berks County Residential Center   Administrative litigation in Pennsylvania over the licensing of the family detention center in Berks County.

A- R- C- G- (Matter of A- R- C- G-)   The 2014 decision of the Board of Immigration Appeals that approved of allowing some domestic violence victims to win asylum.

Castro   United States Third Circuit Court of Appeals decision denying habeas corpus review for recently-arrived mothers detained at Berks who challenged the adequacy of their credible fear interviews.

Doe   Suit that required Customs and Border Protection officials to provide migrants in custody at the border with certain necessities, such as mattresses.

Dora   Suit by mothers who were separated from their children during the Trump administration, challenging negative credible fear determinations based on interviews that DHS conducted while they were distraught.

East Bay Sanctuary Covenant v. Trump   Suit challenging the presidential proclamation and related regulation denying asylum to persons who had crossed the Rio Grande rather than presenting themselves at an official border crossing.

East Bay Sanctuary Covenant v. Barr   Suit challenging the July 2019 rule denying asylum to non-Mexican persons arriving from Mexico who had not applied for asylum in Mexico or another country en route, and been finally rejected by that country, before seeking asylum in the United States.

Flores   The class action brought in 1985 by Peter Schey and Carlos Holguín, attempting to end the federal government's detention of migrant children.

Grace   Challenge to Homeland Security's application of Attorney General Jeff Sessions's A- B- decision in expedited removal interviews.

Grassroots Leadership   Texas state court suit to prevent the state of Texas from licensing Karnes and Dilley.

Innovation Law Lab   The ACLU's suit challenging the Trump administration's "Remain in Mexico" plan.

J.O.P.   Suit challenging new DHS practice of "redetermining" the status of migrant children who turn eighteen.

L- E- A-   A 2019 case in which Attorney General Barr reversed a Board of Immigration Appeals decision that had allowed asylum based on persecution of a member of the applicant's family.

Matter of Hutto   The ACLU's suit challenging the legality and conditions of detention at the Hutto family detention center.

Ms. L   The ACLU's lawsuit to prevent the separation of migrant families.

O.A.   Suit in which the trial-level court vacated the regulation that was at issue in *East Bay Sanctuary Covenant v. Trump*.

Orantes-Hernandez   Case that required the government to refrain from misleading Salvadoran migrants, and to provide them with written notice of their right to apply for asylum.

Osorio-Martinez   Pennsylvania suit holding that notwithstanding the Castro decision, habeas corpus review of a negative credible fear determination was possible for children who could qualify for special immigrant visas.

Padilla   Case challenging Attorney General's decision to deny bond hearings to adult asylum applicants who had received favorable credible fear determinations.

Ramirez   Class action to require ICE to end the practice of automatically placing children who are in ORR custody in adult detention facilities when they turn eighteen.

Ramos   Lawsuit to prevent the Trump administration from summarily ending Temporary Protected Status for Salvadorans and Haitians.

R. I. L- R-   Class action preliminarily enjoining the government from using deterrence as a rationale to justify keeping asylum-seeking families in detention.

Thuraissigiam   Decision by the Court of Appeals for the Ninth Circuit holding that asylum-seekers in expedited review cases who are found to lack credible fear, and therefore are subject to immediate deportation, can obtain judicial review through a writ of habeas corpus. The court declined to follow the Third Circuit's holding in Castro.

Acronyms

ACLU   The American Civil Liberties Union, which compiled some of the reports and brought several of the cases discussed in this book.

AILA   The American Immigration Lawyers Association, the largest organization of immigration lawyers, with chapters in all major urban areas.

AMSCP   Alien Minor Shelter Care Program, a 1987 plan by the Community Relations Service of the Department of Justice to contract with child care agencies to take physical custody of children, replacing INS custody.

BIA   The Board of Immigration Appeals, which considers appeals from decisions of immigration judges.

CARA   The coalition of the Catholic Legal Immigration Network, the American Immigration Council, the Refugee and Immigrant Center for Education and Legal Services, and the American Immigration Lawyers Association, which came together to represent families in immigration detention in 2014.

CBP   Customs and Border Protection, a division of the Department of Homeland Security. It houses both the Border Patrol and the Office of Field Operations.

DACA   Deferred Action for Childhood Arrivals, the program created by President Barack Obama to provide temporary relief from deportation to certain individuals who had been brought to the United States by their parents without documentation.

DFPS   Texas Department of Family and Protective Services, the agency that attempted to issue licenses to the family detention centers in Texas.

DHS   The Department of Homeland Security, which houses (among other agencies having little to do with immigration), Customs and Border Protection, Immigration and Customs Enforcement, and the United States Citizenship and Immigration Services.

IACHR   The Inter-American Commission on Human Rights, a body of the Organization of American States.

ICE   Immigration and Customs Enforcement, a division of DHS, is responsible for apprehending undocumented persons in the United States (except at the border), for detaining them, and for representing the United States in immigration court hearings.

INS   The Immigration and Naturalization Service, which managed all immigration functions until 2003, when by statute it was dissolved and its functions distributed to three agencies (UCSIS, ICE, and CBP) of the Department of Homeland Security, with the immigration courts and the BIA remaining in the Department of Justice.

MPP   Migrant Protection Protocols (also known as the "Remain in Mexico" plan). The Trump administration's program to require thousands of migrants from Central America and elsewhere to wait in Mexico for months or years before participating in immigration court hearings to resolve their claims for asylum or other relief from deportation.

OFO   CBP's Office of Field Operations. Its officers process individuals, including asylum-seekers, who arrive at official ports of entry, including airports, seaports, and land border crossings.

ORR   The Office of Refugee Resettlement in the Department of Health and Human Services. The Homeland Security Act assigned it responsibility for the custody of UACs.

RAICES   The Refugee and Immigrant Center for Education and Legal Services, in San Antonio, Texas.

TRLA   Texas RioGrande Legal Aid. It represents Grassroots Leadership in the litigation to prevent licensing of the family detention centers in Texas.

TVPRA   The Trafficking Victims Protection Reauthorization Act of 2008, which provided new procedural protections to unaccompanied undocumented children.

UAC   Unaccompanied Alien Children, foreign nationals under the age of eighteen who arrive in the United States and who either have no parent or legal guardian in the United States, or who have no parent or legal guardian in the United States who can provide for their care and physical custody.

UNHCR   United Nations High Commissioner for Refugees, the agency that advises national governments on what the UN believes are their obligations toward refugees under the 1951 Refugee Convention and its 1967 Protocol.

USCIS   United States Citizenship and Immigration Services, the division of DHS in which asylum officers make decisions on applications for immigration benefits, including asylum (for individuals who apply for it before being apprehended, and, after 2008, for unaccompanied minors). Those officers also conduct "credible fear" and "reasonable fear" interviews for asylum-seekers in expedited removal proceedings.

Notes

Dates and headlines for major newspaper and magazine articles which appeared beginning in the late 1990s refer to the online versions. Occasionally headlines will vary from the stories in the print editions, which may have been published the day before or the day after the online version. Articles appearing prior to the advent of digital editions refer to the print editions, retrieved for the most part from Lexis or WestLaw.

These notes include many references to documents filed in federal courts. Documents filed after 2004 can be found on the federal court documents website PACER, www.pacer.gov. Many of those documents may also be viewed and copied for free on the RECAP website, https://free.law/recap. The documents in the Flores case can be found, through PACER or RECAP, on the website of the Federal District Court for the Central District of California. The docket number is 2:85-cv-04544.

INTRODUCTION

1. "Letter to Members of Congress from President Donald J. Trump," January 4, 2009, https://perma.cc/CZ8N-4S5V.

2. In 2018, the average immigration court case took 578 days from the time the immigrant was summoned to court until the case was completed. On average,

a case in which the immigrant sought asylum took three years. See Denise Lu and Derek Watkins, "Court Backlog May Prove Bigger Barrier for Migrants Than Any Wall," *New York Times*, January 24, 2019.

3. A Lexis search suggests that the term was apparently first used by Rebecca Schoenkopf, a blog editor who had once been a writer for the Orange County Weekly. See Rebecca Schoenkopf, "House GOP Has Final Solution For Border Children: Keep Them All in Baby Jail," *Wonkette*, July 17, 2014, https://perma .cc/D27W-86HK.

4. Foreign nationals who have a well-founded fear of persecution on account of race, religion, nationality, political opinion or membership in a particular social group are eligible for asylum. See Chapter 5.

5. A former client and I described what a client and lawyer have to do to present an asylum case in David Ngaruri Kenney and Philip G. Schrag, *Asylum Denied* (Berkeley: University of California Press, 2008), 95–171.

6. In addition to asylum, children can avoid deportation if they achieve "Special Immigrant Juvenile Status" (SIJS). This requires them to obtain both a state court order determining that they were neglected or abandoned by a parent, and a subsequent grant of that status by the Department of Homeland Security. Children found to have been trafficked may also obtain relief from deportation, and permanent resident status, through the issuance of special "T" visas.

7. For a broader look at the impact of Trump administration policy on immigrants and refugees, adults as well as children, see Shoba Sivaprasad Wadhia, *Banned: Immigration Enforcement in the Time of Trump* (New York: New York University Press, 2019).

CHAPTER ONE. JENNY FLORES, 1985–1988

1. Lisa Belkin, "Lonely Young Aliens Pose Problem for U.S.," *New York Times*, May 19, 1989.

2. This INS policy was based on the standard applied by U.S. magistrate judges for releasing juveniles charged with federal offenses under Sec. 504 of the Juvenile Justice and Delinquency Prevention Act of 1974. That standard is now codified at 18 U.S.C. Sec. 5034.

3. "Harold W. Ezell is Dead at 61; Immigration Official in West," *New York Times*, August 27, 1998.

4. Jane Applegate, "Help for Refugees: Activist Attorneys Battle INS to Protect Rights of Immigrants," *Los Angeles Times*, June 1, 1986.

5. Nancy Cleeland and Patrick J. McDonnell, "Harold Ezell, Co-author of Prop. 187, Dies," *Los Angeles Times*, August 26, 1998.

6. Philip Hager and Laurie Becklund, "Ezell's Ouster Urged Over Statements Called Racist," *Los Angeles Times*, September 24, 1987. A spokesman for Ezell

stated that this remark had been directed only at those who participated in the criminal fabrication of fraudulent immigration documents. Id.

7. *Flores v. Meese*, 942 F. 2d 1352, 1355 (9th Cir. 1991) (en banc).

8. Patrick McDonnell, "Children of Poverty, War Stagnate in Camps; Resurgence of Central American Immigration Points Up Plight of Youths Held by the INS," *Los Angeles Times*, April 17, 1988.

9. Bond, like bail in the criminal justice system, is a cash payment to the court to ensure that a detained person, if released, will return to court for a hearing on the merits of whether he or she has any right to remain in the United States. A person who absconds will be ordered deported, the bond will be forfeited, and the absconder is subject to arrest and deportation. In immigration proceedings, bond may not be paid by undocumented persons, so an incarcerated child would have to find a citizen or lawful permanent resident to post bond.

10. Claudia Weinstein, "The Children San Diego Forgot," *American Lawyer*, September 1987, 103–8.

11. Complaint in *Flores v. Meese*, Case 85 4544 RJK (C.D. Calif.), filed July 11, 1985.

12. According to the company's website, it was originally an alcohol and drug rehabilitation service, but in the early 1980s, it began working with the INS, "operating the first privately operated . . . holding facilities." See "Behavioral Systems Southwest History and Mission Statement," https://perma.cc/75HP-STEN.

13. Lorelei Laird, "Meet the Father of the Landmark Lawsuit that Secured Basic Rights for Immigrant Minors," *ABA Journal*, February 1, 2016; for the name of motel, Weinstein, supra n. 10, at 106. In 1989, Los Angeles forced the INS to close the building because it did not meet health and safety standards. See Marc Lacey, "Troubled Motel is Proposed Site of Parolee Home," *Los Angeles Times*, February 23, 1990.

14. Jenny Lisette Flores, affidavit executed on June 26, 1985, filed in the District Court in *Flores v. Meese*.

15. *Flores v. Meese*, 681 F. Supp. 665 (C.D. Calif. 1988).

16. Complaint, supra n. 11.

17. Laird, supra n. 13.

18. Affidavit of William Arroyo, M.D., executed July 17, 1985, filed in the District Court in *Flores v. Meese*.

19. Weinstein, supra n. 10. By 1990, the number had risen to 8500 per year, 15 percent of whom where female and 15 percent of whom were under fifteen years of age. *Reno v. Flores*, 507 U.S. 292 (1993).

20. James N. Baker with Ginny Carroll, Linda Buckley and Bill Hart, "Plight of the 'Border Orphans,'" *Newsweek*, July 24, 1989.

21. Id.

22. Miriam Jordan, "The Flores Agreement Protected Migrant Children for Decades. New Regulation Aims to End It," *New York Times*, Aug. 20, 2019. See

Suzanne Gamboa, "When Migrant Children Were Detained Among Adults, Strip Searched," *nbcnews.com*, July 24, 2014.

23. Circle 047: Charlie Clements, Ed Asner, and Uma Pemmaraju, "Central America in Turmoil," May 12, 1987, Southern New Hampshire University Academic Archive, https://perma.cc/8583-BTHU.

24. Interview with Peter Schey in Los Angeles, California, September 29, 2017.

25. Matthew Heller, "Déjà vu for Rights Lawyer: Peter Schey is Jumping Into the Fight Against Prop. 187—Much Like the Battle He Helped Win for Texas Students," *Los Angeles Times*, November 10, 1994; Susan Goldsmith, "Los Angeles Lawyer Peter Schey Ruining America by Helping Hordes of Illegal Immigrants Stay Here," *New Times Los Angeles*, June 20, 2002.

26. Goldsmith, supra n. 25.

27. Id.

28. Id.

29. For the history of what became known as the Plyler lawsuit, see Michael A. Olivas, *No Undocumented Child Left Behind* (New York: New York University Press, 2012).

30. *Plyler v. Doe*, 457 U.S. 202 (1982).

31. Laird, supra n. 13.

32. Complaint, supra n. 11.

33. Four children were plaintiffs in the suit, but Schey no longer recalls why he selected Flores as the "lead" plaintiff. His policy in class actions, however, was to choose plaintiffs who would be representative of the class (a legal requirement) and among those to consider their credibility, the absence of a personal adverse history (such as juvenile delinquency), the availability of an adult who could authorize participation, and their age—that is, he didn't want to sue on behalf of a minor who would confuse the issue by soon reaching the age of eighteen. In the case of Ms. Flores, "it might have been a relatively random decision" (Schey, supra n. 24).

34. Claire Noland, "Robert J. Kelleher Dies at 99; Pivotal Tennis Official Became Federal Judge," *Los Angeles Times*, June 20, 2012.

35. Complaint, supra n. 11, para 8.

36. Congress abolished the distinction when it amended the immigration law in 1996, creating a single type of case called a "removal" proceeding.

37. 8 U.S.C. Sec. 1226, as it existed in 1985.

38. Fed. R. Civ. P. 23(a)(4).

39. For immigration cases, bond is similar to the criminal law's bail system, except that bond is subject to more restrictions. For example, only a person who has lawful status can post bond for an undocumented migrant. See 8 U.S.C. Sec. 1226 and Catholic Legal Immigration Network, "Immigration Bond: How to Get Your Money Back," https://perma.cc/SWW8-ZCSX.

40. Order in *Flores v. Meese*, July 19, 1985.

41. Michael C. Tipping, untitled story, *United Press International*, July 19, 1985 (available on LEXIS).

42. David Holley and Elizabeth Lu, "Judge Orders INS to Free 2 Children: Advocates Say Ruling Could Aid Hundreds of Illegals," *Los Angeles Times*, July 20, 1985.

43. Tipping, supra n. 41.

44. Dan Weikel, "Juveniles: They Endure Hardship at Detention Sites," *Orange County Register*, February 1, 1987. See biography of Pegine E. Grayson (graduate of USC Law), https://perma.cc/9N3C-W337.

45. Weinstein, supra n. 10, at 107. See also Youth Advocate Programs, Paul DeMuro, https://perma.cc/LV7F-S6EL.

46. Faye Fiore, "Alien Child 'Hostage' Suit Gains," *San Diego Union-Tribune*, June 3, 1986.

47. Id.

48. Weinstein, supra n. 10, at 107.

49. Weikel, supra n. 44.

50. Marita Hernandez, "Court Eases Rule on Freeing Alien Minors," *Los Angeles Times*, June 3, 1987.

51. *Flores v. Meese*, Transcript of Proceedings, August 24, 1987, at 5.

52. Id., at 6.

53. Id., at 42.

54. Id., at 31.

55. Id., at 31–35.

56. Letter to Kenneth G. Leutbecker, U.S. Department of Justice, from R. David Cousineau, Executive Director, Catholic Charities, Archdiocese of Los Angeles, January 13, 1987.

57. McDonnell, supra n. 8.

58. Schey, supra n. 24.

59. Department of Justice, Community Relations Service, "Alien Shelter Care Program—Description and Requirements," April 28, 1987 (emphasis added), available online as an attachment to *Flores v. Meese*, Memorandum of Understanding re Compromise of Class Action: Conditions of Detention, https://perma.cc/RQ4R-KNY9.

60. Id.

61. *Flores v. Meese*, 681 F. Supp. 665 (C.D. Calif. 1988), quoting, as to the nature of strip searches, *Bell v. Wolfish*, 441 U.S. 520 (1979).

62. Department of Justice, Detention and Release of Juveniles, 53 Fed. Reg. 17449 (May 17, 1988) (final regulation).

63. Order of the District Court, May 25, 1988, attached as Appendix C to the petition for certiorari in *Reno v. Flores*, 507 U.S. 292 (1993); "Judge Rules Against INS," *Los Angeles Times*, May 27, 1988.

64. Catherine Gewertz, "Illegal Aliens Win Children-as-'Bait' Suit," *United Press International*, May 26, 1988.

CHAPTER TWO. "GOOD ENOUGH," 1988–1993

1. Mission statement of the People's College of Law, https://perma.cc /X6ZS-QMRE.

2. See Brennan Center for Public Justice, "The Restriction Barring LSC-Funded Lawyers From Assisting Certain Immigrant Groups," https://perma .cc/3XXS-HPGJ.

3. Lorelei Laird, "Meet the Father of the Landmark Lawsuit That Secured Basic Rights for Immigrant Minors," *ABA Journal*, February 1, 2016.

4. *Orantes-Hernandez v. Smith*, 541 F. Supp. 351, 356 (C.D. Calif. 1982).

5. Refugee Act of 1980, codified at 8 U.S.C. Sec. 1158.

6. U.S. Department of State, Country Reports on Human Rights Practices for 1981.

7. Letter from Amnesty International to Secretary of State Alexander Haig, May 6, 1981, cited in *Orantes-Hernandez*, supra n. 4, text following n. 6.

8. *Orantes-Hernandez*, supra n. 4, n. 9.

9. Id., following n. 10.

10. Id., following n. 26.

11. Id., following n. 42. Another case pending at the same time challenged INS's practice of coercing voluntary departure agreements from detained children of all nationalities. It also resulted initially in an injunction barring INS from using "threats, misrepresentations, subterfuge, or other forms of coercion" to secure voluntary departure agreements and required INS to give them lists of free legal services providers. See *Perez-Funez v. INS*, CIV 81–1457-ER (C.D. Calif. 1984). Several months later, the court made its order permanent, though it modified the injunction by striking the language about "threats, misrepresentations, subterfuge, or other forms of coercion" as "no longer necessary" and merely required the government to refrain from attempting to persuade the children to accept voluntary departure, as well as requiring the government to read a statement of rights to the children and to allow them to call parents, relatives, or free legal services providers before agreeing to voluntary departure. See *Perez-Funez v. INS*, 691 F. Supp. 656 (C.D. Calif. 1985). The relief granted in the Perez-Funez and Orantes-Hernandez injunctions overlapped somewhat. But the injunction in *Orantes-Hernandez*, while applying only to Salvadorans, provided much greater relief. It applied to adults as well as to children and explicitly prohibited "threats, misrepresentation, subterfuge or other forms of coercion," the words omitted from the final Perez-Funez injunction. It allowed lawyers to rescind voluntary departure agreements. It also specified that detention centers had to have at

least one telephone per twenty-five detainees and required that privacy be afforded to lawyer-client communications.

12. *Orantes-Hernandez v. Meese*, 685 F. Supp. 1488 (C.D. Calif. 1988). The expansion directed, e.g., that because INS was giving detained persons inaccurate lists of legal services organizations (e.g., incorrect phone numbers for organizations and names of organizations that no longer existed), it had to provide accurate lists in the future.

13. *Orantes-Hernandez v. Thornburgh*, 919 F. 2d 549 (9th Cir. 1990).

14. Interview with Peter Schey in Los Angeles, California, September 29, 2017.

15. 8 U.S.C. Secs. 1103(a) and 1252(a)(1).

16. *Gerstein v. Pugh*, 420 U.S. 103, 114 (1975).

17. *Bush v. Gore*, 531 U.S. 98, in which the Supreme Court divided along party lines to decide the winner of the presidential election of 2000, is the most well-known example of this proposition, but there is also an extensive academic literature supporting it. See, e.g., Richard L. Revesz, "Environmental Regulation, Ideology, and the D.C. Circuit," *Virginia Law Review* 83 (1997): 1717. Judges don't always follow the political ideologies or predilections of the presidents who appointed them, but since presidents tend to favor candidates who share their outlooks, lawyers in public policy cases, particularly constitutional cases, are almost always interested in who appointed the judges who will decide their cases.

18. U.S. Court of Appeals for the Ninth Circuit, Court Structure and Procedures, Sec. E(4), https://perma.cc/P35U-HRCV.

19. Id., at Sec. eE(5); 28 U.S.C. Sec. 292(a).

20. Alan Abrahamson, "Law and Order Judge Takes Over Key Appeals Court Post," *Los Angeles Times*, February 4, 1991. This article was written one year after the panel decided the Flores case.

21. Id.

22. "Federal Appeals Court Judge J. Clifford Wallace Seeks the Inspiration of the Lord," *LDS Church News*, January 5, 2017.

23. Gene Johnson, "Appeals Judge Was Pioneer: Ninth Circuit's Fletcher Dies at 89," *Spokane Spokesman-Review*, October 24, 2012.

24. Brigham Young University, One Hundred and Twenty-Sixth Spring Commencement Exercises 19 (April 26, 2001), https://archive.org/stream/commence mentexer2001brig#page/18/mode/2up.

25. "With predominantly liberal appointees, the 9th Circuit was reversed 27 of 28 times by the U.S. Supreme Court in 1984, inviting comparisons in news accounts to the 1961 Philadelphia Phillies baseball team, which lost a then-record 23 games in a row" (Abrahamson, supra n. 20).

26. Schey, supra n. 14.

27. *Flores v. Meese*, 934 F. 2d 991, 997–1002 (1990).

28. *Bowers v. Hardwick*, 478 U.S. 186 (1986). *Bowers* was overruled by *Lawrence v. Texas*, 539 U.S. 558 (2003), but the decision in *Lawrence* came thirteen years after Judge Wallace wrote his opinion.

29. To justify framing the right narrowly rather than broadly, he cited a recent Ninth Circuit decision in which a property owner had challenged the Endangered Species Act. A man had killed a grizzly bear for eating his sheep. To contest his fine for violating the Act, he had asserted the right to "possess and protect property." The court instead redefined the right, which it found not to be fundamental, as the "right to kill federally protected wildlife in defense of property," and the fine stood. See *Christy v. Hodel*, 857 F. 3d 1324 (1988).

30. *Flores*, supra n. 27, at 1002–10.

31. Id., at 1010–12.

32. Id., at 1014 (Fletcher, J., dissenting).

33. Id., at 1018. Regarding the Christy case that Judge Wallace had cited as authority, she said that it should be read only as a refusal to find that property owners had no right to kill endangered species, not for the general principle that constitutional rights should be narrowly framed.

34. *Schall v. Martin*, 467 U.S. 253 (1983).

35. *Flores*, supra n. 27, at 1025. In a footnote, the majority took issue with Judge Fletcher's use of the word "unfeeling." "We cannot agree that the court's decision . . . should be resolved by attempted characterizing or mischaracterizing of the judges' personal feelings. We suggest that an objective analysis of the INS's rule demonstrates it to be a reasonable compromise reached by an agency with limited resources." See *Flores*, supra n. 27, at 1003 n. 2.

36. Id., at 25.

37. U.S. Court of Appeals for the Ninth Circuit, Circuit Rule 35–3.

38. U.S. Court of Appeals for the Ninth Circuit, Ninth Circuit En Banc Procedure Summary, https://perma.cc/EE8H-LUHG.

39. The selection would be almost but not entirely random, as the court rules provided that the chief judge of the Circuit would be one of the eleven members of the panel. By the time the case was argued, Judge Wallace had become the chief judge as a result of the retirement of Chief Judge Goodwin. That meant that the author of the panel opinion would again participate in deciding the case, but Judge Fletcher would not necessarily be chosen—and she was not.

40. David G. Savage, "INS Detention of Children Upheld," *Los Angeles Times*, March 24, 1993.

41. American Bar Association, Honorable Mary Murphy Schroeder, https://perma.cc/3JVS-787J.

42. American Law Institute, The Hon. Mary M. Schroeder, https://perma.cc/496E-LYWD.

43. In re: Gault, 387 U.S. 1 (1967).

44. *Flores v. Meese*, 942 F. 2d 1352 (1991) (en banc).

45. Wolfgang Saxon, "Thomas Tang, 73, Senior Judge for a Federal Court of Appeals," *New York Times*, July 21, 1995.

46. *Flores* (en banc), supra n. 44, at 1365–68 (concurring opinion).

47. Maura Dolan, "Judge William A. Norris, Author of Early Ruling That Boosted Gay Rights, Dies at 89," *Los Angeles Times*, January 27, 2017.

48. *Flores* (en banc), supra n. 44, at 1371 (concurring opinion).

49. Id., at 1374–77 (concurring in part and dissenting in part).

50. Id., at 1377–84.

51. See supra n. 25.

52. Schey, supra n. 14.

53. Memorandum to Robert E. Kopp, Director, Appellate Staff, Civil Division, from Grover Joseph Rees, INS General Counsel, October 7, 1991. In addition to budgetary concerns, the memorandum cited the agency's alarm that the decision seemed to recognize a fundamental right to physical liberty, and its worry that INS might be sued if it released a child to an adult who harmed the child.

54. Susan Freinkel, "INS Moving Away From Its No-Settle Strategy," *New Jersey Law Journal*, January 20, 1992.

55. Brief for the United States in *Barr v. Flores*, 1992 U.S.S. Ct. Briefs LEXIS 498 (1992).

56. The major features are summarized in chapter 1.

57. Brief for Respondent, *Barr v. Flores*, 1992 U.S. S. Ct. Briefs LEXIS 499, fn. 8 (1992). The footnote cited only one specific instance of alleged mistreatment: a 1990 California state legislative committee report stating that a twelve-year-old child was taken to immigration court in handcuffs, that the use of handcuffs was not uncommon, and that the food was inadequate.

58. Id., at 41.

59. Reply brief for petitioners, *Barr v. Flores*, 1992 U.S.S. Ct. Briefs LEXIS 446.

60. Transcript of oral argument, *Barr v. Flores* (October 13, 1992), 1992 WL 687875.

61. Id. The transcript does not reveal which justice asked the question.

62. Laird, supra n. 3.

63. This concession may not have been necessary. In connection with the en banc argument in the Ninth Circuit in 1991, years after the Shelter Care Agreement requiring detention to meet the AMSCP standards had gone into effect, the Mexican-American Legal Defense and Educational Fund and the Southwest Refugee Rights Project had filed a brief amicus curiae citing published sources to the effect that "current" conditions in INS detention facilities continued to be harsh, and in violation of those standards. It pointed out that in Yuma, Arizona, detained children were "placed in the county juvenile court facility and mixed with local youths charged with crimes, . . . required to wear orange and green uniforms [and] offered little to occupy their time. . . . Most of the time, the

children sit around a concrete table. If they try to stand up and stretch, a guard orders them back down. . . . [Another detention center in California] has a high fence topped with hoops of razor wire. Children are locked into the facility at all times and must report for several 'head counts' each day. [That facility has] two 'punishment rooms' where some children have been restricted for over a week" (Brief Amicus Curiae of Immigrant, Refugee and Civil Rights Groups, *Flores v. Meese*, Court of Appeals for the Ninth Circuit, at 5–6 [March 1, 1991.])

64. *Reno v. Flores*, 507 U.S. 292, 305 (1993).

65. Id., at 345–46 (dissenting opinion).

CHAPTER THREE. THE SECOND SETTLEMENT, 1993–1997

1. James N. Baker with Ginny Carroll, Linda Buckley and Bill Hart, "Plight of the 'Border Orphans,'" *Newsweek*, July 24, 1989.

2. Lisa Belkin, "Lonely Young Aliens Pose Problem for U.S.," *New York Times*, May 25, 1989.

3. Tracy Wilkinson, "Boy, 12, Facing Deportation Held on $12,000 Bail," *Los Angeles Times*, May 2, 1990. After the *Los Angeles Times* published a story about Caballero, the INS was "flooded with calls" from people who offered to take care of him. The judge then reduced the bail to $2000, and he was released to a Franciscan friar. See Tracy Wilkinson, "Friars in Glendora Receive Custody of Boy from INS," *Los Angeles Times*, May 5, 1990.

4. Department of Justice, Community Relations Service, "Alien Shelter Care Program—Description and Requirements," April 28, 1987 (emphasis added), available online as an attachment to *Flores v. Meese*, Memorandum of Understanding re Compromise of Class Action: Conditions of Detention, https://perma.cc/YLB9-NZRD.

5. This document is not available online, but selected articles from it are reproduced as Appendix D to Human Rights Watch, "Slipping Through the Cracks: Unaccompanied Children Detained by the U.S. Immigration and Naturalization Service," April, 1997, https://perma.cc/VNC3-HKYC.

6. An exception occurred during 1994 when seven thousand Cubans, more than half of whom were unaccompanied minors or families with small children or elderly adults, arrived in Florida by boat during a seven-month period. The INS announced that it had changed its policy, in order to deter further migration, and incarcerated the children along with adult migrants at its Krome detention center in Miami, stating that they would remain there indefinitely. See John M. Broder, "Clinton Halts Special Treatment For Cubans; Refugees: Decades-old Program Favoring Immigrants is Reversed, Sweeping New U.S. Policy Called Permanent," *Los Angeles Times*, August 20, 1994. But a month later, after being

sued and criticized in the press, the government began releasing the children and any accompanying parents, citing "compelling humanitarian concerns." See "Refugee Children Released," *Ft. Lauderdale Sun-Sentinel*, September 20, 1994.

7. The government's petition for certiorari is at 21, its brief at 10–13, and the oral argument transcript at 7.

8. Casa San Juan was similar to a group home. There were no barred cells or armed guards, and the children had daily classroom instruction provided by the Catholic Church. The average stay for those with adult relatives in the U.S. was only nine days, but one boy without such relatives was confined for nine months. See Patrick McDonnell, "Casa San Juan, Hailed as Best INS Youth-Detention Facility, Keeps Homelike Atmosphere," *Los Angeles Times*, April 17, 1988.

9. These summaries of the evidence that Holguín collected are drawn from the plaintiffs' Motion to Enforce Consent Decree, *Flores v. Reno*, filed in the U.S. District Court for the Central District of California on Nov. 15, 1993, accessible from https://www.clearinghouse.net/detail.php?id = 9493.

10. Michael A. Olivas, "'Breaking the Law' On Principle: An Essay On Lawyers' Dilemmas, Unpopular Causes, and Legal Regimes," University of Pittsburgh Law Review 52 (1991): 822.

11. Email to the author from Michael A. Olivas, June 25, 2018.

12. Interview with Peter Schey, September 29, 2017.

13. Id.

14. Id.

15. See letter to Alex Aleinikoff, Office of the General Counsel, INS, from Peter A. Schey, et al., September 14, 1994.

16. Human Rights Watch, supra n. 5.

17. Apparently the Human Rights Watch staffers were able to talk with certain children at California prisons only because those children happened to be material witnesses to trafficking and had been transferred temporarily from the legal custody of the INS to the custody of the U.S. Marshals. Id., at 57–58. In Arizona, Human Rights Watch was allowed to visit the facility with which INS had contracted but only on the condition that the location not be revealed. Id., at 45, n. 88.

18. Id., at 76–77.

19. Douglas Montero, "Three Hellish Months in a Juvenile Jail," *New York Post*, January 29, 2001.

20. Prepared testimony of attorney Linton Joaquin before the California Legislature's Joint Committee on Refugee Resettlement, International Migration and Cooperative Development, July 19, 1990.

21. The history of the Berks County Family Detention Center is the subject of chapter 11.

22. Human Rights Watch, "Detained and Deprived of Rights, Children in the Custody of the U.S. Immigration and Naturalization Service" (1998), https://www.hrw.org/legacy/reports98/ins2/index.htm.

23. Meki Cox, "Report: INS Violating Illegal Child Immigrant Rights," Associated Press, December 23, 1998.

24. Prepared testimony of Wendy A. Young, Washington Liaison, Women's Commission for Refugee Women and Children, before the Senate Judiciary Committee, Subcommittee On Immigration, September 16, 1998.

25. Stipulated settlement agreement, *Flores v. Reno*, U.S. District Court, Central District of California (January 17, 1997), available at https://perma.cc /R7EY-GNBA.

26. Schey, supra n. 12.

27. Id.

28. Stipulated settlement, supra n. 25, at paragraph 12A.

29. Children who could be charged with serious crimes or engaged in behavior that threatened the health or safety of other children, or who were escape risks, could be held in secure facilities (id., at paragraph 21.)

30. Id., at paragraph 12B.

31. Stipulation Extending Settlement Agreement in *Flores v. Reno*, December 7, 2001, available at https://perma.cc/G2FN-UD7A.

32. Schey, supra n. 12.

33. See chapters 6, 9, and 10.

34. See chapter 12.

35. Patrick J. McDonnell, "INS Adopts Reforms on Custody of Minors: Immigration Settlement Aims to Ensure that Unaccompanied Children Arrested by the Agency Are Treated Humanely and Quickly Reunited With Their Families," *Los Angeles Times*, April 30, 1997.

CHAPTER FOUR. CONGRESS INTERVENES,
1997–2002

1. See the graph of Mexican and non-Mexican apprehensions in Allen McDuffee, "Who Really Crosses the U.S.–Mexico Border?," *The Atlantic*, December 31, 2014.

2. In fiscal year 2000, "the INS detained 4,136 unaccompanied illegal juveniles [one quarter of whom were female] for longer than 72 hours [actually for an average of 33 days]." See U.S. Department of Justice, Office of the Inspector General, Report I-2001–009, September 28, 2001.

3. Id.

4. Tanya Weinberg, "Teen's Ordeal in Federal Custody Ends in Freedom: Advocates Push Changes for Kids," *Chicago Tribune*, December 25, 2002.

5. Telephone interview with Peter Schey, January 24, 2018.

6. Motion to enforce the Flores settlement, docket entry 19 (January. 26, 2004) in *Flores v. Meese*.

7. Notice of withdrawal of motion, docket entry 88 (November 14, 2005), in *Flores v. Meese.*

8. For the timeline of the case, see PBS, *Frontline,* https://perma.cc/YJH7-W2CX. On protests in Miami, see also "U.S. Ruling on Cuban Boy Ignites Protests," *Chicago Tribune,* January 7, 2000.

9. "Grandmothers, Elian Meet for Hour in Private," *Los Angeles Times,* January 27, 2000.

10. Robert D. McFadden, "Angry Crowds in 2 States Protest Seizure of Cuban Boy," *New York Times,* April 23, 2000.

11. CBS News, "Panel Wants Elian Raid Documents," June 9, 2000, https://perma.cc/V343-XT7X.

12. Rick Bragg, "Boy's Cuba-Based Family to be Issued U.S. Visas," *New York Times,* April 4, 2000.

13. Todd Richissin, Scott Calvert and Chris Gray, "Cuban Family Finds Quiet at Pastoral Shore Retreat," *Baltimore Sun,* April 27, 2000.

14. Tom Brune, "INS Housing Children in Jails: Few Places Left for Unaccompanied Kids," *Newsday,* February 4, 2000.

15. "Elian Had It Good," *The [Lakeland, FL] Ledger,* February 28, 2002, https://perma.cc/PN2U-V9B6.

16. S. 3117 (106th Cong.)

17. Cong. Rec. S9382 (September 27, 2000).

18. Id., at S9383.

19. Id.

20. Scott Martelle, "A KIND of Justice," *Williams Magazine,* Spring 2013.

21. Jacqueline Bhabha and Wendy Young, "Not Adults in Miniature: Unaccompanied Child Asylum Seekers and the New U.S. Guidelines," *International Journal of Refugee Law* 11 (1999): 84–125, building on a shorter version published in 1998.

22. See Cong. Rec. S9383 (Senator Feinstein's report of what she had learned from the Women's Commission and Human Rights Watch); Testimony of Wendy Young before the Senate Judiciary Committee, February 28, 2002, https://perma.cc/A2BL-2KAC.

23. Women's Commission for Refugee Women and Children, "Prison Guard or Parent? INS Treatment of Unaccompanied Refugee Children" (2002), https://www.womensrefugeecommission.org/resources/document/253-prison-guard-or-parent-ins-treatment-of-unaccompanied-refugee-children. In later years, Young went on to increasingly important jobs but remained an advocate for refugee children. After leaving the Women's Commission, Young worked for the United Nations High Commissioner for Refugees and then became the Chief Counsel for Immigration Policy of the Senate Subcommittee on Immigration, serving under Senator Edward M. Kennedy. In 2009, she became Executive Director of Kids in Need of Defense (KIND), an international organization

founded by Angelina Jolie and Brad Smith, president of Microsoft, with a mission of protecting child refugees.

24. Id.

25. See Unaccompanied Alien Child Protection Act of 2001, S. 121 (107th Cong.).

26. 6 U.S.C. Sec. 279.

27. See Office of Refugee Resettlement, Sponsors and Placement, https://perma.cc/WX5W-F6PJ.

28. 6 U.S.C. Sec. 279(b)(2)(B).

CHAPTER FIVE. ASYLUM, 1980–1997

1. Protocol Relating to the Status of Refugees, 31 January 1967, 66 U.N.T.S. 267.

2. P.L. 96–212.

3. The provision allowing the Department of Homeland Security or the Department of Justice to grant asylum to a person who has been determined to be a "refugee" is now codified at 8 U.S.C. Sec. 1158. Some exceptions, codified at 8 U.S.C. Secs. 1158(a)(2) and (b)(2), bar asylum grants to limited categories of individuals such as terrorists and certain felons.

4. 8 U.S.C. Sec. 1101(a)(42) defines who may be considered a "refugee".

5. Migration Policy Institute, "Central Americans and Asylum Policy in the Reagan Era," April 1, 2006, https://perma.cc/8UWU-TD3A.

6. Like the immigration judges, members of this Board, to which immigration judge decisions can be appealed by either the immigrant or by ICE, are Justice Department employees.

7. Matter of O-Z- and I-Z-, 22 I&N Dec. 23 (BIA 1998). This was a case in which hoodlums beat up a father and son in their native Ukraine because of the victims' Jewish religion.

8. Matter of Toboso-Alfonso, 20 I&N Dec. 819 (BIA 1990).

9. Matter of Kasinga, 21 I&N Dec. 357 (BIA 1996).

10. Matter of A- R- C- G-, 26 I. & N. Dec. 388 (BIA 2014). Long before the Board of Immigration Appeals rendered this precedential decision, some immigration judges and DHS asylum officers were granting asylum to victims of domestic violence.

11. See, e.g., Crespin-Vallidares v. Holder, 632 F. 3d 117 (4th Cir. 2011).

12. Form I-589, https://perma.cc/F7AN-8SXR.

13. Form I-589 instructions, https://perma.cc/P6C2-AXM5.

14. Id.

15. The law also permitted a person to apply for asylum "affirmatively" if the applicant had not first been apprehended. In affirmative cases, eligibility for asylum was initially determined by an asylum officer after a non-adversarial

interview. For a detailed description and analysis of the affirmative asylum process, see Andrew I. Schoenholtz, Philip G. Schrag, and Jaya Ramji-Nogales, *Lives in the Balance: Asylum Adjudication by the Department of Homeland Security* (New York: New York University Press, 2014).

16. See, e.g., *Aden v. Holder*, 589 F. 3d 1040 (9th Cir. 2009).

17. See Mina Fazel, Ruth V. Reed, Catherine Panter-Brick and Alan Stein, "Mental Health of Displaced and Refugee Children Resettled in High-Income Countries: Risk and Protective Factors," *Lancet* 379 (2012): 266–82, https://perma.cc/W9YF-BCWB.

18. Nestor P. Rodriguez and Ximena Urrutia-Rojas, "Undocumented and Unaccompanied: A Mental-Health Study of Unaccompanied, Immigrant Children from Central America," Institute for Higher Education Law and Governance, University of Houston (1990), https://perma.cc/49DC-M77J.

19. Barry Holman and Jason Ziedenberg, "The Dangers of Detention: The Impact of Incarcerating Youth in Detention and Other Secure Facilities," Justice Policy Institute (1978), https://perma.cc/6DHN-7H9K.

20. Id., at 8.

21. Women's Commission for Refugee Women and Children, "Prison Guard or Parent? INS Treatment of Unaccompanied Refugee Children," May 2002, https://www.womensrefugeecommission.org/resources/document/253-prison-guard-or-parent-ins-treatment-of-unaccompanied-refugee-children, at 26.

22. Al Kamen, "INS's Unofficial Open Door: Illegal Aliens Swamp N.Y. Holding Capacity," *Washington Post*, January 27, 1992.

23. Robert O'Harrow, Jr., and Bill Miller, "CIA Suspect Left Trail of Conflicting Personal Data," *Washington Post*, February 18, 1993. Kasi fled to Pakistan, was abducted by American operatives, and was sentenced to death. See Tim Weiner, "Killer of Two at C.I.A. Draws Death Sentence," *New York Times*, January 24, 1998.

24. Yousef (which may not be his real name) was sentenced to 240 years in prison. See Benjamin Weiser, "Mastermind Gets Life for Bombing of Trade Center," *New York Times*, January 9, 1998.

25. Tim Weiner, "Pleas for Asylum Inundated System for Immigration," *New York Times*, April 25, 1993. See also Ira Mehlman, "The New Jet Set: How Questionable Political Asylum Claimants Enter the US at New York, New York's John F. Kennedy Airport Without Any Difficulty," *National Review*, March 15, 1993; Wendy Lin and Jack Sirica, "An Invitation to Terrorists? INS Admits It Can't Stop All Undesirables," *Newsday*, March 6, 1993; Jim Mann, "Chinese Refugees Take to High Seas," *Los Angeles Times*, March 16, 1993; CBS, *60 Minutes*, March 14, 1993. Stephen Legomsky has noted that the *60 Minutes* broadcast, in particular, generated "massive media attention" (Stephen H. Legomsky, "The New Techniques for Managing High-Volume Asylum Systems," 81 Iowa Law Review 671, 693 [1996]).

26. The full story of the *Golden Venture*, including the smugglers who arranged it, the passengers, and the federal officials who dealt with it, is told in Patrick Radden Keefe's marvelous book *The Snakehead: An Epic Tale of the Chinatown Underworld and the American Dream* (New York: Doubleday, 2009).

27. In 1986, Congress had passed a law barring persons from employment unless they were citizens or lawful permanent residents or had some other legitimate status such as asylum. Before Martin reformed the system through a regulation that took effect in January, 1995, a person who applied for asylum before being arrested and was therefore entitled to an interview by an INS asylum officer could get a work permit upon filing the application. Many people with weak or nonexistent asylum claims came to the United States simply to get that permit so that they could get work and send money home during the months before they were told to present themselves for interviews. This "magnet" swelled the number of asylum applicants and caused an ever-larger backlog and, as processing times increased, an ever-more-powerful magnet. Martin's solution was to impose a six-month waiting period for a work permit and to prioritize interviews for new claimants rather than those in the backlog. That enabled the INS to interview applicants and reject most weak cases within the six months, and work permits were never issued to the unsuccessful applicants whose cases were decided within that time frame. In fact, when those failed applicants were told of the interviewer's decision, they were also served with process summoning them to a deportation hearing in immigration court. With the incentive to migrate for the purpose of obtaining a work permit eliminated, the number of applicants and the backlog fell. New claims fell by 75 percent over a five-year period. See U.S. Department of Justice, "Asylum Reform: Five Years Later," February 1, 2000, https://perma.cc/Z525-QA4A.

28. Persons entitled to enter the United States without visas included American citizens and green card holders (lawful permanent residents) as well as visitors from most Western European countries, Japan, and a few other industrialized countries. The "visa waiver" program for such visitors is still operative. See Department of Homeland Security, Visa Waiver Program Requirements, https://www.dhs.gov/visa-waiver-program-requirements (accessed Aug. 29, 2019).

29. Illegal Immigration Reform and Immigrant Responsibility Act of 1996, Division C of Pub. L. 104–208, 110 Stat. 3009–546, enacted September 30, 1996. The short paragraph in the text conceals a great deal of sausage-making in the legislative meat grinder. The full story of the enactment of the refugee-related aspects of the legislation is told in Philip G. Schrag, *A Well-Founded Fear: The Congressional Battle to Save Political Asylum in America* (New York: Routledge, 2000).

30. This section is denominated as Sec. 235 of the Immigration and Nationality Act. In the U.S. Code it is 8 U.S.C. Sec. 1225.

31. Id.

32. INS (and later DHS) Form I-867AB.

33. U.S. Commission on International Religious Freedom, "Report on Asylum Seekers in Expedited Removal" (2005), http://www.uscirf.gov/reports-briefs /special-reports/report-asylum-seekers-in-expedited-removal, at 6.

34. Id.

35. Many migrants, particularly Central Americans fleeing through Mexico by foot, are too poor to afford lawyers, though those who pass the credible fear stage and are referred for full hearings before immigration judges are entitled to be represented by counsel (but not to have counsel appointed for them at government expense) in that final stage. Those without lawyers are at a severe disadvantage. The Commission's 2005 report stated that immigration judges granted relief to 25 percent of represented asylum applicants but only 2 percent of unrepresented applicants (id., at 56).

36. Id., at 10.

37. Id., at 52.

38. USCIS, "Questions and Answers: Reasonable Fear Screenings," June 18, 2013, https://perma.cc/94D7-HSAS.

39. See 8 C.F.R. Sec. 1208.16.

40. Designating Aliens for Expedited Removal, 69 Fed. Reg. 48,877 (2004).

41. See ICE, Detention and Removal Operations, DRO Policy and Procedure Manual, at Sec. 2.2 (March 2006), https://perma.cc/EC2H-DVM5. The guidance was apparently based on a 1997 memorandum from the INS General Counsel: Paul Virtue, "Unaccompanied Minors Subject to Expedited Removal," Immigration and Naturalization Service, Policy Memorandum, Washington, DC, August 21, 1997.

CHAPTER SIX. HUTTO, 2003–2007

1. Congressional Research Service, "Gangs in Central America 2," RS22141, May 10, 2005.

2. Ninety-four percent of gang members in El Salvador lacked a secondary education. See International Crisis Group, "El Salvador's Politics of Perpetual Violence" (2017): 9, https://perma.cc/62WS-FLPY.

3. Jose Miguel Cruz, "Central American Gangs Like MS-13 Were Born Out of Failed Anti-Crime Policies," *The Conversation*, May 8, 2017, https://perma .cc/9YV3-7LCQ.

4. Congressional Research Service, supra n. 1, at 1.

5. Office of Inspector General, Department of Homeland Security, "A Review of DHS' Responsibilities for Juvenile Aliens," OIG-05–45 4 (2005).

6. There were 1.6 million apprehensions of Mexican nationals near the border in FY 2000, but only 1 million in FY 2005. See U.S. Border Patrol, "Illegal Alien Apprehensions from Mexico by Fiscal Year," https://perma.cc/L9FB-JLAU.

7. Id.

8. Jacqueline Bhabha and Susan Schmidt, "Seeking Asylum Alone: Unaccompanied and Separated Children and Refugee Protection in the U.S." (2006): 16, https://www.researchgate.net/publication/267042020_Seeking_Asylum_Alone_Unaccompanied_and_Separated_Children_and_Refugee_Protection_in_the_US.

9. This is the estimate of Amanda Levinson, who was then Director of Policy Programs and Operations at Hope Street Group, in "Alone in America," August 22, 2005, https://perma.cc/S99H-Q57R. As of 2006, Customs and Border Patrol did not keep statistics that separately accounted for accompanied and unaccompanied children. See Bhabha and Schimdt, supra n. 8, at 18.

10. Id.

11. Id.

12. Office of Inspector General, supra n. 5, at 7 (800); Levinson, supra n. 9 (700).

13. Christopher Nugent, "Whose Children Are These? Towards Ensuring the Best Interests and Empowerment of Unaccompanied Alien Children," *Boston University Public International Law Journal* 15 (2006): 223.

14. Office of Inspector General, supra n. 5, at 15–16 n. 20.

15. Bhabha and Schmidt, supra n. 8, at 86.

16. Office of Inspector General, supra n. 5, at 17–18.

17. Nugent, supra n. 13, at 231.

18. Human Rights Watch, "Detained and Deprived of Rights" (1998), excerpted at https://perma.cc/ZA87-7CR2. This report is described in more detail in chapter 11.

19. Eric Schmitt, "New Shelter Seeks to Place Asylum-Seeking Families in More Hospitable Surroundings," *New York Times*, June 14, 2001.

20. Levinson, supra n. 9, quoting Maureen Dunn, division director of the Unaccompanied Children's Services of ORR.

21. Office of Inspector General, supra n. 5, at 19–20.

22. Interview with Michelle Brané, May 22, 2018.

23. H.R. Rep. 109–79 (2005), at 38.

24. Associated Press, "Chertoff: End 'Catch and Release' at Borders," Fox News, October 18, 2005, https://perma.cc/Q8J4-GLH3.

25. Brané, supra n. 22. Before the facility in Taylor was selected for family detention, senior staff at ICE assessed the suitability of that location for housing migrant families. The staff recommended that families be housed in the Laredo Detention Facility, near the border, rather than in Taylor, in part because "Austin . . . has a broader NGO . . . base that have typically been very strong advocates for immigrants." See memorandum, "Implementation of Familty [sic] Detention," anonymously leaked to Barbara Hines by an ICE employee in San Antonio, shared with the author in an email from Barbara Hines, July 10, 2018.

26. Interviews of ICE officials by the Women's Refugee Commission, reported in Women's Commission for Refugee Women and Children and Lutheran Immigration and Refugee Service, "Locking up Family Values: The Detention of Immigrant Families" (2007), https://www.womensrefugeecommission.org/component/zdocs/document/150-locking-up-family-values-the-detention-of-immigrant-families-locking-up-family-values-the-detention-of-immigrant-families, at 11.

27. Clark Lyda and Jessy Lyda, *The Least of These* (documentary film) (2009), at 3:28, http://theleastofthese-film.com/ and https://vimeo.com/179342261.

28. Interview with Barbara Hines in Austin, Texas, July 9, 2018.

29. *Roe v. Wade*, 410 U.S. 113 (1973).

30. Hines, supra n. 28.

31. See *The Least of These*, supra n. 27, at 18:50.

32. Women's Commission for Refugee Women and Children and Lutheran Immigration and Refugee Service, supra n. 26, at 2.

33. Nina Pruneda, ICE spokesperson, speaking in *The Least of These*, supra n. 27, at 40:25.

34. Margaret Talbot, "The Lost Children," *The New Yorker*, March 3, 2008.

35. *The Least of These*, supra n. 27, at 5:15.

36. Women's Commission for Refugee Women and Children and Lutheran Immigration and Refugee Service, supra n. 26, at 2.

37. Id., at 17.

38. Talbot, supra n. 34.

39. Complaint, *Emptage v. Chertoff*, A07-CA-158 SS (W.D. Texas 2007), para. 57.

40. Id.; Tony Cantu, "Barbara's Fire," *Austin Chronicle*, December 12, 2014.

41. *The Least of These*, supra n. 27, at 6:42. The fifteen-minute period began when the first person in the cafeteria line arrived, so those in the middle or back of the line had only ten minutes. See Women's Commission for Refugee Women and Children and Lutheran Immigration and Refugee Service, supra n. 26, at 19.

42. Women's Commission for Refugee Women and Children and Lutheran Immigration and Refugee Service, supra n. 26, at 19.

43. Id., at 14–15.

44. Ralph Blumenthal, "U.S. Gives Tour of Family Detention Center That Critics Liken to a Prison," *New York Times*, February 10, 2007.

45. *The Least of These*, supra n. 27, at 24:53.

46. Talbot, supra n. 34; Women's Commission for Refugee Women and Children and Lutheran Immigration and Refugee Service, supra n. 26, at 27.

47. Women's Commission for Refugee Women and Children and Lutheran Immigration and Refugee Service, supra n. 26, at 32.

48. Talbot, supra n. 34.

49. *Emptage* complaint, supra n. 39, para 76.

50. *The Least of These*, supra n. 27, at 5:40.

51. Talbot, supra n. 34.

52. Women's Commission for Refugee Women and Children and Lutheran Immigration and Refugee Service, supra n. 26, at 20–21.

53. Id., at 29.

54. *The Least of These*, supra n. 27, at 17:55.

55. Women's Commission for Refugee Women and Children and Lutheran Immigration and Refugee Service, supra n. 26.

56. *The Least of These*, supra n. 27, at 45:26.

57. *Emptage v. Chertoff*, supra n. 39.

58. *Bunikyte v. Chertoff*, Case A-07-CA-164-SS, filed March 6, 2007 (W.D. Tex 2007).

59. Nina Hess Hsu and Marc Vockell, "Hon. Sam Sparks," *The Federal Lawyer*, May 2010.

60. *Hopwood v. Texas*, 861 F. Supp. 551 (W.D. Tex. 1994), reversed in *Hopwood v. Texas*, 78 F. 3d 932 (5th Cir. 1996); *Grutter v. Bollinger*, 539 U.S. 306 (2003).

61. Hsu and Vockell, supra n. 59.

62. *Bunikyte* Complaint, supra n. 58. The nine other complaints were similar.

63. Hines, supra n. 28.

64. Plaintiff's motion for a temporary restraining order to prevent separation from her mother, *Bunikyte v. Chertoff* (March 6, 2007).

65. Hines, supra n. 28.

66. Michael Meltsner and Philip G. Schrag, *Public Interest Advocacy* (Boston: Little, Brown, 1974), 88.

67. A new lawsuit in Texas, rather than in California, was possible because the Flores settlement explicitly provided, in Paragraph 24B, that an *individual* lawsuit to enforce the agreement with respect to a particular child could be brought in the federal court for the district in which the child was being kept in custody.

68. Order, March 6, 2007.

69. A month earlier, ICE had allowed a small group of reporters to tour Hutto, but they were not allowed to talk to the detainees. In anticipation of the press tour, "plastic plants had been hurriedly installed and some areas repainted, . . . and officials acknowledged that pizza was on the lunch menu for the first time." Blumenthal, supra n. 44.

70. Defendants' Reply to Equitable Remedies Sought by Plaintiff Saule Bunikyte (March 16, 2007).

71. Plaintiff's Reply in Support of Her Motion For a Preliminary Injunction (March 19, 2007).

72. Id.

73. Id.

74. Transcript of argument, March 20, 2007, not available on PACER but on file with the author.

75. The Corrections Corporation of American had requested the exemption on May 24, 2006, and it was granted on June 14, 2006. See letter to Mickey Liles, Administrator, Corrections Corporation of America, from Michele Adams, Policy Specialist, Texas Department of Family and Protective Services, June 14, 2006, attached as part of Exhibit 2 to the Second Amended Petition Seeking a Restraining Order in *Grassroots Leadership Inc., v. Texas Dept. of Family and Protective Services*, May 3, 2016.

76. Order in *Bunikyte v. Chertoff* (April 9, 2007), supra n. 58.

77. Defendants' motion to dismiss, In re Hutto Detention Center (April 18, 2007).

78. Order in In re Hutto Dentention Center (May 10, 2007).

79. Hines, supra n. 28.

80. Id.

81. Settlement agreement filed in In re: Hutto Family Detention Center (August 26, 2007).

82. Talbot, supra n. 34.

CHAPTER SEVEN. THE TVPRA, 2007–2008

1. See House of Representatives Subcommittee On Border, Maritime, and Global Terrorism, "Crossing the Border: Immigrants in Detention and Victims of Trafficking," March 15 and 20, 2007; House Subcommittee on Immigration, Citizenship, Refugees, Border Security, and International Law, "Detention and Removal: Immigration Detainee Medical Care," October 4, 2007.

2. Clark Lyda and Jessy Lyda, *The Least of These* (documentary film) (2009), http://theleastofthese-film.com/ and https://vimeo.com/179342261.

3. Juan Castillo, "Delegation Examining Detention Facilities," *Austin American-Statesman*, October 2, 2008.

4. After they were promulgated, these standards were criticized as inadequate. See chapter 8.

5. Department of Health and Human Services, Office of the Inspector General, "Division of Unaccompanied Alien Children's Services: Efforts to Serve Children," OEI-07-06-00290 (2008).

6. See Uki Go-i, "Jews Targeted in Argentina's Dirty War," *The Guardian*, March 24, 1999.

7. Interview with Michelle Brané, May 22, 2018.

8. Testimony of William Canny, Executive Director, United States Conference of Catholic Bishops' Migration and Refugee Services, before the Permanent Subcommittee on Investigations of the Senate Homeland Security and Governmental

Affairs Committee, January 28, 2016. As of 2016, ORR was able to provide studies of the home to which children would be released for only 5 percent of the children before their release. Id.

9. Women's Refugee Commission and Orrick Herrington Sutcliffe LLP, "Halfway Home: Unaccompanied Children in Immigration Custody," 2009, https://www.womensrefugeecommission.org/component/zdocs/document/196-halfway-home-unaccompanied-children-in-immigration-custody, at 1.

10. Id., at 5.

11. Center for Public Policy Priorities, "A Child Alone and Without Papers: A Report on the Return and Repatriation of Unaccompanied Undocumented Children by the United States," 2008, https://perma.cc/7MZ2-PFX6, at 25.

12. Women's Refugee Commission and Sutcliffe, supra n. 9, at 11.

13. Id.

14. Id., at 9. An HHS Inspector General's report confirmed that 16 percent were not transferred to ORR within three days but noted that only 6 percent were not transferred within five days. The Inspector General was not able to ascertain from government records whether the 10 percent who were transferred after three days but before five days fell into the exception permitted by the Flores agreement with respect to situations in which there was no licensed facility with space available in the DHS district where the child was apprehended. HHS Inspector General, supra n. 5, at 11.

15. Id., at 7.

16. Id., at 8.

17. Id.

18. Id., at 14.

19. Id., at 16.

20. Id., at 15. A staff-secure facility, in contrast to a "shelter," is one that "reflects" a "home-like" setting but has "stricter security measures . . . to prevent escape." Unlike secure facilities, most do not have internally locked units but may have a "secure perimeter with a 'no climb' fence." See Office of Refugee Resettlement, "Children Entering the United States Unaccompanied: Guide to Terms," https://perma.cc/6AFS-G2EW.

21. Id., at 20.

22. Inspector General, supra n. 5, at 12.

23. Id., at 8.

24. Id., at 9.

25. Id., at 14.

26. Id.

27. Id., at 15.

28. Id., at 17.

29. See S. 119, 109th Cong.

30. Michelle Brané credits the idea for using the reauthorization process to obtain new protections for children to Christopher Nugent, an immigration advocate at the community services team of the law firm of Holland and Knight (Brané, supra n. 7). Nugent had previously been a director of the American Bar Association's Commission on Immigration Policy and had served as the Executive Director of the Florence Immigrant and Refugee Rights Project in Arizona, which served detained migrants. See "Taking on Tough Cases: Holland and Knight's Community Services Team," *Corporate Counsel Business Journal*, August 1, 2007, https://perma.cc/3R9U-XA39.

31. Brané, supra n. 7.

32. To avoid singling out Mexico, the statute referred to children who were nationals of countries contiguous to the United States, but very few UACs are Canadians.

33. P.L. 457, 110th Cong., Sec. 235(a).

34. In 2012–13, the office of the United Nations High Commissioner for Refugees made four monitoring trips to observe operations of the Customs and Border Patrol. It reported that despite the TVPRA, CBP officials "continue to reinforce the presumption of an absence of protection needs" of Mexican children and used "overly restrictive standards by which to assess trafficking and fear of persecution," with the result that "children with needs that Congress intended to protect are likely rejected at the U.S. border." See United Nations High Commissioner for Refugees, Regional Office Washington D.C. for the United States and the Caribbean, 2014, https://perma.cc/83RQ-QXZ4, at 5.

35. Lisa Seghetti, Alison Siskin, and Ruth Ellen Wasem, "Unaccompanied Alien Children: An Overview," Congressional Research Service Report 7–5700, 2014, at 5 n. 26.

36. ICE, Detention and Removal Operations, DRO Policy and Procedure Manual as of March 2006, Sec. 2.2, reads, in part, "if a decision is made to pursue formal charges against the unaccompanied juvenile, the juvenile will normally be placed in removal proceedings under Section 240 of the [Immigration and Nationality] Act [the Section providing for full hearings before immigration judges] rather than expedited removal." The manual is attached to "Memorandum to Field Office Directors from John P. Torres, Acting Director, Office of Detention and Removal Operations," March 27, 2006, https://perma.cc/43F6-EASV.

37. P.L. 457, supra n. 33, Sec. 235(b).

38. Id., Sec. 235(c)(2).

39. Id., Sec. 235(d)(7).

40. Seghetti et al., supra n. 35, at 10–11.

41. Id.

42. P.L. 457, supra n. 33, Sec. 235(c)(4) and (5). The act also allowed but did not require ORR to appoint "independent child advocates for child trafficking

victims and other vulnerable UACs." These persons would advocate "for the best interest of the child," while a legal representative, on the other hand, would be obligated by ethical rules to advocate for what the child expressly wanted. See id., Sec. 235(c)(6), and American Bar Association, Model Rules of Professional Conduct, at 1.14 and comment 1.

CHAPTER EIGHT. ARTESIA, 2009–2014

1. ICE, "Family Residential Standards, Background," March 25, 2011, https://www.ice.gov/detention-standards/family-residential

2. Interview with Michelle Brané, May 22, 2018.

3. ICE, supra n. 1.

4. "Mayor Bloomberg Appoints Dora B. Schriro as Correction Department Commissioner," press release, September 9, 2009, https://perma.cc/N97Q-FYD3.

5. Dora Schriro, "Obstacles to Reforming Family Detention in the United States," Global Detention Project Working Paper No. 20 (2017), https://perma.cc/LQ4K-GCLL. See also Dora Schriro, "Weeping in the Playtime of Others: The Obama Administration's Failed Reform of ICE Family Detention Practices," *Journal on Migration and Human Security* 5 (2017): 452.

6. Magistrate Judge Andrew W. Austin, quoted in Nina Bernstein, "U.S. to Reform Policy on Detention for Immigrants," *New York Times*, August 5, 2009.

7. Brané, supra n. 2.

8. Anna Gorman, "Family Detention Sites in Works," *Los Angeles Times*, May 18, 2008.

9. Schriro, supra n. 5; Bernstein, supra n. 6.

10. Anabelle Garay, "Families Slowly Leaving Texas Detention Facility," *Newsday*, September 9, 2009.

11. Department of Homeland Security, Immigration and Customs Enforcement, "Immigration Detention Overview and Recommendations," 2009, https://perma.cc/RDF7-LNSB.

12. Press release, supra n. 4.

13. Council on Foreign Relations, "Central America's Violent Northern Triangle," 2018, https://perma.cc/L7JV-QALA (85,000 members in Central America); International Crisis Group, "El Salvador's Politics of Perpetual Violence," December 2017, https://perma.cc/62WS-FLPY, at 8–9 (60,000 members in El Salvador). Total estimates of gang size vary considerably, and many of the estimates are out of date. See International Crisis Group, "Mafia of the Poor: Gang Violence and Extortion in Central America," April 2017, https://perma.cc/88GS-ZZZ8, at 11.

14. Douglas Farah and Kathryn Babinau, "The Evolution of MS-13 in El Salvador and Honduras," *Prism* 7, no. 1 (2017): 59, https://perma.cc/TPR3-AAY9. (*Prism* is a publication of the National Defense University).

15. Human Rights Watch, "You Don't Have Rights Here," 2014, https://perma.cc/U7AQ-RDBJ, at 12.

16. Oscar Martinez, Efren Lemus, Carlos Martinez, and Deborah Sontag, "Killers on a Shoestring: Inside the Gangs of El Salvador," *New York Times*, November 20, 2016.

17. Annie Hylton and Sarah Salvadore, "They Said We Would Pay With Our Lives," *Slate*, August 31, 2016, https://perma.cc/8BBZ-3QNA.

18. Members were occasionally allowed to leave a gang for an exceptional reason, such as joining an evangelical church. See International Crisis Group, "El Salvador's Politics of Perpetual Violence," supra n. 13, at 8 n. 37.

19. Id., at 18.

20. Id., at 12–13.

21. KIND, "Neither Security Nor Justice: Sexual and Gender-Based Violence in El Salvador, Honduras and Guatemala," 2017, https://perma.cc/U9WX-FDML, at 5–6.

22. Center for Gender and Refugee Studies, University of California, Hastings College of the Law, "Guatemala's Femicides and the Ongoing Struggle for Human Rights," 2006, https://perma.cc/WV2K-YTNQ, at 8–9, 12.

23. International Crisis Group, "Mafia of the Poor," supra n. 13, at 6–7.

24. Id., at 8–10.

25. Id., at 16–17.

26. CNN, "Which Countries Have the World's Highest Murder Rates? Honduras Tops the List," April 11, 2014, https://perma.cc/L7RF-M3ZW.

27. Joshua Partlow, "Why El Salvador Became the Hemisphere's Murder Capital," *Washington Post*, January 5, 2016.

28. See, e.g., the description of the motivations of the Pulex family from Guatemala in Kirk Semple, "Deported From U.S., and Picking Up Pieces of a Shattered Dream," *New York Times*, July 18, 2018.

29. United Nations High Commissioner for Refugees, "Women on the Run," 2015, https://perma.cc/8GFY-UTRM, at 4.

30. Id., at 5.

31. Id., at 10.

32. Id.

33. Id., at 25–27.

34. United Nations High Commissioner for Refugees, "Children on the Run," 2014, https://perma.cc/4WHH-AWMU, at 9–10.

35. Id., at 36.

36. Women's Refugee Commission, "Forced from Home: The Lost Boys and Girls of Central America," 2012, https://www.womensrefugeecommission.org

/uncategorized/2057-forced-from-home-the-lost-boys-and-girls-of-central-america-background-and-report, at 1.

37. KIND, supra n. 21, at 4–5.

38. Id., at 8.

39. Kids in Need of Defense & Human Rights Center Fray Matias de Cordova, "Childhood Cut Short: Sexual and Gender-based Violence Against Central American Migrant and Refugee Children," 2017, https://perma.cc/Z3LD-JDKJ, at 12–13.

40. Medecins Sans Frontieres, "Forced to Flee Central America's Northern Triangle: A Neglected Humanitarian Crisis," 2017, https://perma.cc/Q23Q-FHVT, at 5.

41. "Long-established immigrant communities in the U.S. undoubtedly are significant 'pull factors,' attracting Central American youth and single-parent families seeking to reunite with relatives already in the U.S. . . . [but] the ever-rising numbers of asylum seekers at other borders in the region [that is, in Mexico, Belize, Costa Rica, Nicaragua and Panama] suggest that conditions in the Northern Triangle countries are the decisive factor driving the exodus" (Dennis Stinchcomb and Eric Hershberg, "Unaccompanied Migrant Children from Central America: Context, Causes and Responses," Center for Latin American & Latino Studies, American University, 2014, https://www.american.edu/centers/latin-american-latino-studies/unaccompanied-minors.cfm, at 13.)

42. Women's Refugee Commission, supra n. 36, at 1.

43. Brané, supra n. 2.

44. This is not a very accurate term, as it may connote some sort of deliberate, active intelligence pushing up the numbers, as in President Obama's "surge" of troops into Iraq to quell the violence there, rather than the spontaneous action of many different people. However, the term was widely used by the United Nations, the United States government, and the press, and it is used here with that caveat. The influx was described as a "surge" by the U.S. Court of Appeals in *Flores v. Lynch*, 828 F. 3d 898 (9th Cir. 2016).

45. Mexican arrivals were treated differently, because after apprehension they were allowed to return to Mexico voluntarily, without an order of removal, and most did.

46. The data regarding members of family units apprehended in FY 2014 includes Mexicans, but the number of Mexicans is small. The Border Patrol did not publish the nationality breakdown for FY 2014, but for FY 2015 and FY 2016, Mexicans apprehended in family units were only 11 percent and 5 percent, respectively. See U.S. Customs and Border Patrol, "Southwest Border Unaccompanied Alien Children FY 2014," https://perma.cc/6VP4-ASM4. Other sources: U.S. Border Patrol, "Unaccompanied Children (Age 0–17) Apprehensions, Fiscal Year 2008 Through Fiscal Year 2012," https://perma.cc/9UX2-3D57; William A. Kandel, "Unaccompanied Alien Children: An Overview," Congressional Research

NOTES TO CHAPTER EIGHT

Service 2 (2017); U.S. Customs and Border Patrol, "Total Family Unit Apprehensions by Month, FY 2013–FY-2018," https://perma.cc/N5S4-C3LR. DHS counts each member of a family as a separate individual for those in the "family units" category. By way of comparison, the figure of 68,684 persons in the "family units" category for FY 2014 includes 38,982 accompanied children. See United States Border Patrol, "Sector Profile—Fiscal Year 2014," https://perma.cc/FZ32-93DL.

47. The number of apprehensions understates the number of migrants because many migrants are able to enter the United States across the Rio Grande without being caught.

48. Office of Refugee Resettlement, "Facts and Data," https://perma.cc /RE7W-FAYQ, gives statistics for FY 2012–17.

49. In FY 2013, 93 percent of apprehended UACs were from the Northern Triangle, with 3 percent from Mexico and 2 percent from Ecuador. See Hannah Rappleye, "Undocumented and Unaccompanied: Facts, Figures on Children at the Border," NBC News, July 9, 2014.

50. Women's Refugee Commission, supra n. 36, at 21.

51. National Immigrant Justice Center, Esperanza Immigrant Rights Project, Americans for Immigrant Justice, Florence Immigrant and Refugee Rights Project, and ACLU Border Litigation Project, letter to Megan H. Mack, Officer for Civil Rights and Civil Liberties, DHS, and John Roth, DHS Inspector General, June 11, 2014, https://perma.cc/56C7-XN5J, at 2.

52. Id., at 7.

53. Letter to Secretary Jeh C. Johnson from John Roth, DHS Inspector General, Aug. 28, 2014, https://perma.cc/B52T-83C9.

54. National Immigrant Justice Center, "DHS Inspector General Fails To Adequately Investigate Abuse of Detained Immigrant Children," press release, September 3, 2014, https://perma.cc/B2TX-EXCR.

55. Statement of the American Civil Liberties Union in House of Representatives, Committee on Homeland Security, Hearings on Unaccompanied Minors, June 24 and July 23, 2014, at 161.

56. "Transcript: Commissioner Kerlikowske's Full Interview," NPR, July 18, 2014, https://perma.cc/6S25-HPY2.

57. Women's Refugee Commission, supra n. 36, at 16.

58. Id., at 15.

59. Manny Fernandez, "Base Serves as Home for Children Caught at Border," New York Times, April 28, 2012.

60. Julia Preston, "U.S. Setting Up Emergency Shelter in Texas as Youths Cross Border Alone," New York Times, May 16, 2014.

61. Graham Lee Brewer and Jennifer Palmer, "Unaccompanied Immigrant Children Begin Their Arrival at Fort Sill," The Oklahoman, June 13, 2014.

62. Jonathan Lloyd and John Cadiz Klemack, "Naval Base Warehouse Converted Into Shelter for Immigrant Children," NBC News, June 13, 2014, https://

perma.cc/P8KY-ZP48. The temporary shelters at the military and naval bases were finally closed in August 2014; see Michael D. Shear, "U.S. to Shut 3 Interim Shelters Housing Immigrant Children," *New York Times*, August 4, 2014.

63. Lauren Aronson, "The Tipping Point: The Failure of Form Over Substance in Addressing the Needs of Unaccompanied Alien Children," *Harvard Latino Law Review* 1 (2015): 18.

64. U.S. Senate Permanent Subcommittee on Investigations, Committee on Homeland Security and Governmental Affairs, "Protecting Unaccompanied Alien Children from Trafficking and Other Abuses: the Role of the Office of Refugee Resettlement," 2016.

65. Appleseed, "Children at the Border: The Screening, Protection and Repatriation of Unaccompanied Mexican Minors," 2011, https://perma.cc/GFW9-UUSE, at 15.

66. Id., at 16.

67. U.S. Citizenship and Immigration Services, "Victims of Human Trafficking: T Nonimmigrant Status," https://www.uscis.gov/humanitarian/victims-human-trafficking-other-crimes/victims-human-trafficking-t-nonimmigrant-status. A four-year visa for a trafficked child could later lead to permanent U.S. residency. See U.S. Citizenship and Immigration Services, "Green Card for a Victim of Trafficking," https://www.uscis.gov/greencard/trafficking-victim-t-nonimmigrant.

68. Appleseed, supra n. 65, at 15.

69. Matter of A- R- C- G-, 26 I & N Dec. 388 (BIA 2014).

70. Appleseed, supra n. 65, at 36–40.

71. USCIS, "Consideration of Deferred Action for Childhood Arrivals," https://perma.cc/6RET-UUZ4.

72. Mark Trumbull, "Immigration is Suddenly No. 1 Issue, but What Do Americans Want Done?," *Christian Science Monitor*, July 16, 2014.

73. Associated Press, "Child Migrant Surge Shifts Politics of Immigration," *Mail Online*, July 18, 2014.

74. Id.

75. If so, this was a misunderstanding of DACA, because DACA benefitted only those who had arrived before June 2007. But some scholars believed that the misunderstanding, along with increased violence in the Northern Triangle, accounted for some of the increased migration by children. See Scott Rempell, "Credible Fears, Unaccompanied Minors, and the Causes of the Southwestern Border Surge," *Chapman Law Review* 18 (2015): 382–83, citing Border Patrol testimony.

76. Stephen Dinan, "DHS Chief to Congress: I Can't Explain the Surge of Immigrant Children," *Washington Times*, June 25, 2014.

77. *All in with Chris Hayes*, MSNBC, July 7, 2014.

78. Associated Press, "Martinez Faults Obama, Congress on Immigrant Surge," July 9, 2014, available on LEXIS.

79. Interview, *Face the Nation*, CBS, July 6, 2014.

80. Statement of the American Civil Liberties Union, supra n. 55, at 2.

81. Mark Sappenfield, "What Will Happen To Immigrant Kids in Border Crisis?," *Christian Science Monitor*, July 6, 2014.

82. Statement of the American Civil Liberties Union, supra n. 55, at 100, 108.

83. Carl Hulse, "Immigrant Surge Rooted in Law to Curb Child Trafficking," *New York Times*, July 7, 2014.

84. On Meet the Press, the President said "we have bipartisan support for that [immigration reform]. We have a Senate bill that would accomplish that. . . . [but] the truth of the matter is that the politics did shift midsummer because of that problem [a perception of an immigration crisis due to the arrival of so many children]" (*Meet the Press*, NBC-TV, September 7, 2014, https://www.nbcnews.com/meet-the-press/president-barack-obamas-full-interview-nbcs-chuck-todd-n197616).

85. "CNN Town Hall—Hillary Clinton's Hard Choices," interview transcript, June 17, 2014, https://perma.cc/VW4M-NL84.

86. Office of the Vice President, "Remarks to the Press with Q&A by Vice President Joe Biden in Guatemala," June 20, 2014, https://perma.cc/D968-DLQH.

87. Bulletin News Network, "DHS Chief Defends Handling of Illegal Immigration Surge Amid GOP Criticism," *The Frontrunner*, June 25, 2014, quoting from McClatchy newspapers.

88. For a history of the administration's budget requests to deal with the immigration "surge" in 2014 and the first half of 2015, see American Immigration Council, "A Guide to Children Arriving at the Border: Laws, Polices and Responses," 2015, https://perma.cc/D6PE-GZGT, at 11–12. Congress eventually appropriated $80 million for the children's care (id., at 12).

89. Statement of the American Civil Liberties Union, supra n. 55, at 9.

90. Dara Lind, "Inside the Remote, Secretive Detention Center for Migrant Families," *Vox*, July 24, 2014, https://perma.cc/L6L7-JUSA.

91. Stephen Manning, "The Artesia Report," 2015, https://innovationlawlab.org/the-artesia-report/the-artesia-report. In the opinion of this author, the online document is a stunning and emotionally compelling combination of reporting, advocacy, and high-tech graphic design.

92. Id.

93. Juan Carlos Llorca, "Immigrant Center Will Expedite Deportations," *Dubuque Telegraph Herald*, June 27, 2014.

94. Detention Watch Network, "Expose and Close: Artesia Family Residential Center," New Mexico, 2014, https://perma.cc/3YLP-7RTL, at 7–9.

95. Sharita Gruberg, "Inside a Converted New Mexico Detention Center, 'Swift Process' May Mean Asylum Claims Overlooked," *ThinkProgress*, July 30, 2014, https://perma.cc/8BW2-TGGY.

96. Wendy Cervantes and Madhuri Grewal, "Family Detention for Central American Refugees is Inhumane," *The Atlantic*, September 16, 2014, https://perma.cc/T9NL-GJEM. See also Wil S. Hylton, "The Shame of America's Family Detention Camps," *New York Times Magazine*, February 4, 2015.

97. U.S. Commission on International Religious Freedom, "Barriers to Protection: The Treatment of Asylum Seekers in Expedited Removal," 2016, https://perma.cc/B3T2-6XTQ, at 19, summarizing the earlier study.

98. Id., at 20.

99. "The Artesia Report," supra n. 91.

100. Llorca, supra n. 93.

101. "The Artesia Report," supra n. 91.

102. Hylton, supra n. 96.

103. See chapter 1.

104. Lind, supra n. 90.

105. Helen Lawrence (one of the volunteer lawyers), "Artesia On Our Minds—an Immigration Attorney's Diary of a Detention Camp," https://perma.cc/YDU9-ZB47; The Artesia Report, supra n. 91.

106. Bill Lascher, "The New Oregon Trail: How Immigration Attorney Stephen Manning is Fighting Exclusion Orders and Deportations," *Oregon Super Lawyers*, August, 2017, https://perma.cc/CS9Z-X5Q7; "The Artesia Project," supra n. 91. Most volunteers paid for their own transportation and lodging, but by September, 2014, AILA and the American Immigration Council provided funds for two lawyers to coordinate and lead volunteers (id).

107. "The Artesia Project," supra n. 91.

108. Id.

109. Alicia A. Caldwell, "U.S. to Close Detention Center in Artesia," *Santa Fe New Mexican*, November 18, 2014.

110. The Artesia Project, supra n. 91.

111. Id.

112. DHS Secretary Jeh Johnson visited Artesia a few weeks after it opened. That night, ICE deported seventy-nine people, flying them on one of its planes to El Salvador, where the gangs were ready to take vengeance on people who had fled. Ten of the children were later killed (Hylton, supra n. 96.)

113. Careen Shannon, "Detaining Families Seeking Asylum is Just Wrong," *The Hill*, December 19, 2014, https://perma.cc/5XXM-LTHR.

114. Jennifer Moore, "Deportations Violate U.S., Global Laws," *Albuquerque Journal*, November 16, 2014; Emily Gogolak, "What's Next for Immigrant Families in Detention?," *The New Yorker*, July 15, 2015.

CHAPTER NINE. KARNES AND DILLEY, 2014–2016

1. Melinda Henneberger, "When an Immigration Detention Center Comes to a Small Town," *Washington Post*, October 2, 2014.

2. Dora Schriro, "Weeping in the Playtime of Others: The Obama Administration's Failed Reform of ICE Family Detention Practices", *Journal on Migration and Human Security* 5 (2017): 462.

3. DHS continued to be responsible, as well, for a small family detention center in Berks County, Pennsylvania, which is the subject of the next chapter. Only mothers with children were detained at Karnes and Dilley; a few fathers with children were sent to Berks. But if a father and mother and one or more children fled to the U.S. together, the father would be sent to a separate adult detention facility to await a hearing, while the mother and child were either released or detained together, at least until the Trump administration began separating them, a subject treated in chapter 12.

4. Emily Gogolak, "What's Next for Immigrant Families in Detention?," *The New Yorker*, July 30, 2015.

5. Rupert Neate, "Welcome to Jail, Inc.: How Private Companies Make Money off U.S. Prisons," *The Guardian*, June 16, 2016.

6. Interview with Denise Gilman in Austin, Texas, July 11, 2018.

7. Interview with Barbara Hines in Austin, Texas, July 9, 2018.

8. University of Texas, Denise Gilman, https://perma.cc/YWB5-HSD6.

9. Gilman, supra n. 6.

10. Hines, supra n. 7.

11. Id.

12. Wil S. Hylton, "American Nightmare," *New York Times*, February 8, 2015; "Mass Detention of Migrant Women and Children Continues to Expand," *Legal Monitor Worldwide*, October 1, 2014.

13. Ironically, undocumented persons who had crossed the border in an irregular manner, such as by rafting across the Rio Grande, were legally eligible to have bond set for them, but those who presented themselves to immigration authorities at an official port of entry, such as a bridge between the U.S. and Mexico, were ineligible for bond. They could, however, be paroled at the discretion of ICE—that is, released with or without ankle monitors and duties to report to ICE officials periodically.

14. Immigration Clinic, University of Texas, "Report to the Inter-American Commission on Human Rights Regarding Grave Rights Violations Implicated in Family Immigration Detention at the Karnes County Detention Center," September 26, 2014, https://perma.cc/U7F4-WCJX,

15. Matter of D- J-, 23 I & N Dec. 573 (A.G. 2003).

16. Julie M. Linton et al., "Detention of Immigrant Children," policy statement, American Academy of Pediatrics, March 2017, https://perma.cc/Y7WZ-7WCM.

17. Olga Byrne, "On the Ground at Karnes: Children Still Harmed by Family Detention," December 18, 2015, https://perma.cc/MC4J-7JLS.

18. Satsuki Ina, "I Know an American 'Internment' Camp When I See One," *Huffington Post*, May 27, 2015.

19. ABA, "Commission on Immigration, Family Immigration Detention: Why the Past Cannot be Prologue," 2015, at 30. (This report is no longer available online but is on file with the author.)

20. See Vivian Kuo and Jason Hanna, "Women Allege Sexual Abuse at Texas Immigrant Detention Center," *CNN*, October 4, 2014, https://perma.cc/94DJ-WFGW.

21. Inter-American Commission on Human Rights, "Refugees and Migrants in the United States: Families and Unaccompanied Children," 2015, https://perma.cc/CC64-4SWL, at 76. Incidents of this nature had been the subject of complaints by detainees to Karnes personnel, but no action was taken. See letter to DHS Secretary Jeh Johnson from Marisa Bono, MALDEF, September 30, 2014.

22. Human Rights Watch, "U.S.: Trauma in Family Immigration Detention," May 15, 2015, https://perma.cc/D3DH-3TRX.

23. Letter to Megan Mack, Office of Civil Rights and Civil Liberties, DHS, from Karen Lucas et al., June 30, 2015, https://www.aila.org/File/Download EmbeddedFile/64983.

24. Lutheran Immigration and Refugee Commission, "Locking Up Family Values, Again," 2014, https://perma.cc/B9B5-72UL, at 8.

25. "Declaration of Luis H. Zayas, Ph.D.," December 14, 2014, https://perma.cc/ZX9A-9YM3.

26. Franco Ordonez, "Detained Mothers Launch Hunger Strike," McClatchy D.C. Bureau, March 31, 2015, https://perma.cc/GY5E-5X3Z; Charles Gonzalez, "Karnes Hunger Strike Organizer Freed," *KSAT*, April 9, 2015, https://perma.cc/CC5C-C9Z7; Wyl S. Hilton, "A Federal Judge and a Hunger Strike Take on the Government's Immigrant Detention Facilities," *New York Times Magazine*, April 10, 2015.

27. Pat Beall, "GEO: Feds Give Karnes Immigrant Center Clean Bill of Health," *Palm Beach Post*, May 1, 2015.

28. Gilman interview, supra n. 6.

29. Chico Harlan, "Why the U.S. Effort to Stop Central Americans from Surging Across the Border Is Failing," *Washington Post*, August 15, 2016.

30. Id.

31. Aseem Mehta, "The Refugee Jail Deep in the Heart of Texas," *Narratively*, December 12, 2015, https://perma.cc/XA47-2EB2.

32. Bree Berwanger and Gracie Willis, "Family Detention is Not the Answer to Family Separation. It's a Failure and a Disgrace," *USA Today*, July 23, 2018.

33. Sambo Dul, "My Turn: What It's Really Like Inside Immigration 'Baby Jails,'" *AZ Central*, September 23, 2016, https://www.azcentral.com/story/opinion /op-ed/2016/09/20/family-detention-immigration-asylum/89930218.

34. Letter from National Immigrant Justice Center et al. to Megan H. Mack, DHS, June 11, 2014, https://cbpabusestest2.files.wordpress.com/2015/03/2014–06-11-dhs-complaint-re-cbp-abuse-of-uics.pdf.

35. International Human Rights Clinic, University of Chicago, ACLU Border Litigation Project, and ACLU Border Rights, "Neglect and Abuse of Unaccompanied Immigrant Children by U.S. Customs and Border Protection," May 2018, https://perma.cc/ZHK5–286U.

36. See the Halfway Home report, discussed in chapter 7; sworn statements by mothers describing experiences in CBP custody, filed by class counsel on February 2, 2015, in *Flores v. Holder*, CV 85 4544 DMG (C.D. Calif. 2015); 225 sworn statements by mothers, describing their experiences in CBP custody, filed by class counsel on July 16, 2018, in *Flores v. Sessions*, CV 85–4544 DMG (C.D. Calif. 2018).

37. International Human Rights Clinic et al, supra n. 35, at 18–19, quoting a DHS inspection report from 2014.

38. Corrected Memorandum Re: Status Conference filed by class counsel on July 16, 2018, in *Flores v. Sessions*, CV 85–4544 DMG (C.D. Calif. 2018) and 225 sworn statements, supra n. 36.

39. See, e.g., Jorge Rivas, "These Unsealed Photos Offer Rare Peek Inside Border Patrol's Notorious 'Ice Box' Detention Cells," *Splinter*, June 29, 2016, https://perma.cc/KRV3-ESEL.

40. Annalisa Merelli, "Those Photos of Immigrant Children 'Caged' by the US? They're From 2014," *Quartz*, June 18, 2018, https://perma.cc/358P-B3VF.

41. Gilman interview, supra n. 6.

42. Jonathan Hiskey et al., "Violence and Migration in Central America," 2014, https://perma.cc/VDL8–72KA.

43. He noted that in an earlier immigration case, *Zadvydas v. Davis*, 533 U.S. 678 (2001), the Supreme Court had said that the due process clause of the Constitution prohibits government detention of a person in the United States unless "ordered in a criminal proceeding with adequate procedural protections, or, in certain special and narrow nonpunitive circumstances, where a special justification, such as harm-threatening mental illness, outweighs the individual's constitutionally protected interest in avoiding physical restraint."

44. *R.I.L-R. v. Johnson*, 80 F. 3d 164 (D.C.D.C. 2015).

45. Motion for reconsideration, *R.I. L-R v. Johnson*, filed March 20, 2015.

46. Notice to the court in *R.I. L-R v. Johnson*, filed May 13, 2015.

47. Order in *R.I. L-R v. Johnson*, June 29, 2015.

48. Gilman, supra n. 6.

49. In addition, for a period of time, Gilman's law school colleague Ranjana Natarajan was one of the co-counsels in the California litigation.

50. Memorandum in Support of Motion to Enforce Settlement of Class Action, filed February 2, 2015, in *Flores v. Johnson*, CV-85–4544-RJK.

51. U.S. District Court, Central District of California, "Passing of Senior District Judge Robert J. Kelleher," https://perma.cc/7B2F-7M2P.

52. Hector Beccera, "Senate OK's Gee as Judge," *Los Angeles Times*, December 26, 2009.

53. Judge Gee, quoted in Kimberly Yam, "Trump Immigration Order Faces Judge Who's Ruled Against Family Detention Before," *Huffington Post*, June 26, 2018.

54. Roque Planas, "Judge Fighting Family Detention Has Personal Connection to Immigration," *Huffington Post*, August 24, 2015.

55. Tim Arango, "Who is Dolly Gee? A Look at the Judge Deciding the Fate of Trump's Executive Order," *New York Times*, June 21, 2018.

56. Beccera, supra n. 52.

57. Defendants' Response in Opposition to Plaintiffs' Motion to Enforce Settlement of Class action in *Flores v. Holder*, filed February 27, 2015.

58. Federal Rule of Civil Procedure 60(b)(5) allows a court to relieve a party from a previous order if applying it in the future is no longer equitable.

59. Defendant's Protective Notice of Motion to Modify Settlement Agreement in *Flores v. Holder*, filed February 27, 2015.

60. For example, the agreement specified that unaccompanied minors could not be transported by INS in vehicles with detained adults. See Flores settlement, 1997, https://perma.cc/R7EY-GNBA, Para. 25.

61. Reply to Opposition to Enforce Settlement of Class Action in *Flores v. Holder*, filed March 13, 2015.

62. See Holland & Knight, "Leon Fresco,", 2019, https://perma.cc/3WNP-4SZK; Franco Ondonez, "Miami's Leon Fresco: The Immigration Mover and Shaker You Don't Know," McClatchy Washington Bureau, June 13, 2013, https://www.mcclatchydc.com/news/politics-government/congress/article24750004.html.

63. Telephone interview with Leon Fresco, October 9, 2018.

64. Id.

65. Id.

66. Tentative ruling re: Plaintiffs' Motion to Enforce Settlement of Class Action and Defendants' Motion to Amend Settlement Agreement in *Flores v. Holder*, CV 85–4544 (April 24, 2015), https://perma.cc/L3C7-H2VJ.

67. Reporter's Transcript of Proceedings in *Flores v. Meese*, April 24, 2015.

68. See, e.g., Nuri Vailbona, "Judge Tentatively Rules Against Restrictive Detention Facilities for Immigrant Families," *National Catholic Reporter*, May 4, 2015, https://perma.cc/ZGW7-M829.

69. Report on Flores hearing on motions to enforce, modify settlement, e-mail to groups concerned with family detention from Center for Human Rights and Constitutional Law, April 27, 2015.

70. Proceedings: Telephonic status conference, May 4, 2015; Order re: Confidentiality of Settlement Discussions, May 12, 2015.

71. Franco Ordonez, "Immigration Lawyer Threatened with Contempt Gets Day in Court," *Miami Herald*, August 24, 2015; Order re: OSC Why Bryan Johnson Should Not Be Held in Contempt of Court for Violating the Court's Order re Confidentiality of Settlement Discussions, August 24, 2015.

72. Letter from Peter Schey to Leon Fresco, May 26, 2015, https://perma.cc /Z6EY-FLTR. Bryan Johnson leaked the letter to the McClatchy news service because he believed the settlement would allow the family detention centers to remain open, even though they would have to release families more promptly. See Franco Ordonez, "Mothers' Proposal on Family Detention Divides Advocacy Groups," *The [Tacoma] News Tribune*, June 26, 2015, https://perma.cc /GKP4-ECNN.

73. Id.

74. Fresco, supra n. 63.

75. Editorial Board, "End Family Detention," *New York Times*, May 15, 2015.

76. Bethany N. Carson, "As Video Spreads of Protest Inside Family Detention During Congressional Tour, DHS Secretary Admits Family Detention Is Flawed," *Grassroots Leadership*, June 24, 2015, https://perma.cc/CT9D-G27G.

77. "Mothers Protest Inside an American Refugee Camp: Dilley, Texas," https://www.youtube.com/watch?v = EB6zo3jrFps.

78. Letter to DHS Secretary Jeh Johnson from 136 House Democrats, May 27, 2015, https://perma.cc/WLV4-EX2J.

79. Michelle Brané said, "We have to actually see it happening." Other immigration advocates complained that Johnson did not plan to close the baby jails. At the same time, House Judiciary Committee chair Robert W. Goodlatte (R-VA) said that Johnson's statement "only encourages more children and families to make the dangerous journey," and called for more detention. See Cindy Carcamo, "Policy Shift Could Free Immigrant Kids, Families," *Los Angeles Times*, June 25, 2015.

80. Statement by Secretary Jeh C. Johnson On Family Residential Centers, June 24, 2015 (press release), filed as Document 164, Ex. 1, in *Flores v. Holder* on July 8, 2015. A month earlier, DHS had issued another press release stating that it would review the detention of each family that was held for more than ninety days ("ICE Announces Enhanced Oversight for Family Residential Centers," May 13, 2015). Evidently DHS concluded that it would need to move further in the direction of adhering to the Flores settlement if it were to have any chance of avoiding losing in the case before Judge Gee.

81. Order Re Plaintiffs' Motion to Enforce Settlement of Class Action and Defendant's Motion to Amend Settlement Agreement, *Flores v. Johnson*, CV 85–4544 DMG, n. 4.

82. Shayna Posses, "Talks Fail on Treatment of Detained Immigrant Children," *Law 360*, July 20, 2015, https://www.law360.com/articles/681100 /talks-fail-on-treatment-of-detained-immigrant-children.

83. Order Re Plaintiffs' Motion to Enforce Settlement, supra n. 81, at n. 4.

84. Id., passim.

CHAPTER TEN. LITIGATION PROLIFERATES, 2015–2016

1. Defendants' response to the court's order to show cause why the remedies set forth in the Court's July 24, 2015 order should not be implemented, filed in *Flores v. Lynch*, August 6, 2015.

2. Plaintiffs' response to order to show cause, filed in *Flores v. Lynch*, August 13, 2015.

3. Order re Response to Order to Show Cause, filed in *Flores v. Lynch*, August 21, 2015.

4. Grassroots Leadership, "Our History," https://grassrootsleadership.org /history.html.

5. Jessie Degollado, "Karnes County Approves Family Detention Center Expansion," *KSAT*, December 16, 2014, https://perma.cc/CX4Z-NGQG; interview with Robert Libal and Cristina Parker, Grassroots Leadership, in Austin, Texas, July 11, 2018.

6. Guillermo Contreras, "Feds Release 7-Year-Old Immigrant Girl with Cancer for Treatment," *Houston Chronicle*, September 3, 2014.

7. Interview with Manoj Govindaiah in San Antonio, Texas, July 10, 2018.

8. CARA Family Detention Project, https://www.aila.org/practice/pro-bono /find-your-opportunity/cara-family-detention-pro-bono-project.

9. Dilley was too far from any city to have a permanent managing attorney on site, so managing attorneys, who served for much longer than the volunteers who came for only a week or so, changed from time to time. Brian Hoffman, who was the manager during my volunteer service in 2015, stayed for about a year. For a description of the Dilley project under his leadership, see Molly Henderson-Fiske, "Immigrant Lawyers Handling a Border Surge: 'This Is Really an Emergency Room Situation,'" *Los Angeles Times*, July 26, 2015.

10. DFPS, Order adopting emergency rules regarding minimum standards for general residential operations (amending 40 TAC Sec. 748.7), September 2, 2015, published in 40 TexReg 6229, September 18, 2015.

11. From "the email strings between them all it's just clear that ICE is calling all the shots on everything," Doggett said. "This was their determination, how can we pile more kids in these rooms?" (interview with Robert Doggett, Executive Director, Texas RioGrande Legal Aid, in Austin, Texas, July 10, 2018).

12. Id.

13. Plaintiffs' original petition in *Grassroots Leadership v. DFPS*, D-1-GN-15-004336 (Dist. Ct., Travis Co. Texas, 353d Judicial District, with proceedings to be conducted in the 250th district, Oct. 26, 2015), amended by Second Amended Petition (May 3, 2016), available at https://perma.cc /45VL-W9NZ.

14. Jennifer R. Lloyd, "The Law Clinics at 25: The Hon. Karin Crump," St. Mary's University, https://www.stmarytx.edu/2016/law-clinics-crump.

15. Id.

16. This order is reference in Transcript of Nov. 12, 2015 hearing in *Grassroots Leadership v. DFPS*, supra n. 13, at p. 16, line. 24. The judge gave DFPS notice that she was considering issuing the order, and a chance to argue against it, but the "State made a decision not to appear" (id., at p. 66, line 2).

17. Id., passim.

18. Temporary injunction in *Grassroots Leadership v. DFPS*, November 20, 2015.

19. Proposed amendment to 40 TAC 748.7, 40 TexReg 8009, November 13, 2015.

20. Minimum Standards for General Residential Operations, 41 TexReg 1493, 1494, February 26, 2016, attached to Second Amended Petition, supra n. 13.

21. The transcript of the hearing is available on the DFPS website: DFPS, Public Hearing Regarding Proposed 40 TAC 748.7, December 9, 2015, https://www .dfps.state.tx.us/About_DFPS/Public_Meetings/Stakeholders/documents/2015-12- 09-Licensing_Hearing_transcript_acc.pdf.

22. DFPS, Family Residential Centers Rule, January 26, 2016, https://perma .cc/7ZV7-P8Z8.

23. This amendment required Karnes to reduce occupancy density from eight persons per room to five persons per room, such as "two mothers and their children." See testimony of Rose Thompson, Karnes' Program Director, in hearing in *Grassroots Leadership v. DFPS*, June 1, 2016, at 152.

24. Minimum Standards, supra n. 20, at 1498–1502.

25. At the hearing on May 13, 2016, the state's attorney admitted that under the regulation, "it is possible that there are multiple family units in one room" and that DFPS did not require single-family rooming "based on the limitations of the facility" (hearing in *Grassroots Leadership v. DFPS*, May 13, 2016, at 70–71).

26. Id., at 76.

27. Associated Press, "Texas Immigrant Family Detention Center Granted Child-Care License," Fox News, May 4, 2016, https://perma.cc/9NPX-AJ8Y.

28. "They surprised us," Doggett later recalled (telephone interview with Robert Doggett, Texas RioGrande Legal Aid, July 31, 2018).

29. See Second Amended Petition of *Grassroots Leadership v. DFPS*, supra n. 13.

30. Tex. Fam. Code Sec. 54.011(f).

31. Application for Temporary Restraining Order and Temporary Injunction in *Grassroots Leadership v. DFPS*, May 3, 2016.

32. Temporary Restraining Order in *Grassroots Leadership v. DFPS*, May 4, 2016.

33. The rejoinder to this, by Barbara Hines, when she was called as a witness, was that every family was being held solely for the purpose of deportation, and each had received deportation orders in which they were advised that they had the burden to overcome by proving credible fear and then winning relief in immigration court (May 13 hearing, supra n. 25, at 92).

34. Id., passim.

35. June 1 hearing in *Grassroots Leadershp v. DFPS*, passim.

36. Final judgment in *Grassroots Leadership v. DFPS*, December 2, 2016.

37. Grassroots Leadership, "Texas Court Blocks Licensing of Family Detention Camps As Childcare Facilities," December 3, 2016, https://grassrootsleadership .org/releases/2016/12/breaking-texas-court-blocks-licensing-family-detention-camps-childcare-facilities.

38. Interview with Denise Gilman, University of Texas Immigration Clinic, July 11, 2018.

39. Id.

40. Gus Bova, "Texas Senate Votes to License 'Baby Jails' as Child Care Facilities," *Texas Observer*, May 9, 2017.

41. Meredith Hoffman (Associated Press), "Prison Company Struggles to Get License to Hold Children," *Washington Times*, April 20, 2017.

42. Id.

43. Interview with Cristina Parker, Grassroots Leadership, in Austin, Texas, July 11, 2018.

44. Bova, supra n. 40.

45. Texas Senate hearing, Committee of Veteran Affairs, March 29, 2017, http://tlcsenate.granicus.com/MediaPlayer.php?view_id=42&clip_id=12028.

46. Interview with Laura Guerra-Cardus in Austin, Texas, July 10, 2018.

47. Bova, supra n. 40.

48. R. G. Ratcliffe, "The Best and Worst Legislators 2017," *Texas Monthly*, July 2017.

49. Interview with Cheasty Anderson, Children's Defense Fund, in Austin, Texas, July 10, 2018.

50. Gus Bova, "Death of 'Baby Jails' Bill a Win for Immigrant Families," *Texas Observer*, May 26, 2017.

51. Brief for Appellants, *Flores v. Lynch*, No. 15–56434 (9th Cir.), filed January 15, 2016.

52. Brief for Appellees, *Flores v. Lynch*, filed February 23, 2016.

53. Reply brief for Appellants, *Flores v. Lynch,* filed March 8, 2016.

54. Telephone interview with Leon Fresco, October 9, 2018.

55. A video of the oral argument appears on the Ninth Circuit's website: https://www.ca9.uscourts.gov/media/view_video.php?pk_vid=0000009764.

56. *Flores v. Meese,* 828 F. 3d. 898 (9th Cir. 2016).

57. *Texas Department of Family & Protective Services v. Grassroots Leadership,* 2018 Tex. App. LEXIS 9643 ((Ct. App. 3d Dist., Nov. 28, 2018); Teo Armus, "A Court Ruling May Allow Migrant Families to Be Held Indefinitely. These Families Know What That Could Be Like," *Texas Tribune,* December 10, 2018.

58. The intermediate appeals court denied the motion for en banc review on November 28, 2018. Grassroots Leadership moved for a rehearing on December 12. The court denied that motion on December 14. Meanwhile, the November 2018 election had produced a new crop of judges for the court, who might be more sympathetic to the plaintiff families. So on January 3, 2019, Grassroots Leadership filed a motion for reconsideration of the denial of its request for en banc review. It remained pending with the court when the new judges arrived later that month. It was not clear under Texas law whether the court still had jurisdiction over the case after the new judges arrived, or whether the first denial of the motion for reconsideration ended the case. So a few days later, Grassroots Leadership filed an motion in the Texas Supreme Court seeking an extension of time for permission to seek review in that court: see *Grassroots Leadership v. Texas DFPS,* Unopposed First Motion for Extension of Time, Case 19-0092 (S. Ct. Texas, Jan. 25, 2019), https://perma.cc/7B5B-F6QB. That court "abated" (temporarily terminated) the case until the intermediate appeals court decided whether to grand the new motion for reconsideration en banc. Texas Supreme Court, Order abating the case, Jan. 25, 2019, https://perma.cc/86GT-JUXQ. That is where the matter stood as of early September 2019.

59. Email to the author from Jerome Wesevich, a Texas RioGrande Legal Aid attorney, January 15, 2019, reporting that the lower court decision will not affected by the appellate court opinion "until the en banc rehearing is decided and the [Texas] Supreme Court decides whether to accept the case."

60. See Flores Settlement Agreement Para. 6.

61. The Office of Hillary Rodham Clinton, "Immigration Reform," https://perma.cc/ZXH5-MM2B. Her campaign book elaborated that "We will end family detention for families and children who arrive at our border in desperate situations. We have alternatives to detention for those who pose no flight or safety risk, such as supervised release, that have proved effective and cost a fraction of what it takes to keep a family in detention" (Hillary Rodham Clinton and Timothy M. Kaine, *Stronger Together* [New York: Simon and Schuster, 2016], 189).

62. Meredith Hoffman, "Everything You Need to Know About Hillary Clinton's Immigration Plans," *The Vice Guide to the 2016 Election*, June 28, 2016, https://perma.cc/F26H-XPHA.

63. Tierney Sneed, "Clinton Criticizes Immigrant Detentions Under Obama," *U.S. News and World Report*, May 6, 2015.

64. Id.

65. "General Election: Trump vs. Clinton (4 way)," *RealClear Politics*, https://perma.cc/D9R9-YF2V.

CHAPTER ELEVEN. BERKS, 1998–2018

1. Molly Hennessy-Fiske, "Quick Shift In Migrant Detention: Processing Time Is Shortened for Many Detainees, But Outcome May Not Be What They Want," *Los Angeles Times*, October 9, 2015.

2. Monica Rhor, "Children Detained: Unlike Elian the Cuban Boy Who Lives with Family, Many Youths Who Arrive in the U.S. Alone Are Held for Months," *Philadelphia Inquirer*, February 21, 2000.

3. Human Rights Watch, "Detained and Deprived of Rights," 1998, https://www.hrw.org/legacy/reports98/ins2/.

4. Id.

5. Eric Schmidt, "New Shelter Seeks to Place Asylum-Seeking Families in More Hospitable Surroundings," *New York Times*, June 14, 2001.

6. Hanna Rosin, "Asylum Seekers Decry Detention by INS," *Washington Post*, June 17, 2001.

7. Id.

8. Chris Mondics, "Illegal-Immigrant Detainees Ill-Treated: Two Family Centers, One in Pa, Are Accused of Being Short on Medical Care, Privacy and Compassion," *Philadelphia Inquirer*, February 22, 2007.

9. Interview with Carol Anne Donohoe in Reading, Pennsylvania, August 7, 2018.

10. Id.

11. Annie Rosenthal, "Berks May be Model for Detention," *Pittsburgh Post-Gazette*, July 8, 2018.

12. Interview with Bridget Cambria in Reading, Pennsylvania, August 7, 2018.

13. Bridget Cambria, "Warning: Content Not Safe for Your Peace of Mind," November 5, 2015, https://perma.cc/DW27-S9WA.

14. Id.

15. Donohoe, supra n. 9.

16. Pennsylvania Bar, "Past PBA Pro Bono Award Winners," https://perma.cc/TXA6-WTHK.

17. See Alexandra Starr, "Standards for Child Migrants Could Force Detention Centers to Close," *National Public Radio*, May 13, 2015, https://perma.cc /Z2E6-NGUW.

18. Human Rights First, "Family Detention in Berks County, Pennsylvania," 2015, https://perma.cc/E9A2-66AT.

19. Dr. Alan Shapiro, Senior Medical Director for Community Pediatric Programs, Children's Hospital at Montefiore, quoted in in Human Rights First, id., at 7.

20. Id., at 8.

21. Id.

22. Human Rights First, "Health Concerns at the Berks Family Detention Center," February, 2016, https://perma.cc/MNW6-WUTB.

23. Only the Flores settlement could restrict DHS's custody of children in family detention, because the TVPRA applied only to unaccompanied children, not to those who arrived with a parent.

24. When a challenge to DHS custody of children at Berks began, in March 2015, it was possible that the Flores agreement did not apply to accompanied children, but very shortly thereafter, Judge Gee ruled that it did. See the discussion in chapter 9.

25. Flores settlement agreement, paras. 6 and 19, https://perma.cc /R7EY-GNBA.

26. See chapter 9.

27. Pa. Code Sec. 3800.5.

28. Letter to Gov. Tom Wolf et al. from Bryan Johnson, Amoachi & Johnson, PLLC, March 23, 2015.

29. Letter to Kathleen Kane from Matthew J. Archambeault, March 23, 2015.

30. Letter to Bryan Johnson from Jay Bausch, April 20, 2015.

31. Letter to Jay Bausch from Bryan Johnson, April 24, 2015.

32. Letter to Jay Bausch from Bryan Johnson, April 30, 2015.

33. Letter to Bryan Johnson from Doris M. Leisch, Chief Counsel to the governor, May 14, 2015.

34. Michael Matza, "U.S. Panel Hears Testimony on Guard Charged over Involvement with Inmate," *Philadelphia Inquirer*, January 31, 2015.

35. See Bridget Cambria et al., Petition to Intervene in the Appeal of Berks County Residential Center, BHA Docket No. 061-16-003, Para. 72 (April 9, 2018), https://perma.cc/WR6H-BAER.

36. Stephanie Weaver, "West Reading Man Sentenced for Sex with Detainee," *Reading Eagle*, April 14, 2016.

37. Ed Pilkington, "Many Migrant Families Held by US Could Soon Be Free from Detention 'Nightmare,'" *The Guardian*, May 11, 2015.

38. American Immigration Lawyers Association, "Ten Individual Case Summaries Documenting ICE's Failure to Provide Adequate Medical Care to Moth-

ers and Children in Family Detention Facilities," AILA Doc. No. 15073004, July 30, 2015.

39. Michael Matza, "House Members Urge End to 'Family Detention,'" *Philadephia Inquirer*, August 1, 2015.

40. Declaration of Bridget Cambria, April 29, 2016, Plaintiff's Exhibit 3 in Support of Motion to Enforce Settlement and for Appointment of Special Master, *Flores v. Johnson*, filed May 19, 2016.

41. Id.

42. Donohoe, supra n. 9.

43. Declaration of Carol Anne Donohoe, May 12, 2016, Plaintiff's Exhibit 4 in Support of Motion to Enforce Settlement and for Appointment of Special Master, *Flores v. Johnson*, filed May 19, 2016.

44. Cambria, supra n. 13.

45. Id.

46. Michael Matza, "Pa. Won't Renew License of Immigrant-Family Detention Center," *Philadelphia Inquirer*, October 23, 2015.

47. Letter to Diane Edwards, Executive Director, Berks County Commissioners, from Matthew J. Jones, Director, Pennsylvania Department of Human Services, January 27, 2016, https://perma.cc/W9RE-QZTS.

48. Id.

49. Estimate from Donohoe, supra n. 9.

50. Id.

51. Adjudication, Appeal of Berks County Residential Center, BHA Docket No. 061–16–0003, April 20, 2017l

52. Id.

53. Donohoe, supra n. 9.

54. Id. See also Anthony Orozco, "Berks County Residential Center Changes Shower Policy," *Reading Eagle*, July 31, 2017.

55. Bridget Cambria, Petition to Intervene on Behalf of Individuals Currently and Formerly Detained at Berks County Residential Center, April 9, 2018, at para. 36.

56. Aldea, "About Us," https://aldeapjc.org/#about.

57. Adjudication, supra n. 51.

58. Memorandum to Stop Berks Coalition from John Farrell, Anthony Sierzga, and Mariya Tsalkovich, Sheller Center for Social Justice, December 11, 2016, linked from https://www2.law.temple.edu/csj/resources.

59. Our Lady of Victory Catholic Church v. Department of Human Services, 153 A. 3d 1124 (Commonwealth Ct. Pa. 2016). The Sheller Center also suggested that the Governor could close Berks down if it presented immediate danger to the children's lives or health, but Governor Wolf's office stated that frequent inspections had not revealed such a danger. See Jeff Gammage, "Berks Family Detention Center: A Model for Jailing Migrant Families?," Philly.com, June 28, 2018.

60. Ivey DeJesus, "Wolf Administration: Only Washington Can Shut down Berks County Immigrant Detention Center," Penn Live, WHYY, July 3, 2019, https://perma.cc/J7TK-K76B.

61. Berks technically has not had a license since 2017, but because of the temporary injunction, all parties are treating it as if it did.

62. Evidence quoted in plaintiffs' Motion for Summary Judgment, *Grassroots Leadership v. Texas Dept. of Family and Protective Services*, October 14, 2016.

63. Flores Settlement agreement Para. 6.

64. Penn. Code. Sec. 3800.5.

65. Jacquelyn Kline, at Oct. 6, 2016 meeting of the Berks County Commissioners, Minute 41, https://www.youtube.com/watch?v=4pD_fpa2KGg&t=0s&index=1 11&list=PLjuI03soTP4H0yFE_m7QjsGlSOZW31nk0, accessed February 18, 2019.

66. "[Commissioner] Barnhardt said the doors out of the center remain unlocked" (Liam Migdail-Smith, "Berks Commissioner Wants County to Defend Residential Center," *Reading Eagle*, October 13, 2016).

67. See, e.g., amicus brief of the Farmworker Legal Aid Clinic, Villanova University and the Sheller Center for Social Justice, Temple University, in Appeal of Berks County Residential Center 12, January 4, 2017.

68. Transcript of Hearing in *Flores v. Meese*, April 24, 2015 at 38–39 (C.D. Calif). As noted in chapter 10, Fresco had not asserted as a fact that Berks was secure, but had stipulated to that fact for purposes of his argument in Flores that the plaintiffs had sat on their rights by years of allowing Berks to operate without any complaint to the federal courts.

69. "ICE has described the center as an unsecured facility" (Anthony Orozco, "What You Need to Know About the Residential Center Holding Immigrant Families in Berks County," *Reading Eagle*, June 23, 2018); "ICE officials confirmed that detainees are not free to leave, but said that the facility is still 'non-secure'" (Annie Rosenthal, "Activists Call for Detention Center to Close; Facility Holds Families, Faces Abuse Allegations," *Pittsburgh Post-Gazette*, July 22, 2018). In August 2019, DHS announced that it "has no intention of running [the family detention centers] as secure facilities. To that end, DHS will be adding additional points of egress to the Dilley and Karnes facilities by September 30, 2019." Department of Homeland Security, Apprehension, Processing, Care and Custody of Alien Minors and Unaccompanied Alien Children, 84 Fed. Reg. 44392, 44443 (Aug. 23, 2019). But DHS warned that leaving a family jail could have "significant immigration consequences." Id. at 44433.

70. Molly Hennessy-Fiske, "Quick Shift in Migrant Detention: Processing Time is Shortened for Many Detainees, But Outcome May Not Be What They Want," *Los Angeles Times*, October 9, 2015.

71. Donohoe, supra n. 9; Cambria , supra n. 12.

72. Declaration of Carol Anne Donohoe, supra n. 43.

73. Donohoe, supra n. 9.

74. Id.

75. Donohoe, supra n. 9; Cambria, supra n. 12.

76. Id.

77. *Boumediene v. Bush*, 553 U.S. 723 (2008).

78. I have used the pseudonyms for the real "Marta Rodriguez" and "Delma Cruz" at the request of their attorneys, who shared their petitions with me. Unlike most federal lawsuits, the documents (including the petitions that initiate the process) in habeas corpus cases are not made available online in PACER.

79. 8 U.S.C. Sec. 1225(b)(1)(B)(iii)(II).

80. Both women were allowed appeals to immigration judges immediately after their interviews, but they were not allowed to have legal representation in the appeals, and those judges affirmed the denials of credible fear. The judge in the Cruz case was male, and Ms. Cruz was too embarrassed to share the details of sexual abuse with him.

81. 8 U.S.C. Sec. 1252(e)(1)(a).

82. 8 U.S.C. Sec. 1252(e)(2).

83. The White House, "Paul S. Diamond," https://perma.cc/MLM2-EU67.

84. Confirmation hearing on the nomination of Paul S. Diamond, https://www.congress.gov/108/chrg/shrg96683/CHRG-108shrg96683.htm.

85. The ACLU also noted that a different provision of the 1996 law provided that "There shall be no [court] review of whether the alien is actually inadmissible or entitled to be any relief from removal." See 8 U.S.C. Sec. 1252(e)(5). It argued that this provision implied that review of the correctness of their credible fear determinations, which was not a review of either of the determinations identified in that sentence, was allowed. This was a weak argument that the court rejected because Congress clearly intended to bar court review in expedited removal cases. In addition to the section of the law quoted in the text, Congress had also said, in another sentence within the very section on which the ACLU relied, "In determining whether an alien has been ordered removed [through expedited removal procedures], the court's inquiry shall be limited to whether such an order in fact was issued and whether it relates [to the person seeking review]." See 8 U.S.C. Sec. 1252(e)(5).

86. U.S. Const. art 1, Sec. 9.

87. For a thorough study showing that Guantanamo detainees had been afforded many more procedural rights than immigrant detainees, see Faiza W. Sayed, "Challenging Detention: Why Immigrant Detainees Receive Less Process Than 'Enemy Combatants' and Why They Deserve More," *Columbia Law Review* 111 (2011): 1833–77.

88. *Castro v. U.S. Department of Homeland Security*, 163 F. Supp. 3d 157 (E.D. Pa. 2016).

89. Federal Judicial Center, "Smith, David Brooks," https://www.fjc.gov/history/judges/smith-david-brooks.

90. *Landon v. Plasencia*, 459 U.S. 21 1982.

91. *Castro v. U.S. Department of Homeland Security*, 835 F. 3d 422 (2016). In 2019, the Court of Appeals for the Ninth Circuit disagreed with the Castro decision and held that recently arrived undocumented foreign nationals could seek habeas review to challenge adverse credible fear decisions. *Thuraissigiam v. U.S. Dept. of Homeland Security*, 917 F. 3d 1097 (9th Cir. 2019). The government asked the Supreme Court to review that decision. Petition for a writ of certiorari, *Dep't of Homeland Security v. Thuraissigiam*, Case 19-161 (S. Ct.), August, 2019, https://perma.cc/7CGR-33Y5. The split between two circuits made it more likely that the Supreme Court would take up the issue.

92. *Castro v. U.S. Department of Homeland Security*, 835 F. 3d 422 (2016), at 450–51.

93. *Castro v. U.S. Department of Homeland Security*, __ U.S. __, 137 S. Ct. 1581 (2017).

94. 8 U.S.C. Sec. 1101(a)(27)(J); 1255(a), (h)(1).

95. Notice of related case and request for reassignment in *Osorio-Martinez v. Johnson*, https://ecf.paed.uscourts.gov/doc1/153116234140 (E.D. Pa. 2017).

96. *Osorio-Martinez v. Sessions*, 2017 U.S. Dist. Lexis 125310 (E.D. Pa. 2017).

97. Alliance for Justice, "Cheryl Anne Krause," https://www.afj.org/our-work/nominees/cheryl-ann-krause.

98. Id.

99. *Osorio-Martinez v. Sessions*, 893 F. 3d 153 (3d Cir. 2018).

100. In footnote 24, the court noted that "in releasing one of the [p]etitioners and his mother," an immigration judge who granted bond for them had stated that the "record was 'completely devoid of any reason, rational or otherwise' justifying their detention for almost two years." That immigration judge had cited a federal regulation, 8 C.F.R. Sec. 212.5(b)(3)(ii), which provides that if a detained child cannot be released to some non-detained relative, the child "may be released with an accompanying relative who is in detention."

CHAPTER TWELVE. TRUMP, 2017–2019

1. Donald J. Trump, Presidential Announcement Speech, June 16, 2015, https://perma.cc/63CR-7K2X. The "wall" idea had been suggested to Trump by his political consultant Roger Stone, who urged him to use "the power of illegal immigration to manipulate popular sentiment" (Stuart Anderson, "Where the Idea for Donald Trump's Wall Came From," *Forbes*, January 4, 2019).

2. Jenna Johnson, "Trump Calls for 'Total and Complete Shutdown of Muslims Entering the United States,'" *Washington Post*, December 7, 2015.

3. Tom Kertscher, "Donald Trump's Racial Comments about Hispanic Judge in Trump University Case," *Politifact Wisconsin*, June 8, 2016, https://perma.cc/D9LZ-RF8Z.

4. Center for Immigration Studies, "A Pen and a Phone: 79 Immigration Actions the Next President Can Take," April 2016, https://perma.cc/PTP9-9LC2.

5. Julia Edwards Ainsley, "Separate Mothers and Children: How a Trump Threat Deterred Illegal Migrants," *Reuters*, April 13, 2017, https://perma.cc/YFD4-3C5Q.

6. "Full Text of Trump's Executive Order on 7-Nation Ban, Refugee Suspension," *CNN*, January 28, 2017, https://perma.cc/4TT3-EAJT.

7. David A. Martin, Trump's 'Refugee Ban'—Annotated by a Former Top Department of Homeland Security Lawyer," January 30, 2017, https://perma.cc/3BMB-AES4.

8. See Donald J. Trump, "Executive Order: Enhancing Public Safety in the Interior of the United States," January 25, 2017, https://www.whitehouse.gov/presidential-actions/executive-order-enhancing-public-safety-interior-united-states.

9. Haley Sweetland Edwards, "'No One Is Safe': How Trump's Immigration Policy is Splitting Families Apart," *Time*, March 8, 2018. The article described how "Alejandro," an undocumented father with no criminal record, was suddenly apprehended on his way to work one morning "before his eldest, Isabella, began talking [and] before Estefania began talking."

10. "Executive Order," supra n. 8. Secretary Kelly followed up with "Memorandum on Enforcement of the Immigration Laws to Serve the National Interest," February 17, 2017, https://perma.cc/X42F-V99Z.

11. "Executive Order: Border Security and Immigration Enforcement Improvements," January 25, 2017. Secretary Kelly followed up with "Memorandum, Implementing the President's Border Security and Immigration Enforcement Improvements Policies," February 17, 2017, https://perma.cc/K7KF-QR5A.

12. Id.

13. Compare the 2014 and 2017 versions of DHS, Credible Fear Asylum Officer Training Manual, Sec. II(C)(6).

14. "Executive Order," supra n. 11.

15. Id., at Sec. K.

16. Id. The memorandum did not refer to the Flores settlement, but two years earlier Judge Gee had interpreted that agreement to apply to accompanied as well as unaccompanied minors, so DHS could not, even by redefining the children as accompanied, incarcerate them for more than twenty days.

17. Michael D. Shear and Julie Hirschfeld Davis, "Trump Moves to End DACA and Urges Congress to Act," *New York Times*, September 5, 2017.

18. *University of California v. Nielsen*, 908 F. 3d 476 (9th Cir. 2018), affirming *University of California v. Nielsen*, C-17–05211 (N.D. Calif.), Order Granting Preliminary Relief, January 9, 2018.

19. *Department of Homeland Security v. Regents of the University of California*, 2019 U.S. LEXIS 4407 (2019).

20. Caitlin Dickerson, "Trump Administration Targets Parents in New Immigration Crackdown," *New York Times*, July 1, 2017.

21. One member of that group, Gene Hamilton, who had worked for Senator Sessions, had become Kelly's senior counselor, and another member, Dimple Shah, who'd been staff director of the National Security Subcommittee of the House, had become the agency's deputy general counsel. See Ainsley, supra n. 5.

22. Ron Nixon and Caitlin Dickerson, "Immigration Officials Taking New Steps to Discourage Smuggling of Children," *New York Times*, September 24, 2017.

23. Dickerson, supra n. 20.

24. Hannah Drier, "Relatives of Undocumented Children Caught up in ICE Dragnet," *ABA Journal*, September 12, 2017.

25. Kelly, supra n. 11.

26. White House, "Remarks by President Trump at a Roundtable Discussion on Immigration, Bethpage, NY," May 23, 2018, https://perma.cc/L5KU-EYEF.

27. Ingrid Eagly and Steven Shafer, "Measuring *In Absentia* Removal in Immigration Court," *University of Pennsylvania Law Review* 168 (forthcoming 2020).

28. Id.

29. Id.

30. Id.

31. Ingrid Eagly, Steven Shafer, and Jana Whalley, "Detaining Families: A Study of Asylum Adjudication in Family Detention," *California Law Review* 106 (2018): 847–48 and Figure 15.

32. $319 is the figure reported in Department of Homeland Security, Congressional Budget Justification FY 2018, U.S. Immigration and Customs Enforcement, II: 50 (2017).

33. ICE, "Family Case Management Program (FMCP) Closeout Report," February 2018, at 7. Also, 99 percent of participants reported positive relationships with their case managers (id., at 8). One reason for this is that most of the participants reported receiving some sort of medical service that they attributed solely to participating in the program, which gave them access to the social workers (id., at 31).

34. Frank Bajak, "ICE Shutters Helpful Family Management Program Amid Budget Cuts," *Christian Science Monitor*, June 9, 2017.

35. Executive Office for Immigration Review, "Cost Savings Analysis—the EOIR Legal Orientation Program," 2012, https://perma.cc/WSL3-G2Y2.

36. Maria Sacchetti, "Justice to Halt Legal Program for Detained Immigrants," *Washington Post*, April 11, 2018.

37. "Sessions Resumes Free Legal Assistance Program for Detained Immigrants—For Now," *CNN*, April 25, 2018, https://perma.cc/3PKL-3YNX.

38. Letter to House and Senate leaders, Immigration Principles & Policies, October 8, 2017, https://perma.cc/DRY9-KCPA.

39. Donald J. Trump, State of the Union Message, January, 2018, https://www.whitehouse.gov/briefings-statements/president-donald-j-trumps-state-union-address.

40. Interview with Mark Morgan, Fox News, January 14, 2019, https://video.foxnews.com/v/5989437509001/#sp=show-clips. See also Nick Moroff and John Dawsey, "Mark Morgan to Replace John Sanders as Border Chief as DHS Shake-up Continues," *Washington Post*, June 25, 2019.

41. The practice apparently originated at the crossings between Tijuana and San Diego in the summer of 2016. Large numbers of Haitians arrived then, and CBP worked with Mexican authorities to keep them in Mexico and provide appointments for them with CBP officers. See Human Rights First, "Crossing the Line: U.S. Border Agents Illegally Reject Asylum Seekers," May, 2017, https://perma.cc/T5AS-3GZN. CBP officers in San Diego then extended the system to Central Americans, but Mexican authorities refused to give appointments to people other than Haitians. See Johnathan Partlow, "U.S. Border Officials Are Illegally Turning Away Asylum Seekers, Critics Say," *Washington Post*, January 16, 2017.

42. Letter to Megan H. Mack and John Roth from American Immigration Council et al., "Re: U.S. Customs and Border Protection's Systemic Denial of Entry to Asylum Seekers at Ports of Entry on U.S.-Mexico Border," January 13, 2017, https://www.americanimmigrationcouncil.org/sites/default/files/general_litigation/cbp_systemic_denial_of_entry_to_asylum_seekers_advocacy_document.pdf.

43. Human Rights First, supra n. 41.

44. Robert Moore, "At the U.S. Border, Asylum Seekers Fleeing Violence Are Told to Come Back Later," *Washington Post*, June 13, 2018.

45. See, e.g, "Asylum Seekers Wait Days and Weeks at U.S.-Mexico Border," *CBS News*, June 7, 2018, https://www.cbsnews.com/news/asylum-seekers-wait-days-and-weeks-at-u-s-mexico-border; Elliot Spagat and Nomaan Merchant, "Undeterred by Trump, Asylum-Seekers Line up at the Border," *U.S. News*, June 7, 2018, https://www.usnews.com/news/us/articles/2018-06-07/us-asylum-seekers-wait-their-turn-on-mexican-border.

46. Masha Gessen, "As the U.S. Shuts Its Doors, Migrants at the Mexican Border Continue to Hope," *The New Yorker*, July 23, 2018.

47. Moore, supra n. 44.

48. Senior CBP officials told Amnesty International that at the San Ysidro port of entry, where both families and unaccompanied children were turned back, CBP had actually reached its detention capacity only during a very short period in 2017. See Amnesty International, "'You Don't Have Any Rights Here':

Illegal Pushbacks, Arbitrary Detention & Ill-Treatment of Asylum Seekers in the United States," 2018, https://perma.cc/2JE8-3J8D .

49. Office of the Inspector General, "Special Review—Initial Observations Regarding Family Separation Issues Under the Zero Tolerance Policy," OIG-18-84, at 5–6 (2018).

50. Robert Strauss Center, University of Texas, "Asylum Processing and Wait-lists at the U.S.-Mexico Border," December, 2018, https://perma.cc/2UFK-N7LW, at 12.

51. Azam Ahmed, "Migrants' Despair Is Growing at U.S. Border. So Are Smugglers' Profits," *New York Times*, January 6, 2019. The price to be ferried by smugglers reportedly went up from $4400 to $5500 as a result of metering (id).

52. See complaint in *Al Otro Lado v. Kelly* (later renamed *Al Otro Lado v. Nielsen*), Case 2:17-cv-5111 (C.D. Calif.), https://perma.cc/HW7C-U7K5. Sworn declarations from migrants who were turned away at a border crossing and who then crossed the Rio Grande because they were desperate to seek safety appear in documents filed in the case (https://perma.cc/Y57T-39DQ).

53. Order granting change of venue in *Al Otro Lado v. Kelly*, November 21, 2017, https://perma.cc/U66Z-CZWT.

54. See Order granting defendants motion to dismiss in part and denying it in part in *Al Otro Lado v. Nielsen*, August 20, 2018, https://perma.cc/5S4U-VJKB.

55. Id.; First amended complaint in *Al Otro Lado*, supra n. 52.

56. Eli Watkins, "Trump: Deport Without 'Judges or Court Cases,'" *CNN Politics*, June 25, 2018, https://perma.cc/R456-EEZT.

57. Gus Bova, "U.S. and Mexican Officials Collaborating to Stop Asylum-Seekers, Attorneys Allege," *Texas Observer*, October 12, 2018; Teo Armus, "U.S. Officials Have Been Keeping Migrants from Crossing Bridges. Now, Mexico Is Doing the Same," *Texas Observer*, October 12, 2018.

58. Elliot Spagat, "Long Odds and Slow Lines Await Migrant Caravan at US Border," *Washington Post*, October 25, 2018.

59. Jean Guerrero, "Trapped in Tijuana: US Asks Asylum-Seekers to Wait Amid Record Homicides," *KPBS*, October 31, 2018, https://perma.cc/LYF2-VVUE.

60. Elizabeth Malkin, "Migrant Caravan Is Just Yards From U.S. Border, but Long Wait Lies Ahead," *New York Times*, November 18, 2018.

61. Id. A December 2018 report by the Robert Strauss Center put the magnitude of the Tijuana backlog even higher, at five thousand refugees (supra n. 50, at 6).

62. *Al Otro Lado v. McAleenan*, 2019 U.S. Dist. LEXIS 12978 (S.D. Cal. Aug. 2, 2019).

63. Kirk Semple, "A Flawed Asylum System in Mexico, Strained Further by U.S. Changes," *New York Times*, August 5, 2017; Kirk Semple, "Migrants in Mexico Face Kidnappings and Violence While Awaiting Immigration Hearings in the U.S.," *New York Times*, July 12, 2019. In 2017, Mexico deported nearly sixteen thousand children to Northern Triangle countries. Women's Refugee

Commission, "Safe Third Countries for Asylum-Seekers: Why Mexico Does Not Qualify as a Safe Third Country," 2018, https://perma.cc/7FBR-GU4M.

64. Dan Weikel, "Detention: INS Holding Sites Draw Heavy Criticism," *Orange County Register*, February 1, 1987.

65. Philip Bennett, "INS Accused of Parting Haitian Families," *Boston Globe*, October 2, 1992.

66. Id. Before Berks opened, there were also a few incidents in which children were separated from accompanying parents, such as a family that arrived from China without immigration documents and sought asylum. The mother was sent to Terminal Island in San Pedro, California, and her sons, twelve and fourteen, were sent to an INS juvenile hall in Los Padrinos, half an hour away. The mother wept for days after the separation, suffered an epileptic seizure, and spent two weeks in a hospital (Shawn Hubler, "The Changing Face of Illegal Immigration is a Child's," *Los Angeles Times*, January 31, 2000). But stories like these were not widespread.

67. Nicole Gaouette and Miguel Bustillo, "Immigration's Net Binds Children Too; Hundreds of Minors Are Being Held with Parents Caught Illegally in The U.S. The Facilties and Conditions Are Like Jail," *Los Angeles Times*, February 10, 2007.

68. Defendant's Response in Opposition to Plaintiffs' Motion to Enforce Settlement of Class Action, in *Flores v. Holder*, Case CV 85–45444, February 27, 2015.

69. Cindy Carcamo, "Immigration Ruling a Blow to Obama," *Los Angeles Times*, July 26, 2015.

70. Julie Hirschfeld Davis and Michael D. Shear, "How Trump Came to Enforce a Practice of Separating Migrant Families," *New York Times*, June 16, 2018.

71. Id.

72. Julie Zauzmer and Keith McMillan, "Sessions Cites Bible Passage Used to Defend Slavery in Defense of Separating Immigrant Families," *Washington Post*, June 15, 2018.

73. Lisa Riordan Seville and Hannah Rappeleye, "Trump Admin Ran 'Pilot Program' for Separating Migrant Families in 2017," *CBS News*, June 29, 2018, https://perma.cc/GV2M-BQ82.

74. Id.

75. Letter to Cameron Quinn, Officer for Civil Rights and Civil Liberies, and John V. Kelly, Acting Inspector General of DHS, from Al Otro Lado, the American Immigration Council, et. al, December 11, 2017, https://perma.cc/8YHX-ZBPB.

76. Amended complaint, *Ms. L. v. ICE*, Case 18-cv-00428-DMS-MDD (S.D. Calif., March 9, 2018); Derek Hawkins, "A Mother and Child Fled Congo Fearing Death. ICE Has Held Them Separately For Months, Lawsuit Says," *Washington Post*, February 27, 2018.

77. Amended complaint, supra n. 76.

78. Samantha Schmidt, "ICE Releases Mother It Detained For Months Far Away from 7-Year-Old Daughter," *Washington Post*, March 7, 2018.

79. Kristina Davis, "Who is Dana Sabraw, the Judge Behind the Family Reunification Case?," *San Diego Union-Tribune*, July 22, 2018.

80. Respondents' Response in Opposition to Petitioner Ms. L's Motion for Preliminary Injunction, *Ms. L. v. ICE*, March 16, 2018.

81. Id.

82. Caitlin Dickerson, "Over 700 Children Taken From Parents at Border," *New York Times*, April 21, 2018.

83. Isaac Stanley-Becker, "Who's Behind the Law Making Undocumented Immigrants Criminals? An 'Unrepentant White Supremacist,'" *Washington Post*, June 27, 2018. Blaise "defended lynching" and believed that "the morals and the mode of living between colored people are not up to the standard adopted and lived up to by white people" (Id).

84. Maria Sacchetti, "Top Homeland Security Officials Urge Criminal Prosecution of Parents Crossing Border with Children," *Washington Post*, April 26, 2018.

85. Dickerson, supra n. 82.

86. Amnesty International, supra n. 48, at 27–42. Beth Van Schaack, former deputy to the U.S. Ambassador-at-Large for War Crimes Issues, later analyzed the administration's policy in terms of the United Nations Convention Against Torture, to which the U.S. adheres, and concluded that it "amounts to government-sanctioned torture" ("The Torture of Forcibly Separating Children from their Parents," *Just Security*, October 18, 2018, https://perma.cc/4FKE-7FME).

87. Sachetti, supra n. 84.

88. Michael D. Shear and Nicole Perlroth, "Kirstjen Nielsen, Chief of Homeland Security, Almost Resigned After Trump Tirade," *New York Times*, May 10, 2018.

89. U.S. Department of Justice, "Attorney General Announces Zero-Tolerance Policy for Criminal Illegal Entry," press release, April 6, 2018, https://perma.cc/6UYS-F589.

90. U.S. Department of Justice, "Attorney General Sessions Delivers Remarks to the Association of State Criminal Investigative Agencies 2018 Spring Conference," press release, May 7, 2018, https://perma.cc/Z83H-BETN.

91. American Immigration Council, "DHS Prosecutes Over 600 Parents in Two-Week Span and Seizes their Children," *Immigration Impact*, May 25, 2018, https://perma.cc/88VG-W878.

92. See, e.g., Miriam G., "At the Border, My Son Was Taken from Me," *CNN.com*, May 29, 2018, https://perma.cc/2N5P-ZKNT; Tom Llamas, Lauren Pearle, Kendall Heath, and James Scholz, "Separated at the Border: A Mother's Story," *ABC News*, May 31, 2018, https://perma.cc/5KGV-PP76. Journalists reported a few weeks earlier that ORR had "lost track" of 1,474 migrant children. See Garance Burke, "Federal Agency Says It Lost Track of 1,475 Migrant Children," *Washington Post*, April 27, 2018. That report added to the furor. But the report was somewhat misleading, in that many of the children in question had merely

been released from ORR's placement program after reaching the age of eighteen, and in any event, the children involved had been unaccompanied rather than separated. See Amy Harmon, "Did the Trump Administration Separate Immigrant Children From Parents and Lose Them?," *New York Times*, May 28, 2018; "Statement by HHS Deputy Secretary on Unaccompanied Alien Children Program," May 28, 2018, https://perma.cc/B79G-FC92.

93. Leahy, "Floor Statement on the Trump Administration's Family Separation Policy," June 5, 2018, https://perma.cc/VYU2-Y2FK.

94. Liz Goodwin, "'Children Are Being Used as a Tool' in Trump's Effort to Stop Border Crossings," *Boston Globe*, June 10, 2018.

95. Order granting in part and denying in part defendants' motion to dismiss in *Ms. L v. ICE*, June 6, 2018, https://perma.cc/F8KW-LANC.

96. Judge Dana Sabraw, in Transcript of Proceedings, Telephonic Status Conference in *Ms. L. v. ICE*, June 25, 2018.

97. Julie Hirschfeld Davis, "Separated at the Border From Their Parents: In Six Weeks, 1995 Children," *New York Times*, June 16, 2018.

98. "Representative Pramila Jayapal, Democrat of Washington [who visited some of the mothers in detention] said some of them reported having been told that they needed to briefly leave their children to be photographed or see a judge, only to return and find the children had been taken away" (id).

99. Michael Scherer and Josh Dawsey, "Trump Cites as a Negotiating Tool His Policy of Separating Immigrant Children from Their Parents," *New York Times*, June 16, 2018.

100. David Yaffe-Bellany, "A Viral Facebook Fundraiser Has Generated More Than $20 Million for Immigration Nonprofit RAICES," *Texas Tribune*, June 27, 2018.

101. Brian Roewe, "US Bishops Condemn Immigration Policies That Separate Families at Border," *National Catholic Reporter*, June 13, 2018; Laurie Goodstein, "Conservative Religious Leaders Are Denouncing Trump Immigration Policies," *New York Times*, June 14, 2018.

102. Jack Crowe, "Pope Condemns Family Separation at the Border," *National Review*, June 20, 2018.

103. Emily Stewart, "Ivanka Trump Speaks Out on Family Separation—After Her Father Said He'd Stop It," *Vox*, June 21, 2018, https://perma.cc/S9DX-W925.

104. For example, *State of Washington v. United States*, Case 18cv0930 (W.D. Wash).

105. Adrienne Masha Varkiani, "The International Condemnation of Trump's Immigration Policy Is Deafening," *ThinkProgress*, June 20, 2018, https://perma.cc/3ANB-NKXQ.

106. Jordain Carney, "13 GOP Senators Ask Administration to Pause Separation of Immigrant Families," *The Hill*, June 19, 2018.

107. Michael D. Shear, Abby Goodnough, and Maggie Haberman, "Trump Retreats on Separating Families, but Thousands May Remain Apart," *New York Times*, June 20, 2018; Donald J. Trump, "Executive Order: Affording Congress an Opportunity to Address Family Separation," June 20, 2018, https://perma.cc/28V3-JNTZ.

108. Id., at Secs. 3(c) and (e). Even the number of families that were separated is controversial. While many news reports used numbers around 2000, Amnesty International reported in October 2018 that CBP had informed it in an email that the Border Patrol had separated 6022 families between April 19 and August 15, 2018, and Amnesty estimated that more than 8000 families had been separated since CBP had begun the practice. See Amnesty International, supra n. 48. The Inspector General of the Department of Health and Human Services reported that the Department had identified 2,737 separated children who had to be reunified under an order from Judge Sabraw, that "thousands" more may have been separated "before the accounting required by the court," and that DHS appeared to be separating more children even after the court ordered it not to do so. See Office of the HHS Inspector General, "Many Children Separated from Parents, Guardians Before *Ms. L. v. ICE* Court Order and Some Separations Continue," January 17, 2019, https://perma.cc/5XHY-5R8L.

109. Shear et al, supra n. 107.

110. Nick Miroff, Amy Goldstein, and Maria Sacchetti, "What Went Wrong with Trump's Family Separation Effort," *Washington Post*, July 29, 2018. The problem was that the ORR computer system used for unaccompanied children "was not built in a way that allowed ORR to add data categories" (such as separated children) or to "quickly sort the information it contains." There was no field for information about the parents of the children in ORR custody. In addition, the computer system "crashed often." The frequent crashes may have made reunification of some of the children easier, because "caseworkers were trained to copy whatever information they were trying to enter about a child into a separate Word document" (id).

111. Office of the Inspector General, supra n. 49, at 10.

112. Order granting plaintiffs' motion for classwide preliminary injunction in *Ms. L. v. ICE*, June 26, 2018.

113. "Fewer than 200 Migrant Children Remain Separated from Their Parents," *The PBS News Hour*, September 21, 2018, https://perma.cc/H38X-C5NR.

114. Id.

115. Miriam Jordan, "Migrant Families Have been Reunited. Now, a Scramble to Prevent Deportations," *New York Times*, July 30, 2018.

116. *Dora v. Sessions*, Case 1:18-cv-01938 (D. D.C.)

117. Fred Barbash and Allyson Chiu, "Settlement Reached in Family Separation Cases: More Than 1,000 Rejected Asylum Seekers to Get Second Chance if Court Approves," *Washington Post*, September 13, 2018.

118. Caitlin Dickenson, "The Price Tag of Migrant Family Separation: $80 Million and Rising," *New York Times*, November 20, 2018, reporting a figure provided by the Department of Health and Human Services to the House Appropriations subcommittee responsible for funding the agency.

119. Id.

120. Julia Ainsley, "Thousands More Migrant Kids Separated from Parents Under Trump Than Previously Reported," *NBC News*, January 17, 2019.

121. Alan Gomez, "Judge May Force Trump Administration to Reunite Thousands More Separated Families," *USA Today*, February 21, 2019.

122. Miriam Jordan and Caitlin Dickerson, "U.S. Continues to Separate Migrant Families Despite Rollback of Policy," *New York Times*, March 9, 2019.

123. Miriam Jordan, "No More Family Separations, Except These 900," *New York Times*, July 30, 2019.

124. Seung Min Kim and Carrie Budoff Brown, "The Death of Immigration Reform," *Politico*, June 27, 2014.

125. Eagly et al., supra n. 31.

126. Order Denying Defendants' "Ex Parte Application for Limited Relief From Settlement Agreement" in *Flores v. Sessions*, 2018 U.S. Dist. LEXIS 115488 (July 9, 2018).

127. Nick Miroff, "Migrant Families Overwhelm Detention Capacity In Arizona, Prompting Mass Releases," *Washington Post*, October 9, 2018; Nick Miroff and Josh Dawsey, "Record Number of Families Crossing U.S. Border as Trump Threatens New Crackdown," *Washington Post*, October 17, 2018; Customs and Border Protection, Southwest Border Migration FY 2019, https://perma.cc/MC75-XDAM (includes apprehensions by both Border Patrol and Office of Field Operations). In June 2019, the number of individuals in family units apprehended at the border fell by 32 percent, and the number of UACs fell by 36 percent, likely as a result of both hotter weather during the summer and a crackdown on migration by Mexico, each of which made transit through Mexico more difficult. See Nick Miroff, "Border Arrests Drop as Mexico's Migration Crackdown Appears to Cut Crossings," *Washington Post*, July 9, 2019.

128. Miroff, supra n. 127.

129. Miriam Jordan, Caitlin Dickerson, and Michael D. Shear, "Trump's Plans to Deter Migrants Could Mean New 'Voluntary' Family Separations," *New York Times*, October 22, 2018; Maria Sacchettti, "Trump's Nominee to Lead ICE Won't Rule Out Separating Migrant Families Again," *Washington Post*, November 15, 2018.

130. At Karnes, Dilley, and Berks, ICE had only about 3,300 detention beds, so most of the 16,658 family members apprehended during September, 2018, had to be released, some with ankle bracelets (id). Asylum-seekers who could not be accommodated in the family jails could not be given credible fear interviews during the short time they were being processed in CBP's border facilities, so

they were not put into expedited removal proceedings. Instead, they were served with notices to appear in immigration court for regular hearings.

131. Robert Moore, "Tornillo Tent City Will Expand to Hold Even More Migrant Kids," *Texas Monthly*, September 11, 2018.

132. Transcript of hearing in *Flores v. Meese*, at 37–38, April 24, 2015.

133. Transcript of argument in *Ms. L v. ICE*, June 22, 2018, filed June 25, 2018.

134. Order Granting Plaintiffs' Motion for Classwide Preliminary Injunction in *Ms. L v. ICE*, June 26, 2018, at 22–23.

135. Notice of compliance in *Flores v. Sessions*, June 29, 2018.

136. Order Denying Defendants' Ex Parte Application (July 9, 2018), supra n. 126, at 5.

137. Id., at 6.

138. Transcript of hearing in *Ms. L v. ICE*, July 10, 2018, at 38.

139. Id., at 43.

140. Telephone interview with Lee Gelernt, October 22, 2018.

141. Joint Motion Regarding Scope of the Court's Preliminary Injunction in *Ms. L. v. ICE*, July 13, 2018.

142. Order Granting Joint Motion Regarding Scope of the Court's Preliminary Injunction in *Ms. L v. ICE*, August 16, 2018.

143. Editorial board, "First, Separation. Now, Incarceration," *Washington Post*, September 8, 2018.

144. Catherine E. Shoichet, "Decision Could Spell Deportation for These 250,000 Immigrants," *CNN*, January 8, 2018, https://perma.cc/H5MB-QWJU.

145. See Sasha Abramsky, "Trump to 200,000 Salvadorans: Drop Dead," *The Nation*, January 8, 2018.

146. Miriam Jordan, "Trump Administration Ends Temporary Protection for Haitians," *New York Times*, November 20, 2017.

147. See Meagan Flynn, "Federal Judge, Citing Trump Racial Bias, Says Administration Can't Strip Legal Status from 300,000 Haitians, Salvadorans and Others—For Now," *Washington Post*, October 4, 2018. The court said that the President's decision might have been "based on animus against nonwhite, non-European immigrants in violation of Equal Protection guaranteed by the Constitution." See Order Granting Preliminary Injunction in *Ramos v. Nielsen*, Case No. 18-cv-01554, Oct. 3, 2018 (D., N.D. Calif.) The government filed its appeal a week later. Notice of Appeal (Oct. 11, 2018) and the case was argued in the Ninth Circuit on August 14, 2109. *Ramos v. Nielsen*, Case 18-16981 (9th Cir. 2019).

148. Obama issued guidance to protect those parents through a program he called Deferred Action for Parents of Americans and Lawful Permanent Residents (DAPA) but a court in Texas had enjoined it from going into effect. See Aria Bendix, "Trump Rolls Back DAPA," *The Atlantic*, June 16, 2017.

149. Eileen Sullivan and Michael D. Shear, "Trump Sees an Obstacle to Getting His Way on Immigration: His Own Officials," *New York Times*, April 14, 2019.

150. Nick Miroff, Seung Min Kim, and Josh Dawsey, "Trump Ditches His Nominee to Lead ICE, Saying He Wants Someone 'Tougher' for Top Immigration Enforcement Role," *Washington Post,* April 5, 2019.

151. Stipulation amending settlement in *Flores v. Reno,* https://perma.cc /G2FN-UD7A.

152. Departments of Homeland Security and Health and Human Services, "Apprehension, Processing, Care and Custody of Alien Minors and Unaccompanied Alien Children," 83 Fed. Reg. 45486, Sept. 7, 2018.

153. Defendant's Response in Opposition to Motion to Enforce Settlement, for a Permanent Injunction and for Adjudication of Civil Contempt, in *Flores v. Sessions,* November 9, 2018, at 2.

154. Departments of Homeland Security and Health and Human Services, "Apprehension, Processing, Care and Custody of Alien Minors and Unaccompanied Alien Children," 84 Fed. Reg. 44392, August 23, 2019.

155. Id. at 44517.

156. Id. at 44526.

157. Id. at 44433.

158. Maria Sacchetti, "ICE's Chief Called Family Detention 'Summer Camp.' Here's What It Looks Like Inside," *Washington Post,* August 25, 2019.

159. Independent cost calculations are detailed in Philip E. Wolgin, "The High Costs of the Proposed Flores Regulation," Center for American Progress, October 19, 2018, https://perma.cc/XFU9-R9P3. DHS's assertion about the impossibility of an estimate are found in its final regulation, supra n. 154, at 44511.

160. 8 U.S.C. Sec. 1103(g)(2).

161. Matter of M- S-, 27 I&N Dec. 509 (Attorney General 1019), overruling Matter of X- K-, 23 I&N Dec. 731 (2005).

162. *Padilla v. ICE,* 2019 U.S. Dist. LEXIS 110755 (W.D. Wa. July 2, 2019).

163. *Padilla v. ICE,* 2019 U.S. App. LEXIS 21846 (9th Cir. July 22, 2019).

164. Motion to enforce Settlement, for Permanent Injunction, and for Adjudication of Civil Contempt, in *Flores v. Sessions,* November 2, 2018, renewed with supplemental brief filed Aug. 30, 2019.

165. See note 151 and accompanying text.

166. Final regulation, supra n. 154, at 44493.

167. Order re: Plaintiffs' Motion to Enforce Settlement and Defendants' Notice of Termination and Motion in the Alternative to Terminate the Flores Settlement Agreement in *Flores v. Barr,* Sept. 27, 2019.

168. KIND et al., "Sexual and Gender Based Violence & Migration Fact Sheet," 2017, https://perma.cc/92U9-7DRJ.

169. Nick Miroff, "The Border is Tougher to Cross Than Ever. But There's Still One Way Into America," *Washington Post,* October 24, 2018.

170. 8 U.S.C. Secs. 1101(a)(42), 1108.

171. Matter of Kasinga, 21 I&N Dec. 357 (BIA 1996).

172. Matter of Toboso-Alfonso, 19 I&N Dec. 819 (BIA 1990).

173. Matter of OZ & IZ, 22 I&N Dec. 23 (BIA 1998).

174. Matter of A- R- C- G-.

175. Matter of A- B-, 27 I&N Dec. 316 (A.G. 2018).

176. Liz Robbins, "She Was Raped and Threatened With Death. Now She Has Lost Hope of Asylum," *New York Times*, June 13, 2018.

177. Human Rights First, "Central Americans Were Increasingly Winning Asylum Before President Trump Took Office," January 30, 2019, https://www .humanrightsfirst.org/sites/default/files/Asylum_Grant_Rates.pdf.

178. U.S. Citizenship and Immigration Services, "Policy Memorandum: Guidance for Processing Reasonable Fear, Credible Fear, Asylum, and Refugee Claims in Accordance with Matter of A- B-," July 11, 2018, https://www.uscis.gov /sites/default/files/USCIS/Laws/Memoranda/2018/2018–06–18-PM-602–0162- USCIS-Memorandum-Matter-of-A-B.pdf.

179. *Grace v. Sessions*, Case 1:18-cv-01853 (D. D.C.)

180. Plaintiff's Memorandum in Support of their Cross Motion for Summary Judgement and Opposition to Defendants' Motion for Summary Judgment in *Grace v. Sessions*, September 26, 2018.

181. *Grace v. Whitaker*, 344 F. Supp. 3d 96, (D. D.C., Dec. 17, 2018).

182. See the government's brief in *Grace v. Barr*, Case 19-5013 (D.C. Cir.), filed June 5, 2019.

183. Memorandum to immigration judges from Susana Ortiz-Ang, Office of the General Counsel, with Guidance on *Grace v. Whitaker*, December 19, 2018, https://uchastings.app.box.com/s/k99txxw746bg7wghirak8w7d86tq1njt /file/381907558796.

184. *Crespin-Valladares v. Holder*, 632 F. 3d 117 (4th Cir. 2011).

185. Matter of L- E- A- 27 I&N Dec. 581 (Attorney General 2019).

186. See Ruth Ellen Wasem, "Asylum Policies for Unaccompanied Children, Compared with Expedited Removal Policies for Unauthorized Adults: In Brief," Cong. Research Svc. Report 7–5700, July 30, 2014.

187. Memorandum to All Asylum Office Staff from Ted Kim, Acting Chief, Asylum Division, USCIS, May 28, 2013, https://www.uscis.gov/sites/default /files/USCIS/Humanitarian/Refugees%20%26%20Asylum/Asylum/Minor%20 Children%20Applying%20for%20Asylum%20By%20Themselves/determ-juris- asylum-app-file-unaccompanied-alien-children.pdf.

188. Graham Lanktree, "Trump Administration Planning Law to Deport Thousands of Unaccompanied Teens From Central America," *Newsweek*, September 21, 2017, https://perma.cc/V85R-YZX3.

189. Memorandum to James R. McHenry III, Acting Director of the Executive Office for Immigration Review, from Jean King, General Counsel of the Executive Office for Immigration Review, Legal Opinion re: EOIR's Authority to Interpret the Term Unaccompanied Alien Child for Purposes of Applying

Certain Provisions of the TVPRA, September 19, 2017, https://perma.cc /XJN4-3ET9.

190. Matter of M- A- C- O-, 27 I&N Dec. 477 (BIA 2018).

191. Memorandum to all Asylum Office Staff, from John Lafferty, Chief, Asylum Division, May 31, 2019, https://perma.cc/8PHK-UAG5.

192. Memorandum Opinion, *J.O.P. v. Dep't of Homeland Security*, Aug. 2, 2019, Case 8:19-cv-GJH (D. Md).

193. 8 U.S.C. Sec. 1232(c)(2)(B).

194. *Ramirez v. ICE*, 310 F. Supp. 3d 7 (D. D.C. 2018).

195. *Ramirez v. ICE*, 2018 U.S. Dist LEXIS 147895 (D. D.C., Aug. 30, 2018).

196. Judge Dana L. Marks, president of the National Association of Immigration Judges, quoted in Julia Preston, "Lawyers Back Creating New Immigration Courts," *New York Times*, February 8, 2018. Stung by criticism from the immigration judges' union, the Trump administration initiated proceedings to decertify the union. Christina Goldbaum, "Trump Administration Moves to Decertify Outspoken Immigration Judges' Union," *New York Times,* Aug. 10, 2019.

197. Seven hundred cases was just above the national average of 678, but the average included judges who handled many more cases a year because they were in courts in ICE detention centers, where few of the immigrants had lawyers and deportation orders could quickly be issued. Others were in areas of the country where even non-detained migrants had trouble obtaining representation. In the San Diego area, on the other hand, the eight judges completed an average of only 380 cases in FY 2016. Kate Morrissey, "Immigration Judges Getting New Performance Metric," *San Diego Union-Tribune*, January 1, 2018.

198. Executive Office for Immigration Review, "EOIR Performance Plan [for] Adjudicative Employees," https://perma.cc/FT7G-SVNH.

199. Memorandum from James McHenry, Director of the Executive Office for Immigration Review, to All of Judges [sic], provided to Michelle Mendez, Catholic Legal Immigration Network on July 24, 2018 in response to Freedom of Information Act request, https://perma.cc/FT5B-L6ZD.

200. Dean DeChiaro, "Trumps Strategy to Shrink Immigration Court Backlogs May Not Work," *Roll Call*, April 16, 2018, https://perma.cc/2KR7-WLQ6 (Tabbador); Liz Robbins, "In Immigration Courts, It Is Judges vs. Justice Department," *New York Times*, September 7, 2018 (Khan).

201. Richard Gonzales, "Trump Administration Seeks Decertification of Immigration Judges' Union," National Public Radio, August 12, 2019, https:// perma.cc/338W-AMC3.

202. DeChiaro, supra n. 200.

203. Presidential Proclamation Addressing Mass Migration Through the Southern Border of the United States, November 9, 2018, https://perma.cc /T7S4-CFYH.

204. Departments of Homeland Security and Justice, "Aliens Subject to a Bar on Entry Under Certain Presidential Proclamations; Procedures for Protection Claims," 83 Fed. Reg. 55934, November 9, 2018.

205. Id., at 55945.

206. Id., at 55944.

207. Id., at 55942.

208. The guidance to asylum officers was issued the same day as the regulations. See "Memorandum to all USCIS employees from L. Francis Cissna, USCIS Director," November 9, 2018, https://www.uscis.gov/sites/default/files/USCIS /Laws/Memoranda/2018/2018-11-09-PM-602-0166-Procedural_Guidance_for_ Implementing_Regulatory_Changes_Created_by_Interim_Final_Rule.pdf. Even before the proclamation was issued, two categories of people were given only reasonable fear screenings and therefore had to meet the higher standard: people who had committed certain crimes, and who previously had been deported from the United States.

209. Complaint in *East Bay Sanctuary Covenant. v. Trump*, Case 18-cv-06810 (N. D. Calif., Nov. 9, 2018).

210. 8 U.S.C. Sec. 1182(f).

211. 8 U.S.C. Sec. 1158(b)(2)(C).

212. 110 Stat.3009-579, codified at 8 U.S.C. Sec. 1158(a)(1).

213. 83 Fed. Reg. at 55936.

214. See Kate Aschenbrenner, "Discretionary (In)Justice: The Exercise of Discretion in Claims for Asylum," University of Michigan Journal of Law Reform 45 (2012): 595-633.

215. See complaint, supra n. 209, at paragraph 62; Jonathan Blitzer, "Donald Trump, the Migrant Caravan, and a Manufactured Crisis at the U.S. Border," *The New Yorker*, November 5, 2018.

216. See complaint, supra n. 209, at paragraph 110.

217. *East Bay Sanctuary Covenant v. Trump*, 2018 U.S. Dist. LEXIS 198092 (Nov. 19, 2018).

218. Maria Sacchetti, "Trump Lashes Out at Judge After Order to Allow Illegal Border Crossers to Seek Asylum," *Washington Post*, November 20, 2018.

219. *East Bay Sanctuary Covenant v. Trump*, 909 F. 3d 1219 (9th Cir., December 7, 2018).

220. *Trump v. East Bay Sanctuary Covenant*, __ U.S. __, 202 L. Ed. 2d 510, 2018 U.S. LEXIS 7304 (December 21, 2018).

221. Memorandum Opinion, *O.A. v. Trump*, Aug. 2, 2019, Case 18-cv-02718 (D. D.C.)

222. Department of Justice, Interim Final Rule: Asylum Eligibility and Procedural Modifications, 84 Fed. Reg. 33,829 (July 16, 2019).

223. 8 U.S.C. Sec. 1158(a)(2)(A). The administration's regulation apparently circumvented the law as amended by requiring neither a "full and fair" procedure in the country of transit nor a government-to-government agreement.

224. U.S.–Canada Safe Third Country Agreement (2002), https://www.uscis .gov/unassigned/us-canada-safe-third-country-agreement.

225. 8 U.S.C. Sec. 1158(b)(2)(A)(vi).

226. 8 C.F.R. Sec. 201.15(a).

227. Brief in Support of Emergency Motion for Stay Pending Appeal in *East Bay Sanctuary Covenant v. Barr,* Aug. 6, 2019, Case 19-16487 (9th Cir. 2019).

228. *East Bay Sanctuary Covenant v. Barr,* 385 F. Supp. 3d 922 (N.D. Calif. 2019).

229. Order, *East Bay Sanctuary Covenant v. Barr,* 934 F. 3d 1026 (9th Cir. 2019).

230. Nomaan Merchant, "Court Sets Limits on Order Halting New Asylum Rules," *San Francisco Chronicle,* Aug. 16, 2019.

231. Opinion of Judge A. Wallace Tashima, dissenting, in *East Bay Sanctuary Covenant v. Barr,* supra n. 229.

232. *Capital Area Immigrants' Rights Coalition v. Trump,* Case 1:19-cv-02117 (D. D.C.).

233. Tal Axelrod, "Federal Judge Allows Trump Asylum Restrictions to Continue," *The Hill,* July 24, 2019, https://perma.cc/YFS5-ZZ3U.

234. Application for a Stay Pending Appeal, *Barr v. East Bay Sanctuary Covenant,* U.S. Supreme Court, August 2019, https://perma.cc/RF6U-J7Y2.

235. Judge Tigar's renewed injunction is Order Granting Motion to Restore Nationwide Scope of Injunction in *East Bay Sanctuary Covenant v. Barr,* September 9, 2019. The Supreme Court's order staying Tigar's original preliminary injunction as amended by the Ninth Circuit's decision is *Barr v. East Bay Sanctuary Covenant,* No. 19A230, 588 U.S. __ September 11, 2019, https://perma .cc/7WAZ-34P7.

236. The rule explicitly states that non-Mexican unaccompanied children crossing from Mexico are subject to the new rule and will be barred from asylum if they did not apply in Mexico or some other transit country and wait for determinations there. Interim Final rule, supra n. 222, at 33839 n. 7.

237. Nick Miroff and Kevin Sieff, "Trump Administration Reaches Deal That Will Force Asylum Seekers to Wait in Mexico As Cases Are Processed, DHS's Nielsen Says," *Washington Post,* December 20, 2018.

238. Patrick J. McDowell, "Mexico Is Unprepared for the Deal It Made with the U.S. on Asylum Seekers, Immigration Chief Says," *Los Angeles Times,* Dec. 21, 2018.

239. Ioan Grillo, "The Mexican Border as Refugee Camp," *New York Times,* December 21, 2018, reported the recent murder of two Honduran teenagers in Tijuana.

240. Roque Planas, "Trump's 'Remain in Mexico' Border Deal Has Serious Legal Problems," *Huffington Post*, November 30, 2018.

241. 8 U.S.C. Sec. 1225(b)(2)(C). This is the section cited by DHS to justify its action. See DHS, "Migrant Protection Protocols," January 24, 2019, https:// www.dhs.gov/news/2019/01/24/migrant-protection-protocols.

242. See 8 U.S.C. Sec 1225(b)(2)(B)(2) and (b)(1); Congressional Research Service, "'Migrant Protection Protocols': Legal Issues Relating to DHS's Plan to Require Arriving Asylum Seekers to Wait in Mexico," February 1, 2009, https://perma.cc /BJ94-CALF. See also the analysis in the concurring opinion of Judge William Fletcher in *Innovation Law Lab v. McAleenan*, 924 F. 3d 503 (9th Cir. 2019).

243. Julian Aguilar, "Migrants on Border Face Confusion and Fear Under 'Remain In Mexico' Policy," *Texas Tribune*, April 26, 2019, reported that "none of the immigrant families [who had been forced to wait in Mexico for hearings] had lawyers" when brought before immigration judges in El Paso.

244. See 8 U.S.C. Sec. 1231(b)(3).

245. See the concurring opinion of Judge Paul J. Watford in *Innovation Law Lab v.McAleenan*, supra n. 242.

246. Rafael Bernal, "Trump Administration Sends Back First Migrant Families to Mexico," *The Hill*, February 14, 2019; Sarah Kinosian and Kevin Sieff, "Entire Families of Asylum Seekers Are Being Returned to Mexico, Leaving Them in Limbo," *Washington Post*, February 15, 2019.

247. Complaint in *Innovation Law Lab v. Nielsen*, Case 3:19-cv-00807 (N.D. Calif. Feb. 14, 2019).

248. See Order re: briefing schedule in *Innovation Law Lab v. Nielsen*, February 21, 2019.

249. Order granting preliminary injunction, *Innovation Law Lab v. Nielsen*, April 8, 2019.

250. See *Innovation Law Lab v. McAleenan*, supra n. 242.

251. Mihir Zaveri, "Asylum Officers' Union Says Trump Migration Policy 'Abandons' American Tradition," *New York Times*, June 26, 2019.

252. Jason Kao and Denise Lu, "How Trump's Policies Are Leaving Thousands of Asylum Seekers Waiting in Mexico," *New York Times*, Aug. 18, 2019; Miriam Jordan, "Migrants in Mexico, Hearings in the U.S. and No Lawyers in Sight," *New York Times*, Aug. 4, 2019; Reade Levinson, Mica Rosenberg, and Kristina Cooke, "Exclusive: Asylum Seekers Returned to Mexico Rarely Win Bids to Wait in U.S.," *Reuters*, June 12, 2019, https://perma.cc/4Q2H-VNVX; Human Rights First, "US Move Puts More Asylum Seekers at Risk," September 25, 2019, http://perma .cc/TRY6-PB7V. Kristina Cooke, Mica Rosenberg, and Reade Levinson, Exclusive: U.S. migrant policy sends thousands of children, including babies, back to Mexico, Reuters, October 11, 2019, https://perma.cc/GD22-CE4V.

253. Joel Rose and Laura Smitherman, "Fear, Confusion and Separation As Trump Administration Sends Migrants Back to Mexico," *National Public Radio*, July 2, 2019.

254. Azam Ahmed, "Mexico Sets Domestic Priorities Aside to Meet Terms of U.S. Trade Deal," *New York Times*, June 8, 2019.

255. Miriam Jordan, "Migrants in Mexico, Hearings in the U.S., and No Lawyers in Sight," *New York Times*, Aug. 4, 2019.

256. Nick Miroff, Kevin Sieff, and John Wagner, "How Mexico Talked Trump out of Tariff Threat with Immigration Crackdown Pact," *Washington Post*, June 10, 2019.

257. U.S.-Mexico Joint Declaration, June 7, 2019, https://www.state .gov/u-s-mexico-joint-declaration.

258. Human Rights Watch, "We Can't Help You Here: US Returns of Asylum Seekers to Mexico (2019)," https://perma.cc/UBV6-XJ38.

259. Human Rights First, "Delivered to Danger: Illegal Remain in Mexico Policy Imperils Asylum Seekers' Lives and Denies Due Process," August 2019, https://perma.cc/22KP-LFCD.

260. Opinion in *East Bay Sanctuary Covenant*, supra n. 228.

261. The White House, "Presidential Memorandum on Additional Measures to Enhance Border Security and Restore Integrity to Our Immigration System," April 29, 2019, https://perma.cc/ATX8-WR22.

262. See Peter Margulies, "New Asylum Limits: A Balancing Act for the Homeland Security Secretary," *Lawfare*, May 1, 2019, https://perma.cc/AUS5-V6JK.

263. Lindsay M. Harris and Joan Hodges-Wu, "Asylum Seekers Leave Everything Behind. There's No Way They Can Pay Trump's Fee," *Washington Post*, May 1, 2019.

264. The result of a challenge to the fee by an indigent asylum seeker is difficult to predict. See Henry Rose, "The Constitutionality of Government Fees as Applied to the Poor," *Northern Illinois University Law Review* 33 (2013): 293–304.

265. Remarks of Attorney General Jeff Sessions to the Executive Office for Immigration Review, October 12, 2017, https://perma.cc/4EFX-FGJJ.

266. Anna Giaritelli, "Trump Administration to Give Border Patrol Agents Authority to Decide Asylum Claims on the Spot: Sources," *Washington Examiner*, May 2, 2019 (Border Patrol officer explanation); Molly O'Toole, "Border Patrol Agents, Rather Than Asylum Officers, Interviewing Families for 'Credible Fear,'" *Los Angeles Times*, September 19, 2019.

267. See Human Rights First, "Allowing CBP to Conduct Credible Fear Interviews Undermines Safeguards to Protect Refugees," April 2019, https://perma .cc/B72P-7RUK; Julia Ainsley, "Stephen Miller Wants Border Patrol, Not Asylum Officers, to Determine Migrant Asylum Claims," CBS-TV News, July 29, 2019, https://perma.cc/2BBC-UZNV.

268. 8 U.S.C. Sec. 1225 (b)(1)(B)(i) and (b)(1)(E).

269. 8 U.S.C. Sec. 208(a)(2)(A).

270. See chapter 5.

271. *INS v. Cardoza-Fonseca*, 480 U.S. 421 (1987).

272. Miroff, Sieff, and Wagner, supra n. 256.

273. Agreement Between the Government of the United States of America and the Government of the Republic of Guatemala For Cooperation in the Examination of Protection Claims, July 26, 2019, https://edition.cnn.com/2019/08/01/politics/guatemala-asylum-agreement-doc/index.html; Agreement Between the Government of the United States of America and the Government of the Republic of El Salvador For Cooperation in the Examination of Protection Claims, undated but signed on September 20, 2019, https://www.document-cloud.org/documents/6427712-US-El-Salvador-Cooperative-Agreement.html (accessed October 7, 2019).; Molly O'Toole, "U.S. and El Salvador Sign Asylum Deal," *Los Angeles Times*, September 20, 2019 (dating the El Salvador agreement); DHS, Acting Secretary McAleenan Signs Agreement with Honduras, September 25, 2019, https://perma.cc/PL5E-YEYV.

274. See, e.g., Guatemalan agreement, supra n. 273, Article 7; Salvadoran agreement, supra n. 273, Article 7.

275. Guatemalan agreement, supra n. 273, Article 2.

276. At the very moment that the agreement with Guatemala was signed, the U.S. State Department travel advisory for that country warned that "violent crime, such as armed robbery and murder, is common" and that "local police may lack the resources to respond effectively to serious criminal incidents." Kirk Semple, "The U.S. and Guatemala Reached an Asylum Deal: Here's What it Means," *New York Times*, July 28, 2019. Michelle Brané noted that "Honduras is one of the most dangerous countries in the world" and that transferring our asylum applicants there is "the opposite of what we are supposed to stand for." Daniella Silva, "U.S. Signs Asylum Deal With Honduras That Could Force Migrants to Seek Relief There." NBC News, September 25, 2019, https://perma.cc/9DVX-LK56.

277. As of this writing, the safe third country agreement with Canada is being challenged in litigation in that country, based on the many ways in which the United States has curtailed refugee protection. *Canadian Council for Refugees v. Minister of Citizenship and Immigration*, IMM-2977-17, 775-17 and 2229-17, Federal Court.

278. Mary Beth Sheridan, "Guatemala's Migrant Pact with the U.S. Threatens to Unleash a Political Crisis," *Washington Post*, July 27, 2019; CBS News, "Guatemala's Next Leader Wants to Alter Immigration Deal with US," August 12, 2019, https://perma.cc/98Y5-QL29. The United States may also have offered a financial incentive to Guatemala in exchange for its agreement. The DHS Acting Secretary announced a month later that the United States would provide $47 million "to build asylum capacity in Guatemala." DHS, Acting Secretary McAleenan's Prepared Remarks to the Council of [sic] Foreign Relations on September 23, 2019, https://www.dhs.gov/news/2019/09/23/acting-secretary-mcaleenans-prepared-remarks-council-foreign-relations. Perhaps other financial incentives were also dangled. The Honduran president, Juan Orlando

Hernández, also had reason to curry favor with the Trump administration; just days before he signed the agreement, he had been named as a co-conspirator in a drug trafficking ring. Amy Guthrie, "US Prosecutors Accuse Honduran President of Drug Conspiracy," *U.S. News*, Aug. 3, 2019.

279. Human Rights First, supra n. 259 (Guatemala); Nelson Rauda Zablan, "El Salvador Signs Agreement to Accept Asylum Seekers the US Won't Protect," *El Faro*, September 29, 2019, https://perma.cc/8KPA-V5M3.

CONCLUSION

1. Michael Grabell, "Pediatrician Who Treated Immigrant Children Describes Pattern of Lapses in Medical Care in Shelters," *Pro Publica*, May 3, 2019, https://perma.cc/2MCY-6RVB; Rebecca R. Ruiz, Nicholas Kulish, and Kim Barker, "Justice Department Investigating Migrants Shelter Provider," *New York Times*, December 20, 2018, reporting an investigation of possible financial misconduct by Southwest Key, the nation's largest shelter provider for migrant children.

2. Instances in this book include testimony by Jenny Flores and children interviewed by Pegine Grayson (chapter 1); the DHS Inspector General's 2005 report (chapter 6); the Halfway Home Report (chapter 7); complaints collected by the Women's Refugee Commission and various NGOs (chapter 8); and the National Immigrant Justice Center/ACLU complaint (chapter 9). See also Human Rights Watch, "In the Freezer: Abusive Conditions for Women and Children in US Immigration Holding Cells," 2018, https://perma.cc/J9BY-LHWS.

3. See chapter 10.

4. Motion to Enforce Settlement and Appoint a Special Monitor in *Flores v. Lynch*, May 19, 2016.

5. She cited the declaration of one child who reported that "there was an open toilet in the room [of 50 people] with no toilet seat for everyone to use. Everyone could see if we were using the toilet" (Order Re: Plaintiffs' Motion to Enforce and Appoint a Special Monitor in *Flores v. Sessions*, June 27, 2017, at 12).

6. She quoted one child who reported asking the officers to make the room a bit warmer, but who responded by making it colder, and then, when children began crying as a result, made it still colder (id, at 16).

7. Id., at 13.

8. Id., at 32–33.

9. Complaint for Injunctive Relief in *ACLU v. Office of Civil Rights and Civil Liberties*, DHS, February 11, 2015, https://perma.cc/K72S-75HD.

10. ACLU, "Neglect and Abuse of Unaccompanied Immigrant Children by U.S. Customs and Border Protection," May 2018, https://perma.cc/ZP4F-C8NY.

11. See Plaintiffs' Corrected Memorandum re: Status Conference and Response to Third Government Monitors' Reports in *Flores v. Sessions*, July 27, 2018.

12. Order Appointing Special Master/Independent Monitor in *Flores v. Sessions*, October 5, 2018.

13. Andrea Sheridan Ordin, Partner, Pepper, Hamilton & Sheetz, https://perma.cc/48NF-C4AE.

14. Order appointing Special Master, supra n. 12, at 11. In a previous order, Judge Gee found that ORR had breached the Flores agreement in several ways, including by administering psychotropic medicines to children in one of its facilities in violation of the settlement, which additionally warranted the appointment of the special monitor. See Status Conference and Plaintiffs' Motion to Enforce Settlement (with tentative ruling) in *Flores v. Sessions*, July 27, 2018.

15. Notice of Appeal to the Court of Appeals for the Ninth Circuit, *Flores v. Whitaker*, December 4, 2018.

16. Order of voluntary dismissal, *Flores v. Sessions*, Case 18-56286, March 22, 2019 (9th Cir.)

17. Helen Christophi, "Feds tell 9th Circuit: Detained Kids 'Safe and Sanitary' Without Soap," *Courthouse News Service*, June 18, 2019, https://perma.cc/7US6-DK5N.

18. Opinion, *Flores v. Barr*, Case 17-56297 (9th Cir. Aug. 15, 2019).

19. Caitlin Dickerson, "'There Is a Stench': Soiled Clothes and No Baths for Migrant Children at a Texas Center," *New York Times*, June 21, 2019. After the *Times*'s story appeared, CBP moved many of the children to a different location operated by ORR. See Caitlin Dickerson, "Hundreds of Migrant Children Are Moved Out of an Overcrowded Border Station," *New York Times*, June 24, 2019.

20. Miriam Jordan, "Judge Orders Swift Action to Improve Conditions for Migrant Children in Texas," *New York Times*, June 29, 2019; Order in *Flores v. Meese* (C.D. Calif., June 28, 2019).

21. Exhibit 1-13 to Ex Parte Application for Temporary Restraining Order in *Flores v. Barr*, June 26, 2019.

22. Office of the DHS Inspector General, "Management Alert—DHS Needs to Address Dangerous Overcrowding and Prolonged Detention of Children and Adults in the Rio Grande Valley," OIG-19-51, July 2, 2019, https://perma.cc/PR23-UDF5. Overcrowding was alleviated, at least temporarily, by a significant drop in apprehensions in June and July 2019, perhaps as a result of tougher Mexican enforcement at its southern border. See Customs and Border Protection, Southwest Border Migration FY 2019 (through June 2019), https://perma.cc/25BV-P536.

23. Julia Ainsley, "Trump Admin: Parents Must Be Fingerprinted to Get Back Migrant Kids," *NBC News*, May 29, 2018, https://perma.cc/7U2C-HMDR.

24. Editorial Board, "Hundreds of Children Rot in the Desert. End Trump's Draconian Policies," *New York Times*, October 2, 2018.

25. Memorandum of Agreement Among the Office of Refugee Resettlement and U.S. Immigration and Customs Enforcement, April 13, 2018, https://perma.cc/G7GT-RXWF.

26. Manny Fernandez and Caitlin Dickerson, "Inside the Vast Tent City Housing Migrant Children in a Texas Desert," *New York Times*, October 12, 2018; Caitlin Dickerson, "The Government is Moving Migrant Children to a Texas Tent City. Here's What's Behind It," *New York Times*, October 1, 2018.

27. Education is required at other ORR shelters, but reportedly "the overall quality of the education they provide largely remains a mystery because much of what happens in the shelters is rarely seen by the public." A big part of the problem of providing a coherent education program is that many children stay in the shelter for only days to months, and given the rapid turnover of students, "it's always like the first day of school." See Dana Goldstein and Manny Fernandez, "In a Migrant Shelter Classroom, 'It's Always Like the First Day of School,'" *New York Times*, July 6, 2018.

28. Dickerson, supra n. 26.

29. Fernandez and Dickerson, supra n. 26.

30. Dianne Gallagher, Devon M. Sayers, and Geneva Sands, "Feds Reverse Fingerprint Policy in Move Expected to Speed Release of Unaccompanied Children in HHS Custody," *CNN politics*, December 18, 2018.

31. Consolidated Appropriations Act, 2019, Sec. 224.

32. Miriam Jordan, "Trump Administration to Nearly Double Size of Detention Center for Migrant Teenagers," *New York Times*, January 15, 2019.

33. Motion to Enforce Settlement Agreement in *Flores v. Barr*, May 31, 2019.

34. Maria Sacchetti, "Trump Administration Cancels English Classes, Soccer, Legal Aid for Unaccompanied Child Migrants in U.S. Shelters, *Washington Post*, June 5, 2019.

35. Monique O. Madan, "Recess Time, Education, and Legal Services Will Be Restored at Homestead Detention Center, Agency Says," *Miami Herald*, June 28, 2019; "4.59B Border Aid Package Signed into Law, *Roll Call*, July 1, 2019.

36. Graham Kates, Angel Canales, and Manuel Bojorquez, "Thousands of Unaccompanied Migrant Children Could Be Detained Indefinitely," CBS News, July 24, 2019, https://perma.cc/6NM2-DSHE.

37. Defendants' response in opposition to plaintiffs' motion to enforce settlement, *Flores v. Barr*, Aug. 2, 2019.

38. In re: Gault, 387 U.S. 1 (1967).

39. See *Lin v. Ashcroft*, 377 F. 3d 1014(9th Cir. 2004) (stopping short of requiring counsel); *J.E.F.M. v. Lynch*, 837 F. 3d 1026 (9th Cir. 2016) holding that the court lacked jurisdiction to decide whether there was a right to counsel for children in immigration court, in a case that did not arise from an appeal from a decision of the Board of Immigration Appeals).

40. TRAC Immigration, "Representation for Unaccompanied Children in Immigration Court," November 25, 2014, https://perma.cc/TV5S-SGP9.

41. Id.

42. Deposition of Assistant Chief Immigration Judge Jack Weil in *J. E. F. M v. Lynch*, Case 2:14-cv-01026-TSZ (W.D. Wash., October 15, 2015), https://perma .cc/CW7B-T9Z4.

43. Id.

44. See, e.g., *Last Week Tonight with John Oliver*, https://www.youtube.com /watch?v = 9fBOGBwJ2QA; Amy Maldonado, "Lilah Wants to be Deported to the Country of PIZZA!," https://www.youtube.com/watch?v=SUQwou7qllc.

45. Annie Nova, "Targeted by Trump, National Service Programs to Aid the Poor are Suffering Cuts," *WNYC News*, October 19, 2017, https://www.wnyc.org /story/targeted-trump-national-service-programs-aid-poor-are-suffering-cuts. Professor Shani M. King has shown that other industrialized countries provide legal assistance at public expense to children who seek asylum. Shani M. King, "Alone and Unrepresented: A Call to Congress to Provide Counsel for Unaccompanied Minors," *Harvard Journal on Legislation* 50:33 (2013).

46. See Vivian Yee and Miriam Jordan, "Migrant Children in Search of Justice: A 2-Year-Old's Day in Immigration Court," *New York Times*, October 8, 2018, reporting on the representation of Fernanda, a two-year-old Honduran toddler, by a lawyer from Catholic Charities, which had received funding from a nonprofit organization to represent migrant children in New York shelters.

47. Miriam Jordan, Caitlin Dickerson, and Michael D. Shear, "Trump's Plans to Deter Migrants Could Mean New 'Voluntary" Family Separations," *New York Times*, October 22, 2018.

48. See the discussion of "secure" facilities in chapter 11 and the report in chapter 12 of the government's plan to remove the locks from its family facilities in favor of unstated "immigration consequences" for any families that leave the premises.

49. As of early April 2019, only sixty-three people remained in Karnes, and part of the facility had been turned into an adults-only jail for women. See Erica Proffer, "How Would Closing the U.S.—Mexico Border Impact the Texas Economy?," *KVUE*, April 2, 2019, https://perma.cc/2TS6-QX4D. But five months later, ICE revealed that it would again use Karnes as a family detention center. Maria Sacchetti, "ICE to Resume Detaining Migrant Families at Texas Facility," *Washington Post*, September 21, 2019. See "ICE: Karnes Family Residential Center to Hold About 700 Women," *KSAT-TV*, March 29, 2019, https://perma.cc /BPA8-TCTX; Molly Hennessey-Fiske, "ICE Detention Centers Preparing for Longer Average Stays by Migrant Families," *Los Angeles Times*, Aug. 23, 2019. See also Nick Miroff, Josh Dawsey, and Rachael Bade, "Trump Administration Considers Revised Version of Family Separation Tactic," *Washington Post*, April 9, 2019. It is possible that Judge Gee's injunction against abrogating the Flores decision will cause ICE to reconsider reopening Karnes for family detention.

50. On the other hand, as an appeals court judge in Colorado and in his first year on the Supreme Court, Justice Gorsuch was particularly skeptical about deference to administrative agencies' interpretations of their statutes, preferring

that judges make their own interpretations as best they could. See Johnathan Adler, "Shunting Aside Chevron Deference," *The Regulatory Review*, August 7, 2018, https://perma.cc/DZ3F-UVJD. Less deference could result in a more expansive interpretation of the term "social group" in the Refugee Act than the Board of Immigration Appeals or Attorney General Sessions have given it. Less deference could also mean that the Court would not uphold the regulations imposing new barriers to asylum, such as the regulation barring protection for non-Mexican refugees who enter from Mexico without first seeking asylum there.

51. Over a long term, wearing the current generation of ankle monitor can result in chafing and pain as well as personal embarrassment. But if Apple can put a computer in a watch, it or some other company should be able to replace the current generation of monitors with a device that is smaller, much lighter in weight, and less obtrusive. Even now, the government requires most migrants to wear the monitors only temporarily, not for the full two years of average waiting time before hearings. If they comply with their other conditions of release, such as periodic reporting in person to ICE, the monitors are often removed. See Jordan et al., supra n. 47. And migrants who post bond are not required to wear monitors.

52. It can't reasonably be reduced much below six months because it takes time to try to obtain counsel and to collect the corroboration needed to win most asylum cases.

53. See the discussions of the A- B- and M- S- cases in chapter 12.

54. The case for an independent immigration court is discussed in Jaya Ramji-Nogales, Andrew I. Schoenholtz, and Philip G. Schrag, *Refugee Roulette: Disparities in Asylum Adjudication and Proposals for Reform* (New York: New York University Press, 2009), 100–116. In 2019, The National Association of Immigration Judges, the Federal Bar Association, the American Bar Association, and the American Immigration Lawyers Association wrote to Congress to urge the creation of such a court, citing an "inherent conflict of interest" between the duty to decide cases impartially and the duty to serve political leadership. See Letter to the House and Senate, "Re: Congress Should Establish an Independent Immigration Court," July 11, 2019, https://perma.cc/Z5FA-W2A9.

55. Recall the findings of Ingrid Eagly et al., that released family members with asylum claims attended their hearings 86 percent of the time, and the report from the Case Management Program of a 96 percent rate. These rates are cited and summarized in chapter 12.

56. The R.I.L- R- case suggests that deterrence is not a valid rationale for civil detention, but of course it was a preliminary decision by a trial court. The issue has not been tested on appeal.

57. These figures represent apprehensions both at ports of entry and of migrant families who crossed into the United States between ports of entry. See U.S. Customs and Border Protection, "Southwest Border Apprehensions by Sector, Fiscal Year 2019," https://perma.cc/H7HS-UGIC; "Southwest Border Migra-

tion, FY 2018," https://perma.cc/T24G-LVH5; and "Southwest Border Migration, FY 2017," https://perma.cc/NQB3-WUHD.

58. U.S. Customs and Border Protection, "Southwest Border Migration, FY 2019," https://perma.cc/QZQ7-9PAP.

59. See Congressional Research Service, "U.S. Strategy for Engagement in Central America: An Overview," June 25, 2018, https://perma.cc/32S9-SRPE; Shannon K. O'Neil, "Trump's Cuts to Central American Aid Will Lead to More Caravans," *Bloomberg Opinion*, October 23, 2018. In March 2019, President Trump abruptly cancelled foreign aid to all three Northern Triangle countries because with migration from the region continuing to increase, "they haven't done a thing for us" (Mary Beth Sheridan and Kevin Sieff, "Trump Cuts Aid in Border Reprisal," *Washington Post*, March 31, 2019).

60. Nicholas Kristof, "This Teenager Knows a Secret to Slowing Guatemalan Migration," *New York Times*, June 8, 2019.

61. In December, 2018, the U.S. State Department announced that the U.S. would commit $5.8 billion in "private and public" investments in the Northern Triangle countries. But the press reported that "much of that amount was previously committed or contingent on the identification of 'commercially viable projects'" (Gardiner Harris and Azam Ahmed, "U.S., Supporting Mexico's Plan, Will Invest $5.8 Billion in Central America," *New York Times*, December 18, 2018).

62. Rachel Anspach, "Unimaginable Cruelty," *Slate*, October 9, 2017, https://perma.cc/V3MW-8WM6.

63. See USCIS, "Central American Minors," https://perma.cc/8X45-KBX4.

64. Human Rights First et al., "Protecting Refugees and Restoring Order: Real Solutions to the Humanitarian Crisis," 2019, https://perma.cc/MUC2-UBGG.

65. United Nations High Commissioner for Refugees/USA, "Figures at a Glance (2018)," https://perma.cc/VD3J-LJEM.

66. Elizabeth Keyes suggests that the U.S. should create a type of temporary protection, perhaps for five years with a renewal option, for those who flee to the United States because they "face a real risk of suffering serious harm," though not for one of the reasons listed in the asylum law. The benefit would be limited to those with "a parent, grandparent, sibling or child already in the United States." See Elizabeth Keyes, "Unconventional Refugees," *American University Law Review* 67 (2017): 89.

67. Max Fischer and Amanda Taub, "In Dismissing Asylum Rights, President Joins Global Chorus," *New York Times*, November 3, 2018, notes that while the European Union and Australia are "two of the biggest offenders" in undermining the postwar global refugee system, Malaysia, Thailand, Peru, Venezuela, and Tanzania, among others, have been refusing to accept refugees who have reached or are trying to reach their borders.

68. See Tim McDonnell, "The Refugees the World Barely Pays Attention To," *NPR*, June 20, 2018, citing, among other data, a World Bank report that

estimates that 143 million people will be displaced by environmental disasters by 2050.

69. Tim Padgett, "Guatemalan Climate Change Refugees Pouring Over U.S. Border—And Into South Florida," WJCT, April 8, 2019, https://perma.cc /M7RE-XCC6.

70. Kirk Semple, "Central American Farmers Head to the U.S., Fleeing Climate Change," *New York Times*, April 13, 2019.

71. See Ted Hesson, "Fact Check: Trump's Speech on Border Crisis," *Politico*, January 8, 2019. Although child and family migration increased during the first two years of the Trump administration, the entry of undocumented migrants remained at one of the lowest levels in decades. In 2000, the Border Patrol apprehended 1.67 million people who were entering the U.S. illegally; in 2018, the number was only 403,479, and in 2017, the ICE Acting Director reported that "the border's under better control than it has been in 45 years." See Brittany Renee Mayes, Aaron Williams, and Laris Karklis, "The History of U.S. Border Patrol Apprehensions," *Washington Post*, January 10, 2019.

72. In 2018, a PRRI survey found that 64 percent of Americans said that immigrants today "strengthen our country because of their hard work" (National Immigration Forum, "Polling Update: American Attitudes on Immigration Steady, but Showing More Partisan Divides," April 17, 2019, https://perma.cc /PNC2-EW9V).

73. Women's Refugee Commission and Lake Research Partners, "Findings on Voters' Attitudes toward Refugees and Asylum Policies," October 24, 2018, https://www.womensrefugeecommission.org/rights/resources/1661-findings-on-voters-attitudes-toward-refugees-and-asylum-policies.

74. Alan Gomez, "Fewer Americans Believe U.S. Should Accept Refugees," *USA Today*, May 24, 2018, reporting a Pew poll showing support for refugees steady among Democrats but falling sharply in recent years among Republicans; Grinnell College, Grinnell College National Poll, December 3, 2018, https:// perma.cc/9HP3-UM94, reporting that "fifty-five percent of people questioned believe this country has a moral responsibility to grant asylum and allow those who are fleeing violence or persecution to live in the United States permanently."

75. Justin McCarthy, "Support for Allowing Border Refugees Into U.S. Edges Up," The Gallup Organization, August 13, 2019, http://perma.cc/W659-YYQY (57 percent support allowing Central American refugees into the United States).

76. Readers of this book who are lawyers, or persons who speak Spanish fluently who want to help as interpreters, can volunteer to assist migrant families at the family detention centers. Training is provided. For a description of volunteer opportunities, see Lindsay M. Harris, "Contemporary Family Detention and Legal Advocacy," *Harvard Latinx Law Review* 21 (2018): 159–163.

77. Miriam Jordan, "The Flores Agreement Protected Migrant Children for Decades. New Regulations Aim to End It," *New York Times*, Aug. 20, 2019.

EPILOGUE

1. Order of the Supreme Court in *Trump v. East Bay Sanctuary Covenant*, Case 18A615, 586 U.S. __ (December 21, 2018). The merits of that case were scheduled to be decided by the Ninth Circuit during the fall of 2019.

2. 8 C.F.R. Sec. 1208.13(c)(4).

3. Order of the Supreme Court in *Barr v. East Bay Sanctuary Covenant*, No. 19A230, 588 U.S. __ Sept. 11, 2019, https://perma.cc/7WAZ-34P7.

4. Id. (Sotomayor, J., dissenting).

5. 8 U.S.C. Sec. 1184(b) directs consular officers to deny visas to those who can't overcome a presumption that they intend to immigrate to the United States.

6. The Supreme Court's September 11, 2019, stay of the injunction, pending appeal, does not preclude the Ninth Circuit from sustaining the injunction as a result of the appeal. The government's appeal to the Ninth Circuit was scheduled to be argued while this book is in press. (Full disclosure: The author is one of many law professors who has filed a friend of the court brief supporting the district court's injunction.) However, the Supreme Court ordered that its stay of the preliminary injunction will remain in force even after a judgment affirming the injunction until "disposition of the Government's petition for a writ of certiorari, if such a writ is sought" and until the Supreme Court finally disposes of the case if it grants review (*Barr*, supra n. 3). In other words, the Supreme Court hinted that it would consider reviewing a decision that was unfavorable to the government, and it stated that its stay of the injunction would remain in force until that final appeal was completed even if the Ninth Circuit affirmed Judge Tigar's injunction.

7. As this book went to press, several other cases challenging the third country transit rule were pending. Unlike the *East Bay* case in which the Supreme Court stayed the preliminary injunction, some of these cases included plaintiff migrants who were at immediate risk of deportation because of the rule.

8. Judge Timothy Kelly, who had earlier denied a temporary injunction in the District of Columbia case challenging the third country transit rule, was asked to stop the deportation of an asylum-seeker who had passed through Mexico. Regarding the Supreme Court's grant of a stay in the California case, he said that he "did not know that he could 'divine' anything from the Supreme Court's order, in which there were no individual plaintiffs." Megan Mineiro, "Honduras Deportation Case Tests Trump Asylum Policy," Courthouse News Service, September 25, 2019, https://perma.cc/3WPT-5PTR.

9. It is possible that the Supreme Court issued its stay because the Court was troubled by the fact that a single federal judge, in just one district, had entered an injunction that barred the enforcement of the regulation throughout the nation, and it did so in a case in which only organizations, and not affected individual migrants, had sued. In recent years, such nationwide injunctions have become controversial. So a case on behalf of a particular migrant who is denied asylum

because of the rule, in which relief was granted only to that migrant, might succeed. That would allow other district judges to deny relief and eventually present the Court with conflicting decisions for the highest court to resolve. Alternatively, a class action for all asylum-seeking migrants entering through Mexico, with all the extrajudicial supervision and regulation applicable to class actions, might be more palatable to the Court than the suit brought by the organizations.

10. The Mexican government might choose to delay rather than deny the applications to avoid international or domestic criticism resulting from unreasonably low asylum grant rates. However, under the third country transit rule, only a denial of asylum would allow the applicant to apply anew in the United States. Ironically, U.S. adjudicators might treat a Mexican denial of asylum, however summary, as evidence that the applicant did not warrant a grant of protection.

11. It is unclear as this book goes to press whether the government will try to apply the third party transit rule to individuals who attempted to come to the United States before the rule was put into place and who were then put on a waiting list for entry under the metering policy or, if the government attempted to do so, whether the courts would enjoin that practice.

12. Maria Sacchetti, "ICE to Resume Detaining Migrant Families at Texas Facility," *Washington Post,* September 21, 2019.

Index